A FIELD GUIDE TO
WESTERN MEDICINAL
PLANTS AND HERBS

A FIELD GUIDE TO

WESTERN MEDICINAL PLANTS AND HERBS

STEVEN FOSTER
AND CHRISTOPHER HOBBS

SPONSORED BY
THE NATIONAL WILDLIFE FEDERATION AND
THE ROGER TORY PETERSON INSTITUTE

HOUGHTON MIFFLIN COMPANY
BOSTON   NEW YORK

For information about permission to reproduce selections from this book, write to
trade.permissions@hmhco.com or to Permissions, Houghton Mifflin Harcourt
Publishing Company, 3 Park Avenue, 19th Floor, New York, New York 10016.

Visit our Web site: www.hmhco.com

PETERSON FIELD GUIDES and PETERSON FIELD GUIDE SERIES
are registered trademarks of Houghton Mifflin Company.

Library of Congress Cataloging in Publication Data
is available
ISBN 0-395-83807-X   ISBN 0-395-83806-1 (flexi)

Book design by Anne Chalmers
Typeface: Linotype-Hell Fairfield; Futura Condensed (Adobe)

Printed in China

SCP 15 14 13
4500681769

PREFACE

The exploration of the flora of the American West by European settlers of North America is a relatively recent undertaking, scarcely two centuries old. In the 1780s the vast expanses of the West beckoned people of a scientific turn of mind as well as those looking to conquer for political and economic gain. Spanish ships had reached the Pacific Northwest by the mid-1770s, and Captain James Cook sailed north along the West Coast on his third expedition to the Pacific in 1778. The British sent Captain George Vancouver to search for the elusive Northwest Passage in 1792. Though that passage proved nonexistent, he did examine hundreds of miles of coastline from California to Alaska.

In 1786 the French Academy of Sciences organized an expedition led by Jean-François de Galaup, comte de La Pérouse, to collect information about plants, particularly those that would grow in the French climate. The explorers were to study roots, woods, barks, leaves, flowers, fruits, and seeds to ascertain their potential as *"matière médicale"* — materia medica, or medicinal plants. The expedition, though primarily scientific in purpose, was also charged with learning the extent and power of Spanish possessions in the American West.

The two ships forming the expedition arrived in California in the summer of 1786, a time when many plants were already dormant from the heat. Potatoes gathered in Chile were left with the Spanish mission at Monterey. After ten days at anchor, the expedition sailed west to Asia. At Kamchatka, in Russia, a member of the scientific crew left the ship and was sent across the great expanse of Asia to France with journals and records of the expedition's finds to date.

In February 1788, the ships stopped at Botany Bay, New South Wales, Australia, and the leaders arranged for the shipment of important journals and records to France. After leaving port on

February 15, 1788, the ships were never heard from again. Their wreckage was discovered forty years later off one of the Solomon Islands. Although most of the scientific records and collections from the voyage were lost, two packets of seeds collected at Monterey by the expedition's gardener did make their way to Paris and were grown at the Jardin des Plantes. Botanists recognized one plant as a new genus, and in 1791 Lamarck published the name *Abronia umbellata*, a common sand verbena from San Diego north to the Columbia River. It was the earliest California plant described in acceptable scientific terms.

Between 1787 and 1793 the eminent British botanist Sir Joseph Banks, who had accompanied Cook on his voyages, sent Archibald Menzies to the West Coast for extensive plant collections. Menzies is honored in numerous species names such as Douglas fir (*Pseudotsuga menziesii*). The plants he collected in what are now Washington, California, and British Columbia were deposited in various European herbaria.

The third American president, Thomas Jefferson, consummated the purchase of vast lands west of the Mississippi River from France in 1803. In May 1804, Jefferson sent Captains Meriwether Lewis and William Clark to explore the territory of the Louisiana Purchase. Lewis and Clark returned to St. Louis in September 1806 with 123 new plant species. Many of those species were published in London in 1814 in Frederick Pursh's *Flora Americae Septentrionalis*, considered the first flora to cover the continent, including species from the Pacific Northwest.

One of America's best-traveled field botanists, the English naturalist Thomas Nuttall (1786–1859), arrived in Philadelphia in 1808, where he met with Dr. Benjamin Smith Barton, author of one of the first treatises on American medicinal plants, *Essays Towards a Materia Medica of the United States*, published in three parts between 1798 and 1804. Backed by Barton's patronage, Nuttall's travels on the Missouri River took him as far north and west as southern North Dakota in 1811. Two decades later, in 1834, he traveled overland to the Columbia River and collected plants along the California coast on his way home. Further government-sponsored scientific expeditions to the West did not occur until 1841. These are just a few of the important botanical explorers of the American West.

Throughout most of the nineteenth century, the botanists who explored the plants of the western United States could be classified as either describers or collectors. The describers primarily worked in the academic institutions of eastern North America and Europe; it was the collectors who did the hard field work in the western wilderness. Both a collector and a describer, Constantine Samuel Rafinesque (1783–1840), author of *Medical Flora; or Manual of the Medical Botany of North America* (2 vols., 1828, 1830), described the experience of a botanist traveling in the western wilderness:

> Let the practical Botanist who wishes like myself to be a pioneer of science, and to increase the knowledge of plants, be fully prepared to meet dangers of all sorts in the wild groves and mountains of America. The mere fatigue of a pedestrian journey is nothing compared to the gloom of solitary forests, where not a human being is met for many miles, and if met he may be mistrusted; when the food and collections must be carried in your pocket or knapsack from day to day; when the fare is not only scanty but sometimes worse; when you must live on corn bread and salt pork, be burnt and steamed by a hot sun at noon, or drenched by rain, even with an umbrella in hand, as I always had.
>
> Musquiotes [sic] and flies will often annoy you or suck your blood if you stop or leave a hurried step. Gnats dance before the eyes and often fall in unless you shut them; insects creep on you and into your ears. Ants crawl on you where ever you rest on the ground, wasps will assail you like furies if you touch their nests. But ticks the worst of all are unavoidable wherever you go among bushes, and stick to you in crowds . . .
>
> The pleasures of a botanical exploration fully compensate for these miseries and dangers, else no one would be a traveling Botanist, nor spend his time and money in vain. Many fair-days and fair-roads are met with, a clear sky or a bracing breeze inspires delights and ease, you breathe the pure air of the country, every rill and brook offers a drink of limpid fluid . . .
>
> Every step taken into the fields, groves, and hills, appears to afford new enjoyments, Landscapes and Plants jointly meet in your sight. Here is an old acquaintance seen again; there a novelty, a rare plant, perhaps a new one! greets your view: you hasten to pluck it, examine it, admire, and put it in your book. Then you walk on thinking what it might be, or may be made by you thereafter. You feel exultation, you are a conqueror, you have made a conquest over Nature, you are going to add a new object, or a page to sci-

ence. This peaceful conquest has cost no tears . . .

To these botanical pleasures may be added the anticipation of the future names, places, uses, history, &c. of the plants you discover. For the winter or season of rest, are reserved the sedentary pleasures of comparing, studying, naming, describing, and publishing [as quoted in McKelvey, 1956, p. xxxix, from Rafinesque, *New Flora of North America*, 1836].

The descriptive botanists who stayed at their desks include the elder Augustin Pyrames de Candolle (1778–1841) in Geneva and Paris; Sir William Jackson Hooker (1785–1865) at the Royal Botanical Gardens at Kew; John Torrey (1796–1873) of New York; the preeminent nineteenth-century American botanist Asa Gray (1810–1888); and the botanical gatekeeper of the West in St. Louis, George Engelmann (1809–1884). Other important collectors and describers of western plants include John M. Coulter (1851–1928), David Douglas (1798–1834), Edward L. Greene (1843–1915), Willis Linn Jepson (1867–1946), Joseph N. Rose (1862–1928), Per Axel Rydberg (1860–1931), and Sereno Watson (1826–1892).

Most of the important early botanists, including Gray, Torrey, Engelmann, and even Linnaeus, were trained as physicians. In the eighteenth century, botany was merely a diversion from pharmacy, which itself had not yet fully emerged as a separate academic pursuit. These medical doctors collected, described, and published articles on plants new to science. Ironically, most of these men had only a passing interest in medicinal plants. By the mid-nineteenth century, botany was accepted as an academic discipline.

As westward settlement continued, professional interest in native plants as sources of medicines declined. Synthetic drugs were on the horizon and plants were considered "crude drugs" peddled as nostrums by quacks, "Indian doctors," and medicine sideshows. As a result, far fewer species of western medicinal plants have found commercial uses even in the modern herb trade than those from eastern North America, particularly from eastern deciduous forests in the first two centuries of European settlement.

When botany matured as a distinct academic discipline, anthropology evolved to include distinct subdisciplines, including, in 1895, ethnobotany, the study of the ways indigenous groups use plants. One rich laboratory for this study was the southwestern United States, where many Native American groups still survived in the late nineteenth and early twentieth centuries. Since many of these groups were culturally intact, and some individuals remembered the old ways, there is far more ethnobotanical information on Native American medicinal plants of the West, compared with those of eastern North America.

Edward Palmer, who collected plants during the heyday of botanical exploration of the American West, from 1853 to 1910, established standards for collecting plants and for noting their uses; in 1871 he published *Food Products of the North American Indians.*

The Smithsonian Institution's Bureau of American Ethnology (BAE), under the direction of John Wesley Powell, produced many important ethnobotanical studies, including Matilda Coxe Stevenson's *Ethnobotany of the Zuni Indians* (1915) and Jesse Walter Fewkes's *A Contribution to Ethnobotany* (1896) on the Hopi Indians' uses of plants. These anthropologists did not call themselves ethnobotanists. Edward F. Castetter was the first botanist of the Southwest to call himself that, followed by Volney H. Jones, who studied under Melvin R. Gilmore at the University of Michigan. Gilmore established the first ethnobotanical laboratory at the University of Michigan Museum of Anthropology in 1930. The Botanical Museum at Harvard University, under the direction of Oakes Ames and students who followed him, including Paul Vestal and the late Richard Evans Schultes, produced significant works on southwestern ethnobotany into the 1970s. From an ethnobotanical perspective, the American Southwest is the best-studied region in the world.

This wealth of data is synthesized in Daniel E. Moerman's 1998 book *Native American Ethnobotany,* which covers the food, material, and medicinal uses of 4,029 species, subspecies, and varieties of plants by 291 indigenous groups of North America (and Hawaii). This work has served as the primary source for much of the literature on western medicinal plants listed in the References.

THE WEST IN THE NORTH AMERICAN FLORA

The flora of North America north of Mexico, including the United States, Greenland, and Canada, consists of at least 21,757 species of vascular plants represented by 3,164 genera in 290 plant families. This area encompasses nearly 60 degrees of latitude and 145 degrees of longitude. Many of the world's major vegetation formations are included in this diverse climatic expanse. Among the plant communities west of the Mississippi River are tundra and polar desert biomes, boreal forests, montane forests, temperate rain forests, prairie, shrub steppes, deciduous and evergreen forests, chaparral, and warm deserts.

Boreal forests, or taiga, with low species diversity and dense stands of coniferous trees, extend from central Alaska to eastern Canada and south to the Great Lakes, spanning 28 percent of the North American landmass north of Mexico. Dominant woody plants include *Abies* (fir), *Larix* (larch), *Picea* (spruce), and *Pinus* (pine). Among these vast expanses of forests are bogs and meadows holding herbaceous plants, many of which have medicinal uses. For instance, the sundew *(Drosera rotundifolia)* has been researched for antiviral and antibacterial activity and is used in phytomedicine preparations in Europe.

The great grassland vegetation of the midcontinent holds mostly herbaceous plants, along with locally restricted woody plants. The grasslands include prairies (humid grasslands with dominant tall-grass species), and high plains or steppes (more arid regions with short grasses). The Great Plains once covered between 21 and 25 percent of the North American landmass north of Mexico. Its most important contribution to plant pharmacy is the genus *Echinacea*, especially *Echinacea angustifolia*.

One of the richest sources of medicinal plants is the winter-deciduous vegetation of the eastern forest, which covers 11 percent of the continent, extending well west of the Mississippi into eastern Texas, Oklahoma, and Kansas. This bioregion was the zone in which European settlement made the greatest impact in the first two centuries of colonization. A disproportionately high number of the American medicinal plant species that have entered commerce, both historically and today, come from this vegetation zone. In the thirteen original colonies in the late eighteenth century, there was an effort to develop medicines from native medicinal plants. Most of the native species used at the inception of the *United States Pharmacopoeia* in 1820 came from eastern deciduous forests, and almost all of the native plant species used in medicine at that time are still commercially traded today, most as ingredients in dietary supplements.

In a sense, the exploration of medicinal plants of western North America is still in its infancy. The ecological diversity forced by the West's harsh environmental extremes has stimulated the evolution of secondary metabolites — chemical compounds that have biological effects in humans — in many plants. Among the western bioregions with the greatest potential for bioactive plants are the vast desert expanses, which are largely dominated by woody plants. The Chihuahuan, Sonoran, and Mojave deserts and the semiarid intermountain regions include the desert scrub biome, which accounts for 5 percent of the North American landmass north of Mexico. These unique floristic zones are home to thousands of potentially bioactive species, among them *Ephedra* (ephedra), *Larrea* (chaparral), *Yucca, Agave, Opuntia* (prickly pear), and *Simmondsia* (jojoba).

Mediterranean/Madrean scrub and woodland vegetation zones extend from Oregon to Mexico. Mediterranean ecosystems are found in only five places in the world — the Mediterranean region, South Africa's Cape of Good Hope, southern and southwestern Australia, central Chile, and the area from southern Oregon to northern Baja California. The ecosystem is characterized by hot dry summers and less than 3 percent annual hours of frost. The North American Mediterranean zone includes a variety of habitats, including mixed evergreen forests, oak woodland, and grasslands, plus various types of scrubland. The Madrean zones, characterized predominantly by evergreen species, such as oaks, extends from central Arizona and southern New Mexico to southwestern Texas.

Both Mediterranean and Madrean zones include many indigenous aromatic plants. The vast majority of these species have not been investigated for biologically active chemicals. Interestingly, most of the culinary and aromatic herbs of European tradition — sage, thyme, rosemary and other familiar herbs — originate from similar climatic conditions in the Mediterranean region.

The richly diverse and productive Pacific Coast coniferous forest, extending from Monterey County, California, to Cook Inlet, Alaska, and covering about 3 percent of North America, contains some of the world's longest-lived massive tree species. Famous trees of this biome are the redwood and giant sequoia of California, western hemlock, Douglas-fir, and Sitka spruce. One common, but historically neglected subcanopy tree — the Pacific yew (*Taxus brevifolia*) — has been the subject of intensive scientific research in recent years. Its bark served as the first commercial source of the anticancer drug paclitaxel (also known by its trade name, Taxol), which the U.S. Food and Drug Administration (FDA) has approved for use in chemotherapy for certain forms of ovarian and breast cancers. In the future it will be approved as a chemotherapeutic agent for other difficult-to-treat forms of cancer. The development of paclitaxel has highlighted the problems of obtaining drugs from natural sources, especially that of securing an adequate, sustainable supply of raw material. At first the compound was derived exclusively from the bark of the Pacific yew, which created both supply shortages and conservation concerns; now, however, it is made by a semisynthetic process from the needles of the widely cultivated English yew (*Taxus baccata*).

Additional western montane coniferous forest floristic regions include the Rocky Mountain forests, Pacific Northwest montane forests, the montane forests of Alta and Baja California, and the forests of the intermountain region. In all of these regions, conifers are the dominant trees.

This rich collection of biomes provides a diverse flora with great potential for discovery of plants with medicinal value. Although we have some knowledge of how Native American groups used the plants of this region, scientific research on medicinal plants of the West still remains to be done. It is hoped that this book will help stimulate some of that needed research.

Steven Foster

ACKNOWLEDGMENTS

We would like to thank several researchers who helped review and compile ethnobotanical and cross-cultural plant uses from numerous sources. Christopher Hobbs wishes to acknowledge the contribution of Steven Brown, N.D., in reviewing, compiling, and writing up information on plant uses. The compiling by Ellen Baker and Patty Baker of ethnobotanical reviews from obscure journal articles and rare books is deeply appreciated. Robin Bencie contributed to research on botanical descriptions; her botanical knowledge of the western flora and her taxonomic expertise were a major help.

Christopher Hobbs would like to thank his dad, Dr. Kenneth Hobbs, for passing on his "green gene," his love of plants and the natural world. Thanks also to his close friend and inspiration, Brian Weissbuch, for his love of native plants and his prodigious and intuitive knowledge of the uses of native plants in a clinical setting. Finally, his love and thanks to his partner, Beth Baugh, for her tremendous support and help.

Steven Foster thanks his current and former staff, including Josie Moore, Wil Moore, Leanna Potts, field colleague Mike Rhodes, Rachel Sullivan, and his partner, Ellen Miller, for many hours they spent in the office and the field producing this book. Abbey Foster, Colin Foster, and Sara Miller provided additional support. Thanks, too, to Lon Ball, Travis Johnson, Logan Chamberlain, Linda Ligon, Sara Smith, and others who have provided places to stay and hosted field trips to the West.

Heartfelt thanks go to many of our American herbalist colleagues with whom we have shared a rich association for more than twenty years, including Cascade Anderson-Geller, Svevo Brooks, Dr. James A. Duke, Rosemary Gladstar, Kathi Keville, Dr. Kelly Kindscher, Dr. Paul Lee, Vinnie McKinney, Ed Smith, Paul Strauss, Michael Tierra, and David Winston.

We are grateful to the staff, curators, gardeners, and collections of numerous botanical gardens and institutions, including the Botanical Research Institute, Fort Worth, Texas; Desert Botanical Garden, Tucson, Arizona; California State, Fullerton, Arboretum; Tilden Regional Botanical Garden, University of California, Berkeley; Quail Botanical Gardens, Encinitas, California; Santa Barbara Botanical Garden, Strybing Arboretum, San Francisco; Missouri Botanical Garden, St. Louis; New Mexico State University; Oregon State University, Corvallis; Kenny Ausebel and the Collective Heritage Institute; and Mark Blumenthal and the American Botanical Council, Austin, Texas. Many photographs for the book were taken in the convenient locations of these rich repositories of rare and native plants of western North America.

We give thanks to the countless generations of Native American Indians who studied, cultivated, and reverently learned about thousands of plants native to North America. Their trials and life experiences have opened up our understanding of plants.

We would also like to thank the kind and diligent work of several individuals and institutions who contributed photographs to the book (see photo credits p. 396). A special thanks to Prof. Ron P. Olowin, Saint Mary's College of California for use of images from the collection of Br. Alfred Brousseau, Saint Mary's College; Scooter Cheatum, Useful Wild Plants of Texas, Inc., Austin; Burr Williams for his photos and those of his late mother, Frances Williams, a longtime member of the Texas Ornithological Society; Dr. Craig Freeman, Kansas Biological Survey, University of Kansas; H. Wayne Phillips, Great Falls, Montana; Robert Skowron, Rocky Mountain Rare Plants, Franktown, Colorado; Dr. Stephen Lee Timme, Pittsburg State University, Pittsburg, Kansas; Larry Blakely, Bishop, California; Pamela Harper, Harper Horticultural Library, Seaford, Virginia; and Karren Elsbernd and the California Academy of Sciences, San Francisco, for use of images in the Academy's archives by Sherry Ballard, Gerald and Buff Corsi, Charles Webber, J. E. (Jed) and Bonnie McClellan, and William R. Hewlett.

Contents

THE LEGACY OF AMERICA'S GREAT NATURALIST, ROGER TORY PETERSON, is preserved through the programs and work of the Roger Tory Peterson Institute of Natural History. RTPI is a national nature education organization with a mission of creating passion for and knowledge of the natural world in the hearts and minds of children by inspiring and guiding the study of nature in our schools and communities. It also preserves and exhibits an extraordinary collection of Dr. Peterson's life's work. You can become a part of this worthy effort by joining RTPI. Just call RTPI's membership department at 1-800-758-6841 ext. 226, fax 716-665-3794, or e-mail (webmaster@rtpi.org) for a free one-year membership with the purchase of this Field Guide.

Visit us on the Web at www.rtpi.org.

A FIELD GUIDE TO
MEDICINAL
PLANTS AND HERBS

How to Use This Book

This book is meant to enlarge people's interaction with plants, and extend the appreciation of them beyond identification and beauty to explore their uses as folk medicines or as potential drugs. A guidebook is not meant to be prescriptive. By learning how various cultures have used plants for food and medicine, we can gain a better understanding of the value and beauty of our native flora and of our relationship with it. When we become familiar with the plants that grow in our back yards, wild places, parks, fields, and forests and discover how important they have been to humans for thousands of years, we are more likely to preserve the plants themselves and, even more important, their habitats.

General Organization

SPECIES COVERED: We have identified more than 1000 native wild plants growing in western North America that have a history of medicinal or herbal use. An herb is loosely defined as any plant used for flavoring, fragrance, or medicinal benefits. In these pages we describe about 500 species of the most commonly encountered medicinal plants—wildflowers, weeds, trees, and shrubs, along with a selection of grasses and ferns—of the western United States, including both native and introduced species. Many, if not most, weeds, ornamentals, and other cultivated plants are used for medicine in their countries of origin or other parts of the world. For instance, more than 1000 species of plants grown in American horticulture have documented medicinal uses in Asian traditional medical systems or folk traditions.

AREA COVERED: This field guide covers the area west of the Mississippi River from the western Great Plains and West Texas through the intermountain West, including Montana, Wyoming, Colorado, and Utah, to the desert Southwest of New Mexico and Arizona and the Pacific states of California, Oregon, and Washington. Many of these plants also occur in adjacent areas of southern Canada, northern Mexico, and Baja California.

BOTANICAL AND MEDICAL TERMS: This guide can be used by anyone who is interested in identifying local plants and learning about their traditional medicinal uses. Some readers may have knowledge of botany and medicine, but most will not. These fields have, in essence, languages of their own, and it is difficult to write about plants and their medicinal effects without using some technical terms, which are often shorthand for a whole concept. Wherever possible, we have used common terms. Less familiar botanical and medical terms are defined in the Glossary on page 389.

PHOTOGRAPHS: Most of the photos are by Steven Foster or Christopher Hobbs. Foster's photographs were taken over a period of 27 years with various Nikon camera bodies and Nikkor lenses, particularly the Micro-Nikkor series. Hobbs used a Canon EOS Elan body, 50 mm and 100 mm Canon macro lenses. Images were shot on Kodachrome 64, Fuji Velvia, Fuji Provia, and other films.

IDENTIFYING PLANTS

Plants are arranged by visual rather than technical features, according to the "Peterson System," which is based on flower color, number of petals, habitat, leaf arrangement, and so on. As in most botanical Peterson Field Guides, white-flowering wildflowers come first, followed by yellow, pink/red, blue/violet, and greenish brown groupings. Shrubs, trees, woody vines, ferns, and grasses or grasslike plants follow. Please note that some species vary greatly in flower color. A plant that one person sees as "purplish" may appear pink to your eye. Be aware of these subtle differences. By thumbing through the correct color section of the book and checking the photos and remarks on similarities to and differences from other plants, you will arrive at the plant you have in hand.

The descriptive plant entries include the key identification characteristics, with primary features in italics. The text describes the plant's growth habit, leaf morphology, flower characteristics, seed features, and so forth. If it is not a herbaceous plant, note whether it is a hardwood (deciduous) tree or softwood (conifer), subshrub (woody only at the base of the plant), or shrub. Be sure to note not only the plant's growth habit but also its habitat — desert, mountain scrub, grasslands, or even lawn.

Many plants look alike, and in the western United States there are large plant groups such as the genus *Astragalus* (Pea Family) that include species that are toxic as well as those that are edible or medicinal. It is very important to correctly identify plants before handling them. Even professional botanists have made incorrect species identifications in the parsley family, which includes the edible Wild Carrot (*Daucus carota*) and the deadly toxic Poison Hemlock (*Conium maculatum*), sometimes with fatal results! All details should correspond to the description, including range, habitat, flowering time, color, and flower or leaf structure (note the headings at the beginning of each plant group). *Never ingest a plant that has not been positively identified*, preferably by a qualified botanist.

COMMON NAMES: One or two common names are given as the heading for each entry. Plants that have some economic importance — used for food, medicine, fiber, dye, or the arts — may have several common names, often depending on regional or cultural differences. We usually list the plant's most widely accepted name or names in its context as a wildflower or medicinal plant. If in doubt, go by the Latin binomial or scientific name, which is much more reliable, though it too may be subject to change.

PART USED: The plant part or parts used by Native Americans or in common herbal practice are listed in bold opposite the common name. "Bark" usually means the inner layer, not the woody outer bark. The dead outer bark of such trees as willow, slippery elm, oak, and others generally is not used medicinally.

SCIENTIFIC NAMES: Beneath the common name in the heading is the scientific name, also called the Latin name or binomial. Most scientific names use roots from classical Greek or Latin to tell something about the plant's history or use or to honor a person, a geographic location, or some aspect of the plant's morphology. The scientific name is always expressed as two words (or, if it is a variety or subspecies, by an additional designation). The first word is the genus (plural is genera). The second is the species name, or specific epithet. There may be many different species in one genus. Often the species name tells us something about the plant. The species name *vulgare*, for example, means common. The name *officinalis* or *officinale* immediately tells us that the plant has been used in medicine, at least historically, for it designates that the plant was sold in apothecary shops. Other species names, such as *canadensis* (of Canada) and *californica*, obviously designate a geographical origin.

Scientific names are changed from time to time to reflect recent discoveries about chemistry, morphology, and genetics, as scientists determine more accurately the plants' common ancestors and how they are related. Unlike common names, the scientific names of plants are the same in China, India, North America, and Europe; hence it is a universal language. Herbalists benefit from understanding the concept of the genus, the major distinct group below family, for it tells them that any individual species of a given genus may have uses similar to those of other members. Although this does not always hold true, it is a good starting point for investigation of lesser-known local species in a genus in which medicinal use has been documented.

Unfortunately, botanists do not always agree on a particular scientific name, depending on who first described the plant or whether good scientific standards were followed. Some taxonomists are "lumpers" and include plants with small differences in a single species, while others create varieties, or subspecies, and still others are "splitters," who endlessly divide plant groups based on minute morphological or genetic features. Native groups and the compilers of their herbal knowledge, upon which this book draws, often did not distinguish between subspecies and varieties. In general, the names given here include any designations below the species rank, such as subspecies, variety, or form.

Botanical synonyms — other scientific names for the plant under discussion — are listed in brackets beneath the main binomial. We have used the most up-to-date and relevant names for each species, based primarily on the works listed in the References, including both print and database sources.

After the binomial, which is always italicized, the heading gives the name, usually abbreviated, of the botanist(s) who first published the species name and description. This citation is called the species author. "Pursh" is Frederick Pursh; "Nutt." is Thomas Nuttall; "DC" represents de Candolle; "Hook." is William Jackson Hooker; "Englm." is George Engelmann. "Torr." is John Torrey; "Gray" is Asa Gray; "Raf." is Rafinesque. The most common abbreviation, "L," stands for the father of modern taxonomy, both in botany and zoology, the Swedish physician Carolus Linnaeus (the Latinized form of Carl von Linné, 1707–1778). Knowing the author's name is a useful reference tool for taxonomists and can be a flag for the layperson as well. For example, many old American herbals list the scientific name of the slippery elm as *Ulmus fulva* Michx., but all modern botanical works cite it as *Ulmus rubra* Muhl. "Michx." is the abbreviation for the French botanist André Michaux (1746–1802), who assigned the name *Ulmus fulva* to this species. "Muhl." is the abbreviation for Gotthilf Henry Ernest Mühlenberg (1753–1815), who first proposed the name *Ulmus rubra*. Mühlenberg's *Ulmus rubra* has priority over Michaux's *Ulmus fulva*, according to the rules of the *International Code of Botanical Nomenclature*, and *Ulmus rubra* thus is the name now used by botanists everywhere.

Why is priority significant? Once Foster spent an afternoon in the living collections of the Arnold Arboretum in Jamaica Plain, Massachusetts, looking for a tree labeled *Ulmus fulva* to photograph, based on the name in an old pocket herbal he carried with him. He never found *Ulmus fulva,* but he did see *Ulmus rubra,* not realizing it was, indeed, the tree he wished to observe! Research on medicinal plants requires delving into historical literature, so it is useful to have the author citation as a point of comparison to help verify the species being discussed. As new information comes to light, a species or genus may undergo a name change. In these instances the author of the first binomial, such as Linnaeus ("L."), is set in parentheses, followed by the abbreviation of the new author's name. For example, Pipsissewa was classified in one genus by Linnaeus, then reclassified by William P. C. Barton; hence its scientific name is *Chimaphila umbellata* (L.) W.P.C. Bart."

FAMILY NAME: The scientific name is followed by the common family name rather than the technical family name. For example, we list the mint family rather than Lamiaceae (Labiatae).

DESCRIPTION: Following the names and the part used is a brief description of the plant, beginning with its growth habit (for example, tree, shrub, perennial), size, and overall appearance.

Next the leaves are described, noting whether they are *opposite* (attached to the stem exactly opposite each other), *alternate* (attached singly along the stem), or in *whorls* (three or more leaves radiating from the same point on the stem). The margin of the leaf is described as *entire* (without teeth), or variously *toothed* or *serrated* (sharp-pointed teeth), *dentate* (more rounded teeth), or *cut* to the midrib. Some leaves are *simple,* meaning that they have only a blade and a stalk, or a blade and no stalk. *Compound* leaves consist of several leaflets, either *palmately compound* (arranged like the fingers of the hand), or *pinnately compound* (arranged along a central axis like a fern). In many plant species the basal leaves (those at the base of the plant) are completely different in form from the leaves on a flowering stem. Other details include the specific shape of the leaf and the characteristics of leaf or stem hairs, if any—stiff, rough, soft, short, or long. All of these features can be important for identification. Check the Glossary (page 389) for the definitions of unfamiliar terms.

A short description of the flower comes next. Because the book is organized by flower color, it is easiest to identify plants when they are in flower. Besides the color, note whether the petals, called collectively the *corolla,* are separate (if they can be pulled out of the flower easily without tearing any tissue) or fused into a single unit, usually with a tube at the bottom, though they may be bell-, saucer-, or urn-shaped. The petals may have lobes. The flower may be radially symmetrical, like a sunflower, or irregular in shape, like the two-lipped flowers of the mint family.

The flowering period for the plant follows, expressed as a range of months in which it blooms throughout its geographical range, such as Mar.–June. The first month listed is usually the time when the flowering period begins in the south. Blooming time in more northerly areas often begins a month or more later. Though the blooming date may be listed as "Apr.–June," the plant may bloom for only two weeks in any particular location. Remember that the flowering period varies according to elevation, latitude, proximity to the ocean, and the weather conditions that year. Many flowering plants of arid regions of the West require moisture to initiate reproduction. The length of the flowering period may vary from a few weeks in a hot, dry year to more than a month or more in a very wet, cold year.

Fragrance can be an identifying feature, and if a plant has a discernible, recognizable fragrance, we note that. You should know something about the plant before you handle it, however. Obviously, you don't want to crush and smell the leaves of poison ivy or poison oak in an attempt to identify them! Many plants in the mint family have fragrant essential oils (also known as volatile oils) and a distinctive and characteristic fragrance. Experience will help you learn the subtle differences among fragrances.

DISTRIBUTION: Under the heading **WHERE FOUND**, we describe the habitat(s) in which the plant grows and its geographical range. Once you have a description and a picture that seem to match the plant or tree you are trying to identify, closely check the geographical range to make sure your plant falls within it. If your plant seems to match a description and picture, but you live in Montana and the range gives only California to Alaska, chances are you don't have the correct identification. If the plant is an introduced alien or a cultivated species that has either escaped from gardens or become naturalized, we note this. Many nonnative plants are well established in fields, forests, waste lots in cities, and parks. They are commonly called weeds, but we like to think of them as herbs.

Remember that some plants are abundant (especially the weedy medicinals), some are rare in some parts of the range, and some occur rarely throughout their range. Fortunately, medicinal plants of western North America are not as well known and thus overharvested as plants in the East. Still, some popular plants, such as Osha (*Ligusticum porteri*) and Lomatium (*Lomatium dissectum*), may easily be overharvested as herbal medicine becomes more popular. Some may also be confused with rarer relatives. For example, there are dozens of western North American species of *Lomatium*, separated according to highly technical characteristics. Currently, the herbal community uses only *Lomatium dissectum*. However, several *Lomatium* species are federally listed endangered species and should be left alone. We strongly urge you to learn by careful observation or by contacting your state or regional native plant society, or conservation groups.

The range of occurrence for each plant is given by state or province, usually starting with the most southwestern state and proceeding first to the Northwest, British Columbia, and Alaska, then to the northeast. The states given usually enclose the entire range, and noncontiguous states are listed separately, preceded by a semicolon. Following the primary range in the West, we note extensions of the range to eastern North America, northern Mexico, and elsewhere if applicable. Because California has a great diversity of habitats and because a majority of the plant species covered are found there, more detailed range information is often given for that state.

USES: This section presents many of the uses of each plant reported by Native American Indian groups. When only one or two tribes used a species, we often give the name of that particular group. When a species was widely known and used, we just say "American Indian groups." We would prefer to use the phrase commonly used in Canada, "First Nation Peoples," but for most readers that is an unfamiliar twist of the English language. Since we cover mostly plant species that are native to western North America, it is the native groups that have the most practical experience with their healing properties. When European settlers first arrived on the continent, the Indians were at times open and friendly, freely sharing their considerable experience and knowledge of the indigenous medicinal plants. The settlers were able to bring some familiar medicines with them, but they had a great need for locally available remedies, especially as their ties with Europe faded. By the time the settlers reached the West, relations with Indian tribes were tense, and they were no longer willing to share their plant knowledge. Some of the information obtained by ethnobotanists may not be reliable because of language difficulties, questions of proper plant identity, and the possibility that native informants gave misleading information because they did not respect the researchers. For more detailed information on Native American uses of many species, see Daniel Moerman's excellent compilation *Native American Ethnobotany* (Portland, Ore.: Timber Press, 1998).

As this Peterson guide is intended for use in the field, we had to consolidate and abbreviate some uses. Even given space limitations, though, we do give a fairly complete picture of the important Native American uses, including cross-cultural uses of given species and of similar species in the same genus. We also provide modern scientific chemical, pharmacological, and clinical data where available and relevant, to help support or clarify a plant's traditional uses.

RELATED SPECIES: Under many species entries, we have included information on related species from western or eastern North America, as well as from Europe, Asia and elsewhere. Cross-cultural uses, contraindications, and warnings about closely related species are especially interesting because generally we have little scientific information on many western species of herbs. Plants from the same genus, even if they are growing in widely divergent habitats and thousands of miles apart, are often quite similar in their chemical makeup and may have similar pharmacological activity when tested in the laboratory. For instance, plants in western North America in the genera *Valeriana, Arnica, Aralia, Ligusticum, Oplopanax, Asarum,* and *Polygala* have counterparts in Asia and Europe for which there is significant scientific evidence of their activity and safety, as well as up to 2,000 years of human experience of their value as medicinal plants. The Chinese herb dang gui (*Angelica sinensis*), a famous female tonic, may have a western counterpart whose use still awaits discovery. *Arnica montana* and *Valeriana officinalis* are two excellent examples of plants used extensively in Europe, even in modern medical practice, that have medicinal counterparts in western North America.

PREPARATIONS: In the Uses section we often include information about the way the plant was processed to release the active constituents and make them easier to assimilate. The most common preparations are chewing, grinding, pounding, or chopping and simmering in water, and steeping in alcohol. Native American Indians didn't have access to grinders or blenders, so they often chewed a plant part, especially leaves, and applied it directly to the skin to soothe and help heal burns, bites, rashes, cuts, or sores. This type of preparation is called a poultice. Denser plant parts, such as roots, bark, and seeds, were crushed or pounded, blended with water to make a paste, and then applied (or poulticed) to the affected area. Sometimes the crushed parts, or even the simmered herbs and then liquid, were spread on a cloth, which was then applied to the affected part as a poultice. Many plant parts were simmered or boiled to make a tea or boiled down to a syrup and applied externally as a wash, lotion, or compress, or mixed with animal fats to make a salve. External preparations such as poultices, salves, and washes were generally freshly prepared as needed.

For internal use, plant parts were traditionally chewed or brewed. Many leaves or flowers could be chewed and swallowed if small amounts were effective, and small pieces of roots or rhizomes of highly active herbs such as Osha and Echinacea were traditionally chewed. Sometimes the plant part was kept in the mouth for hours and the saliva swallowed. Since many denser plant parts have a high fiber content, which can upset the stomach, they were prepared as a decoction or infusion.

In many cases we do not distinguish between these two preparations. A simple infusion is generally made by soaking or steeping an herb (usually the leaves or flowers) in freshly boiled water for 10 to 20 minutes. A cold infusion is made by soaking the plant material in cold water for a longer period of time (varying from 2 hours to overnight) or by simply letting the hot infusion sit until it is cool. A decoction is made by simmering the plant material—usually the root, bark, or seeds—over low heat for up to 30 or 60 minutes. In general, the word "infusion" is reserved for leaves and flower material and "decoction" for roots, barks, or seeds. Check the plant part used to determine whether it should be decocted or simply infused. The difference was often not noted in ethnobotanical reports, and all hot water extractions are simply called teas.

Alcoholic extractions, often in wine or brandy, are made by adding crushed or pounded herbs to the liquid and letting them steep for a week or so. A teaspoon of the liquid is taken several times daily. The alcohol acts as a solvent for some of the herb's active principles, preserving and concentrating them and making them more easily absorbed from the digestive tract. Only ethyl alcohol is used, never isopropyl (rubbing) alcohol, which is toxic.

ABSORPTION: There are many compounds that the body does not absorb as they travel through the digestive tract. Many *Lobelia* species contain the toxic alkaloid lobeline, and ingesting it could lead to serious consequences, except that it is also a powerful emetic. The body rejects it before much absorption takes place.

Over millions of years of evolution, humans have been exposed to many compounds in plants that challenged our immune systems or other defense mechanisms, ultimately bringing adaptation and resistance to the ill effects of those compounds. Have we now become hothouse plants, pampered and unchallenged by any of nature's forces? We do insulate ourselves from the environment and, increasingly, from natural compounds in foods and herbs, perhaps to our detriment. For instance, Japanese women get up to 200 mg daily of natural estrogenic compounds called isoflavones in soy and other beans, while women in North America get only a few milligrams a day. Although some toxicologists argue that isoflavones and natural plant estrogens may *increase* the risk of cancer, just as synthetic estrogens do, Japanese women have the highest life expectancy of any developed country in the world and lower rates of cancer and heart disease than women in the United States, so they must be doing something right. It is interesting to note that many wild plants in the pea family, used traditionally for teas, food, and medicine, contain high levels of isoflavones. Examples discussed in this book include alfalfa (*Medicago sativa*), leather root (*Hoita macrostachys*), and California tea (*Rupertia physodes*).

DOSAGE: Since this book is not intended to be prescriptive or to take the place of a health care provider, we rarely list dosages in the Uses section.

WARNINGS: Pay special attention to the warnings. Some species are highly toxic and could injure you or, at the very least, cause nausea and vomiting. Remember that many plants may cause skin irritation or unpleasant rashes or blisters when handled. And many plants, especially when no flowers are present, may resemble something quite different. We stress the importance of making absolutely certain of identification before handling or ingesting any plant.

CONSERVATION AND HARVESTING

Many guidelines of wildcrafting are simply common sense. At its best, the time-honored practice of wildcrafting—the harvesting of wild herbs—depends upon conscious and respectful practices. At its worst, wildcrafting results in the careless extirpation of plant populations purely for profit. Recently the body of the Iceman, a Stone Age cave dweller, was found in the Tyrolean Alps, well preserved and carrying a pouch with several pieces of some hard, fibrous mushrooms that are still used as medicines today in Asia and Siberia. Researchers speculate that the Iceman used the mushrooms as medicine more than 5000 years ago. He, like many of his contemporaries, was of necessity a wildcrafter.

The most important rule is, if a plant is rare in your area, don't pick it and don't disturb it. Even a relatively common species may be rare at the edges of its ranges, and small populations of any species that is not widespread should be left alone. Contact your local Audubon Society, native plant societies, botanical gardens, or state conservation agencies to find out about a plant's abundance and range. Contact United Plant Savers (www.plantsavers .org) to view a list of plants that are thought to be under especially intense harvesting pressure.

You should harvest less than 10 percent of the plants growing in a plant population, particularly if you are seeking roots. If there are ten plants, take only one. If there are fewer than ten individuals, leave them alone. If you are pruning the flowering tops, leaves, shoots, or fruits, you can be more liberal, because the plant will regenerate, but do exercise restraint. Even if a plant is abundant in your area, preservation and the sustainable future of the plant should be your first consideration.

Do not harvest plants without the landowner's permission. In some states, such as Montana and North Dakota, it is now illegal to harvest certain plants for medicinal purposes without written permission from the owner. Vast expanses of the western United States are owned by government agencies, such as the U.S. Forest Service, National Park Service, or Bureau of Land Management. In most instances it is illegal to harvest plants from federal lands without special permits. In national parks you may not disturb anything. Many states also require permits for harvesting on state lands, including the roadside rights of way of most highways.

THANKFULNESS AND RESPECT: American Indians had great reverence for the plants they used as medicine. Some Native American healers fasted, participated in sweat-lodge ceremonies, and went off alone to pray before harvesting them. Often a gift of tobacco or another offering was buried in the vicinity before harvest. We have much to learn from this reverence for nature. Today, appropriate consciousness toward wild living things could go a long way toward preserving them for future generations.

HARVEST AT THE RIGHT TIME OF THE YEAR: Herbalists study the life cycles of plants so that they can harvest herbs when their potency is greatest. Flowers and flowering tops should be picked when they are at the peak of flowering, in the early morning after the dew has dried and before they are pollinated and begin to fade for the day— say by 10 or 11 a.m. Barks are generally harvested in the fall when the constituents are migrating down toward the roots or, as a second choice, in the spring when the sap is rising. Roots are traditionally harvested in the late fall and early winter after the plant tops have died back. Spring-harvested roots are sweeter and less bitter. Some biennials, such as burdock root, should be harvested at the end of the first year or the beginning of the second. After that, the quality is poor. Fruits are usually harvested when mature but still green, but in some cases when fully ripe. Seeds are harvested when mature. If you wait too long after the fruits mature, quality of both seeds and fruits can decline, especially with prolonged exposure to rain or sun. When collecting herbs, use paper bags or baskets with handles. Avoid keeping them in plastic bags, especially on a hot day. Plants can darken, begin fermenting, and lose quality within a few hours under these conditions.

Toxins in the environment can adversely affect the quality of medicinal plants and herbs. Do not harvest near roads, areas where pesticides and herbicides are sprayed, or factories. Avoid plants that are yellowing or dying. As a general rule, harvest at least 100 feet from a major road, 50 feet from a secondary road, and 10 feet from a poorly traveled road. Studies have shown that wild-harvested herbs near roadsides in Eastern Europe, where leaded gas was prevalent during the days of communist rule, have high levels of heavy metals such as lead.

GARBLING, DRYING, AND STORAGE: Garbling is the practice of separating the usable parts of plants from those that are unusable. When you harvest thyme from your garden, for example, you strip the leaves and flowering tops from the stems, dry the leaves, and store them for later use. The stems are tough and don't contain much of the flavor and fragrance components of the plant. Carefully wash roots with a brush or by hand. Cut thick roots into diagonal slices to allow more surface area for drying. Thin roots and rhizomes can be dried whole.

Dry herbs as quickly as possible, ideally by placing them on screens for increased air flow. Hang or place them in an area that has good air flow to hasten moisture evaporation, but out of direct sunlight. Excessive heat and direct sunlight can quickly degrade constituents. Make sure all plant parts are dry all the way through before storing them. Test a root for dryness by snapping it. Sometimes root slices look dry on the outside, but they may be still moist inside. These will mold if you store them for an extended time in a sealed jar.

Store herbs in sealed glass jars if possible, out of direct sunlight and in a cool dry place. Many roots, if carefully dried and stored well, will retain their value for one to three years. Leaves and flowers are best stored for no more than one year.

A FINAL WORD OF CAUTION

Even after taking the proper precautions, you might have an adverse reaction to handling and/or ingesting any plant. *Please be sure to read the warnings in each species account before handling the plant. Never eat or taste any part of a wild plant or use it in any medicinal preparation unless you are certain of its identification, safety, the correct dosage, and the proper preparation.*

This book is intended to extend appreciation of the plants around us beyond their intrinsic beauty to an understanding of their medicinal properties. It is not intended as an aid to self-medication. If you wish to explore herbal medicine as a health care regime, seek the advice of a qualified medical practitioner.

Symbols:

 = **Poisonous**. Dangerous or deadly to ingest, or perhaps even to touch.

 = **Caution**. See warning in text.

 = Known to cause **allergic reactions** in some individuals.

 = Known to cause **dermatitis** in some individuals.

 = Used in **modern medicine** in the U.S.

SPECIES
ACCOUNTS

MISCELLANEOUS SHOWY FLOWERS

BUNCHBERRY   **Leaves, roots, berries**
Cornus canadensis L.   Dogwood Family
    Low-growing, *spreading perennial*, 3–8 in., often forming large colonies. *Oval leaves in whorls of 6 beneath showy "flowers"* (bracts); *veins arch* from leaf base toward tip; margins entire. Small, greenish white flowers tightly clustered above *4 large, white, petallike bracts*; May–July. Fruit scarlet, single-seeded. **WHERE FOUND:** Moist, cool forests, meadows, bogs. Alaska to Idaho, Mont. south to N.M., nw. Calif. eastern N. America. **USES:** American Indians toasted the leaves, then sprinkled the powder on sores. Berries were a snack source, dried and stored for winter; also chewed to treat insanity. Leaf tea drunk as a strong laxative and to treat paralysis. The Paiutes mashed and strained the roots and used the liquid as a wash for sore eyes. Tea of the whole plant was taken for coughs, fevers, and tuberculosis. Tea from roots, leaves, and berries was drunk for fits. A root tea was given to babies for colic. Bark tea drunk for body pains.

ICE-PLANT, SEA FIG   **Leaves**
Mesembryanthemum crystallinum L.   Carpet Weed Family
    Multibranched, *bumpy-stemmed* perennial, spreading along ⚠ ground; to 24 in. high. Leaves succulent, alternate, flat, ovate to spoon-shaped; margins wavy. Flowers *stalkless in leaf axils*, showy, white to red-tinged, with many stamens and 5 linear petals; Mar.–Oct. Bumpy fruit opening when moist. **WHERE FOUND:** Saline soils near coast, bluffs, disturbed sites, coastal sage scrub. Along

Bunchberry (Cornus canadensis) blankets patches of the floor of northern forests.

In autumn, Bunchberry produces brilliant red fruits.

Note the bumpy stems and thick, succulent leaves of Ice-plant (Mesembryanthemum crystallinum).

Canada violet (Viola canadensis). Medicinal uses of violets are generic rather than species-specific.

the cen. and s. coast of Calif. to Ariz.; Baja Calif., Mexico; S. America, Mediterranean. Alien (South Africa). **USES:** Historically, physicians used leaf juice to soothe inflammation of the mucous membranes of the respiratory or urinary system; to treat painful or difficult urination and involuntary urination. In Europe the fresh juice has been used to treat water retention and painful urination and to soothe lung inflammation. **RELATED SPECIES:** *M. edule* L. (*Carpobrotus edulis* [L.] N. E. Br.), or Hottentot Fig, a common escape in California, is used externally in S. Africa for burns and thrush and internally for dysentery. **WARNING:** High in oxalates, potentially toxic in high doses, especially in flower and fruit.

CANADA VIOLET
Viola canadensis L.

Whole plant
Violet Family

Perennial with short, thick rhizome and slender stolons; to 10 in. Leaves *heart-shaped* or oval on *long stalks*; tips pointed; margins toothed. Flowers solitary from leaf axils. Petals white above, purple beneath, *yellow-centered; bottom petal dark-lined, spurred; side petals hairy at base*; Apr.–July. Pod splitting into 3 valves. **WHERE FOUND:** Moist to dry woods. Ore. to ne. Wash., Idaho, Utah, Ariz. Rockies from Mont. to N.M.; eastern N. America. **USES:** Native Americans used a root tea for pains in the bladder region. Externally, a poultice was used to treat skin abrasions and boils. In European traditions violet species were listed as soothing and softening for coughs and colds, urinary tract ailments, and skin conditions. **WARNING:** Roots of most if not all violet species may induce vomiting.

YERBA MANSA, YERBA DEL MANSO
Whole plant

Anemopsis californica (Nutt.) Hook. & Arn.   Lizard Tail Family

Aromatic perennial with thick, woody rhizomes. Leaves large, basal, oblong, to 6 in. long, bases somewhat heart-shaped; margins without teeth. Flowers tiny in dense, conical spike. Showy petallike bracts below flower spike are white, *often red-tinged or spotted*, so that the inflorescence resembles a single flower; Mar.–Sept. **WHERE FOUND:** Wet or moist sites in saline or alkaline soils, coastal marshes, seeps, springs. Colo., w. Utah, Nev., south to w. Tex., nw. Ariz., Mexico, Baja Calif. to s. Calif., s. Ore. **USES:** An important remedy of the Indians of the Southwest for many conditions. After they showed it to early Spanish settlers, it became known as the "herb of the Manzo," as the Indians who worked in the missions were called. American Indians made a root tea for colds, stomachache, ulcers, diabetes, tuberculosis, pleurisy, menstrual cramps, gonorrhea, itchy throat, and general pain. Dry roots were held in the mouth to treat sore throat. Externally, root tea used as an antiseptic wash and for venereal sores; boiled and mashed, the root was applied to swellings. Leaf tea drunk to treat stomach ulcers, constipation, colds and chest congestion, blood disorders, and lung hemorrhages. Externally, used

(Above) *The broad oval leaves of Yerba Mansa* (Anemopsis californica) *have a peculiar fishlike fragrance. White flowers are often mottled pink.* (Right) *White Marsh Marigold* (Caltha leptosepala) *has round, deeply notched leaves with scalloped margins.*

Buckbean (Menyanthes trifoliata) *is found in wet habitats. Note the white "beard" on inside of petals.*

to bathe muscular pains and sore feet and as a disinfectant for open sores. Powdered leaf used to disinfect sores and knife wounds and to encourage growth of healthy tissue. A poultice of chewed green leaves was applied to burns and open wounds. The fragrant, spicy roots are gaining popularity today as a digestive and respiratory tea. Research confirms their anti-inflammatory activity.

WHITE MARSH MARIGOLD, MARSH MARIGOLD
Caltha leptosepala ssp. *howellii* (Huth) P.G. Sm.   **Whole plant**
[*C. biflora* DC., *C. howellii* Huth]   Buttercup Family

Perennial with short, upright, *thick, fleshy stems*, to 14 in. Leaves broadly round on long, fleshy stalks; deeply notched at base; margins scalloped. Flowers white on long, leafless stalks, 1–2 flowers per plant, rising above leaves; May–Aug. Short-beaked fruit oval, many-seeded. **WHERE FOUND:** Marshes, pond edges, bogs, streambanks in montane, coniferous forests. S. Alaska to cen. Calif., east to nearly every western state. **USES:** American Indians chewed or crushed plant and poulticed it to wounds to ease pain and reduce inflammation. **RELATED SPECIES:** An infusion of leaves of Yellow Marsh Marigold, *C. palustris* L., was used by Eskimos for relieving constipation. The Chippewa used root tea to treat colds. Mashed roots were applied to sores. The plant was considered to have diuretic, diaphoretic, expectorant, and emetic properties. The Iroquois favored a tea of the mashed roots as an emetic to counteract a love potion. **WARNING:** The whole plant is irritating to the gastrointestinal tract when fresh. All parts may irritate and blister skin or mucous membranes. Sniffing bruised stems induces sneezing.

BUCKBEAN, BOGBEAN, MARSH TREFOIL   **Root, leaves**
Menyanthes trifoliata L.   Buckbean Family

⚠ Thick, submerged rhizomes *covered by old leaf bases*. Leaves on long petioles, divided into 3 *oval, cloverlike leaflets*; rising to 15 in. above water. White to pink, *ill-smelling flowers* on naked racemes. Petals 5, spreading, covered in *long, frilly hairs*; Apr.–Aug. Fruit a thick-walled oval pod, remaining unopened. **WHERE FOUND:** Lake and pond edges, bogs, swamps, wet meadows, seeps, marshes. Every western state except N.M., Tex., from s. and n. Sierra, and n. coast ranges of Calif. to Alaska; eastern N. America; Eurasia. **USES:** Native Americans used the root or leaves in a compound with other plants to treat gas pains, constipation, nausea, spitting of blood, and rheumatism. The tea was used as a general tonic for weight gain. Physicians historically used bogbean leaf extracts as a potent digestive tonic, also for weak blood and uterine problems, and to treat water retention. European herbalists recommend bogbean for liver-related headaches, loss of appetite, gout, and rheumatoid arthritis. Leaf approved in Germany for treatment of dyspeptic discomfort and loss of appetite. Pharmacological studies show bogbean constituents have bile-stimulating and liver-protective effects. **WARNING:** Fresh plant may cause gastrointestinal upset and vomiting. Contraindicated in cases of colitis or diarrhea.

FRAGRANT WATER-LILY, WHITE PONDLILY   **Root, leaves**
Nymphaea odorata Ait.   Water-lily family

Aquatic perennial with large, round, *floating leaves*, notched at base. Flowers white to pinkish, floating, *sweetly fragrant*. Flowers open in morning, close in evening; June–Sept. **WHERE FOUND:** Ponds, lake edges, marshes, slow waters; widely cultivated. Native to eastern N. America; introduced in all western states except Idaho, Wyo., N.M. **USES:** Herbalists recommended a root tea as a gargle, wash, or tea to treat mouth sores, sore throat, dysentery, chronic diarrhea, and gonorrhea; in cough compounds for bronchitis. Used as a douche

Fragrant Water-lily (Nymphaea odorata) has sweet-scented flowers.

for vaginal yeast infections and for uterine fibroids and as an eye-wash. Root and leaf poultices were used on sores, boils, tumors, and rashes. Native Americans placed the stems on teeth for toothache; root tea used to diminish men's libido. Alcoholic extracts of the rhizomes contain the sedative and antispasmodic alkaloid nymphaeine. Antitumor and antimicrobial activity confirmed in laboratory tests. **RELATED SPECIES:** *N. caerulea* Sav. and *N. ampla* DC. were used in ancient Egypt and among Mayan priests, respectively, as ritual narcotics.

AQUATIC PLANTS; 3 PETALS

COMMON WATER-PLANTAIN
Whole plant
Alisma plantago-aquatica L.   Arrowhead Family

Aquatic perennial with very short, upright stem, 1–3 ft. tall when in flower. Leaves glossy, *oval, on long, thick petioles from base*; tips pointed, bases rounded; margins without teeth. Flowers small, white to pink, 3-parted, in open, multibranched panicles, rising well above leaves; June–Sept. Fruits flat, curved on back. **WHERE FOUND:** Shallow water or muddy soils, marshes, pond edges, wet ditches, roadsides. Colo. to Ariz., west to Calif., B.C., eastern N. America; Eurasia, also e. Africa, Australia, S. America. **USES:** Cree and Woodland Indians ate the dried stem base or grated it and took it in water for heart troubles and heartburn. It was also taken for stomachaches, cramps, constipation and stomach flu and to prevent fainting during childbirth. The Iroquois used a leaf tea as a runner's liniment. Plant tea was used for female ailments. Root tea was used for back injuries or kidney problems. Raw roots were chewed to strengthen veins. In the late 1800s physicians used a liquid extract from the roots as a compress for nasal catarrh and touted the dried-leaf tea to treat urinary calculi and ease burning urination with a feeling of having to urinate too often. Used similarly in China. *Alisma* species contain diuretic and cholesterol-lowering triterpenes.

BROAD-LEAVED ARROWHEAD
Roots, leaves
Sagittaria latifolia Willd.   Arrowhead Family

Perennial with tuberous, white to blue, oblong rhizomes. Leaves arrowhead-shaped on long stalks; *basal lobes long, pointed*; submerged leaves linear or lacking. Flowers white, 3-parted, 3 per node on long, leafless flowering stalks. Petals spreading or reflexed; stamens many; June–Sept. Fruits sharp-beaked from side, flat, winged, in round clusters. **WHERE FOUND:** Marshes, pond and lake edges, wet ditches, slow streams. Widespread from Calif. to B.C., in every western state except Nev. There are 30-plus species of arrowhead in N. America, separated on technical characteris-

Common Water-plantain (Alisma plantago-aquatica) *has delicate white flowers on thick stalks.*

About 30 species of Sagittaria *are found in North America. Note the arrow-shaped leaves.*

tics. **USES:** The roots, an important potatolike food for Native Americans, were also used as a tea for indigestion, constipation, boils, rheumatism, and in very small quantities for fever in infants. It was added to other herbal teas for constipation and to calm children who screamed in the night. Root poulticed to treat wounds and sores. The whole plant was considered an effective love charm; also used to ward off witches. Science has not investigated these uses. **WARNING:** Some *Sagittaria* species are reported to cause contact dermatitis.

CURIOUS FLESHY PLANTS WITH SPECIALIZED GROWTH HABITS OR LACKING CHLOROPHYLL

DODDER, CHAPARRAL DODDER
Whole plant
Cuscuta californica Hook. & Arn.   Morning-glory Family
⚠ *Very slender, orange to yellow, chlorophyll-lacking stems densely twining over plant.* Parasitic via many knoblike suckers on stems. Leaves reduced to minute scales. Small, waxy, white flowers, 5-parted, on short stalks in spikelike clusters; May–Aug. **WHERE FOUND:** Roadsides, chaparral, grasslands, yellow pine forests. S. and n. coastal ranges, s. Sierra of Calif. to every western state except Mont., N.M. **USES:** American Indians made an infusion of the

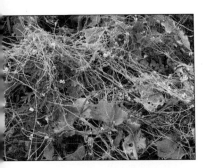

(Above) *Dodder* (Cuscuta *spp.*) *is a yellow, chlorophyll-lacking parasite.* (Right) *Roundleaf Sundew* (Drosera rotundifolia) *is usually found in acidic bog habitats.*

plant as a cure for black widow spider bites. Juice from chewed stem or plant powder was snuffed up the nose to treat nosebleeds. The whole plant was eaten as a contraceptive. **RELATED SPECIES:** C. *epithymum* (L.) L., found in many parts of the world, is used as a folk medicine for liver problems, urinary tract ailments, and as a laxative. C. *compacta* Juss. ex Choisy, Compact Dodder, was used by Pawnee girls as a love medicine to reveal the intentions of suitors. The seeds of C. *chinensis* Lam. are the traditional Chinese drug tu-si-zi, used in prescriptions to "strengthen the kidneys" and to treat impotence, nocturnal emission, premature ejaculation, ringing in the ears, and frequent urination, sometimes accompanied by a chronically sore lower back. The drug is also taken for eye problems associated with liver ailments and is believed to benefit the digestion, stop diarrhea, and calm the fetus during threatened abortion. **WARNING:** Some parasitic flowering plants take up toxins from their hosts.

ROUNDLEAF SUNDEW   **Whole plant**
Drosera rotundifolia L.   Sundew Family
   Insectivorous perennial to 1 ft. Small, *round leaves in basal rosette*, covered with *sticky, red hairs* that trap prey. Flowers few, white to pinkish on *one side of 2–9-in.-long flowering stalk*; June–Sept. **WHERE FOUND:** Sphagnum bogs, marshes, wet meadows. N. Calif. to Alaska, Idaho, Mont., Colo.; eastern N. America. **USES:** American

Indians poulticed Sundew for corns, warts, and bunions. The plant is commonly used in European herbal medicine to ease coughs and respiratory infections. Laboratory experiments show antibacterial, immunostimulating, antifungal, and antiviral quinones as well as muscle-relaxing effects on the bronchial airways. **REMARKS:** Conservation concerns have arisen about overharvesting of the herb for use in European herbal medicine.

INDIAN PIPE
Whole plant

Monotropa uniflora L.

Indian-Pipe Family

Entire plant translucent white, fleshy; generally clumped; to 10 in. Flowers solitary, bell-shaped, nodding at stem tip (becoming upright in fruit); June–Oct. Thick-walled pod splitting, many-seeded. **WHERE FOUND:** Shady, moist, mixed coniferous forests in rich humus; low elevations. N. coastal forests of Calif. to Alaska, Idaho, Mont., Tex.; eastern N. America, n. Mexico; C. and S. America, e. Asia, Japan. Parasitic on conifers via mycorrhizal associations. **USES:** Historically, herbalists used the root as an antispasmodic and sedative for convulsions, epilepsy, spasms, restlessness, and nervous irritability and as an opium substitute for pain. They also used the juice or infusion to treat stubborn eye in-

Indian Pipe (Monotropa uniflora) *has a single flower and lacks chlorophyll.*

Giant Bird's Nest (Pterospora andromedea) *often has reddish stems; the flowers are white.*

flammations, ulcers, gonorrhea, and cystitis. Native Americans used it for similar conditions, as well as for colds, fevers, pain from colds, and toothache and as an application to bunions or warts. **WARNING:** Safety undetermined; possibly **toxic**—contains several glycosides.

GIANT BIRD'S NEST, PINEDROPS
Plant, berries, root
Pterospora andromedea Nutt.   Wintergreen Family
    Sticky stems reddish-brown, with clammy hairs, unbranched, upright to 1–4 ft. Leaves practically absent, only bractlike, basal, scales. Flowers cream to pinkish, drooping urns on elongated racemes; June–Sept. Dry, rounded fruit opens base to tip, releasing many large-winged seeds. **WHERE FOUND:** Mixed or coniferous forests. S. and n. Calif. to B.C., all western states, Midwest, Great Lakes, New England; Mexico. Parasitic on conifers via mycorrhizal associations. **USES:** The Cheyenne prepared a solution from the stems and berries for bleeding from the lungs; it was snorted for nosebleed. Keres Indians used plant to induce vomiting. Thompson Indians used root to treat gonorrhea. As a folk remedy, the plant was used for pleurisy and skin eruptions.

ORCHIDS (3-PARTED WITH EXPANDED LOWER LIP)

WESTERN RATTLESNAKE PLANTAIN
Whole plant
Goodyera oblongifolia Raf.   Orchid Family
    Perennial from slender rhizome, to 18 in. (in flower). *Dark green*, oval to oblong leaves in *basal rosette, white veins forming simple or dense netted pattern*. Small white to greenish flowers in dense, *one-sided spike; top petal hooded*; July–Aug. **WHERE FOUND:** Dry to moist, shaded coniferous forest, mossy areas. Cen. Sierra and n. Calif. to Alaska, east to Idaho, Utah, Ariz.; also in Rockies from Mont. to N.M.; eastern N. America, Mexico. **USES:** Pregnant women of Northwest American Indian groups chewed the leaves to determine the sex of their babies. If they could swallow the leaves, the baby would

Western Rattlesnake Plantain (Goodyera oblongifolia) *has mottled leaves with white veins.*

Flower spike of Downy Rattlesnake Plantain (Goodyera pubescens) *has tiny white flowers.*

Ladies'-tresses (Spiranthes spp.) *has a distinct double-spiraling flower spike.*

be a girl, if not, a boy. Leaves were also chewed to make childbirth easier. Externally, leaf poulticed for cuts and sores; a wash was used for stiff muscles by canoers and sprinters. **RELATED SPECIES:** Downy Rattlesnake Plantain (*G. pubescens* [Willd.] R. Br. ex Ait. f.), with prominent white veins in a rattlesnake pattern, earned this plant its common name, as well as use of the root for snakebites, based on the doctrine of signatures. The Cherokee used the leaves externally as a poultice to heal burns in the mouth and for toothaches, and internally to improve the appetite, as a cleansing emetic, and to benefit the kidneys. Other tribes used the leaves and roots variously for rheumatism, following childbirth, for pleurisy, and for babies with sore mouths. **REMARKS:** Of historical interest only. Too scarce to harvest.

LADIES'-TRESSES

Spiranthes romanzoffiana Cham.

Whole plant

Orchid Family

Perennial from tuberous roots, to 20 in. Leaves *mostly basal*, linear to lance-shaped. Small, *fragrant*, white to greenish flowers in *dense, spiraled spikes*; May–Sept. Top petals *hooded; lip short, narrowed below wavy tip*. Oval pod upright. **WHERE FOUND:** Wet meadows, streamsides, freshwater marshes. S. Calif. to Alaska, every western state except Tex.; eastern N. America. **USES:** Ladies'-tresses was used to treat venereal disease. Other unidentified native species were used to treat urinary tract disorders and as blood purifiers. **RELATED SPECIES:** Other N. American, European, and S. American species have also been used as a diuretic and aphrodisiac.

FLOWERS 3- TO 6-PARTED (LILY FAMILY); LEAVES AT BASE OR IN WHORLS WITH PARALLEL VEINS

GARLIC   Bulb
Allium sativum L.   Lily Family

To 3 ft. Leaves extend *almost to middle of stem*. Note the 2- to 4-in. long, *narrow, papery green spathe* around flowers. **WHERE FOUND:** Fields, roadsides. Alien. Escaped from cultivation in Calif., Ore., Wash. Garlic has evolved through cultivation by humans for over 7000 years. Believed to have originated in the Asian steppes, it is not now found in the wild except when escaped from cultivation. It is entirely dependent upon humans. California is the main commercial producer of fresh garlic. **USES:** Garlic has been used to treat hundreds of ailments. Fresh garlic cloves and preparations

California is the largest grower of garlic (Allium sativum) *in the United States.*

Wavyleaf Soap Plant (Chlorogalum pomeridianum) *has broadly linear leaves with strongly wavy margins.*

have been used for colds, fevers, coughs, earaches, bronchitis, sinus congestion, headaches, stomachaches, high blood pressure, arteriosclerosis, diarrhea, dysentery, and many other conditions. Used for centuries in China primarily for diarrhea and amoebic dysentery. Experimentally, it lowers blood pressure and serum cholesterol; it is antibacterial, antifungal, and diuretic. Clinical studies suggest it is effective in gastrointestinal disorders, hypertension, heart ailments, and arteriosclerosis. Garlic has been the subject of more than 2500 scientific studies over the past 25 years, including more than 18 clinical studies, involving more than 3000 patients, to evaluate its effects in lowering blood lipids (cholesterol). Results are mixed, but generally positive. Epidemiological studies show that garlic significantly decreases the incidence of cancers, especially those of the gastrointestinal tract. **WARNING:** The highly concentrated essential oil can cause irritation and chemical burns.

WAVYLEAF SOAP PLANT, SOAP-ROOT, AMOLE
Root, bulb, stalk
Chlorogalum pomeridianum (DC.) Kunth. Lily Family

Hairless perennial from long bulb covered with *thick, fibrous scales*; to 6 ft. Stem *leafless*, with whitish film. Leaves long, *broadly linear* in *basal rosette*; margins *strongly wavy*. Flowers small, solitary on open-branched stalks; petals linear with *purple or green midvein, recoiled*, twisted above round fruit; Mar.–Aug. **WHERE FOUND:** Dry, open hills, grasslands, banks, valleys. Coast ranges, n. Sierra of Calif. to sw. Ore. **USES:** An important fish poison, food, and fiber plant of western tribes. Juice rubbed on skin to treat poison oak. Roasted bulbs used as an antiseptic poultice for sores. Fresh bulbs were rubbed on the body for cramps and rheumatism; also used as a wash to prevent lice. Bulb tea used as a diuretic and laxative and for stomachache caused by gas. Stalks used as a shampoo for dandruff. **WARNING:** The bulbs contain saponins that are highly irritating to the mucous membranes and are considered poisonous unless well cooked. May cause dermatitis.

QUEENCUP, BRIDE'S BONNET
Whole plant
Clintonia uniflora (Menzies *ex* J. A. & J. H. Schultes) Kunth. Lily Family

Perennial from slender, *spreading* rhizome; to 6 in. Leaves 2–3, *oblong, basal, shiny*; veins parallel. Flowers solitary (or 2) on *stalks shorter than leaves*; May–July. *Berry dark blue* to black. **WHERE FOUND:** Moist, shaded forests. N. Calif. to Alaska, east to Idaho, Mont. **USES:** The Bella Coola and other tribes used plant tea as a body wash. The juice, plant, or toasted leaves were poulticed to cuts and wounds. The root juice, mixed with water, was taken for urinary calculi.

Queencup (Clintonia uniflora)
has a single flower with parallel-veined, shiny leaves.

WESTERN TRILLIUM, WAKEROBIN, TRILLIUM   Root
Trillium ovatum Pursh   Lily Family

⚠ Single-stemmed, hairless perennial to 2½ ft. Leaves 3, *stalkless, broadly ovate,* in whorls beneath showy flower. Flowers on *evident stalk,* white, turning rose; petals 3, larger than the 3 narrow sepals; Feb.–June. **WHERE FOUND:** Moist, shady forests, streambanks, redwood forest. Mont., Wyo., Colo. cen. to n. coast ranges and Cascade Mts. from Calif. to B.C. **USES:** Trillium roots traditionally used to stop uterine, respiratory tract, and urinary tract bleeding; externally for skin problems. American Indians used roots for uterine bleeding, as an aid in childbirth, and for other gynecological problems; externally as a poultice on boils. **RELATED SPECIES:** The eastern N. American species Red Trillium or Bethroot (derived from "birth root"), *T. erectum* L., was used to prepare a woman's system for childbirth. **WARNING:** The fresh rhizome is intensely acrid and can cause nausea and vomiting.

DEATH CAMAS   Root
Zigadenus venenosus S. Wats.   Lily Family

☠ Hairless, *slender-stemmed* perennial from deep *bulb with dark scales,* to 2 ft. *Basal* leaves narrow, *grasslike,* rough, clasping at base. Flowers white to cream, dense along branches of upper stalk; petals with *yellowish green gland at base;* stamens 6, *longer than petals;* Apr.–July. **WHERE FOUND:** Moist meadows to dry, rocky slopes. S. B.C. to Calif.; all western states except Ariz. **USES:** Externally only, the root was used fresh or dried, poulticed for aches, pains, bruises, sprains, boils, burns, rattlesnake bites, rabid coyote bites, and broken bones. There is mention of its use as a strong emetic, and small pieces were placed in the mouth for mouth sores, sore throats, and to ease toothache (bear in mind that the number one cause for suicide in pre-industrial societies was toothache). There is one reference to the bulb being used as

Western Trillium (Trillium ovatum) *has three stalkless leaves below the white flower (turning pink with age).*

Death Camas (Zigadenus venenosus) *somewhat resembles a wild onion but is highly toxic.*

food, but one has to wonder whether this was the result of miscommunication or of the desire to be rid of a pesky ethnobotanist. **WARNING: Highly toxic.** Fatalities have been reported; hence the common name Death Camas.

FLOWERS 3- TO 6-PARTED (LILY FAMILY); PETALS AND SEPALS ALIKE; LEAVES ALONG STEM

FALSE SOLOMON'S SEAL
Maianthemum racemosum ssp. *racemosum* (L.) Link
[*Smilacina racemosa* (L.) Desf.]

Root, leaves
Lily Family

Perennial from creeping rhizome, to 1–2 ft.; *stems zigzag, arching.* Leaves alternate, *ovate*, base clasping stem. Flowers small, *densely arranged along tightly branched* stem tip; *stamens longer than petals*; Mar.–July. *Berry red*, often dotted purple. **WHERE FOUND:** Moist, shady areas, streambanks, meadows. Calif. to Alaska; every western state; widespread throughout eastern N. America. **USES:** The astringent and demulcent properties of root and leaf preparations made them useful for sore throats and colds, to soothe a cough, for upset stomach, constipation, and ulcers, and as a poultice on boils, swellings, itching, rashes, and cuts. Root tea used to regulate menstrual cycles, for short-term birth control, for kidney problems, sore backs, arthritis, cancer, and heart problems. Leaf tea also used to soothe coughs, itchy rashes, and rheumatism. A decoction of the root and leaves was used to ease internal pain and injuries.

STAR-SOLOMON'S SEAL
Smilacina stellata (L.) Desf.
[*Maianthemum stellatum* (L.) Link]

Root, leaves
Lily Family

Perennial from creeping rhizome, to 2½ ft. Stems straight or zigzag. Leaves alternate, *lance-shaped*, often folded. Flowers *few on loosely branched* stem tip; stamens shorter than petals; Mar.–June. *Red-purple berry becoming black.* **WHERE FOUND:** Moist, shady places, meadows, streambanks. Throughout most of northern N. America; every western state except Tex. **USES:** Star-Solomon's Seal used similarly to False Solomon's Seal, especially to ease menstrual disorders and stomach problems, for colds, earaches, sore throat, swollen glands, and internal pain and injury. Root poulticed for sprains, boils, earaches, eye inflammation, swellings, and arthritis. Leaf tea used to prevent contraception and as an eyewash.

CLASPING TWISTED-STALK
Streptopus amplexifolius (L.) DC.

Root, plant
Lily Family

Well-branched perennial from long rhizomes, to 4 ft. Leaves alternate, ovate, *clasping stem, with heart-shaped bases*; whitish film

False Solomon's Seal (Maianthemum racemosum) has flowers in terminal clusters.

Star-Solomon's Seal (Smilacina stellata) has a zigzag stem.

The bell-shaped flowers of Clasping Twisted-stalk (Streptopus amplexifolius) *are on a twisted stalk.*

beneath. Flowers greenish white, *bell-shaped, nodding, solitary (or 2) on slender, twisted stalks from below leaf axil, petals curved back* or spreading; May–July. Berry yellow or red, sometimes becoming dark purple. **WHERE FOUND:** Moist, shady woods, streambanks. N. Calif. to Alaska; all western states except Nev., Tex., to e. Canada and New England. **USES:** American Indians chewed the roots to initiate labor; tea used to treat hemoptysis, gonorrhea, kidney problems, internal pains, and stomachache and as an appetite stimulant. A tea of the berries and stems was drunk as a general tonic.

FLOWERS 4-PARTED; PETALS SEPARATE; STAMENS 6; FRUIT PODLIKE (MUSTARD FAMILY)

HORSERADISH   Root
Armoracia rusticana P. G. Gaertn., B. Mey. & Scherb.
[*A. lapthifolia* Gilib.]   Mustard Family

 Large-rooted herb, 1–4 ft. Leaves large, broad, lance-shaped (sometimes jagged); *long-stalked;* leaves much reduced on flowering stalks. Flowers white, tiny, 4-petaled; May–July. Pods tiny, egg-shaped. **WHERE FOUND:** Moist *fields.* Throughout. Alien (Europe), it persists after cultivation. **USES:** Root used in many cultures as a condiment. Root tea weakly diuretic, antiseptic, and expectorant; used for bronchitis, coughs, and bronchial catarrh. Root poultice used for rheumatism, respiratory congestion. Research confirms antibiotic activity against bacteria and pathogenic fungi. Experimentally, it has antitumor activity. In Germany the root is approved to treat inflammation of the respiratory tract and in supportive treatment of urinary tract infections. Externally, root preparations have been approved to treat lung congestion and minor muscle aches. **WARNING:** May irritate digestive system or cause blistering if applied directly to the skin. Plant tops are a **fatal poison** to livestock in large amounts.

SHEPHERD'S PURSE
Whole plant

Capsella bursa-pastoris (L.) Medik.
Mustard Family

Fine-haired annual, to 23 in. Leaves mostly in *basal rosette*, oblanceolate, *pinnately lobed.* Stem leaves small, clasping. Flowers small, on spreading stalks from upper stem; flowering all year. Seedpods *heart-shaped, flattened.* **WHERE FOUND:** Disturbed sites, roadsides. Alien (Eurasia). Widespread weed throughout N. America; every state. **USES:** American Indians adopted European use of tea to treat dysentery and diarrhea and as a wash for poison ivy. The Cheyenne drank a tea of powdered leaves and stems in small quantities for headache. The Chippewa boiled the whole

Horseradish (Armoracia rusticana) is often found near gardens. Note the large leaves and tiny white flowers.

Shepherd's Purse (Capsella bursa-pastoris) has purse-shaped seedpods.

root and drank tea for stomach cramps. An infusion of seedpods was used for stomach pains and to rid the body of worms. Modern herbalists recommend it for nosebleed and excessive menstrual flow; also as a laxative and diuretic. In European phytotherapy, tincture of shepherd's purse is prescribed for mild high blood pressure, postpartum bleeding, excessive or irregular menstrual bleeding, and to stop nose bleed. The plant contains choline, acetylcholine, and polypeptides that have been demonstrated to affect the tone of the uterus. Externally used as a hemostatic and styptic to stop bleeding. **WARNING:** Seeds are known to cause rare cases of blistering of skin.

SPECTACLE POD, TOURIST PLANT   **Whole plant**
Dimorphocarpa wislizeni (Engelm.) Rollins   Mustard Family
Soft-haired, light gray annual, to 20 in. Hairs star-shaped or multibranched. Leaves alternate, pinnately lobed, densely hairy. Flowers along reduced branches on upper stem; base of petals sometimes purplish. *Flat pods much broader than long with 2 rounded lobes*, each single-seeded; remaining unopened. **WHERE FOUND:** Sandy soils, deserts. Colo. N.M., Tex., to Mexico, west to Utah, Nev., and Ariz. **USES:** American Indians used crushed seeds and leaves as an inhalant for catarrh or sore nose. Plant tea used externally as a compress for throat problems and swellings. Ground stalk used as a salve for sores. Both leaves and seedpods were powdered and sprinkled on abrasions. Plant tea was taken internally and applied externally as a lotion for centipede or sand cricket bites. In Zuni medicine, plant tea was drunk to treat delirium.

Spectacle Pod (Dimorphocarpa wislizeni) is a soft-haired, light gray annual.

Shining Peppergrass (Lepidium nitidum) *has shiny oval seedpods.*

SHINING PEPPERGRASS
Whole plant

Lepidium nitidum Nutt. (and other *Lepidium* spp.)   Mustard Family

Slender-stemmed annual, to 16 in. Leaves mostly basal, *deeply pinnately dissected* into *pointed, linear segments.* Flowers minute, dense along branches of mostly leafless stems; Feb.–May. *Round, shiny pods shallowly notched at top, beakless, on flattened, hairy stalks.* Varieties distinguished by hairless or densely hairy stems and pods and by beaked or nonbeaked fruit tips. **WHERE FOUND:** Open places, meadows, alkaline soils. Calif. to Wash., Nev.; Baja Calif. **USES:** Cahuilla Indians used leaves to make a wash to cleanse the scalp and prevent baldness. Diegueño Indians used seeds to treat indigestion. Other tribes used the plant as a vitamin C source and to speed healing of poison oak rashes. **RELATED SPECIES:** Members of the Keres tribes used *L. densiflorum* Schrad. for headaches, kidney problems, sunburn, and to counteract the effects of swallowing an ant. Navajo used *L. montanum* Nutt., Mountain Pepperweed, to treat biliousness and stomach problems, palpitations, and dizziness. *L. apetalum* Willd. seeds are used in Chinese medicine to decrease phlegm and congestion in the lungs, for wheezing and coughs, and to reduce edema. In India the leaves of garden cress, *L. sativum* L., are used as a stimulant and diuretic and for liver ailments. Seeds are eaten or brewed to stimulate milk flow, regulate the menses, as a tonic and aphrodisiac, and as a poultice for sprains. Studies confirm antibacterial and antioxidant properties.

WATERCRESS, WHITE WATERCRESS
Whole plant

Rorippa nasturtium-aquaticum (L.) Hayek   Mustard Family
[*Nasturtium officinale* Ait. f.]

⚠ *Weak stems submerged or lying flat on mud, rooting at nodes,* to 4–36 in. Leaves pinnately divided into 3–11 ovate to oblong leaflets; largest leaflet at tip; margins wavy to entire. Small, white

(Left) *Watercress* (Rorippa nasturtium-aquaticum) *leaves have a peppery flavor.* (Above) *Watercress* (Rorippa nasturtium-aquaticum) *grows in slow-moving streams.*

flowers 4-parted in compact racemes; Mar.–Nov. Linear pods upright, pointed, with 2 rows of seeds per valve. **WHERE FOUND:** Watercress, well known for its edible, mustardlike leaves, forms large colonies in cool running water. It begins its life cycle in early spring, growing in fresh water, streamsides, springs, ditches, marshes, lake margins. Native to Eurasia, widely naturalized and cultivated throughout N. America. **USES:** Watercress has been used since ancient times, throughout Europe and Asia, as a savory fresh vegetable in salads to promote good appetite and health. Herbalists use it to treat kidney problems, sluggish liver, cirrhosis, gallstones, gout, hormone imbalances, mild digestive upset, vitamin C deficiency, anemia, and respiratory congestion and inflammation. Other uses include treatment of fevers, hypotension, fungal infections, and skin problems such as eczema. Okanagan-Colville Indians used a poultice on the forehead for aches or dizziness. Costanoans and other tribes used an infusion to reduce fevers and as a kidney, liver, and gallbladder remedy, especially for liver stagnation and gallstones. Laboratory tests demonstrate antimutagenic activity. Approved in Germany for treatment of respiratory tract inflammation. **WARNING:** Leaves from polluted waters may accumulate toxins, such as heavy metals and pesticides.

FLOWERS 4-PARTED; PETALS SEPARATE (NOT IN MUSTARD FAMILY)

WHITE-MARGIN SANDMAT, RATTLESNAKE WEED

Chamaesyce albomarginata (Torr. & Gray) Small **Whole plant**
[*Euphorbia albomarginata* Torr. & Gray] Spurge Family

⚠ *Hairless, trailing* perennial with milky sap, to 1 ft. Leaves opposite, ovate to round; margins without teeth. *Stipules fused into white, triangular, papery scale.* Flower cup surrounded by *4 white, petallike bracts with maroon gland at base*; Mar.–Nov. Pod sharply 3-angled; seeds white, smooth. **WHERE FOUND:** Dry slopes, plains. S. Calif., Nev., Utah, Ariz., N.M., Tex.; n. Mexico. **USES:** American Indians used tea of whole plant to wash sores. Internally used as a strengthening tonic for general weakness. The Ramah Navajo and other tribes used cold tea as a remedy for stomachaches. Nursing mothers ate both leaf and root to increase milk flow. Leaves and flowers were ground and applied to rattlesnake bites. Crushed plant was placed on the eyes to alleviate soreness and on wounds to stop bleeding. **RELATED SPECIES:** Numerous other species were used in N. America. In the western U.S., *C. fendleri* (Torr. & Gray) Small was used by the Navajo and other tribes as a tea for easing stomachaches and diarrhea. *C. lata* (Engelm.) Small was used by the Navajo as a purge for upset stomachs. The milky sap of *C. melanadenia* (Torr.) Millsp. was applied to bee stings and sores by

(Above) *White-margin Sandmat* (Chamaesyce albomarginata) *has four white, petallike bracts with a maroon gland at the base.* (Right) *The slender stems of Cleavers* (Galium aparine). *Note the hooked hairs.*

the Cahuilla. The Miwok used a decoction of *C. ocellata* (Dur. & Hilg.) Millsp. as a blood purifier and rubbed mashed leaves into snakebites to prevent swelling. The Luiseño used *C. polycarpa* (Benth.) Millsp. ex Parish in several forms for snakebite, as an eyewash and general tonic, and for stomach and bowel troubles. **WARNING:** Members of the genera *Chamaesyce* and related *Euphorbia* are known to contain highly irritating and potentially mutagenic diterpenoid esters. Historical use only; keep milky juice away from the eyes.

CLEAVERS, BEDSTRAW
Galium aparine L.

Whole plant
Madder Family

Sprawling, rough annual covered with hooked prickles; to 1 3 in. Stems square, weak, *raspy*, with prominent hooked hairs. Leaves lance-shaped, in *whorls of 6–8*, bristle-tipped. Flowers small, on *slender stalks* from leaf axils; Apr.–Sept. **WHERE FOUND:** Moist, shaded areas, open forests, gardens as a weed. Throughout N. America. Alien (Europe). **USES:** Tea traditionally used for nodules or lymphatic swellings, fevers, painful urination, kidney inflammation, urniary calculi, kidney stones, cystitis, and edema. Used as a blood purifier, folk cancer remedy, and diuretic. Externally, tea applied as wash for inflammation, infections, rashes, eczema, psoriasis, leprosy, and burns. American Indians adopted European use to treat skin problems, including poison ivy and itch and for urinary tract problems, including gonorrhea. *Galium* spp. contain iridoid glycosides that are laxative, anti-inflammatory, and diuretic in laboratory tests. **RELATED SPECIES:** Other species common to Europe and N. America are used interchangeably, including *G. verum* L., *G. asprellum* Mich., *G. trifidum* L., and *G. triflorum* Mich.

FLOWERS 5-PARTED; PETALS SEPARATE; STAMENS MANY AND CHIEF SHOWY FEATURE OF FLOWER

RED BANEBERRY, WESTERN BANEBERRY
Actaea rubra (Ait.) Willd.

Roots, leaves
Buttercup Family

Hairless perennial to 3 ft. Leaves alternate, divided 3 times into ovate to lance-shaped leaflets; margins lobed, sharply toothed. Flowers small with many *showy stamens* in dense, *rounded racemes on long stalks*; Apr.–July. Smooth, *shiny red berry* (rarely white). **WHERE FOUND:** Moist, shady areas, streambanks. Cen. to n. coast ranges of Calif. to s. B.C.; eastern N. America. **USES:** American Indians used root tea for colds and coughs, rheumatism, syphilis, emaciation, and menstrual difficulties. Externally,

Red Baneberry (Actaea rubra) *has
delicate white petalless flowers.*

*Red Baneberry produces fleshy red
fruits.*

chewed leaves were applied to boils and wounds. **RELATED SPECIES:**
The Cheyenne used an infusion of the root and stems of *Actaea
arguta* Nutt. (*A. rubra* ssp. *arguta* [Nutt.] Hultén) to stimulate
milk flow. In Europe, *A. spicata* L. is known as an emetic and
cathartic used for asthma. **WARNING:** The berries and root are potentially poisonous, causing irritation to the gastrointestinal tract
and vomiting.

GOAT'S-BEARD, BRIDE'S FEATHERS

Stems, roots

Aruncus dioicus (Walt.) Fern.

Rose Family

Robust, hairless perennial from stout rhizome, to 6 ft. Leaves
large, alternate, pinnately divided 2–3 times into ovate to lance-
shaped leaflets; margins sharply toothed. *Small flowers in dense
spikes* in highly branched sprays; May–July. *Male and female flowers on separate plants.* **WHERE FOUND:** Moist streambanks in forests.
Calif. to B.C.; eastern N. America. **USES:** In American Indian
medicine ashes from the stem
were mixed with grease and
used as a poultice for swelling

Goat's-Beard (Aruncus dioicus)
occurs in wooded habitats.

and paralysis. Root and stem tea was taken for indigestion and general stomach disorders. Root tea taken in small doses for flu and by pregnant women to prevent excessive bleeding during childbirth. Externally, root tea was used to bathe swollen feet and pouticed to treat bee stings. The plant was infused for excessive urination and for stomach and other internal ailments.

WESTERN BUGBANE, TALL BUGBANE
Cimicifuga elata Nutt.
[*Actaea elata* (Nutt.) Prantl.]

Root
Buttercup Family

⚠️ *Unpleasant-smelling* perennial, to 6 ft. Leaves large, 3-divided into ovate, shallowly lobed, finely toothed leaflets; tips pointed; *teeth gland-tipped; angled petioles clasping stem.* Flowers small, white to pinkish, in dense racemes; stamens many, *showy*; June–Aug. Oblong pod with *small beak off-centered at top*; seeds without scales. **WHERE FOUND:** Moist sites in woods, roadsides, streambanks. Nw. Ore. to s. B.C. **USES:** A close relative of the widely used black cohosh (*C. racemosa* [L.] Nutt.) of eastern N. America, whose limited occurrence and destruction of habitat recommend against its use. Very little ethnobotanical or traditional use exists for *C. elata*. **RELATED SPECIES:** Black cohosh, *C. racemosa*, is one of the most widely used N. American native plants, commonly prescribed by early 20th-century physicians, especially for menstrual and reproductive disorders. Black cohosh has become a standard herbal medicine for easing symptoms of hot flashes and other unpleasant symptoms that can occur during menopause. European clinical studies confirm use in menopause, and it is approved in Germany for treatment of menopausal and premenstrual

Western Bugbane (Cimicifuga elata), like its eastern cousin Black Cohosh (C. racemosa), pictured here, has petalless flowers dominated by showy stamens.

symptoms and painful or difficult menstruation. C. *foetida* L. and
C. *dahurica* (Turcz. ex Fish. & C. A. Mey.) Maxim. and other
species are used in Chinese medicine as sheng ma in prescriptions to treat symptoms of flu and measles and painful sores on
the skin, lips, gums or in the mouth or throat. Also used for muscle pain, shortness of breath, fatigue, and prolapsed uterus. **WARN-
ING:** Concentrated solutions, such as teas and tinctures, can cause
digestive upset. Avoid use during pregnancy except under advice
of qualified medical practitioner.

FENDLER'S MEADOW-RUE
Roots, seeds
Thalictrum fendleri Engelm. ex Gray
Buttercup Family

Hairless perennial to 6 ft. *Stems and leaves purplish.* Leaves *thin,*
alternate, 3-divided into round to ovate, 3-lobed leaflets, *minutely
glandular below; petioles short*; margins scalloped. Flowers many,
small, white to greenish, nodding in open-branched clusters;
male and female flowers on separate plants; stamens many, *showy,
yellow or purplish*; May–Aug. **WHERE FOUND:** Moist, shady places,
streamsides, meadows. Calif. to Wash., every western state except
Mont.; Baja Calif., n. Mexico. **USES:** Root tea once used to treat

Fendler's Meadow-rue (Thalictrum fendleri) *has white to greenish flowers nodding in open-
branched clusters.*

Western Meadow-rue (Thalictrum
occidentale). *Note the purplish
stamens.*

colds and gonorrhea. Leaf and stem tea used by American Indians to relieve stomach cramps and fevers. Externally, as a wash for fevers and heat prostration. Smoke from the burning plant was inhaled for colds and headaches, and a pillow was stuffed with the leaves to relieve headaches. **RELATED SPECIES:** The stems and leaves of *T. fendleri* var. *polycarpum* Torr. [*T. polycarpum* (Torr.) S. Wats.] were pounded and used as a poultice for sprains by applying a hot rock over the herb on the site, and the juice was made into a wash for headaches. A root decoction was used for colic. **WARNING:** *T. fendleri* is reported to have heart-stimulating properties similar to digitalis. The root of *T. fendleri* var. *polycarpum* has caused death in cows and horses, and the stems are considered poisonous.

WESTERN MEADOW-RUE
Thalictrum occidentale Gray

Root, leaves, fruit, seeds
Buttercup Family

⚠ Hairless perennial from rhizome, to 4 ft. Young stems purplish. Leaves alternate, *bluish green*, 3-divided into round to obovate, 3-lobed leaflets; margins coarsely scalloped. Flowers numerous, small, white to greenish or purple-tinged, nodding in open panicles; male and female flowers on separate plants; stamens many, *showy, purplish*; June–Aug. **WHERE FOUND:** Moist, shaded places, meadows, open forest. Calif. to se. Alaska, Idaho, Mont., Wyo. **USES:** Juice from a small piece of chewed root was swallowed to stimulate blood circulation, as an expectorant, and to treat headache, eye problems, and sore legs. A decoction of the root was used as a wash for body pains and stiffness. An infusion of the seeds was taken for chest pains and as a tonic. Mashed root poultice applied to open wounds. **WARNING:** Of unknown toxicity.

FLOWERS 5-PARTED; PETALS SEPARATE; LEAVES 3-PARTED OR PALMATELY LOBED

BEACH STRAWBERRY
Fragaria chiloensis (L.) P. Mill.

Leaves, fruit
Rose Family

Perennial, to 6 in. tall. Leaves leathery, divided into 3 oval leaflets with distinctly *rounded bases, shiny green above*. Flowers white, like those of wild strawberry; Apr.–Aug. Fruits look like strawberries but are tasteless or insipid. **WHERE FOUND:** Coastal regions, ocean beaches, grasslands. Alaska to Calif., S. America, Hawaii. **USES:** Though the fresh berries lack the flavor we associate with strawberries, American Indian groups of the West Coast ate them to prevent scurvy and as a general food source. Leaves were also dried and used to make a beverage tea. A poultice of the dried leaves was used to treat burns.

(Above) *Beach Strawberry* (Fragaria chiloensis) *has leathery leaves with rounded bases.* (Right) *Wild strawberry* (Fragaria vesca) *has seeds on the surface of the fruit.*

WILD STRAWBERRY
Fragaria vesca L.

Whole plant
Rose Family

Perennial from scaly rhizomes and *obvious runners*; to 1 ft. *Thin* leaves basal, divided into 3 *oval*, sharply toothed leaflets; sparsely hairy above, denser below; *tips bluntly pointed, base wedge-shaped*. Flowers on long stalks *above leaves*; Mar.–Aug. *Fleshy, red fruit dotted with minute seeds*. **WHERE FOUND:** Forest openings, partial shade, banks. Throughout N. America; every western state except Nev. **USES:** American Indians used all parts of the plant as a remedy for diarrhea and dysentery. Root tea used for stomach disorders. Poultice of leaves (or leaves mixed with deer fat) applied to sores. Early 20th-century physicians recommended mildly astringent leaf tea for urinary stones, gout, and diarrhea. A cordial from the fruit was used for relieving fevers. Root tea used as a mild diuretic and was applied to sunburns. Root used as a chewing stick (toothbrush).

POKER HEUCHERA, ROUNDLEAF ALUMROOT
Heuchera cylindrica Dougl. ex Hook.

Roots, leaves
Saxifrage Family

Stiff-haired perennial with creeping rhizome, to 3 ft. Leaves in *basal rosette on long*, short-haired petioles, palmately lobed, glandular; margins *scalloped*. Flowers small, whitish to yellowish, bell-shaped, in branched clusters on leafless upper white-haired stalks; *stamens 5, styles 2*; May–June. **WHERE FOUND:** Rocky slopes. Calif. to s.

Poker Heuchera (Heuchera cylindrica) *has thick pokerlike flower spikes.*

B.C., Idaho, Mont., Colo., Nev. **USES:** Native Americans and early European explorers and hunters mashed or boiled the roots or leaves for external use on sores, cuts, wounds, snakebites, and rashes and for sore muscles and rheumatism. Root tea or chewed roots used for rheumatic pains, sore muscles, stomach cramps, diarrhea, sore throat, mouth and gum sores, liver problems, and tuberculosis. Externally, root tea used as an eyewash, and a small, cleaned, peeled piece of root was chewed and held in the mouth to relieve mouth and gum sores and infections. An antifungal compound has been found in root extracts. **RELATED SPECIES:** Early 20th-century physicians considered this and other species of alumroot to be powerful astringents useful in treating rashes, wounds, ulcers, skin cancer, diarrhea, hemorrhoids, and bleeding, and as a douche for vaginitis, but felt that its strength was such that internal use should be moderate.

CREVICE HEUCHERA OR ALUMROOT
(Not shown)   **Roots, leaves**
Heuchera micrantha Dougl. ex Lindl.   Saxifrage Family
Rhizomatous perennial, to 2 ft. Palmately lobed leaves in *basal rosette, hairy veins below*; margins toothed; stalks with long, soft hairs; *stipules at base of leaf stalk fringed with hairs.* Flowers numerous, small, in open, upper *red-stemmed branches*; May–Aug. *Stamens 5; styles 2.* **WHERE FOUND:** Moist, shady, rocky slopes, streambanks. S. and n. coast ranges of Calif. to s. B.C., Idaho. **USES:** American Indians used root tea as a tonic astringent to treat fevers, liver conditions, mouth and gum sores, and sore throat and as an eyewash. Externally, root poulticed for cuts, wounds, sores, and swellings; a piece was chewed to relieve mouth sores and infections. The Skagit pounded the plants and rubbed them on hair and scalp to encourage hair growth.

FLOWERS 5-PARTED; PETALS SEPARATE; STAMENS 10 OR LESS; LEAVES NOT PALMATELY LOBED

INDIAN HEMP
Root, stems, berries, sap

Apocynum cannabinum L.   Dogbane Family

Shrublike; *1–2 ft.* Leaves (except lowermost ones) with *definite stalks*, to ½ in. long. Flowers *terminal, whitish green*; bell-like, 5-sided; June–Aug. Seedpods paired, 4–8 in. long. **WHERE FOUND:** Fields, prairies, roadsides. B.C. to Calif., eastward. **USES:** See *A. androsaemifolium* (p. 165). Stems an important source of fiber and cordage, hence the common name. Milky sap a folk remedy for venereal warts. American Indians used fruits and root in weak teas for heart ailments and as a diuretic. Components have been found to raise blood pressure and experimentally show antitumor activity. **WARNING: Poisonous.** Contains toxic cardioactive (heart-affecting) glycosides.

INDIAN MILKWEED, WOOLYPOD MILKWEED
Whole plant

Asclepias eriocarpa Benth.   Milkweed Family

Perennial with milky sap, *densely covered in white-woolly hairs*, to 3 ft. Leaves oblong to lance-shaped, usually *3–4 per node*. Flowers cream-colored, in *dense umbels*; petals reflexed, sometimes tinged pink; hoods *as long as central stamen column*, with small

(Left) *Indian Hemp* (Apocynum cannabinum) *flowers in late summer.* (Above) *Indian Milkweed* (Asclepias eriocarpa) *has white-woolly leaves.*

Miner's Lettuce (Claytonia perfoliata) *has distinctly rounded leaves sitting atop the stem.*

California Horkelia (Horkelia californica) *has white petals, but reddish sepals.*

horns; May–Aug. Seedpods long, slender; seeds many, with long, silky hairs. **WHERE FOUND:** Dry areas, washes, slopes. S. and n. Calif.; n. Baja Calif. to Nev. **USES:** Costanoan Indians made a salve from plant tea for colds. Milky juice was applied to corns, cuts, sores, and warts. Smoke from burning the dried plant was inhaled as a remedy for asthma. **WARNING:** This species is considered too poisonous for internal use. Many species of *Asclepias* contain cardiac glycosides that stimulate the heart muscle.

MINER'S LETTUCE
Whole plant
Claytonia perfoliata Donn *ex* Willd.   Purslane Family
   Fleshy, hairless annual from slender taproot, to 16 in. Leaves mostly in basal rosette, oval to triangular or diamond-shaped on long petioles; 2 *opposite stem leaves fused into round disk* below small, white to pinkish flowers; Jan.–July. *Petals notched; sepals 2;* styles 3. Oval pod 3-valved, opening from tip; seeds 3, black, shiny. **WHERE FOUND:** Moist, shady places; under oaks; disturbed sites. Calif. to B.C., Idaho, Nev., Utah, Ariz.; Rockies from Mont. to Wyo.; Baja Calif., Mexico. Highly variable in size and leaf shape. **USES:** The Shoshone applied leaf poultice for syphilis and rheumatism. The plant was also used to soothe sore eyes and to improve vision. Leaves used as food, fresh or cooked.

CALIFORNIA HORKELIA,
CALIFORNIA DEWBERRY
Roots
Horkelia californica Cham. & Schlect.   Rose Family
   Fragrant, glandular perennial, to 4 ft. Leaves mostly basal, pinnately divided into ovate, generally 3-lobed leaflets; margins

Common Chickweed (Stellaria media) *is a widespread weed.*

sharply toothed. Flowers *cup-shaped*, in open upper branches; sepals *red to purple, mottled inside*; 5 ovate bractlets below; May–Sept. **WHERE FOUND:** Open, grassy places, streambanks. Coastal areas from cen. to n. Calif. **USES:** Pomo Indians used a decoction of the roots as a blood purifier. Arapaho used an infusion of the roots as a general tonic.

COMMON CHICKWEED
Stellaria media (L.) Vill.

Leaves
Pink Family

Low-growing, weak, *sprawling* annual or perennial; to 15 in. Stems *slender*, with *line of hairs between leaf nodes*. Leaves opposite, ovate to oval on *short petiole*. Flower petals *deeply 2-cleft* (appearing as 10), shorter than sepals; Feb.–Sept. **WHERE FOUND:** Disturbed areas, lawns, meadows, and gardens. Cosmopolitan weed throughout N. America. Alien (Europe). **USES:** Mild-tasting chickweed greens are used in salads and as a potherb worldwide. An ancient European folk remedy, used in ointments for relieving skin inflammations, acne, boils, bruises, eczema, hemorrhoids, psoriasis, poor-healing ulcers, and eye inflammation. A tea was drunk to relieve constipation, coughs, and hoarseness. Fresh juice was applied to the eyes to relieve soreness, redness, and itchiness. Chickweed tea, juice, or salad was a well-known folk remedy for obesity, and it still has this reputation today. In Asia the herb tea is drunk by women after giving birth as a cleansing tea, to encourage milk flow, and also to regulate menstrual cycle.

FLOWERS 5-PARTED; PETALS FUSED; TUBULAR; NOT LARGE

EYEBRIGHT
Euphrasia spp.
[*Euphrasia officinalis* L.]

Whole plant
Figwort Family

⚠ Slender, semiparasitic (root is attached to grasses) annual; 4–8 in. Leaves tiny, bristle-toothed; June–Sept. The 3 *lower lobes notched*, with purple lines. Highly variable. **WHERE FOUND:** The

Eyebright (Euphrasia *spp.) is a low-growing plant of the far north.*

Salt Heliotrope (Heliotropium curassavicum) *grows in dry, alkaline soils.*

plants in this complex group, with over 200 named species (mostly European), are separated by botanists on minute technical details. Western N. American material, mostly from Alaska or n. Wash., is generally assigned to the species *E. mollis* (Ledeb.) Wettst or *E. disjuncta* Fern. & Weig. Mostly harvested from northern Europe, the plants are referred to by herbalists collectively as *Euphrasia officinalis.* Most species used interchangeably. **USES:** The genus name *Euphrasia* comes from the Greek meaning "to delight," perhaps referring to medicinal uses. The tea is astringent. A folk remedy (as a wash or poultice) for eye ailments with mucous discharge; also used for coughs, hoarseness, earaches, and headaches with congestion. The small flowers, somewhat eyelike, suggested its use for eye ailments, according to the medieval doctrine of signatures. Poorly researched, *Euphrasia* species contain anti-inflammatory and antibacterial compounds, perhaps providing a basis for traditional uses. A recent retrospective clinical analysis by European ophthalmologists found that single-dose treatments of an eyebright preparation effectively and safely treated catarrhal conjunctivitis in over 65 patients. **WARNING:** Avoid use without a qualified health practitioner's advice. **RELATED SPECIES:** Other *Euphrasia* species have been used similarly and interchangeably.

SALT HELIOTROPE
Heliotropium curassavicum L.

Whole plant, roots
Borage Family

Low-growing, fleshy perennial *covered with a whitish film, to 2 ½* ft. Leaves alternate, oblanceolate, without stalks. Flowers small, tubular, white to bluish, in *2–4 coiled spikes at stem tips;* Mar.–

Oct. **WHERE FOUND:** Moist or dry saline soils. Throughout western N. America. **USES:** American Indians used plant tea to treat diarrhea, venereal disease, bloody discharges, and water retention. Plant tops were used to hasten measles development by bringing out the rash. Root tea used as a gargle for sore throat and to induce vomiting. Powdered, dried juice applied to wounds, sores, and abrasions. *H. currassavicum* var. *argentatum* is used in S. America to treat gout, rheumatism, neuralgias, arteriosclerotic disorders, myalgia, phlebitis, and varicosities. **WARNING:** *Heliotropium* species contain liver-toxic pyrrolizidine alkaloids that cause veno-occlusive disease of the liver. Use not recommended.

WESTERN BISTORT   **Root**
Polygonum bistortoides Pursh   Buckwheat Family
Unbranched perennial, to 2 ft. Basal leaves oblong to lance-shaped on long stalks; upper leaves reduced, clasping stem; brownish, *papery stipules surrounding stem at swollen leaf base.* Flowers small, white to pinkish, in dense, oval spikes on long, nearly leafless stalks; May–Aug. **WHERE FOUND:** Moist to wet mountain meadows and streambanks; subalpine and alpine. S. Calif. to Alaska; every western state except Tex. **USES:** A poultice of the roots used on sores and boils, and roots chewed to check diarrhea. **RELATED SPECIES:** The closely related *P. bistorta* L. occurs in Alaska, Europe, and Asia. The roots are used traditionally as a tea, douche, or mouth rinse to stop internal bleeding from the lungs or stom-

Western Bistort (Polygonum bistortoides) *has a tight, cylindrical flower head.*

Douglas's Nightshade (Solanum douglasii) *has white, flattened, star-shaped flowers.*

ach and to alleviate symptoms of irritable bowel syndrome, diverticulitis, incontinence, vaginal and uterine infections with discharge, mouth ulcers, spongy gums, and nasal polyps. Laboratory studies have shown plant extracts to possess anti-inflammatory properties.

DOUGLAS'S NIGHTSHADE
Solanum douglasii Dunal

Root, leaves, berries
Nightshade Family

Multibranched perennial to 3 ft., mostly reclining; stems angled, roughened by curved, white hairs. Leaves ovate with *tapering tip*; margins mostly entire or coarsely toothed. Flowers white, 5-lobed, in umbellike clusters from leaf axils; petals somewhat star-shaped, flattened, with *greenish spots at base*; yellow stamens upright, hairy, opening by pores at tip; Jan.–Dec. Fruit blackberrylike, with many yellowish seeds. **WHERE FOUND:** Dry woodland, chaparral, partly shaded slopes, canyons, streamsides. Calif. coast ranges to Ariz., N.M., Tex.; Baja Calif., n. Mexico. **USES:** The fresh berry juice was strained directly into sore, inflamed, or infected eyes. It was also said to help alleviate presbyopia (aging eyes). **WARNING:** *Solanum* species contain the toxic alkaloid solanine in varying amounts, especially in the leaves and unripe berries. It disrupts the gastrointestinal tract and nervous system, leading to feelings of dryness and heat in the throat as well as nausea and diarrhea. Deaths have been reported. *Solanum* species should be avoided by pregnant women because of potential toxicity to the fetus.

JIMSONWEED, THORNAPPLE
Datura stramonium L.

Leaves, seeds
Nightshade Family

Upright or sprawling, *ill-smelling* annual, to 5 ft. Leaves alternate, oval to oblong; *wavy margins coarsely lobed into sharp points.* Flowers *large*, showy, *trumpet-shaped*, white to purplish, *solitary in branch axils*; May–Sept. Fruit a spiny pod, *upright*, splitting into 4 parts. **WHERE FOUND:** Sandy soils, desert washes, streambanks, disturbed areas. Widespread weed throughout N. America; every western state except Wyo. Native to Mexico. **USES:** Both the leaves and seeds were used externally in American Indian medicine. A poultice of crushed leaves was applied to boils and cuts. The seeds were ground and mixed with tallow as a salve for hemorrhoids. A tea of fresh or dried leaves was used on wounds and as a wash for fever or inflammation. The leaves were smoked for asthma. The seeds were considered poisonous. Both the leaves and seeds were listed as official medicines in the *United States Pharmacopoeia* from 1820 to 1950, and preparations are still used today for asthma and spasmodic coughs. *Datura* contains many toxic alkaloids. It also contains scopolamine, which is used in patches behind the ear for vertigo. **WARNING: Violently toxic**; teratogenic and abortifacient. Contains the poisonous alkaloids atropine, hyoscyamine, and hyoscine, among others. Many deaths have been reported.

(Above) *Jimsonweed* (Datura stramonium) *is highly toxic, causing fatalities each year.* (Right) *Indian tobacco* (Nicotiana quadrivalvis) *has long, wrinkled, trumpet-shaped flowers.*

INDIAN TOBACCO

Nicotiana quadrivalvis Pursh var. *bigelovii* (Torr.) DeWolf
[*N. bigelovii* Torr.]

Nightshade Family

Malodorous, glandular annual, to 6 ft. Leaves alternate; lower ones lance-shaped to ovate, petioles short; upper leaves lance-shaped, *sessile*; margins entire. Flowers long, trumpet-shaped, white with green or purple tinge, in loose racemes; petals a long, slender tube with flared, pleated lobes; May–Oct. Round pod releasing many minute seeds. **WHERE FOUND:** Dry washes, slopes, disturbed areas. S. Calif. to n. Sierra north to Wash., w. Nev., Idaho; cen. N. America. **USES:** Kawaiisu Indians put leaves in the ear to treat earache, in the nose for headache, between the teeth for toothache, on the chest for internal pains, and on a woman's abdomen during childbirth. Leaves were smoked as a ceremonial purgative and chewed to induce vomiting. A snuff was used to treat a stuffy nose, smoke blown into the ear for an earache, and a poultice used on bleeding cuts and itching bites. The plant was used to commit suicide and infanticide. **WARNING:** Plant contains deadly nicotine alkaloid. **RELATED SPECIES:** *N. quadrivalvis* Pursh, Indian Tobacco, of eastern U.S. was used for many of the same purposes.

FLOWERS 4- OR 5-PARTED; PETALS FUSED, 2-LIPPED (MINT FAMILY); LEAVES NOT STRONGLY AROMATIC

CUT-LEAVED WATER HOREHOUND BUGLEWEED

Lycopus americanus Muhl. ex. W. Bart.

Mint Family

Hairless perennial from slender rhizome, to 1–2 (3) ft. Leaves opposite, lance-shaped, *deeply pinnately lobed to sharply toothed*, on square stems; *stalks short.* Flowers small, in *whorls in leaf axils*; petals 4-lobed (upper lobe notched); *sepal lobes linear, awn-tipped*; stamens 2, rising slightly beyond petals; July–Sept. **WHERE FOUND:** Moist areas, marshes, streambanks. Throughout U.S. and Canada; every western state except Nev. **USES:** Meskwaki Indians used bugleweed to treat stomach cramps. **RELATED SPECIES:** Used similarly to Bugleweed, *L. virginicus* L., and European Bugleweed, *L. europaeus* L., which were widely used historically as a sedative and a tonic in cases of general debility. It was also used to improve circulation and appetite and to treat insomnia associated with chronic disease; for painful indigestion, gastritis, diarrhea, and dysentery; acute and chronic lung problems; hyperthyroidism, diabetes, and light hemorrhage. Recent laboratory studies show that extracts have a hormone-regulating effect and inhibit iodine metabolism and thyroxine release in the thyroid. Approved in

Germany for thyroid hyperfunction and thyroid enlargement (without functional disorders). **WARNING:** Avoid use during pregnancy or nursing. In rare cases, Bugleweed has been found to enlarge the thyroid. If therapy is discontinued, symptoms may return.

HOREHOUND
Marrubium vulgare L.

Whole plant
Mint Family

Low-growing, *white-woolly* perennial, to 2 ft. Leaves opposite, round to ovate, *gray, woolly, crinkled*, on square stems; margins scalloped. Flowers small, in dense whorls from leaf axils; May–Oct. Hooked sepal lobes forming a bur when dried. **WHERE FOUND:** Disturbed sites, fields, roadsides. Widespread weed throughout N. America; every state except N.D. Alien (Europe). **USES:** This European species has traditionally been used in syrups, candies, or tea for colds, coughs, chronic respiratory congestion, asthma, and other lung problems. American Indians adopted the plant for respiratory afflictions. Herbalists use warm tea for jaundice, hepatitis, asthma, hoarseness, dyspepsia, and worms and to calm overactivity of the heart. Tea or leaves were used on skin conditions. Pharmacological studies show that horehound extracts contain diterpenes and other compounds that have anti-inflammatory, expectorant, and antibacterial properties. In Ger-

Cut-leaved Water Horehound (Lycopus americanus) *is our most common bugleweed.*

Horehound (Marrubium vulgare) *has woolly, strongly wrinkled leaves.*

California Skullcap (Scutellaria californica) *is one of the few skullcaps with white flowers.*

many horehound preparations are approved for supportive treatment of coughs and colds and as a digestive aid and appetite stimulant. **WARNING:** Plant juice may cause dermatitis.

CALIFORNIA SKULLCAP
Leaves
Scutellaria californica Gray
Mint Family

Hairy perennial from slender rhizome, to 16 in. *Hairs short, curved.* Leaves opposite, narrowly oval to oblong; margins scalloped. Flowers white to pale lavender; *top lip arched, hoodlike; sepal tube with uplifted crest on upper side* (skullcap); *stamens 4,* under upper lip; June–July. **WHERE FOUND:** Dry, open areas, gravelly soils, along dry streambanks. N. Calif. **USES:** The bitter leaves and flowering tops were used by American Indian tribes and early European Americans as a substitute for quinine to reduce fevers. **RELATED SPECIES:** A number of native species were used in N. America. The whole plant of *S. tuberosa* Benth., Dannie's Skullcap, a common species of the western U.S., was used by Indian tribes as a sedative, nerve tonic, digestive tonic, and antispasmodic. A tincture or tea of Mad-dog Skullcap, *S. lateriflora* L., harvested in flower, was once popular for improving digestion and appetite and reducing recovery time from chronic illness, especially with nervousness, mental and physical exhaustion, and weak blood or anemia. A respected remedy for quieting the nerves, improving sleep, helping to eliminate addictions, for teething pain, muscle twitches, tics, and muscle spasms. Others species are used in China and India.

FLOWERS 5-PARTED; PETALS FUSED, 2-LIPPED (MINT FAMILY); LEAVES STRONGLY AROMATIC

LEMON BALM, MELISSA
Whole plant
Melissa officinalis L.
Mint Family

Strongly *lemon-scented* perennial, to 2½ ft. Leaves opposite, ovate, *crinkled,* on square stems; margins coarsely scalloped. Flowers *few,* white to pale lavender, clustered in *leaf axils;* sta-

mens 4, in 2 pairs, lying under upper lip; June–Sept. **WHERE FOUND:**
Disturbed places, open woods. Widespread garden escape in
Calif. n. to Wash.; also eastern N. America. Alien (Europe). **USES:**
Though once listed in official drug books, by the 1870s Lemon
Balm was considered too weak to be of benefit. Modern studies
reawakened interest in the herb after studies demonstrated antioxidant, antiviral (herpes), antimicrobial, anti-inflammatory,
thyroid-regulating, and sedative properties. Current uses include
treatments for a wide range of respiratory, digestive, neurological,
psychological, gynecological, and skin problems, including
asthma, flatulence, intestinal cramps, headaches, toothache,
melancholy, insomnia, painful menstruation, sores, bites, and
fevers. Creams are available for treatment of herpes simplex. In
Germany Lemon Balm preparations are approved for treatment of
sleeplessness due to nervous conditions and digestive tract
spasms.

WILD OREGANO, HORSEMINT
Monarda pectinata Nutt.

Flowering tops
Mint Family

Aromatic, *rough-haired* annual to 20 in. Leaves opposite, lance-
shaped, on square stems; margins wavy. Flowers showy, white to
pinkish, in *dense whorls from leaf axils; top petal arched;* lower lip
often *purple-spotted,* central lobe larger; *sepals densely white hairy,
long bristle-tipped; stamens 2;* May–Sept. **WHERE FOUND:** Dry, open,
rocky places. Se. Calif., Utah, Ariz. Rockies from Wyo. to N.M.,
Tex.; n. Mexico. **USES:** The Ramah Navajo used Wild Oregano both
internally and as a poultice to treat headache, general aches and
pains, cough, fever, and flu. The Kayenta Navajo drank a tea for

Lemon Balm (Melissa officinalis)
*has pleasantly lemon-scented
leaves.*

*Lemon Balm has white to pale
lavender flowers.*

Wild Oregano (Monarda pectinata) *has tiered flower heads.*

Catnip (Nepeta cataria) *is a favorite of felines.*

(Left) *Mountain Mint* (Pycnanthemum californicum) *has lightly
woolly and nearly clasping leaves.*
(Above) *Yerba Buena* (Satureja
douglasii), *common in the redwood
forests, has pleasant minty flavor.*

stomach problems. A flower infusion was used as a wash for bites and stings. The flowers were infused in cool water and applied as a perfume.

CATNIP
Flowering tops
Nepeta cataria L.
Mint Family

Aromatic, *gray-green*, hairy perennial, to 3 ft. Leaves opposite, *triangular-ovate*, on square stems; margins coarsely toothed. Flowers in *dense, clustered whorls at stem tips*; *lower lip purple-spotted, flattened, margin wavy*; top lip hooded; sepals densely hairy, tips sharply pointed; *stamens 4, under upper lip*; June–Sept. **WHERE FOUND:** Moist, disturbed sites, roadsides, streambanks. Throughout N. America. Alien (Europe). **USES:** Catnip is popular as a tea for children's ailments; used for colds, coughs, sore throats, pneumonia, fevers, restlessness, chills, upset stomach, indigestion, nausea, vomiting, gas, colic, diarrhea, and constipation. The herb is also indicated for worms, anemia, pain, headache, toothache, insomnia, hives, swellings, and measles. Tea used as a soothing bath for tiredness or to raise the body temperature. Many American Indian tribes adopted these uses and others in the 18th and 19th centuries. Catnip contains nepetalactone, a sedative and analgesic compound whose action involves opioid receptors. Best known as a feline euphoric, Catnip produces in housecats and larger felines the "Catnip response," which includes sniffing, licking, chewing, head shaking, rolling, and rubbing. This phenomenon is the result of an inherited autosomal dominant gene, absent in about one-third of cats. Human use of Catnip does not produce similar effects.

MOUNTAIN MINT, SIERRA MINT
Whole plant
Pycnanthemum californicum Torr.
Mint Family

Strongly aromatic, *gray-haired* perennial from creeping rhizome, to 3 ft. Leaves opposite, ovate to lance-shaped, *gland-dotted below*, on square stems; margins coarsely toothed. Flowers in dense whorls in leaf axils; lower petal lip *purple-spotted*; sepal tips *densely covered in short, white hairs*; *stamens 4, slightly exserted*; June–Sept. **WHERE FOUND:** Moist montane areas, canyons, streambanks. N. Sierra, s. Cascades, and lower mountains of Calif. **USES:** Miwok Indians made a tea of Sierra Mint for colds. **RELATED SPECIES:** Several species from the eastern U.S. were used by American Indian tribes for fevers and colds, including *P. albescens* Torr. & Gray, *P. flexuosum* (Walt.) B.S.P.; also used for headaches, diarrhea, and for stomach and heart problems.

YERBA BUENA
Leaves, stems

Satureja douglasii (Benth.) Briq. **Mint Family**

Aromatic, low-growing perennial to 6 in. with *long, trailing, slender, square stems*; rooting at nodes. Leaves opposite, ovate to round, stiff and shiny; *margins scalloped*. Flowers small, white- or purple-tinged, *solitary in leaf axils*; Apr.–Oct. **WHERE FOUND:** Shady areas in woodlands, chaparral. Along the coast ranges of Calif. to s. B.C., n. Idaho, Mont. **USES:** This aromatic minty herb, whose name means "good herb," makes one of the best-tasting wild teas. (The original name of the city of San Francisco was Yerba Buena.) The fragrant leaves and stems were used as tea to treat colds and fevers, strengthen the blood, for kidney problems, as a love medicine, and as a panacea. The tea was reputed to make one sleepy after a few cups. It was used to calm upset stomach and colic. **RELATED SPECIES:** *Satureja* means "culinary herb," and summer savory, *S. hortensis* L., and winter savory, *S. montana* L., were both formerly used in traditional European herbal medicine to ease gas pains, as an expectorant, and to stop diarrhea. Both contain essential oils that have antimicrobial and muscle-relaxing qualities.

FLOWERS IN UMBELS; 5 TINY PETALS; LEAVES FINELY DISSECTED (UMBELLIFERAE)

WESTERN WATER HEMLOCK
Root

Cicuta douglasii (DC.) Coult. & Rose **Parsley Family**

Tuberous *rhizomes containing air chambers* (cut lengthwise to see vertical walls separating chambers) *and orange-yellow resin.* Hollow stems hairless, reddish at base, to 6 ft. Leaves pinnately 1 - to 3-divided into lance-shaped leaflets; petiole base sheathing; leaflet tips pointed; margins sharply toothed. Leaflet veins end at base of teeth rather than tip. Dense clusters of many small, white to greenish flowers in umbels; June–Sept. Corky fruits

Western Water Hemlock (Cicuta douglasii) has toxic roots with orange-yellow resin.

flattened, round, short-ribbed. **WHERE FOUND:** Fresh water, marshes, streamsides, ponds, wet ditches. S. to n. coast ranges, s. and n. Sierra of Calif. to Alaska, Idaho, Mont., Nev.; n. Mexico. **USES:** American Indians drank a very dilute infusion as an emetic and tonic. A decoction of the root was used as a poultice or wash for aching or broken bones, arthritis, and stiffness and as a bath for tired, aching feet. The roots poulticed for sores, to draw out splinters and thorns, poison from snakebites, as well as for leg and back pains. They were also used as a purgative, and the tubers were infused and taken as an emetic. A cold infusion of the roasted powdered bark was taken for diarrhea. **WARNING: Deadly poisonous.** Never ingest the root or seeds or its preparations. Contains cicutoxin, which is highly toxic. Considered the most toxic N. American genus. Many fatalities reported.

POISON HEMLOCK
Conium maculatum L.

Whole plant

Parsley Family

Robust, *hairless* biennial, 2–6 ft. Musty, ill-smelling when crushed. Stems hollow, *purple-blotched or streaked*. Leaves alternate, pinnately dissected into *fernlike* segments; petiole *base inflated*, clasping. Small flowers in umbellets, arranged into larger umbel; Mar.–Sept. Oval fruit with *wavy ribs.* **WHERE FOUND:** Moist, disturbed areas, roadsides. Widespread throughout N. America. Alien (Europe). **USES:** Native Americans ate the root or took it in strong drink to commit suicide. All parts of the plant were considered poisonous. Poison Hemlock was an official drug in the *United States Pharmacopoeia* (1890–1920) and was formerly

Poison Hemlock (Conium maculatum) *has spotted stems. It is highly toxic.*

Coriander (Coriandrum sativum) *has fine leaves above, wider leaves below. Note the pink pollen.*

used by medical doctors in minute doses as an antispasmodic, sedative, and pain reliever. Full-grown but unripe fruit was carefully dried and preserved and made into an extract for use as a medicine. **WARNING: Deadly toxic.** All parts of the plant, but especially the ripe fruits and mature root, contain the toxic alkaloid coniine. The ancient Greek philosopher Socrates drank the fresh juice of poison hemlock as a punishment for inciting political unrest. In a famous account, he described going slowly numb from his feet up until the paralysis stopped his breathing, and he died.

CORIANDER, CHINESE PARSLEY, CILANTRO

Fruits, leaves

Coriandrum sativum L.

Parsley Family

Annual to 4 ft. Leaves have distinctive fragrance. Leaves pinnate; on lower stem, ovate with scalloped edges; greatly reduced on upper stem, finely divided, threadlike. Flowers small, in umbels, white to pinkish; *pollen pink*. Mar.–June. Fruits, about ⅛ in. in diameter, globular, ribbed, light brownish when ripe, are the coriander seeds of commerce. **WHERE FOUND:** Alien (Mediterranean), widely naturalized in Europe and Asia. Disturbed ground, often near gardens. Throughout. **USES:** The fresh leaves are called cilantro in Hispanic traditions, Chinese parsley in Asian traditions; used as salad or flavoring. Use dates back at least 7000 years. Traditionally, the fresh leaves or tea were used to allay nausea and stomachache. Fruits used in traditional Chinese medicine to promote sweating, as an aromatic appetite stimulant, and to treat diabetes. Fruits considered carminative and diuretic. In Germany coriander is allowed to be labeled for medicinal use to treat dyspeptic complaints and loss of appetite. Recent research, at least in laboratory animals, suggests the fruits may have a protective effect against colon cancer, plus antioxidant, antidiabetic, and potential cholesterol-lowering effects. **WARNING:** May produce rare allergic reactions in some individuals.

QUEEN ANNE'S LACE, WILD CARROT
Daucus carota L.

Flowers, roots, leaves, fruit
Parsley Family

Bristly, taprooted biennial, to 4 ft., with *ribbed stem.* Leaves alternate, *fernlike*, pinnately dissected into narrow, linear segments; petiole base clasping *ribbed stem.* Flowers tiny, in umbellets arranged in larger, *flat-topped umbel*; central umbel flower often *dark maroon to purple*; bracts below umbel long, thin, sharp-pointed; Apr.–Oct. Flat, oval fruits covered in *barbed bristles*; umbel becoming nestlike in fruit. **WHERE FOUND:** Disturbed sites, roadsides, moist ditches. Widespread throughout N. America. Alien (Eurasia). **USES:** American Indians used flower tea for diabetes. Tests on rodents showed no beneficial effect on blood sugar levels. Root tea traditionally used as a diuretic and to prevent or eliminate urinary stones, worms, and pimples. Seeds used as a folk "morning-after" contraceptive. Laboratory models have confirmed an anti-implantation effect on fertilized eggs. The dried flowering tops are currently used in European herbal medicine as a mild diuretic. **WARNING:** May cause dermatitis and blisters. Fatal results have occurred from mistaking deadly members of the parsley family, such as Poison Hemlock, for Queen Anne's Lace. Avoid use during pregnancy.

Queen Anne's Lace (Daucus carota) has a purple floret in the center of the umbel.

KISHWOOF, GRAY'S LICORICE ROOT

Root

Ligusticum grayi Coult. & Rose

Parsley Family

Hairless, aromatic perennial, to 3 ft. Taproot topped with old, fibrous leaf bases. Leaves mostly basal, *pinnately divided into narrow, deeply lobed leaflets*; stem leaves few, much smaller; leaf stalks clasping base. Flowers small in umbellets, arranged in *larger, dome-shaped umbel; 1–2 side umbels below main umbel*; June–Oct. Oval fruits *narrowly winged; spicy-smelling when crushed*. **WHERE FOUND:** Moist to dry montane meadows, slopes, forests. Cen. Sierra and n. Calif. to Wash., east to Idaho, Mont., Utah, Nev. **USES:** Atsugewi Indians chewed or brewed the roots to treat colds, coughs, stomachaches of children, "to avoid pain," and as a panacea for any ailment. **RELATED SPECIES:** See *L. porteri* Coult. & Rose. The root of *L. wallichii* Franch. (*L. chuaxiong* Hort.) is an important herb in China used to invigorate blood flow and treat gynecological problems such as dysmenorrhea, colds and flulike symptoms, and to alleviate pain in the chest and head. Clinical and animal studies show hypotensive properties, improvement in cerebral blood flow, relief of asthma, antianginal and anti-inflammatory effects. The roots of *L. sinense* Oliv. or *L. jeholense* Nakai et Kitag. are prescribed for the common cold, headaches, and acute lower-back pain.

Kishwoof (Ligusticum grayi) *is pleasantly fragrant throughout.*

Osha (Ligusticum porteri) *is becoming one of the best-known western medicinal plants.*

Yampah (Perideridia kelloggii) *Note the narrow leaves.*

OSHA, PORTER'S LICORICE ROOT Root
Ligusticum porteri Coult. & Rose   Parsley Family
Hairless perennial, to 4 ft. Taproot with old, fibrous leaf bases at top. Leaves alternate, pinnately divided into *numerous deeply lobed leaflets*; leaf stem bases clasping. Flowers small, in *loose umbellets*, arranged in larger umbel; main umbel with *several side umbels below*; June–Aug. Oval fruits *narrowly winged, spicy-smelling when crushed*. **WHERE FOUND:** Damp woods, high mountain meadows. Rockies, w. Mont., Colo. to N.M., Idaho, Nev., Ariz.; n. Mexico. **USES:** Osha is popular because of reputed antiviral effects and used widely in today's herbal practice for colds, flu, and infections. Hispanic Americans use osha to treat colds, sore throats, fevers, and stomachache and to improve digestion. Carrying a small piece in a bag is thought to help avoid sickness. Zuni Indians used Osha to relieve body aches and sore throats.

GAIRDNER'S YAMPAH Root
Perideridia gairdneri (Hook. & Arn.) Mathias   Parsley Family
Slender, hairless perennial from a *single fibrous, slightly thickened* tuber; to 5 ft. Leaves mostly basal, pinnately divided into *long, linear leaflets*; margins entire; petioles *inflated*, clasping. Flowers small, in umbellets, arranged in larger, dense umbel; June–July. Oval, slightly flattened fruits *hairless, ribbed*; *smell like caraway* when crushed. **WHERE FOUND:** Moist areas in heavy soils, meadows,

grasslands. S. to n. coast ranges of Calif. to B.C.; east to Alta. and N.M. **USES:** American Indians used root tea to reverse the effects of an emetic or cathartic; as a diuretic and mild laxative, also for sore throats, coughs, and to promote endurance during hunts. Root poulticed on sores and wounds; powdered root snorted to clear nasal congestion. The sweet, slightly aromatic, starchy roots of this and other yampah species were an important food. **OTHER SPECIES:** *P. kelloggii* (Gray) Mathias, found in w. Calif., had similar uses.

UMBELS; STEMS THICK OR SUCCULENT; LEAF SEGMENTS NOT FERNLIKE (UMBELLIFERAE)

BREWER'S ANGELICA
Roots
Angelica breweri Gray
Parsley Family

Robust perennial from stout taproot, to 6 ft. Stems hollow, hairy. Large, *thin, green* leaves pinnately 3-divided into *lance-shaped, toothed* leaflets, *hairless*; leaf stems long, clasping at base. Flowers small, in umbellets arranged in larger umbel; *petals and ovary hairy*; June–Sept. *Fruit flattened, oblong, ribbed; side ribs more broadly winged* than midribs; aromatic when crushed. **WHERE FOUND:** Rocky slopes, inland conifer forests above 3000 ft. Cen. to n. Sierra of Calif. to w. Nev. **USES:** American Indians used boiled roots for colds, coughs, bronchitis, tuberculosis, flu, kidney ailments, and venereal diseases; mixed with whiskey for chest colds and severe coughs, including whooping cough. Root tea drunk instead of water for kidney ailments. Small pieces of dried root were chewed for sore throats, colds, coughs, and headaches. The dried, shaved roots were smoked in cigarettes for head colds or infused for flu or bronchitis. Externally, root tea used as a wash for venereal disease. Mashed root poultice was applied to cuts, sores, swelling, and rheumatic areas and to the chest for pneumonia. The Washo Indians used this plant to flavor and enhance the effectiveness of medicines. **RELATED SPECIES:** *A. atropurpurea*

Brewer's Angelica (Angelica breweri) *has purple stems.*

L., a common species of eastern N. America, was a favorite remedy of many tribes for menstrual, respiratory, digestive, and other ailments. *A. archangelica* L., native to northern Europe, is now a common garden plant. The aromatic seeds and roots are included in many digestive tonics. *A. sinensis* (Oliv.) Diels is the famed dang gui (also called dong quai) of Chinese medicine. It is one of the most commonly used herbal treatments for menstrual difficulties, fatigue and general weakness due to weakness of the blood, and problems of menopause. All *Angelica* spp. contain a complex essential oil, lactones, coumarin derivatives, and other compounds that experimentally show blood-thinning, immune-system-modulating, and muscle-relaxing effects. **WARNING:** Contains furocoumarins, which can cause photosensitivity. Avoid misidentification with toxic members of the parsley family.

HAIRY ANGELICA, CALIFORNIA ANGELICA   Whole plant
Angelica tomentosa S. Wats.   Parsley Family

Very similar to *A. breweri*. Robust, *long-haired* perennial, *covered with a whitish film*; to 6 ft. Leaves large, pinnately 3-divided, into lance-shaped to oblong, entire to minutely toothed leaflets; leaf stems long, clasping at base. Flowers small, in umbellets arranged in larger umbel; June–Sept. Flattened fruit oblong, ribbed; *side ribs broader than midribs; aromatic when crushed.* **WHERE FOUND:** Moist or dry shady areas, woods. S. Calif to n. coast ranges to s. Ore. **USES:** American Indians burned the twigs, then beat aching joints with them. Juice from the heated leaves was rubbed on sores. Root chewed or held in the mouth to treat sore throat, hoarseness, and bad breath and relieve stomachache. Root boiled to make a wash for bathing sores. Root tea used for diarrhea, menstrual cramps, menopause complaints, stomachaches, and colds. Externally,

Hairy Angelica (Angelica tomentosa) leaves are covered with white down.

The root of Angelica genuflexa *was used as a laxative.*

Angelica hendersoni *grows near the coast.*

root poulticed to treat headache. Smoke from the burning plant was inhaled as a headache remedy. **RELATED SPECIES:** *A. hendersoni* Coult. & Rose, a larger coastal species, was used by American Indians to ease symptoms of food poisoning, especially from mussels. Root tea of *A. genuflexa* Nutt. used as a purgative; also for colds or chest ailments. **WARNING:** Contains furocoumarins, which can cause photosensitivity. Avoid misidentification with toxic members of the parsley family.

COW PARSNIP

Leaves, roots, stems

Heracleum maximum Bartr.
[*H. lanatum* Michx.]

Parsley Family

Stout, densely hairy perennial, to 10 ft. Stems hollow. Leaves *very large,* 3-divided into *palmately lobed leaflets;* margins coarsely lobed and toothed; leaf stem clasping, *widely inflated.* Flowers small, in umbellets arranged in larger umbel; Feb.–Sept. *Flattened* fruits ribbed, winged at margins. **WHERE FOUND:** Moist, shaded places. Throughout N. America; every western state except Tex. **USES:** Historically, physicians used root to treat gas, dyspepsia, epilepsy, asthma, colic, dysmenorrhea, amenorrhea, stroke, palsy, and intermittent fever. American Indians used leaf poultices on aching joints and muscles, sore arms and legs, cuts, and on the

Cow Parsnip (Heracleum maximum), *one of the largest members of the carrot family, can cause severe contact dermatitis.*

eyelids for eye problems; wash used for swellings and rheumatism. Leaf or root tea used as a hair tonic and scalp cleanser to prevent dandruff and graying hair; internally for colds and sore throats. Root tea used as a purgative and tonic and to treat influenza, tuberculosis, diarrhea, gut pain, colic, stomach cramps, cholera, rheumatism, erysipelas, syphilis, and bladder problems. Root poultice used on rheumatic areas, neuralgias, bruises, boils, sores, chronic swelling, wounds, syphilitic chancres, sore eyes, severe headaches, and pain in lungs, hips or back. Stems poulticed for wounds and as wart removal wash. A piece of root was placed in a tooth cavity to alleviate toothache. Smoke from the plant tops was used for fainting and convulsions, and smoke from the root for head colds. The plant was used in a steam bath for headaches and rheumatism, and the seeds to treat headaches. Flowers were rubbed on the body as a mosquito and fly repellent. **WARNING:** Plant can cause severe contact dermatitis in sensitive individuals. Acrid stem sap can cause blisters on contact. Foliage toxic to livestock.

MOUNTAIN SWEET CICELY
Osmorhiza chilensis Hook. & Arn.
[*O. berteroi* DC.]

Root, plant
Parsley Family

⚠ *Slender*, coarse-haired perennial, to 4 ft. Roots and fruits *licorice-scented*. Leaves alternate, twice pinnately 3-divided into 9 *ovate to lance-shaped, toothed leaflets*; leaf-stem bases clasping. Flowers tiny, in umbellets arranged in larger, *open umbel*; Apr.–July. *Long, slender* fruits *beaked at top*, with *bristly tail below*. **WHERE FOUND:** Coniferous forests, oak woodlands, usually in shade. Widespread throughout U.S.; every western state except Tex. **USES:** Native Americans used roots (as tea or chewed) to treat sore throat,

Mountain Sweet Cicely (Os-morhiza chilensis) has licorice-scented roots and fruits.

coughs, colds, headache, sores, skin ulcers, and eye problems, to facilitate birth, and to induce weight gain. The Cheyenne added the root to any remedy, apparently to improve the taste. Considered a panacea by some tribes. Root chewed "to bring one around" and as a potent love charm. Karok Indians put roots under their pillows to prevent disease. A tea made from the plant was used as a hair wash for killing fleas. **RELATED SPECIES:** European American herbalists and American Indians used the root of *O. longistylis* (Torr.) DC. as a stomachic and carminative to treat indigestion, gas, and debilitated stomachs. It was also taken for anemia, kidney problems, and amenorrhea, and as an expectorant to treat coughs and mucous congestion. **WARNING:** Do not confuse with Poison Hemlock (*Conium*); see p. 60.

FLOWERS 5-PARTED, TINY; IN GLOBELIKE UMBELS

CALIFORNIA SPIKENARD
Aralia californica S. Wats.

Whole plant
Ginseng Family

Stout, hairless perennial, to 9 ft. Leaves very *large,* 3-divided, each with 3–5 *ovate, finely toothed leaflets; petioles long,* clasping at base. Flowers small, in compact umbels arranged in large panicle; June–Sept. *Red berry becoming black,* 3–5-seeded. **WHERE FOUND:** Moist, shady forest, streambanks. Lower Calif. to sw. Ore. **USES:** American Indians drank root tea and ate the fruit as a tonic. Root tea was highly valued as a medicine; taken for stomach pain, lung disorders, consumption, colds, and fever; in a bath as a soak for arthritis. Root cooked, then poulticed for various kinds of open sores and itching. **RELATED SPECIES:** *A. nudicaulis* L., Wild Sarsaparilla, grows on high e. slope of the Rockies and eastward. It was commonly used by American Indians to cleanse and strengthen the blood and for numerous other purposes. As a folk remedy, *A. nudicaulis* was popular as a pleasant-tasting tea and

(Left) *California Spikenard* (Aralia californica) *is sometimes offered falsely as a type of ginseng.* (Above) *California Spikenard has globular flower heads on red stalks.*

used in many patent medicines to cleanse the blood and as a health tonic. Physicians used it as a minor remedy for lung problems and as a wash to treat shingles and slow-healing ulcers.

BUTTON SNAKEROOT

Whole plant

Eryngium alismifolium Greene

Parsley Family

Low-growing, hairless perennial, to 1 ft. Leaves basal, *narrowly oblanceolate, often longer than flower stalks*; teeth spine-tipped; leaf-stem bases clasping. Flowers small, in dense, headlike umbels; *linear bracts below longer than head, spiny*; July–Aug. Oval fruit covered with *flat, white scales*. **WHERE FOUND:** Wet meadows, spring pools, above 4000 ft. High Cascades of n. Calif. to Ore., Idaho, Nev. **USES:** An infusion of the whole plant was used for diarrhea and for snakebites in American Indian medicine. **RELATED SPECIES:** *E. campestre* L. was used by the ancient Greeks to relieve water retention, to cleanse the liver and bowels, relieve gas, and to treat venomous bites. *E. yuccifolium* Michx. and *E. aquaticum* L. of the eastern U.S. were both widely used by American Indians and prescribed historically by physicians as an expectorant for laryngitis and bronchitis and to improve the appetite and relieve nausea; for genitourinary tract disorders such as urinary calculi, cystitis with painful urination, bladder inflammation, kidney infections, water retention, prostate inflammation, and vaginitis. Research has confirmed an anti-inflammatory activity from the root.

Button Snakeroot (Eryngium *spp.*) *has tight flower heads with spiny bracts beneath. The widespread species* Eryngium yuccifolium *is pictured here.*

FLOWERS 5-PARTED; PETALS FUSED, SMALL, TUBULAR IN LOOSE CLUSTERS (VALERIAN FAMILY)

CAPITATE VALERIAN
Valeriana capitata Pallas ex Link
[*V. californica* Heller]

Root
Valerian Family

 Hairless perennial from *stout, strong-scented rhizome*, to 2 ft. Leaves mostly in basal rosette, *oblanceolate to spoon-shaped*; opposite stem leaves pinnately divided, *sessile*; margins entire. Small, *tubular*, white to pinkish flowers in dense, rounded clusters at stem tips; petals above ovary; stamens 3, *well exserted*. Sepal lobes becoming *feathery bristles* in fruit; July–Sept. **WHERE FOUND:** Mountain meadows, slopes, streambanks. High e. cen. Sierra to high n. coast ranges of Calif. to Ore., w. Nev. **USES:** Valerian species are used for their sedative properties. Species vary in strength. See description under *V. sitchensis* (p. 73). *V. capitata* was used by Native Americans for stomach problems. **WARNING:** Chronic use may lead to depression.

WILD VALERIAN, TOBACCO ROOT
Valeriana edulis Nutt. ex Torr. & Gray

Root
Valerian Family

 Robust, hairless perennial from *stout, strong-scented* taproot, to 4 ft. Leaves mostly basal, *pinnately divided into narrowly lanceolate lobes*; stem leaves opposite; leaf-stem base *clasping*; margins entire. Flowers small, *funnel-shaped*, in dense, rounded clusters; May–Sept. **WHERE FOUND:** Moist areas, streambanks, meadows, valleys. Se. Ore. and Wash. to B.C., Idaho, Nev., Utah, Ariz.; Rocky Mts. from Mont. to N.M.; n. Mexico; also in northeastern N. America. **USES:** Native Americans considered the roots of *V. edulis* to be poisonous.

Capitate Valerian (Valeriana capitata) *has distinct globular flower
heads.*

Valerian (Valeriana edulis) *has
leaf stalks that clasp the stem.*

Valerian (Valeriana officinalis)
flowers may be white or pink.

Mountain Valerian (Valeriana
sitchensis). *Note the square stems
and divided leaves.*

They rubbed the raw roots on aches, pains, and swollen bruises. A poultice of the roots was put on painful or bleeding cuts and wounds and was used to draw out boils. Root used internally to expel tapeworm. **WARNING:** Chronic use may lead to depression.

ALERIAN

Root

...leriana officinalis L.

Valerian Family

Perennial; 4–5 ft. Leaves strongly divided, *pinnate*; lower ones toothed. Tiny, pale pink to whitish flowers, in tight clusters; June–July. **WHERE FOUND:** Widely cultivated, escaped from gardens. Occasional. **USES:** A well-known herbal calmative, antispasmodic, nerve tonic, used for nervous headaches, irritability, mild spasmodic affections, depression, despondency, insomnia. Research confirms that it is a CNS depressant, antispasmodic, and sedative when agitation is present but also a stimulant in fatigue; antibacterial, antidiuretic, liver-protective. Valerian is a leading over-the-counter tranquilizer and sleep aid in Europe. More than 10 controlled clinical studies have been published on Valerian preparations. A recent study found that it works best as a sleep aid if used continuously over a period of a month rather than as a single dose. Approved in Germany for use as a sedative and in sleep-inducing preparations for nervous restlessness and difficulty in falling asleep. Cats are said to be attracted to the scent of the root much as they are to Catnip. In 18th-century apothecaries, the quality of Valerian root was determined by how cats reacted to it. Folklore says the root repels rats. **WARNING:** Chronic use may lead to depression.

OUNTAIN VALERIAN,
TKA VALERIAN

Roots, leaves, flowers

...leriana sitchensis Bong.

Valerian Family

Hairless perennial from *malodorous* rhizome, to 4 ft. Leaves opposite, on square stems *pinnately divided into ovate to lance-shaped, coarsely toothed leaflets. Small, sweet-scented*, white to pinkish flowers in dense, rounded clusters at stem tip; Apr.–Sept. **WHERE FOUND:** Moist montane areas, streambanks, meadows. Cascade range from n. Calif. to Alaska; coast ranges of Ore., Wash; Idaho, Mont. **USES:** Valerian is used for anxiety and insomnia. In 19th century, Valerian root infusions were used for muscle cramps, headache, backache, menstrual pain, menopausal symptoms, depression, hysteria, hypochondriasis, epilepsy, nervous disorders, and restlessness. American Indians used root tea for pains, colds, influenza, and diarrhea and the whole plant for ulcers and stomach problems. **WARNING:** Chronic use may lead to depression.

CANADIAN MILKVETCH
Astragalus canadensis L.

Roots
Pea Family

Robust, upright perennial spreading by rhizome, to 3 ft. Rough-haired; *hairs forked at base, tips spreading along stem surface.* Leaves alternate, pinnately divided into many oblong leaflets; tips rounded to slightly notched; *papery stipules fused into sheath* around stem. Flowers cream-colored, *nodding, in dense, spikelike raceme*; May–Sept. Blackish pods *upright, with curved beak at top.* **WHERE FOUND:** Heavy, moist soils; prairies, ditches, vernal pools; low to mid-elevation. Widespread in eastern N. America: Cen. Calif. to B.C.; every western state except Ariz. **USES:** American Indians used root tea for fever in children and for coughs. Roots ground and chewed for chest and back pains; externally, applied to cuts. **RELATED SPECIES:** In Chinese medicine, *A. membranaceus* (Fisch.) Bge., Astragalus or huang-qi, is used as a spleen and blood tonic and for suppressed urination. Research confirms immunostimulant activity. Astragalus is included in many formulas for treatment of immune suppression related to AIDS, cancer, and other conditions. **WARNING:** Some species of *Astragalus* are known to contain toxic alkaloids and to concentrate high levels of toxic metals.

PRAIRIE CLOVER
Dalea candida Willd.

Whole plant
Pea Family

Aromatic low-growing perennial with upturned branch tips or upright, to 2½ ft. Stems, underside of leaves, and sepals *gland-dotted.* Leaves pinnately divided into 5–7 obovate leaflets, generally folded upward; margins entire. Flowers white, 5-parted, in dense, oblong spikes at branch tips; May–Sept. **WHERE FOUND:** Dry, sunny areas, prairies, sandy drainages, rock ledges, gravelly knolls, desert shrubland, pinyon-juniper woodland. Widespread from Midwest to s. cen. Canada to s. Utah, Ariz., N.M., Tex.; Mexico. **USES:** The Navajo chewed the roots to alleviate pain; root tea used for abdominal pain and toothache. Ramah Indians used plant tea externally on poisonous snakebites; internally for stomachache and fever. Plant poultice used for arrow wounds. Root tea used as a wash to prevent baldness. The plant was also used as a tonic and disease preventative, called a "life medicine." **RELATED SPECIES:** Other prairie clovers were popular remedies with American Indian groups. An infusion of the leaves of *D. aurea* Nutt. ex Pursh, Golden Prairie Clover, was given for stomachaches and dysentery. The whole crushed plant of *D. lanata* Spreng., Woolly Prairie-Clover, was poulticed to ease centipede bites; tea from *D.*

Canadian Milkvetch (Astragalus canadensis) *has cream-colored, nodding flowers in dense, spikelike raceme.*

White Prairie Clover (Dalea candida) *has tiny pealike flowers in a dense thimblelike head.*

nana Ton. ex Gray, Dwarf Prairie Clover, used to strengthen weak children. An infusion of the fresh, crushed leaves of *D. purpurea* Vent., Purple Prairie Clover, was applied to wounds. Leaf and blossom tea used for easing heart problems. Root tea was used for diarrhea and to prevent disease.

MERICAN LICORICE, WILD LICORICE   **Roots, leaves**
ycyrrhiza lepidota Pursh   Pea Family

Sticky perennial with *aromatic, sweet rhizome*; to 4 ft. Leaves alternate, *pinnately divided* into many lance-shaped leaflets, *bristle-tipped, gland-dotted.* Flowers white to cream in dense racemes from leaf axils; May–Aug. Oblong *pods covered in hooked prickles.* **WHERE FOUND:** Moist open or disturbed sites, streambanks, roadsides. Widespread throughout U.S.; every western state, n. Mexico, s. Canada. **USES:** Licorice has been used for over 3000 years in many cultures. Native Americans used root tea as a tonic or laxative, to aid the voice for singing, and to treat sore throats, for childhood fevers, diarrhea, swellings, and chest pains. Chewed root used for flu; for their cooling effect, roots were held in the mouth for toothache. **RELATED SPECIES:** In Europe, *G. glabra* L. used as a demulcent to treat mucous membrane irritation and inflammation, for coughs, asthma, hoarseness, and other respiratory conditions; for ulcers, urinary tract irritation, bladder infections, and painful diarrhea. *G. uralensis* Fischer ex DC. used in Chinese medicine to temper the harshness of other herbs and to treat sore throat, coughs, wheezing, skin sores, and lower body spasms. All licorice species contain glycyrrhetic acid, glycyrrhizin, and other plant steroids with confirmed anti-inflammatory, expectorant, liver-protective, antibacterial, and antiviral effects. **WARNING:** Overuse can exacerbate or cause hypertension and sodium retention. Avoid use during pregnancy. In Germany use is limited to 4 to 6 weeks.

WHITE SWEETCLOVER
Melilotus alba Medik.

Flowering plant
Pea Family

Straggly biennial, 2–6 ft. Leaves cloverlike, leaflets elongate, slightly toothed. Flowers small, white, pealike, in long, tapering spikes; Apr.–Oct. **WHERE FOUND:** Roadsides. Throughout N. America. Alien (Europe). **USES:** White Sweetclover is used interchangeably with Yellow Sweetclover. Dried flowering plant once used in ointments for external ulcers. Navajo Indians drank plant tea for

American Licorice (Glycyrrhiza lepidota) *has spiny seed pods.*

White Sweetclover (Melilotus alba) *is an abundant late-summer roadside weed.*

colds brought on by being chilled. Iroquois used it externally on acne and sunburn and drank a tea to treat a typhoid fever–like condition caused by smelling a dead snake. Keres Indians used the plant as a bedbug repellent. In animal studies, components of sweet-clover found to lower blood pressure. **WARNING:** Don't use sweet-clover internally if you are taking a pharmaceutical blood thinner such as warfarin. May affect blood clotting.

COMMON SCURFPEA, INDIAN TURNIP   Root, leaves
Psoralidium lanceolatum (Pursh) Rydb.   Pea Family

Perennial, 6–24 in., spreading, branched perennial herb from creeping roots with long wavy hairs and scented oily glands. Small, white, pealike flowers in dense glandular-hairy racemes; May–July. Pod globular, densely hairy. **WHERE FOUND:** Dry sandy hills, ridges in sagebrush scrublands. Ne. Calif. to e. Wash.; every western state eastward through Great Plains. **USES:** Arapaho Indians used the leaves in a snuff. Leaf tea used externally to relieve headaches. Leaves chewed for sore throat. Navajo used plant tea in lotions and applied a poultice to sores and itchy skin. Cold tea drunk for stomachache, menstrual cramps, and as protection from witches. Root used to treat venereal disease. Zunis ate the fresh flowers to assuage stomach pain. **WARNING:** Contains photo-toxic compounds, which can cause photodermatitis if one ingests it and is then exposed to sunlight.

(Left) *Scurfpea (Psoralidium spp.) have small pealike flowers. In P. lanceolatum the flowers are cream-colored with prominent blue keels.* (Above) *White Clover (Trifolium repens) is the familiar clover found in lawns.*

WHITE CLOVER
Trifolium repens L.

Flowers, leaves
Pea Family

⚠ Low, *mat-forming*, hairless perennial, 4–10 in.; rooting at nodes. Leaves alternate on *long petioles*, 3-divided, *broadly obovate*, finely toothed leaflets, often with whitish "V." Flowers white to pinkish, *drooping in age*, in *dense, round heads*; Apr.–Oct. **WHERE FOUND:** Disturbed places, lawns, pastures, roadsides. Widespread throughout N. America. Alien (Europe). **USES:** White clover has been used for coughs, colds, and fevers, in asthma compounds, for urinary tract infections, and for kidney disease. Externally, as an eyewash, a wash for liver spots and athlete's foot. An alcoholic tincture is added to ointments to relieve the pain of gout. **WARNING:** White clover contains coumarins, which may interact with pre-scription blood thinners such as warfarin, to reduce clotting time.

FLOWERS WITH MORE THAN 5 "PETALS" (SEPALS); MANY STAMENS

WINDFLOWER, GLOBE ANEMONE
Anemone multifida Poir.
[*Pulsatilla patens* ssp. *multifida* (Pritz.) Zamels]

Whole plant, leaves
Buttercup Family

☠ Long-haired herbaceous perennial from a woody base, to 1 ft. *Basal leaves with 3-dissected, narrowly oblong leaflets* with acute tips. Silky-haired stem leaves in 1 or 2 whorls on long stalks. Flowers showy, petals separate, purple, maroon, yellow or white, *hairy on back*; June–July. The small, dry fruits are *silky-haired*. **WHERE FOUND:** High mountain sagebrush, ponderosa pine, aspen, Douglas-fir, alpine tun-

Windflower (Anemone multifida) has silky-haired, feathery dry fruits.

dra. Every western state except Tex. **USES:** American Indians used a whole plant tea as a wash to kill lice and fleas. Leaves were eaten or a tea of aboveground parts consumed during sweat baths for rheumatism. Leaves or fruit pappi were stuffed in the nostrils to treat nosebleed. Leaves crushed and fumes inhaled for colds and lung problems. The ripe seed-head "cotton" was burned on hot coals and the smoke inhaled for headaches. Plant used to induce abortions. **WARNING:** The undried plant is highly irritating and toxic. Dried or fresh plant is a potentially dangerous urinary tract irritant and may damage the kidneys.

WESTERN PASQUEFLOWER
Pulsatilla occidentalis (S. Wats.) Freyn
[*Anemone occidentalis* S. Wats.]

Whole plant, roots
Buttercup Family

Soft, *long-haired* perennial, to 2½ ft. Basal leaves on long petioles, *deeply pinnately dissected into narrow, rounded lobes.* Flowers solitary, *bowl-shaped*, with showy cream to purplish petals and many stamens; May–Sept. Hairy fruits with *long, feathery tails in dense, oblong heads.* **WHERE FOUND:** Dry open, rocky areas, moist meadows; mid- to high elevations, alpine. Sierra and Cascade ranges of Calif. to B.C., Idaho, Mont., Colo. **USES:** Okanagan and Thompson Indians used the root or plant to treat stomach and intestinal problems, and a plant preparation as an eyewash or a bath for rheumatism. **RELATED SPECIES:** The European *A. pulsatilla* L. demonstrated antispasmodic properties in early experiments and was a favorite remedy of 19th-century physicians for treating nervous exhaustion and menstrual disorders, especially with pain and cramps. *A. chinensis* (Bge.) Regel extracts are

Western Pasqueflower (Pulsatilla occidentalis) has showy, bowl-shaped, white to violet flowers.

commonly used in China to treat amebic dysentery. Laboratory studies show that extracts have potent antibacterial and antiamebic activity. Western herbalists used *Pulsatilla* species to treat anxiety and depression and a wide range of neurological, respiratory, cardiovascular, digestive, and reproductive tract disorders. **WARNING:** *Pulsatilla* species contain a highly irritating alkaloid and other toxic compounds and are potentially fatal in high doses. The undried plant is highly irritating and toxic. Dried or fresh plant is potentially dangerous urinary tract irritant and may damage the kidneys. Use is not allowed in Germany because of potential toxicity and lack of scientifically documented effectiveness.

CRESTED PRICKLY POPPY
Roots, seeds

Argemone polyanthemos (Fedde) G. B. Ownbey — Poppy Family
[*A. intermedia* auct. non Sweet; *A. platyceras* auct. non Link & Otto.]

Stout annual or biennial covered with *yellow spines*, 6–24 in. Leaves oblong with wavy spiny margins, dissected to midrib. Flowers white, to 4 in. across, 6 large petals, *stamens numerous, yellow*; June–Aug. Capsules cylindrical, spiny. **WHERE FOUND:** Dry washes and sandy flats. S. Calif. to every western state except Ore. and Nev.; e. Tex., n. Mexico. **USES:** American Indians ground the ripe seeds into an oily paste to apply to burns, sores, or cuts. Ground cooked seeds were used as a poultice to bring boils to a head. Ripe seeds were roasted, finely mashed, and taken as a laxative and to induce vomiting. Tea of seeds or the sap was used to treat sore eyes. Ripe seeds were pulverized and moistened, then rubbed into the hair to kill

Crested Prickly Poppy (Argemone polyanthemos) *has thistlelike leaves with yellow juice.*

head lice. Warmed root mash was applied to gums or inserted in tooth cavities to relieve toothache. **RELATED SPECIES:** *A. mexicana* L. was historically prescribed by physicians for similar conditions. The Kawaiisu roasted and mashed the ripe seeds of *A. munita* Dur. et Hilg., Flatbud Prickly Poppy, and used it in salves for burns.

OREGON GOLDTHREAD, CANKER ROOT Whole plant
Coptis laciniata Gray   Buttercup Family

Hairless perennial from *threadlike, bright yellowish rhizome*, to 10 in. Leaves basal, divided into 3 *leaflets, each deeply 3-lobed, sharply toothed.* Flowers small, white to greenish, nodding on *long stalks; only slightly taller than leaves*; Mar.–Apr. Oblong pods hairless, with minute curved beak. **WHERE FOUND:** Wet sites, streambanks, forests. Southwestern coast ranges of Calif., Cascade Mts. of Ore. and Wash. **USES:** A substitute for the eastern N. American Goldthread or Canker-root (*C. trifolia* [L.] Salisb.) as a bitter tonic for treating dyspepsia and stimulating the appetite; used as a mouthwash or applied directly as a tincture for mouth sores, inflamed gums, and sore throat. Externally, as a poultice for skin eruptions and genital herpes or as a douche or eyewash. The root's yellow color derives from the antibacterial alkaloid berberine. **RELATED SPECIES:** The important Chinese drug huang lian consists of the roots and rhizomes of *C. chinensis* Franch and related species. Preparations containing huang lian are frequently used to treat infections of the urinary, respiratory, and digestive tracts.

Oregon Goldthread (Coptis laciniata) *has a bright yellow rootstock.*

LEAVES MORE CONSPICUOUS THAN FLOWERS; LEAVES IN SERIES OF 3 (BARBERRY FAMILY)

VANILLA LEAF
Achlys triphylla (Sm.) DC.

Leaves
Barberry Family

⚠ Hairless perennial from creeping, scaly rhizome, to 20 in. Leaves on long petioles divided into 3 *fan-shaped leaflets*; margins shallowly lobed; vanilla fragrance when dry. Flowers small, white, in *dense spike on slender stalk*; Apr.–July. Fruit *red-purple*, single-seeded. **WHERE FOUND:** Moist, shady sites in forests, streambanks. N. Calif. to s. B.C. west of Cascade crest. **USES:** American Indians used leaf tea to induce vomiting for ceremonial cleansing; also to treat tuberculosis. Leaf tea used as a hair wash. A tea of shredded

(Top left) *The leaves of Vanilla Leaf* (Achlys triphylla) *are divided into three distinct fan-shaped leaflets.* (Bottom left) *Inside-out-flower* (Vancouveria hexandra) *has thin thrice-divided leaves.* (Below) *Inside-out-flower. Note the parachute-like flowers.*

roots used as a wash for cataracts. The plant was hung to dry to repel flying insects; leaf tea used as a household insecticide. The plant is rich in coumarins, which accounts for the pleasant vanilla smell exuded by the drying leaves. **WARNING:** Avoid internal use if taking pharmaceutical blood thinners such as Coumadin.

INSIDE-OUT-FLOWER, PARACHUTE FLOWER
Root, leaves
Vancouveria hexandra (Hook.) Morr. & Dcne.　　Barberry Family
　　Perennial from scaly rhizome, to 16 in. *Thin* leaves on long, slender petioles, 3-*divided* into oval leaflets, 3-*lobed toward tip*; leaf stalk becoming *straw-colored*. *Delicate, nodding* flowers in open panicles on *hairless stalks*; May–July. **WHERE FOUND:** Moist, shady forests. N. coast ranges of Calif. to sw. Wash. west of Cascade crest. **USES:** American Indians ate leaves to treat coughs. An anti-inflammatory flavanol glycoside, isolated from the root, has been used in a nasal inhaler for treating allergic rhinitis.

PETALS 6; FLOWERS SMALL, IN HEADS

UMBRELLA PLANT, HERCULES ERIOGONUM
Roots, stems, leaves
Eriogonum heracleoides Nutt.　　Buckwheat Family
　　Loosely matted, *white-woolly* perennial, sometimes woody at base; to 16 in. Tufted basal leaves oblanceolate to oblong, *densely hairy below*. Small, cream-colored flowers in dense umbellike heads; *bracts whorled at middle of flowering stem and below umbels*. Petals 6, hairless on outside; *bases fused into short*

Umbrella plant (Eriogonum heracleoides) has dense flower heads in an umbellike arrangement, similar to those of the closely related E. umbellatum, pictured here.

stalks; May–Aug. **WHERE FOUND:** Dry sandy or gravelly slopes, ridges. E. Calif. to B.C.; Idaho, Nev., Utah, Rockies from Mont. to Colo. **USES:** American Indians used root and stem tea as a cold remedy; externally as a wash for infected cuts. Root tea taken for diarrhea. Plant tea used to treat stomach pain, other internal pains and general debility, for syphilis and tuberculosis. Externally, leaves poulticed or used as a wash for cuts and sore. The plants were used in steam baths for rheumatism, stiff and sore joints and muscles, for general illness, and as a ceremonial purification remedy. The dried leaves or leaf ash was mixed with grease and applied as a salve to swellings.

COAST BUCKWHEAT   **Roots, stems, leaves**
Eriogonum latifolium Sm.   Buckwheat Family
   White-woolly perennial, sometimes woody at base; to 2 ft. Leaves in basal rosette, *oval to round*, densely hairy below; margins wavy to entire. Flowers small, white to rose, in *dense heads* on *velvety, leafless stalks*; petals 6, hairless; sepals *not fused into stalklike base*; June–Dec. **WHERE FOUND:** Coastal bluffs and dunes. S. to n. cen. coast ranges of Calif. to Wash. **USES:** American Indians used a tea of root, stalk, and leaves for colds, coughs, menstrual disorders, stomach pains, and headaches. The Sanpoil used a root decoction for diarrhea, and the Thompson, to ease stomachaches and other pains. The whole plant was used in steam baths to ease the pain of rheumatism and aching joints, as a ceremonial medicine in the sweat lodge, and decocted for general illnesses or lung problems, especially tuberculosis. A decoction of the leaves was used to relieve sore eyes. **RELATED SPECIES:** American Indians used numerous other western species of *Eriogonum*. The root of *E. jamesii* Benth. was held in the mouth to relieve a sore tongue. The leaves, stems, and roots of *E. latifolium* Sm. were used to relieve stomach and head pain, ease menstrual difficulties, and as a wash for sore eyes. Paiutes used a tea of the roots and tops of *E. microthecum* Nutt. as a remedy for tuberculosis. A leaf, stem, and root tea of *E. nudum* Dougl. ex Benth. was taken to ease stomachaches, head pains, and menstrual problems. Root tea used for colds and coughs. As a folk medicine, the plant was boiled to ease kidney and bladder problems. The Navajo used the stems, leaves, and roots of *E. alatum* Torr. internally to treat pain and as a "life medicine," externally as a wash for rashes. The Ramah Navajo took a cold infusion of the roots for diarrhea, bad coughs, sore gums, and as a ritual medicine and panacea. The Zuni made an infusion of the powdered root for falls and general illness. The fresh root was eaten as a purgative to relieve stomachaches. The Thompson Indians made a decoction of *E. androsaceum* Benth. for any internal pains, especially stomachaches, for general ill-

ness, and in steam baths for rheumatism and stiff joints and muscles. A salve from the dry leaves or leaf ash was applied to swellings. The Lakota drank an infusion of *E. annuum* Nutt. for urinary difficulties and used it as a rinse for a child's sore mouth. The Ramah Navajo considered it "the boss of all medicines," effective for keeping witches away.

BUCKWHEAT
Fagopyrum esculentum Moench

Leaves, seeds
Buckwheat Family

Annual, stems weak, somewhat succulent, 1–4 ft. Leaves broadly triangular to arrow-shaped, to 3 in. long. Flowers white or pink, small, loosely crowded together in drooping terminal inflorescence; May–Sept. Fruit is the familiar buckwheat of commerce, a smooth, shining, triangular achene; July–Oct. **WHERE FOUND:** Near cultivated ground. Alien (Europe). Escape from cultivation. Occasional throughout. **USES:** Leaf tea used to treat erysipelas. A poultice of the powdered seeds in buttermilk was an English folk remedy to stimulate milk flow. In Europe the herb has been used to treat venous and capillary problems, for it increases the tone of veins and is taken to prevent hardening of the arteries. A recent controlled clinical study of a buckwheat herb tea in the treatment of chronic venous insufficiency found that it lowered edema (water retention), improved blood flow through the femoral vein, and enhanced capillary resistance.

(Above) *Coast Buckwheat* (Eriogonum latifolium) *has white to rose flowers in dense heads.*
(Right) *Buckwheat* (Fagopyrum esculentum) *is a weak-stemmed, white-flowered annual.*

SMALL FLOWERS IN FLAT-TOPPED CLUSTERS WITH RAY AND TUBULAR FLOWERS (COMPOSITE FAMILY)

YARROW
Whole plant

Achillea millefolium L.   Composite Family

   Aromatic perennial, to 3 ft. Alternate leaves *finely pinnately dissected*, fernlike. Small heads of white to pink flowers in *dense, flat-topped clusters*; ray flowers, 5 per head, *short, rounded*; tip 3-notched; Mar.–Oct. **WHERE FOUND:** Dry to moist open places, woods, roadsides. Widespread throughout N. America. **USES:** Flowers and leaves are used in tea or extracts to lessen symptoms of colds and flu, such as fever and pain. American Indians chewed the leaves and applied them to burns, bruises, sores, sprains, swellings, and wounds. The leaves and roots were also chewed for toothache or rolled and inserted into the cavity of a painful tooth. Crushed dried leaves were used as a snuff for headaches. A poultice of the leaves was applied to rheumatic joints, to the chest during colds, and to breasts following childbirth, to desensitize them. The leaves were used in steam baths to treat rheumatism or general sickness. Dried stems and leaves were powdered and used for skin problems and to stop bleeding. A tea made from the whole plant was used as a wash for sore eyes, insect stings, and snakebites.

(Left) *Yarrow* (Achillea millefolium) *has finely divided fernlike leaves. The flowers are in flat-topped heads.* (Above) *Western Coltsfoot* (Petasites frigidus *var.* palmatus) *has broad leaves with 5 to 7 lobes. It forms large colonies.*

The tea was used for headaches, stomachaches, blood purification, and fever. European settlers used the plant as a bitter digestive aid. In recent times the herb and flowering tops have been commonly used in an infusion to regulate menstruation and relieve menstrual pain; also for hemorrhoids and colon polyps. The tea or tincture is used for gastrointestinal complaints and as a bitter aromatic and bile stimulant. Yarrow contains a number of proven anti-inflammatory and hemostatic compounds. **WARNING:** May cause contact dermatitis in sensitive individuals. Large doses taken over a long period of time could be potentially toxic. Some strains contain the toxic compound thujone.

WESTERN COLTSFOOT
Leaves, root

Petasites frigidus (L.) Fries var. *palmatus* (Ait.) Cronq.
[*P. palmatus* (Ait.) Gray]   Composite Family

⚠ Perennial from creeping rhizome to 2 ft. *Often forming colonies.* Leaves large, basal, *deeply palmately lobed* into 5–7 coarsely toothed segments; green above, *densely white-woolly beneath.* Flowers white to pinkish, on single thick stem, in flat-topped clusters, *appearing before leaves*; Feb.–May. **WHERE FOUND:** Shaded, moist forests, streambanks; roadsides. N. Calif. to Alaska; Mont. **USES:** *Petasites* species are used worldwide, especially to treat respiratory-tract conditions. American Indians used infusions for colds, flu, head and chest congestion, tuberculosis, and in cough syrups. Roots were also used for coughs. Externally, for boils, sores, scabies, rheumatic pains, swellings, and sore eyes. **RELATED SPECIES:** In Chinese herbal traditions *P. japonicus* (Sieb. & Zucc.) Maxim. is used as an expectorant for congestion, asthma, and "pulmonary deficiency." **WARNING:** Pyrrolizidine alkaloids found in all parts of *Petasites* species can cause cumulative and irreversible liver damage. Not recommended for internal use.

WOOLLY PLANTS; EVERLASTING FLOWERS, TUBULAR FLOWERS; NO RAY FLOWERS (COMPOSITE FAMILY)

PEARLY EVERLASTING
Whole plant

Anaphalis margaritacea (L.) Benth.   Aster Family

Aromatic perennial with slender rhizomes, 1–3 ft. Stems and undersides of leaves covered in white-woolly hairs. Leaves alternate, narrowly lance-shaped; tips pointed; margins entire, often rolled under. Flowers white, in persistent round heads arranged in attractive flat-topped clusters; June–Sept. Dry, papery white bracts below head. **WHERE FOUND:** Open clearings in woods, meadows, roadsides, disturbed sites, rocky slopes. Calif. to Alaska, every

Pearly Everlasting (Anaphalis margaritacea). *The flowers remain intact after drying.*

western state except Tex. Common in eastern North America, Eurasia. **USES:** American Indians used the whole plant in a steam bath for rheumatism. Flowers were applied as a poultice to sores and swellings and used as a bath or powder for ulcers and sores. Inhaling smoke from powdered dried flowers was said to revive a stroke victim. Flower tea once used for rheumatic fever, colds, and throat infections, and the steam inhaled for headache or blindness caused by the sun. Dried leaves were smoked for catarrh and bronchial cough. Leaves were smoked or chewed for colds. A poultice of boiled leaves was applied to burns. A tea of stalks and roots was taken as an emetic and laxative, and also for the opposite effect of allaying diarrhea and dysentery. The juice was said to be aphrodisiacal.

FIELD PUSSYTOES
Antennaria neglecta Greene

Whole plant
Aster Family

Mat-forming perennial, to 16 in. Stems and undersides of leaves white-woolly. Leaves mostly in basal rosettes, spoon-shaped; stem leaves alternate, reduced, lance-shaped; margins entire. Upper leaf green, hairless or thinly hairy. Flower heads densely clustered at stem tips; May–July. Whitish bracts below head are dry, papery, narrow, with pointed tips. **WHERE FOUND:** Dry to moist forest openings, rocky

Field Pussytoes (Antennaria neglecta) *has white-woolly leaves and stems.*

slopes. Utah, Idaho, Mont., Wyo., n. Colo., eastward. **USES:** American Indians chewed the plant for coughs and colds. It was taken as a tea for body pain but not pain in the limbs. **RELATED SPECIES:** *A. rosea* Greene is a widespread species used by a number of tribes. The smoke from the burning leaves was used to drive away bad spirits and revive dancers who had fainted. The fresh leaves were chewed to improve male potency. *A. luzuloides* Torr. and Gray was used similarly. The Rocky Mountain species, *A. rosulata* Rydb., was used by the Gosiute to treat snow blindness.

HOARY CHAENACTIS, DOUGLAS'S DUSTY MAIDEN

Whole plant

Chaenactis douglasii (Hook.) Hook. & Arn.   Composite Family

White-woolly perennial, to 2 ft. Leaves alternate, *deeply pinnately lobed* into oblong segments; *segments shallowly lobed*; margins rolled under. Flower head of white to pinkish flowers in mostly flat-topped clusters; *glandular bracts below*; May–Sept. **WHERE FOUND:** Dry, open, often sandy or rocky areas. E. and n. Calif. to all other western states except Tex. **USES:** American Indians made a mild tea for use as a stomach tonic. Whole plant tea was used to slow heartbeat. Both the leaves and whole plant tea were used for colds and coughs. Whole plant tea was taken as an emetic for indigestion or sour stomach. Externally, used as a wash for swollen limbs or dropsy, chapped hands, pimples, boils, tumors, swellings, insect bites, and snakebites. Mashed leaves were poulticed to treat sprains, sore limbs, rattlesnake bites, and to reduce swelling. Tea or poultice of young leaves used for headache. An infusion of the roots was applied as a wash to the eyes. Root tea used as a purgative by all members of the

Hoary Chaenactis (Chaenactis douglasii) *has deeply divided, soft hairy leaves.*

family of a person who died to ward off sickness, especially tuberculosis. **RELATED SPECIES:** A number of other species were also used by American Indians. The Kawaiisu used root tea of *C. santolinoides* Greene for sore chest or shoulders and other internal soreness. Indians in Nev. used a tea of the whole plant of *C. stevioides* Hook. & Arn. to slow the heartbeat and to lower fevers in children.

CALIFORNIA LIFE EVERLASTING   Whole plant
Pseudognaphalium californicum (DC.) A. Anderb.   Composite Family
[*Gnaphalium californicum* DC.]

Sweet-scented, glandular annual or biennial, to 3 ft.; *feels oily to the touch.* Leaves alternate, narrowly (ob)lanceolate to linear, without stalks; *green on both sides;* margins entire. Flowers in small, *round heads,* densely clustered at stem tips, somewhat flat-topped; Jan.–July. Bracts below head *white, round, papery, shiny,* enclosing flowers. **WHERE FOUND:** Dry, open sites; disturbed places. Baja Calif. to Ore. **USES:** The Miwoks, Costanoans, and other Indian tribes made a pleasant-tasting leaf tea to treat colds and stomach problems. Externally, leaves and flowers poulticed to treat swelling. **RELATED SPECIES:** Indians dipped a cloth in a strong tea of rabbit tobacco, *Pseudognaphalium obtusifolium* ssp. *obtusifolium* (L.) Hilliard & Burtt (*G. obtusifolium* L.), and applied it to the throat for healing mumps. The tea was drunk for colds and to calm restless sleep and used to bathe the faces and heads of old

California Life Everlasting (Pseudognaphalium californicum) *leaves are green above and below and feel oily to the touch.*

Povertyweed (Iva axillaris) *was a favorite children's herb of the Shoshone.*

people. The leaves and blossoms were historically recommended by physicians to be chewed, then the juice swallowed to heal mouth and throat ulcers. A warm tea was drunk to induce sweating and reduce fevers, to treat lung problems and vaginal yeast infections, and to shrink tumors. The fresh juice reportedly has aphrodisiacal qualities. Several species are used medicinally throughout Asia, including *G. luteoalbum* L., used for lung diseases, fevers, and ulcers of the stomach and intestines.

POVERTYWEED
Iva axillaris Pursh

Leaves, roots
Composite Family

Perennial from creeping roots; to 2 ft. Leaves alternate, oblanceolate, *without stalks, red gland-dotted*; margins *entire*. Flowers in many small heads, *nodding on short stalks from leaf axils*; May–Sept. Bracts below head few, *fused into shallow cup*. **WHERE FOUND:** Saline habitats; weedy in disturbed places. Throughout western N. America; cen. coast ranges, e. cen. Sierra of Calif. to B.C. **USES:** This was a favored children's herb with the Shoshone Indians, who used a leaf tea to treat stomachache, cramps, diarrhea, and colds. Raw or cooked root was eaten for indigestion. Paiute Indians used a wash of the leaf tea or poultice to treat sores, rashes, or itching. The Mohuna used the whole plant as an abortifacient and for birth control.

MAYWEED, DOGFENNEL
Whole plant

Anthemis cotula L.
Composite Family

  Malodorous, stout annual, to 3 ft. Chamomile lookalike. Leaves alternate, pinnately *dissected into many narrow segments.* Flowers in *conical heads* on short stalks; disk flowers yellow; ray flowers becoming reflexed; *each flower with linear bract below;* Apr.–Nov. **WHERE FOUND:** Moist, disturbed places, gardens, roadsides, fields. Widespread weed throughout U.S. Alien (Europe). **USES:** Plant tea once used as a tonic, diaphoretic, blood purifier, and, in large doses, an emetic; used to treat asthma, biliousness, colds, diarrhea, dropsy, epilepsy, fevers, hysterics, rheumatism, stomach

(Top left) *Mayweed* (Anthemis cotula) *has foul-smelling leaves.* (Bottom left) *English Daisy* (Bellis perennis) *is a common weed on lawns.* (Bottom right) *Eclipta* (Eclipta prostrata) *is a common tropical weed.*

cramps, shortness of breath, and venereal disease. Externally, used as a wash for rheumatism and severe colds, poulticed to draw out blisters. Juice from the plant was used as an eyewash. The roots were chewed to relieve toothaches. Tea from the dried roots and stems was used as a sedative. European settlers made an ointment by frying the older blossoms with lard to treat sore throat and rheumatism. European herbalists used Mayweed for sluggish menses plus intestinal and menstrual cramps. **WARNING:** Touching or ingesting plant may cause allergic reactions.

ENGLISH DAISY
Bellis perennis L.

Leaves, root
Composite Family

Small perennial, 2–4 in. tall. Leaves mostly basal, soft-hairy, obovate to oblanceolate, tapered to winged stem, entire or minute-toothed. Flowers small, white to light pink daisies, to ½ in. across; May–Sept. or year-round. **WHERE FOUND:** Lawns, waste places, damp grassy areas. Throughout, mostly near homes. Alien (Europe). **USES:** In European folk traditions leaves used as a potherb, for fevers, inflammatory liver conditions, gout, and gastrointestinal disorders; as a gargle for sore throat or mouth ulcers. Externally, leaves used in ointments or poulticed for inflammatory skin conditions, aches, pains, bruises, and wounds. Once called Bruisewort in England. Primarily used for soothing, demulcent action coupled with mild anti-inflammatory activity. Root tea used to prevent scurvy. Research confirms antifungal and antibacterial activity. **WARNING:** May cause allergic reactions.

CHICORY
Cichorium intybus L.

Roots, leaves
Composite Family

Flowers usually blue (rarely white or pink). See p. 216.

ECLIPTA, FALSE DAISY
Eclipta prostrata (L.) L.
[*Eclipta alba* (L.) Hassk.]

Whole plant
Composite Family

Rough-haired annual, to 1½ ft. Leaves opposite, narrowly lance-shaped, with or without stalks, to 4 in. long. Margins apparently entire but with a few marginal teeth. Flowers white in small heads, *solitary in leaf axils*; ray flowers *very short*; all flowers with *bristlelike bract below*; Mar.–Nov. **WHERE FOUND:** Waste places, cultivated fields, ditches in damp sandy soils. Widespread weed from Calif., Ariz., N.M., Tex. to eastern N. America; Baja Calif. Alien (Eurasia). **USES:** Traditionally used for snakebites, and recent studies suggest that extracts have a protective effect against muscle toxicity and bleeding caused by snake venom. In Chinese medicine the plant is used to control bleeding from the respira-

Ox-eye Daisy (Leucanthemum vulgare) is a widely naturalized weed throughout the United States.

tory tract, urinary tract, or intestinal tract, and also to treat dizziness. The herb is added to prescriptions to treat vomiting and coughing of blood, vertigo, and premature graying of the hair. Preparations are applied externally for eczema. Research confirms antibacterial, anticandidal, astringent, anti-inflammatory and immunostimulating activity.

OX-EYE DAISY

Whole plant

Leucanthemum vulgare Lam.
[*Chrysanthemum leucanthemum* L.]

Composite Family

The familiar daisy of roadsides; a hairless perennial from *creeping rootstock*, to 3 ft. Basal leaves spoon-shaped, lobed, on long petioles; stem leaves alternate, *oblong, pinnately lobed*, stalkless. Flowers with white petals and yellow disk flowers, to 2 in. across; May–Sept. **WHERE FOUND:** Disturbed sites, roadsides. Widespread throughout temperate regions of N. America; every state. Alien (Europe). **USES:** Flowers and leaves used since ancient times for menstrual problems and as a folk remedy for whooping cough, asthma, and nervousness. Externally in salves to heal wounds. Historically, physicians prescribed tea for whooping cough, asthma, and nervous excitability. Used externally as a wash or poultice for vaginal yeast infections, excess perspiration, wounds, ulcers, and dandruff. American Indians used tea as a

Townsendia (Townsendia exscapa) is mat-forming, with gray-green linear leaves.

spring tonic and for fevers. **WARNING:** May cause contact dermatitis or allergic cross-reactions with other composite family members.

TOWNSENDIA

Townsendia exscapa (Richards.) Porter

Leaves, roots
Composite Family

Mat-forming, *rough-haired* perennial, to 3 in. Leaves *linear*, grayish, with *apparent midvein*. Ray flowers white to pinkish; disk flowers yellow, *below upright leaves*; May–June. **WHERE FOUND:** Dry, open places, meadows; widespread on high plains. Ariz., Nev., Idaho, Rockies from Mont. to N.M., Tex.; Great Plains. **USES:** American Indians used tea to aid labor and help with delivery of both baby and placenta; also used to assure pregnancy and to guarantee that it be a boy. The plant was used to clear one's throat, as a snuff for nose and throat problems, and to improve a singer's voice in ceremonies. A decoction was used for stomach problems. **RELATED SPECIES:** *T. incana* Nutt. [*T. arizonica* Gray], and *T. strigosa* Nutt. used similarly.

MISCELLANEOUS AQUATIC PLANTS

YELLOW WATERWEED, FLOATING PRIMROSE WILLOW
Whole plant

Ludwigia peploides ssp. *glabrescens* (Kunth) Raven
[*Jussiaea repens* L.]   Evening Primrose Family
Floating, mat-forming perennial. Leaves alternate, oblanceolate, hairless; margins entire. Flowers 5-parted, solitary in leaf axils, petals arising *from* ovary; stamens 1 o, in 2 unequal sets; May–Sept. **WHERE FOUND:** Wet sites, ditches, streambanks, lake edges. Calif. to Ariz., N.M., Tex.; eastern U.S. Sometimes a serious wetland weed. **USES:** In India the plant is poulticed for ulcers and other skin problems, swollen testicles, and swollen lymph glands in the neck. Tea taken for diarrhea, dysentery, intestinal gas, vaginal yeast infections, and urinary problems. In China the plant is used to relieve inflammation, promote urination, and detoxify in cases of coughs, jaundice, gonorrhea, measles, carbuncles, and inflammatory skin ailments.

YELLOW SKUNK CABBAGE
Root, leaves

Lysichiton americanus Hultén & St. John   Arum Family
Fleshy perennial with *skunklike odor*; up to 4 ft. Leaves large, oblanceolate, from basal rosette; margins entire. Tiny, yellow-green flowers in *dense spikes surrounded by yellow bract*; Apr.–June. Berries greenish white, embedded along fleshy stalk.

(Above) *Yellow Waterweed* (Ludwigia peploides *ssp.* glabrescens) *is a mat-forming yellow perennial.* (Right) *Yellow Skunk Cabbage* (Lysichiton americanus). *Note the distinct lanternlike flower spathe.*

WHERE FOUND: Swamps, marshes, stream edges, seeps, wet forests. Northern coast ranges of Calif. to Alaska, Idaho, Mont., Wyo. **USES:** Bella Coola and other tribes used root as a blood purifier and for asthma, coughs, stomach cramps, constipation, and bladder problems. In steam baths, root was used to treat arthritis, low back pain, and stroke. Fresh warmed or crushed leaves were also used in sweat baths and as a poultice to treat headaches, fevers, and arthritis. Roots were chewed both to induce an abortion and to ease labor in childbirth. Smoke from the burned roots was inhaled to treat influenza and rheumatism and to bring good dreams. Poultices made by pulverizing the dry or charred root or baking the fresh root were used externally on sores, boils, infections, fungal infections, burns, animal bites, thorns, splinters, and swellings; for rheumatism, arthritis, lung hemorrhage, and chest pain, and to make a child's hair grow. **RELATED SPECIES:** Early American physicians prescribed root preparations of the eastern Skunk Cabbage, *Symplocarpus foetidus* L., as an expectorant and antispasmodic to alleviate symptoms of asthma, whooping cough, and chronic lung conditions and for nervous-system problems like epilepsy. **WARNING:** Fresh roots are extremely acrid and contain high levels of oxalic acid. Internal use may cause nausea and vomiting. Externally may cause burning or dermatitis.

ROCKY MOUNTAIN YELLOW POND LILY   Roots, leaves
Nuphar lutea (L.). Sm. ssp. *polysepalum* (Engelm.) E. O. Beal
[*N. polysepalum* Englm.]   Waterlily Family

⚠ Aquatic perennial. Leaves heart-shaped, *floating*; notched at base, margins entire, leaf stalks long. Flowers large, to 2 in. across, solitary on long stalks, sometimes tinged red; petals thick, cup-shaped; *many red-tipped stamens* surround stigma disk at center; Apr.–Sept. **WHERE FOUND:** Ponds, shallow lakes, slow-moving water. Throughout the West. **USES:** American Indian groups used

Rocky Mountain Yellow Pond Lily (Nuphar lutea ssp. polysepalum) has thick yellow flowers, sometimes with reddish tint.

root tea as a blood purifier and an analgesic for back pain, chest pain, sore joints, tuberculosis, heart disease, gonorrhea, and rheumatism. The root was used for protection during epidemics, as a contraceptive, and to treat stomach ulcers and lung hemorrhage. Root shavings were toasted and eaten for bleeding from the lungs. Leaf poultice used for pain, bites, and infections. **RELATED SPECIES:** The rhizomes of the common eastern N. American Yellow Pond Lily, *N. lutea* (L.) Sm., were used to treat spermatorrhea, nocturnal emissions, to tone and strengthen the sexual organs, and for digestive problems with chronic diarrhea. Modern herbalists recommend an extract of the rhizomes for easing menstrual cramps; the demonstrated antispasmodic properties of alkaloids from *Nuphar* support this use. **WARNING:** Large doses of root potentially **toxic.**

FLOWERS 3-PARTED; PETALS AND SEPALS ALIKE

GLACIER LILY, YELLOW FAWN LILY
Erythronium grandiflorum Pursh

Roots, corms
Lily Family

Perennial from slender bulb, to 12 in. *Two basal*, broadly oblong leaves *not mottled*; margins wavy. Flowers *nodding; petals strongly curved backward, bases pale;* stamens 6; *stigma lobes recurved;* May–July. **WHERE FOUND:** Moist, open areas, meadows; mid-elevation to alpine; N. Calif. to sw. Canada; Idaho, Mont., Wyo., Colo., Utah, N.M. **USES:** Montana Indians applied the mashed roots as a poultice to boils. The corms were used as a remedy for bad colds. **RELATED SPECIES:** *E. americanum* Ker-Gawl. was prescribed by 19th-century physicians for swollen lymph nodes related to tuberculosis and to relieve water retention, hiccups, vomiting, and spitting of blood. **WARNING:** The fresh root may cause vomiting.

Glacier Lily (Erythronium grandiflorum). *Note the strongly recurved petals.*

FLOWERS 4-PARTED; PETALS SEPARATE; STAMENS 6; FRUIT A PAPERY POD (MUSTARD FAMILY)

BLACK MUSTARD

Seeds, leaves

Brassica nigra (L.) W. D. J. Koch

Mustard Family

Stiff-haired, widely branched annual, to 6 ft. Leaves alternate, *deeply pinnately lobed at base; terminal lobe broadly rounded*; margins toothed. Flowers small, dense along elongated upper branches; Apr.–Oct. *Short, upright pods pressed against stem, beaked at top.* **WHERE FOUND:** Disturbed sites, fields; widespread weed throughout N. America; every western state except Wyo. Alien (Europe). **USES:** Cherokee Indians used seeds as an appetite stimulant and tonic and for fever, dropsy, ague, palsy, croup, and asthma. It was mixed with flour and water and taken to induce vomiting. The powdered seeds were snuffed up the nose to relieve congestion from head colds. Externally, fresh or wilted leaves were poulticed for headaches and toothaches. Oil from the seed has been used traditionally as a counterirritant, rubefacient, and stimulant. The seed and the seed oil were official in the *United States Pharmacopoeia* from 1820 to 1950. Black mustard seed is

Black Mustard (Brassica nigra) has leaves deeply lobed at base.

The petals of Golden Prince's Plume (Stanleya pinnata) are densely hairy at the base.

used as a plaster for rheumatism, bronchitis, and lumbago. Seed tea taken for coughs and to improve digestion. **RELATED SPECIES:** White mustard seed, *B. alba* Rabenh., non L., is used similarly and is prescribed in China to expel mucus, relieve coughs, and to ease joint pain and swelling. Both species contain abundant mucilage and 1–2 percent of a volatile mustard oil rich in the glucosinolate sinigrin, which changes to the more active and highly irritating allyl isothiocyanate (responsible for mustard flavor) when the seeds are crushed. **WARNING:** Mustard-seed preparations can cause painful chemical burns if left on the skin too long. Internal use may cause skin welts and sometimes blisters. The oil is highly irritating and toxic.

GOLDEN PRINCE'S PLUME

Root, leaves, seeds

Stanleya pinnata (Pursh) Britt.

Mustard Family

Perennial with whitish film, to 5 ft. Leaves alternate, gray-green; *lower ones deeply pinnately lobed* into lance-shaped segments; upper leaves lance-shaped *on short petioles*. Flowers dense along upper stalks; *stamens and style long; petals densely hairy at base;* Apr.–Sept. Linear pods drooping on *long, slender stalks jointed at base.* **WHERE FOUND:** Dry, open areas; sandy soils. S. Calif. to every western state but Wash.; Great Plains. **USES:** Warm root poulticed for earaches, arthritis, throat pain, congestion, and swollen glands. Root tea taken for general weakness after an illness. The powdered plant was poulticed on syphilitic sores. A piece of chewed root was placed next to an aching tooth. Fruits chewed and applied to the skin to relieve itching.

SHOWY FLOWERS 4-PARTED

EVENING PRIMROSE

Root, plant, seed oil

Oenothera biennis L.

Evening Primrose Family

Rough, hairy biennial, to 6 ft. Basal rosette and alternate stem leaves oblanceolate, *lobed at base;* margins slightly toothed. Flowers in dense spikes, petals 4, shallowly notched; *sepals green to yellowish, reflexed; stigma deeply 4-lobed, not extended beyond 8 stamens;* opening at dusk or on cloudy days; June–Sept. Oblong pod 4-sided, splitting to release abundant small brown seeds. **WHERE FOUND:** Disturbed sites, roadsides. Widespread weed throughout N. America. Calif., Ore., Nev., Wyo., N.M., Tex. **USES:** American Indian groups used plant tea to treat obesity. Roots were rubbed on muscles to strengthen and used both internally and as a poultice for hemorrhoids. The plant was used as a poultice on boils and sores. Early settlers used the plant to treat rashes, coughs, and depression and to stimulate digestion. Seed oil is high in linoleic acid and gamma linolenic acid (GLA), which have

Evening Primrose (Oenothera biennis) *blooms in the evening.*

cholesterol- and blood pressure–lowering effects, and are used in the treatment of high blood pressure, premenstrual syndrome (especially breast tenderness), eczema, acne, and arthritis. Laboratory tests and human trials showing anti-inflammatory, blood-thinning, and immune-modulating effects support some of these uses. Research has demonstrated that extracts of this plant can alleviate imbalances and abnormalities of essential fatty acids in prostaglandin production. Approved in Britain for treatment of atopic eczema, premenstrual syndrome, and prostatitis. Seeds formerly collected and eaten with food.

HOOKER'S EVENING PRIMROSE
Root, flowers, plant
Oenothera elata ssp. *hookeri* (Torr. & Gray) W. Dietr. & W. Wagner
[*O. hookeri* Torr. & Gray]
Evening Primrose Family
Densely rough-hairy biennial, to 3 ft. *Hair bases red, blisterlike.* Basal rosette *crowded*; stem leaves alternate, lance-shaped; margins wavy. Large flowers in dense spikes, opening at dusk; petals shallowly notched; *sepals reddish, reflexed*; *stigma deeply 4-lobed, extended beyond 8 stamens*; June–Sept. **WHERE FOUND:** Moist places, coastal areas. Every western state. **USES:** Zuni Indians poulticed the flowers (mixed with saliva) for swellings. The Navajo used a plant poultice on sores and mumps; root poultice used on swellings and as a life medicine, or panacea. The plant tea was used to treat colds and to win the heart of a desired person.

SYRIAN RUE, AFRICAN RUE
Seeds, root
Peganum harmala L.
Caltrop Family
 Densely foliaged, spreading, hairless, or slightly hairy herbaceous plant from a perennial rootstock; to 1 ft.. Leaves alternate, fleshy, *irregularly pinnately divided* into linear segments. Flowers on stalks, with 4–5 yellow to whitish separate petals; *sepals longer*

(Left) *Hooker's Evening Primrose* (Oenothera elata *ssp.* hookeri) *has large, showy flowers.* (Above) *Syrian Rue* (Peganum harmala) *is a weed introduced from Old World deserts.*

than petals; Apr.–Nov. **WHERE FOUND:** Scattered throughout deserts of se. Calif. to e. Ore., e. Wash.; Nev., Ariz., N.M., Tex. Introduced from North African and Asian deserts. Considered a noxious weed. **USES:** Syrian Rue has a long history of use as a narcotic and aphrodisiac. It has been used in the treatment of asthma, hysteria, rheumatism, gallstones, malaria, worms, and uterine complaints. A tea of the seeds is used in India for menstrual difficulties and as an abortifacient and mild intoxicant. Syrian Rue contains psychoactive b-carbolines similar to those found in the hallucinogenic ayahuasca vine (*Banisteriopsis caapi* [Spuce ex Griseb.] Morton) of the Amazon. The plant extract has strong antibacterial, antifungal, and antiprotozoal activity. **WARNING:** Hallucinogenic and poisonous; can cause hypertensive crisis with certain foods because of its monoamine oxidase–inhibiting activity.

FLOWERS PEALIKE

YELLOW SWEETCLOVER
Melilotus officinalis (L.) Lam.

Flowering plant
Pea Family

⚠ Bushy biennial, to 6 ft.; *sweet vanilla scent when crushed.* Leaves alternate, divided into 3 *oblong, toothed leaflets.* Flowers small, pealike, densely arranged along upper stalks; Apr.–Oct. *Round,* yellowish brown pods *not opening, coarsely ridged,* single-seeded. **WHERE FOUND:** Disturbed sites, roadsides. Widespread weed across northern N. America. Alien (Europe). **USES:** Though once an offi-

Yellow Sweetclover (Melilotus officinalis) *has a vanilla fragrance when dried.*

cial medicine, by the 1870s Sweet-clover was considered of no value by many physicians, finding favor only as a local application for inflammation. Eclectic physicians of the late 19th and early 20th century reinstated its use for neuralgia and in treating idiopathic headaches, lameness, soreness, rheumatic pain, colic, gastralgia, neuralgia of the stomach and other abdominal viscera, painful diarrhea, ovarian neuralgia, dysmenorrhea, and menstrual cramps. Modern herbalists recommend it for these uses and especially for varicose veins, hemorrhoids, and bruises internally and externally. The Navajo took it for colds. Flower and leaf extracts show pain-relieving, muscle-relaxing, and mild blood pressure–lowering effects in laboratory tests. **WARNING:** Don't take Sweet-clover internally if you are taking a pharmaceutical blood thinner like warfarin. Anticoagulant effects should not be expected from Sweetclover taken by itself.

MISCELLANEOUS 5-PARTED FLOWERS

BUFFALO GOURD, STINKING GOURD
Whole plant
Cucurbita foetidissima Kunth
Gourd Family

Coarse, viny, rough-hairy, *ill-smelling* perennial, to 15 ft. long. Leaves alternate, *triangular,* with branched tendrils; margins finely toothed. Flowers large, bell-shaped; Apr.–Sept. Round *gourds mottled green with white stripes.* **WHERE FOUND:** Sandy sites. S. Calif., Nev., Utah, Ariz., Rockies from Wyo. to N.M., Tex., Baja Calif. **USES:** American Indians held this plant in high esteem and used it for numerous ailments. According to the doctrine of signatures, the large, sometimes human-shaped roots were considered either male or female. The powdered root was mixed with cold water and used to treat pain; sometimes only the part of the root that corresponded to the painful part of the body was used. Soaked in cold water, the root was used on ulcers or made into laxative tea. The crushed roots were poulticed on sores. The Omaha, Pawnee, and Ponca considered the root a panacea and tonic and used it for a wide range of ailments. A root tea was used as an emetic, for chest pains, to kill maggots in wounds, and for venereal disease. The seeds were ground and sprinkled on venereal sores. Zunis applied a poultice of powdered seeds and flowers mixed with saliva to rheumatic swellings.

WESTERN PUCCOON, GROMWELL, STONESEED

Whole plant

Lithospermum ruderale Dougl. ex Lehm.   Borage Family

Rough-hairy perennial, to 2 ft. Leaves alternate, *narrowly lance-shaped, crowded* at stem tip; margins entire. Flowers in *coiled inflorescence*; petal lobes spreading, sometimes green-tinged; Apr.–June. *Hard, white nutlets smooth, shiny.* **WHERE FOUND:** Dry, open slopes and plains. Ne. Calif. to s. B.C., Idaho, Mont., Wyo., Nev., Utah, Colo. **USES:** American Indian groups used Stoneseed to treat diarrhea, especially bloody diarrhea, internal bleeding, kidney problems, itching hemorrhoids, and as a permanent form of birth control. Rheumatic pain was treated externally. **RELATED SPECIES:** The hard seeds of the European *L. officinale* L. were used to treat kidney stones. **WARNING:** Species of *Lithospermum* contain hepatotoxic pyrrolizidine alkaloids. Internal use should be avoided.

(Above) *Buffalo Gourd* (Cucurbita foetidissima) *has white striped fruits.* (Right) *Western Puccoon* (Lithospermum ruderale) *flowers are arranged in a coil.*

PURSLANE

Portulaca oleracea L.

Purslane Family

Branching, low-spreading, *succulent annual,* to 1 ft. Leaves alternate, *spatula-shaped,* smooth, shiny; tips rounded. Upper leaves clustered beneath flowers, hairless in axils. Flowers yellow, *stalkless, with only 2 sepals,* solitary or in clusters at stem tips; petals 5; stamens several; style deeply 5–6-branched; May–Nov. **WHERE FOUND:** Widespread weed of disturbed sites, cultivated areas and gardens. Throughout. Alien (Europe). **USES:** An ancient European and Asian remedy, also used as a food. American Indians adopted its use after it was introduced to North America in the 18th century. The Keres used a leaf tea to treat diarrhea and rubbed the leaves inside the mouth to treat difficulty opening the mouth. The Cherokee used leaf juice for earache. Iroquois poulticed the fresh plant on bruises and burns. Navajo used the plant for pain, stomachaches, and as a lotion for scarlet fever. Hawaiians used the juice as a tonic for general debility. In European folk tradition the fresh juice is used for slow and painful urination, liver heat with headaches, insomnia, gout, and sore gums. Juice mixed with honey as a syrup to relieve dry coughs. The juice was applied externally for dermatitis and sores. The crushed seeds were taken to kill intestinal worms. Laboratory tests show the juice to have antimicrobial properties. Studies have also demonstrated the presence of anti-inflammatory and cardiovascular-protective omega-3 fatty acids. Science confirms antibiotic and antioxidant activity. One of

the few plants reported to contain L-dopa and noradrenaline (norepinephrine). This hormone reduces bleeding at the tissue level, suggesting a rational scientific basis for the plant's use in traditional Chinese medicine to stop postpartum bleeding.

Purslane (Portulaca oleracea) *has succulent leaves.*

PACIFIC STONECROP, PACIFIC SEDUM

Sedum spathulifolium Hook. Stonecrop Family

Rhizomatous perennial, to 8 in. Leaves obovate or spoon-shaped, flat in basal rosettes, sage green *covered with whitish hue, becoming red*; tips rounded or minutely pointed. Yellow flowers 5-parted in flat-topped clusters at stem tips; petals lance-shaped, pointed, upright or widely spreading; stamens 10; May–July. **WHERE FOUND:** Rocky outcrops, coastal bluffs, forest openings. S. to n. coast ranges and n. Sierra of Calif. to B.C. **USES:** Pacific Stonecrop is astringent. The juice or crushed succulent leaves were applied externally to boils and other infections, wounds, burns, stings, ringworm, swollen glands, and hemorrhoids. Internally, the tea has been used for sore gums and sore throat, also for lung ailments, stomachache, diarrhea, and fever. American Indian women ate or poulticed the leaves during the last month of pregnancy in hopes of having an easier labor and to increase milk flow. They also used it as a laxative for infants and for calming fussy babies. **RELATED SPECIES:** *S. divergens* S. Wats. was used by the Okanagan as a children's laxative and as a hemorrhoid remedy. The most widely used western sedum is *S. acre* L., a European species, sparingly naturalized in some western states. It is acrid and will cause blistering externally and vomiting and diarrhea internally if used fresh. The plant was taken in small amounts for fever and epilepsy and externally applied to swollen lymph nodes and to warts or corns to help remove them. In traditional Chinese medicine, *S. malacophyllum* var. *japonicum* (Maxim.) Fröd. is used to treat skin diseases. *S. fimbriatum* (Turcz.) Franch. and other species are used internally to stop intestinal bleeding, for dysentery, irregular menses, kidney stones, and dog bites. A number of Asian species are poulticed for abscesses, poisonous snakebites, eruptions, and burns.

Pacific Stonecrop (Sedum spathulifolium) *leaves are covered with a white film.*

Common Mullein (Verbascum thapsus) *flowers in the second year.*

COMMON MULLEIN
Leaves, fruits, flowers
Verbascum thapsus L.
Figwort Family

Stout, densely white-woolly biennial, to 1–8 ft. Leaves large, to 12 in. or more long, in basal rosette (in first year), broadly oblanceolate; alternate stem leaves lance-shaped, *bases fused against stem; margins entire.* Flat flowers in dense, tall, thick spikes; lower petal larger; stamens 5, *upper 3 filaments yellow-hairy;* June–Sept. **WHERE FOUND:** Disturbed sites, poor soils. Throughout N. America. Alien (Europe). **USES:** Leaf tea used for coughs, colds, bronchitis, catarrh, asthma, hoarseness, sore throat, fever, and muscle and joint pain. Tea of roots and sometimes flowers used for respiratory problems, hiccups, bloody diarrhea, and female complaints. Leaves smoked to alleviate respiratory congestion. Leaf poultices, sometimes with flowers, used for painful skin inflammation, sprains, bruises, sores, cuts, wounds, swellings, infections, abscesses, muscle aches, hemorrhoids, toothaches, and swollen glands. Juice has been used on warts. Drops of flower oil are a traditional earache remedy. In Europe the flowers are preferred to the leaves. Widely used in European phytomedicine for anti-inflammatory and soothing effect on inflamed mucous membranes; widely used in cough preparations. Leaves are high in mucilagin and contain the antiseptic, antitumor, and immunosuppressant compound verbascoside. German health authorities approve the use of the flowers as an expectorant in inflammatory conditions of the upper respiratory tract. **WARNING:** Hairs may irritate the skin.

Contains some potentially toxic compounds, though the herb is generally not associated with toxicity.

FLOWERS 5-PARTED, PETALS FREE; LEAVES OPPOSITE

ST. JOHN'S WORT, KLAMATH WEED   Plant, flowers, roots
Hypericum perforatum L.   St. John's Wort Family

Perennial, to 3 ft. *Leaves opposite,* narrowly oblong; margins rolled under, *with translucent dots* when held up to light. Flowers yellow, in flat-topped clusters, stamens numerous in bushy clusters; sepals lance-shaped, *hairless; petals 5,* with *black glandular dots on margins, twisted after flowering;* June–Sept. **WHERE FOUND:** Dry soils, disturbed sites. Widespread throughout N. America. Alien (Europe). **USES:** European herbal uses include topical application of a flower oil as a liniment for sprains, swellings, bruises, wounds, sores, and ulcers. For at least 2000 years the plant has been used internally for insomnia, anxiety, mild depression, and other nervous conditions. Used also as an expectorant and to treat diarrhea, dysentery, stomachache, colic; to control uterine cramping and for chronic urinary tract problems, especially suppressed urination. American Indian groups such as the Cherokee used the plant to treat fever, suppressed menstruation, bloody diarrhea, and gut problems. The sap was rubbed on venereal sores; crushed plant was sniffed to treat nosebleed. Roots chewed, then

(Above) *St. John's Wort* (Hypericum perforatum). *Note the black dots on flower margins.* (Right) *Arizona poppy* (Kallstroemia californica) *flowers have a poppylike form.*

swallowed; also poulticed for snakebites. Montagnais Indians used a plant decoction to treat coughs. Iroquois used the plant to treat fever and the root to enhance fertility. Modern clinical research supports its use as an antidepressant for mild to moderate forms of depression; also antibacterial, antifungal, and anti-inflammatory compounds have been identified. St. John's Wort is said to outsell the antidepressant Prozac by as much as 20 to 1 in Germany and is approved as a treatment for depression. Over 30 controlled clinical trials have confirmed its safety and effectiveness. Several compounds are believed to contribute different mechanisms to help relieve depression. **WARNING:** Taken internally or externally, hypericin may cause photodermatitis (skin burns) on sensitive persons exposed to light. As an antidepressant, St. John's Wort is used only for mild to moderate depression, not severe forms. Recent evidence suggests the herb may interfere with a digestive enzyme that helps metabolize drugs into the bloodstream. Concurrent use of St. John's Wort preparations with prescription drugs should be discussed with a physician.

CONTRAYERBA, ARIZONA POPPY
Kallstroemia californica (S. Wats.) Vail

Leaves, roots
Caltrop Family

Low-growing annual, to 2 ft. White-haired stems radiating from central point. *Leaves opposite, pinnately divided* into oval leaflets; *terminal leaflet lacking.* Flowers small, solitary in leaf axils; stamens 10; June–Oct. *Round fruit splitting into 10 bumpy nutlets.* **WHERE FOUND:** Sandy or gravelly soils; disturbed areas. San Diego Co., Calif., Nev., Utah, Ariz., N.M., Tex.; n. Mexico, Baja Calif. **USES:** Tewa Indians used a poultice of chewed leaves on sores and swellings. Internally, the root tea was used to treat diarrhea.

PUNCTURE VINE, GOATS HEAD, LITTLE CALTROP
Tribulus terrestris L.

Whole plant
Caltrop Family

Bristly-branched annual sprawling along ground, to 3 ft. Silky-hairy stems radiating from central point. *Leaves opposite, pinnately divided* into many small, oblong leaflets; *terminal leaflet lacking.* Flowers small, solitary in leaf axils; stamens 10; Apr.–Oct. *Spiny fruits flat, 5-parted.* **WHERE FOUND:** Roadsides, fields, disturbed areas. Throughout N. America; Mexico. Alien (Mediterranean). **USES:** The spiny fruits of *Tribulus* have been prescribed by East Indian and Chinese herbalists for centuries to treat ailments of the genitourinary tract. In India the fruits are made into tea capsules, tablets, and liquid extracts for treating painful urination, incontinence, kidney stones, Bright's disease, impotence in men, nocturnal emissions, and gonorrhea. A leaf tea is used to

Puncture Vine (Tribulus terrestris). *Note the hairy, ladder-arranged leaves.*

calm the stomach and dissolve kidney stones; root tea used to improve the appetite. In China the fruits are prescribed in herbal formulas to calm and regulate the liver, to ease headaches, vertigo, dizziness, red and painful eyes, insufficient lactation, and suppressed menses, as well as skin ailments such as hives with intense itching. The fruits are also recommended to stop postpartum bleeding, nosebleeds, and bleeding in the gastrointestinal tract. A recent controlled clinical study found that the herb does not strengthen the body or enhance exercise performance in trained athletes. Another clinical study suggests its potential usefulness in treating angina pectoris. Several steroidal saponins and alkaloids have been identified in the plant. **WARNING:** Avoid use during pregnancy. Sheep feeding on the plant have been reported to contract photodermatitis and to develop locomotor disorders such as staggers.

FLOWERS 5-PARTED, PETALS FREE; LEAVES ALTERNATE, PALMATELY LOBED OR DIVIDED (BUTTERCUP FAMILY)

TALL BUTTERCUP
Ranunculus acris L.

Roots, leaves, flowers
Buttercup Family

Rough-hairy perennial, to 3 ft. *Leaves deeply palmately lobed into 3–5 segments; each segment further deeply lobed.* Flowers with shiny petals; *sepals spreading;* stamens many; May–Sept. **WHERE FOUND:** Disturbed sites, moist meadows. Nevada Co., Calif. to every western state except Ariz., Colo., Tex.; eastern N. America. Alien (Europe). **USES:** Roots poulticed on abscesses and boils and used on the torso by the Iroquois for chest pains and colds. Inhaling the odor of crushed leaves or flowers was a headache remedy. Leaves were used to make a gargle for sore throat. The plant was made into a tincture in Europe and given as a folk remedy in small, diluted doses to relieve neuralgia in the rib area. The fresh juice was used directly on warts to remove them and as a counterirritant blistering agent to relieve the pain of gout. The leaves were included in a famous cancer remedy from 1794. **RELATED SPECIES:** Several species of *Ranunculus* are used in Asia for their analgesic and anti-inflammatory properties. **WARNING:** All buttercup species contain varying amounts of toxic and acrid blistering compounds and should not be used internally or externally. The volatile acrid principle is destroyed by drying or boiling. All fresh parts of *R. acris* contain especially potent irritants and can cause blistering in sensitive individuals after contact with the plant juice.

WOODLAND BUTTERCUP, BONGARD'S BUTTERCUP

Whole Plant

Ranunculus uncinatus D. Don ex G. Don   Buttercup Family

Perennial, to 3 ft. *Leaves deeply 3-lobed on soft, hairy petioles; segments shallowly lobed and coarsely toothed.* Flowers with *very small,* shiny petals; *sepals reflexed;* stamens many; Apr.–Aug. Many flattened single-seeded fruits in round clusters; *beak strongly hooked.* **WHERE FOUND:** Moist, shaded areas. N. Calif. to B.C., all western states except Utah. **USES:** Thompson Indians used it in a wash to allay muscle soreness and stiffness and aching bones. Used as a purifying wash or steam and to relieve pains of rheumatism in sweat houses. **WARNING:** Buttercups contain an acrid compound that can cause blistering of the skin and dangerous, even fatal, excoriation of mucous membranes if swallowed.

Tall Buttercup (Ranunculus acris) *is a common weed introduced from Europe.*

Woodland Buttercup (Ranunculus uncinatus) *has deeply three-lobed leaves.*

FLOWERS 5-PARTED, PETALS FREE; LEAVES ALTERNATE, PINNATELY LOBED OR PALMATELY DIVIDED (ROSE FAMILY)

AGRIMONY, TALL HAIRY AGRIMONY

Whole plant

Agrimonia gryposepala Wallr.

Rose Family

Glandular, long-hairy perennial, to 4 ft. Leaves pinnately divided into *alternating large and small oval leaflets*; margins sharply toothed. *Flowers small, numerous, in long, spikelike racemes*; stamens many; July–Sept. Hard, oblong fruits *ringed with hooked prickles*. **WHERE FOUND:** Moist places. N. coast ranges, San Diego Co., Calif., to eastern N. America; Mexico. **USES:** Cherokees used root tea to build the blood. A tea of the burs was taken for diarrhea, vaginal discharge, and fever. A root tea was given to satisfy children's hunger. The Iroquois made a root tea for children's diarrhea and vomiting. The root was also used as a styptic for nosebleeds. **RELATED SPECIES:** *A. eupatoria* L. contains about 8 percent tannins as well as coumarins and flavonoids. For centuries the root has been used for easing diarrhea, gallbladder disorders, nosebleeds, sore throats and laryngitis (as a gargle), and as a simple digestive stimulant. *A. pilosa* Ledeb. var. *japonica* (Miq.) Nakai is the Chinese drug xian he cao, used in prescriptions to stop abnormal bleeding from the lungs, urinary tract, nose, and gums and to check bleeding after operations. Also used to ease diarrhea and to kill parasites such as *Trichomonas vaginalis* and tapeworms.

(Above) *Agrimony* (Agrimonia eupatoria). *Most species of this genus are used similarly, for their astringent properties.* (Right) *Large-leaf Avens* (Geum macrophyllum) *has a large terminal leaflet.*

LARGE-LEAF AVENS
Roots, leaves
Rose Family
Geum macrophyllum Willd.

Bristly-haired perennial, to 3 ft. Leaves pinnately divided into *alternating large and small, round* leaflets; *terminal leaflet much larger; margins finely toothed.* Flowers few; *5 or fewer linear bractlets below sepals*; stamens many; Apr.–Aug. Hairy, single-seeded fruit with *hooked awn, borne in round clusters.* **WHERE FOUND:** Moist sites, meadows. Calif. to Alaska, every western state but Tex.; eastern N. America. **USES:** American Indian groups considered Avens a panacea, good for any illness. They chewed leaves during and after childbirth for uterine healing and drank leaf tea as a contraceptive. Root tea used to treat stomach pain, acid reflux, teething, and rashes from measles, chickenpox, and smallpox. Leaves poulticed on boils, cuts, and bruises. Salish Indians ate the leaves as protection against infection from being exposed to a dying person. Root extracts have antifungal activity. **RELATED SPECIES:** Studies of *G. japonicum* Thunb., used in Asia as an astringent to stop bleeding and as a diuretic, show antiviral activity of root extracts for herpes simplex, cytomegalovirus, and HIV. *G. urbanum* L. is used in Europe as a tonic and astringent.

STICKY CINQUEFOIL
Leaf, root
Rose Family
Potentilla glandulosa Lindl.

Sticky or soft-hairy upright perennial, to 3 ft. Leaves pinnately divided, mostly basal; obovate leaflets coarsely toothed. Flowers

(Left) *Sticky Cinquefoil* (Potentilla glandulosa) *is usually sticky to the touch.* (Above) *Graceful Cinquefoil* (Potentilla gracilis). *Note the silver-gray hairs on underside of leaves.*

several, sometimes white; 5 *linear bractlets below sepals*; stamens many; May–Aug. *Finely ridged*, single-seeded fruit with *thick style easily detaching from middle or below*. **WHERE FOUND:** Open sites, banks, mostly at low elevations. Throughout western N. America. **USES:** Okanagan and Thompson Indians used Sticky Cinquefoil as a mild stimulant and tonic for general rundown feeling. The plant was used to treat colic, stomach acidity, and headaches. Gosiute Indians used a poultice of the leaves on swellings.

GRACEFUL CINQUEFOIL   **Roots, leaves**
Potentilla gracilis Dougl. ex Hook.   Rose Family
     Long-hairy perennial, to 3 ft. Leaves *palmately divided*, mostly basal; oblanceolate leaflets sharply toothed, *densely white-woolly beneath*. Five lance-shaped bractlets below sepals; stamens many; May–Aug. *Smooth*, single-seeded fruit with *slender style easily detaching from tip*. **WHERE FOUND:** Moist places, meadows. Sierras, all western states except Ariz., to n. Great Plains. **USES:** Okanagan and Colville Indians used the mashed roots as a tonic and blood fortifier, for treating aches and pains, diarrhea and gonorrhea and for washing sores. Thompson Indians macerated the roots with pitch as a salve for wounds. **RELATED SPECIES:** The European species *P. erecta* (L.) Raeusch. and *P. tormentilla* Stokes have antioxidant and anti-inflammatory constituents. They are used for their astringent properties to treat mild inflammations of the mouth and throat, oral and gum sores, diarrhea, and excessive menstrual bleeding. The Mexican herb Sinfito, *P. candicans* Hum. et Bonpl., contains a potent aldose reductase inhibitor, which has been shown to help relieve symptoms of diabetic neuropathy by increasing blood flow and to enhance nerve conduction to the sciatic nerve. Extracts of *P. arguta* Pursh from British Columbia have been shown to inhibit respiratory syncytial virus in vitro.

FLOWERS 5-PARTED; PETALS FUSED: FLAT TO BELL-SHAPED (NIGHTSHADE FAMILY)

HENBANE   **Leaves, seeds**
Hyoscyamus niger L.   Nightshade Family
     Malodorous, sticky annual or biennial, to 3 ft. Leaves large, alternate, oval, sessile, with *few, pointed teeth*. *Large, bell-shaped flowers, greenish yellow with purple center and veins*, on one-sided racemes; June–Sept. Sepal tube bristle-tipped, *enclosing and hardening around fruit*; stamens 5. Fruit *opening by cap at tip*, many-seeded. **WHERE FOUND:** Disturbed places, roadsides. Widely introduced in western N. America, except Calif., Ariz., to ne. U.S. and Canada. Alien (Europe). **USES:** Henbane has a long tradition of use as a narcotic, sedative, and antispasmodic. It has been used to

Henbane (Hyoscyamus niger) *is a toxic plant.*

treat internal organ pain, including uterine pain and intestinal colic. Also used for hemorrhoid pain, urinary irritation, gout, rheumatism, earache, and headache. It was considered useful for mania, restlessness, nervous excitability, delirium, and nymphomania. Its antispasmodic properties made it useful in the treatment of chronic coughs, bronchitis, pneumonia, and asthma. Henbane was reportedly used by witches in the Middle Ages as a ritual and visionary plant; it contains the potent alkaloids atropine, hyoscyamine, and scopolamine. **WARNING: Deadly poison.** All parts of the plant are highly toxic, causing respiratory paralysis and death.

GRAPE GROUND CHERRY
Root, fruit
Physalis viscosa L.
Nightshade Family

Low, spreading perennial with *star-shaped* hairs, to 3 ft. Leaves alternate, ovate; margins entire. Flowers *nodding,* bell-shaped, on slender stalks; *petals not spotted, center dark yellow or purplish;* stamens 5; May–Oct. *Berry enclosed by inflated, papery sepals.* **WHERE FOUND:** Disturbed places, roadsides. Native to Ark. and Okla. southwest to Tex., N.M.; e. Mexico. Introduced along s. coast of Calif. **USES:** American Indian groups used the root as a dressing for wounds. Plains tribes drank a root decoction for headaches and stomach problems. **RELATED SPECIES:** Estrogen-antagonistic, tumor-inhibiting and immunostimulatory compounds have been isolated from various species of ground cherry. In Chinese and European herbal traditions, *P. alkekengi* L. is used to lower fever, to relieve bouts of rheumatism, and as an expectorant, diuretic, and laxative. It is said to be antibiotic to *Staphylococcus.* The Navajo used the dried leaves and roots of *P. pubescens* L. as a panacea, or life medicine. **WARNING:** May be toxic in large amounts. Contains liver enzyme–inhibiting compounds.

Grape Ground Cherry (Physalis viscosa) *has nodding, star-shaped flowers, with papery inflated seedpods.*

Buffalo Berry (Solanum rostratum) *has formidable spines.*

BUFFALO BERRY

Root, leaves, berries

Solanum rostratum Dunal   Nightshade Family

Annual, densely covered with yellow prickles and star-shaped hairs, to 2½ ft. Leaves alternate, deeply lobed. Flowers flat; large anthers opening by pores, standing upright in center, one larger and purple; May–Sept. Densely prickly sepals enclosing dry berry. **WHERE FOUND:** Disturbed sites, roadsides. Widespread weed throughout southwestern N. America; every state. Native to Great Plains. **USES:** Powdered root was used for upset stomach and headache. The oily juice squeezed from the fruit was applied to skin eruptions by American Indians. A root decoction was drunk for bowel problems. **WARNING:** Potentially toxic.

FLOWERS 4- OR 5-PARTED; FLOWERS IRREGULAR, PETALS FUSED: TUBULAR

GOLDEN CORYDALIS

Whole plant, root

Corydalis aurea Willd.   Bleeding-heart Family

Highly branched, diffuse biennial with a leafy base, to less than 12 in. Leaves alternate, doubly divided, *fernlike*. Golden flowers few, in short racemes, long tubular with *two lips*; May–Aug. **WHERE**

The various species of Corydalis (Corydalis) are used interchangeably.

Western Jewelweed (Impatiens noli-tangere) is very closely related and used interchangeably with Common Jewelweed (I. capensis) pictured here.

FOUND: Disturbed places in loose, open ground. Sagebrush scrub, yellow pine forests, ne. Calif. to e. Ore., Wash., B.C. to Alaska; all western states to eastern U.S. **USES:** The plant was used by American Indian groups to treat diarrhea and sores on the hand and to prevent and treat postpartum puerperal infections. Smoke from burning roots was inhaled by patients who had lost consciousness. Historically, physicians used tea for menstrual irregularities, dysentery, diarrhea, recent syphilitic nodes, and related afflictions. **RELATED SPECIES:** *C. aurea* ssp. *occidentalis* (Engelm. ex Gray) G. B. Ownbey [*C. montana* Engelm.] was used by the Navajo for rheumatism. The Ramah Navajo drank a cold tea for stomachache and sore throats. The tea was applied as an external wash for backaches, which is an important use of the Chinese drug yan hu suo, from the tubers of *C. yanhusuo* W. T. Wang. Yan hu suo is added to prescriptions to treat pain from traumatic injuries and is considered especially effective for easing pain in the chest and abdomen, menstrual pain, and discomfort from hernias. The tubercles, or small bulblets, contain the alkaloid tetrahydropalmatine, which has a sedative and tranquilizing effect. **WARNING:** *Corydalis* species are potentially **toxic** in moderate doses.

WESTERN JEWELWEED
Impatiens noli-tangere L
[*I. occidentalis* Rydb.]

Whole Plant
Touch-me-not Family

⚠ Hairless annual, to 3 ft. Leaves alternate, oval; margins coarsely toothed. Showy flowers with *curved spur, spotted red-brown to or-*

ange; July–Sept. Narrow *pod explosively opening when touched* into 5 coiled valves. **WHERE FOUND:** Wet places. W. Ore. to Alaska. **USES:** Closely related to and used interchangeably with the more eastern Common Jewelweed (*I. capensis*). Historically, tea of the plant used as an emetic, cathartic, and diuretic. It is not considered safe, however. An ointment made from the plant boiled in lard has been used to treat hemorrhoids. Fresh raw juice or fresh plant poultice of jewelweed is a traditional remedy for relief from poison oak or poison ivy. Mucilaginous stem juice (harvested before flowering) also applied to rashes. A 1957 study by a physician found it effective (in 2–3 days) in treating 108 of 115 patients. Some people swear by the leaf tea as a poison-ivy rash preventative. However, in 1997, a randomized double-blind paired comparison was done on the effects of fresh jewelweed. It was found to not be effective in treatment of allergic contact dermatitis from poison ivy or poison oak. **WARNING:** Do not use internally; it is potentially toxic, especially when fresh.

FLOWERS 5-PARTED; PETALS FUSED, WITH 2 LIPS (BILABIATE)

BUTTER-AND-EGGS   **Whole plant**
Linaria vulgaris P. Mill.   Figwort Family
    Hairless perennial, to 3 ft. Leaves alternate, *linear*, crowded, not stalked. Flowers in dense racemes at stem tips; top lip 2-lobed;

(Left) *Butter-and-eggs* (Linaria vulgaris) *has bicolored flowers.* (Above) *Musk Monkeyflower* (Mimulus guttatus) *flowers have a red-spotted lip.*

spurred bottom lip orange-hairy; stamens 4; June–Oct. Capsule with many *flat, winged seeds*. The snapdragon-like flowers, in two shades of yellow, earn the common name Butter-and-Eggs. **WHERE FOUND:** Disturbed sites. Widespread throughout N. America. Alien (Europe). **USES:** The Iroquois used the plant to treat diarrhea, for babies who cry too much, and as an emetic antilove medicine to remove bewitching. Ojibwa used it in a sweat-lodge inhalant mixture. Western herbalists use it as a diuretic and cathartic to treat jaundice, gallbladder problems, stones, spleen or liver enlargement, congestive heart disease, cystitis, "bad blood," sciatica, skin diseases, and hemorrhoids. Diuretic and fever-reducing effects have been confirmed.

MUSK MONKEYFLOWER, SEEP-SPRING MONKEYFLOWER

Whole plant

Mimulus guttatus DC.

Figwort Family

Annual or perennial, to 3 ft. Leaves opposite, round to ovate; margins coarsely toothed. Flowers on *stalks longer than sepals*; bracts below flowers fused at base, surrounding stem; *lower lip red-spotted, hairy*; *2-parted style flat*, closing when touched; Mar.–Sept. Capsule hidden by *inflated, strongly pleated sepals; the top sepal lobe longest*. **WHERE FOUND:** Wet or moist places. Throughout western N. America, Alaska; n. Mexico. **USES:** Native American groups used varieties of this plant to treat many different conditions. Wounds, cuts, sores, and rope burns were treated with a poultice. Colds, flu, epilepsy, stomachache, and poisoning were treated with a tea. Chest and back soreness was treated with a steam bath made by boiling the stems and leaves. **RELATED SPECIES:** Historically, physicians used a poultice, tea, or tincture of *Mimetanthe pilosa* (Benth.) Greene [*Mimulus pilosa* (Benth.) S. Wats.] to treat painful rheumatism, neuralgia, erysipelas, and burns and used it as a spray for bronchitis or laryngitis.

HOT-ROCK PENSTEMON, SCABLAND PENSTEMON

Leaves, root

Penstemon deustus Dougl. Ex Lindl.

Figwort Family

Hairy, glandular shrub; stems flexible, woody at base; to 2 ft. Leaves opposite, oblanceolate, bright green; *margins toothed*. White to yellowish flowers *dark-veined, clustered in leaf axils*; May–July. Petal tube hairy, glandular inside; fertile stamens 4, sterile stamen slender, *not hairy*. Pod 2-parted, opening at tip. **WHERE FOUND:** Dry, rocky sites; sagebrush or juniper woodland. N. Calif. to e. Wash., to Mont., Wyo., n. Nev., nw. Utah. **USES:** The astringent properties of Penstemon make it especially useful as a poultice or powder applied to swellings, sores, boils, chapped or

Hot-Rock Penstemon (Penstemon deustus) *has dark-veined flowers.*

cracked skin, itching or eczematous rashes, and mosquito and tick bites. The leaves, stems, or roots were a valued remedy for venereal disease, both internally and as a wash or douche. A decoction of the plant was taken for stomachaches, colds, and rheumatic aches, put in the ear for ear infections, used as a bath for sore feet and swollen legs, and as an eyewash. **RELATED SPECIES:** A poultice of *P. centranthifolius* Benth. was applied as a poultice for deep and infected wounds and sores. An infusion of *Keckiella breviflora* (Lindley) Straw [*P. breviflorus* Lindl.] was steeped and drunk for colds. *P. eatoni* Gray was decocted and applied to burns to allay pain and promote healing. Plant infusions of Shrubby Penstemon, *P. fruticosus* (Pursh) Greene, were taken for colds, flu, headache, internal ailments, ulcers, urinary tract disorders, and backache and used as a wash for rheumatic aches and pains, acne, red sore eyes, and sore or itching scalp. A piece of raw root was put on an intensely hurting tooth. Penstemon was used in an emetic compound as an antidote to having taken a love potion.

FLOWERS WITH 7 OR MORE PETALS; PETALS MOSTLY FREE

DWARF MENTZELIA, STICKLEAF   **Root**
Mentzelia pumila (Nutt.) Torr. & Gray.   Loasa Family
   Rough-haired, upright, *white-stemmed* biennial or short-lived perennial with few branches. Leaves alternate, thick, light or yellowish green, narrow, with large teeth, or pinnately parted. Flowers large, with 10 bright yellow petals; calyx fused to ovary: Feb.–Oct. Fruit a cylindrical capsule. **WHERE FOUND:** In dry streambeds, along roads. Ariz., Nev., Utah; Rockies from Mont. to N.M., Tex. questionable. **USES:** Zuni Indians treated constipation with a rectal sup-

Smooth-Stemmed Blazing Star Mentzelia (Mentzelia laevicaulis) pictured here, also has large, showy flowers like those of Dwarf Mentzelia (M. pumila).

pository made from the powdered root. Hopi used it as a toothache remedy. **RELATED SPECIES:** The Cheyenne used the roots of *M. laevicaulis* (Dougl. Ex Hook.) Torr. & Gray, Smooth-stem Blazing-star, to ease pain and stiffness of rheumatism and arthritis; to reduces swellings from bruises; and for earaches, fevers, mumps, and measles. The roots were chewed to allay thirst. The Mendocino and other tribes used leaf tea for stomachache; externally as a wash for skin diseases. The seeds of *M. albicaulis* (Dougl. ex Hook.) Dougl. ex Torr. & Gray, White-stem Blazing-star, were used by the Gosiute as a burn remedy, by the Hopi for toothaches. A poultice of the crushed, soaked seeds was used by the Ramah Navajo for toothaches. An infusion of *M. multiflora* (Nutt.) Gray, Many-flowered Mentzelia, was used as a diuretic and tuberculosis remedy.

PLAINS PRICKLYPEAR CACTUS
Opuntia polyacantha Haw.

Whole plant
Cactus Family

Flat, jointed stems forming small, rounded clumps to 10 in. high and 1 ft. across. Joints round to oblong, not easily detached, *covered with woolly, gray knobs from which minute tan spines and stout rigid spines up to 2 in. long emerge.* Flowers yellow, solitary, with many stamens and sharp-tipped petals; Apr.–July. Fruits dry, spiny; seeds white. **WHERE FOUND:** Deserts, gravelly washes and slopes, pinyon-juniper woodland, sagebrush scrub, mixed conifer forests. Every western state eastward to the Great Plains. **USES:** Sioux Indians applied the peeled stems to wounds. Flathead Indians applied the pulped stems to aching backs and used a stem infusion to treat diarrhea. The Okanagan-Colville Indians applied the peeled plant to skin sores and infections and ate it as a diuretic to promote urination.

Plains Pricklypear Cactus (Opuntia polyacantha). *Note the long, rigid spines.*

FLOWERS SMALL IN UMBELS; LEAVES COMPOUND, FINELY DISSECTED, MOSTLY BASAL

CALIFORNIA DESERT PARSLEY

Root

Lomatium californicum (Nutt.) Mathias & Constance   Parsley Family

⚠ Parsleylike perennial from stout, thickened taproot, to 4 ft. Hairless stem with whitish film. Basal leaves broadly divided into groups of 3 coarsely toothed leaflets or lobes; petiole sheathing at base. Smaller, dense umbellets arranged in umbels; Apr.–June. Oval fruit flat, hairless; margins narrowly winged; wings thick, corky. **WHERE FOUND:** Moist, shaded, or brushy slopes, woodlands. S. to n. coast ranges of Calif. to s. Ore. **USES:** Dried roots were smoked to treat colds and clear nasal passages, burned as moxa for treating rheumatic pains, and chewed for sore throat or bad breath. Root decoctions were used to treat colds, as a wash for bathing sores, as an appetite stimulant, and for menstrual cramps, irregular menstruation, and menopausal symptoms. Pounded roots were rubbed on the stomach to relieve stom-

California Desert Parsley (Lomatium californicum) *has parsley-like leaves.*

Lomatium (Lomatium dissectum).
Note the finely divided leaves.

achache. The dried roots were strung around the neck as a talis-
man to ward off rattlesnakes and illness. **WARNING:** Strong doses
can cause gastrointestinal irritation with nausea.

LOMATIUM, DESERT PARSLEY · Root

Lomatium dissectum (Nutt.) Mathias & Constance · Parsley Family

Perennial from stout, thickened taproot, to 4 ft. Stems hollow,
hairy. Leaves mostly basal, hairy; segments deeply lobed into
many small, round-tipped divisions; petioles sheathing at base.
Flowers yellow or maroon-purple in small, dense umbellets arranged in umbels; Apr.–Aug. Bracts below umbellets linear, hairless. Oblong to oval fruit flat, hairless; margins narrowly winged;
wings thick, corky. **WHERE FOUND:** Rocky, wooded, or brushy slopes,
often coniferous forests. Kern Co., n. Sierra of Calif., to B.C., every western state but N.M. and Tex.; Baja Calif. **USES:** Root preparations are currently prescribed by naturopathic physicians for vi-
ral conditions such as AIDS and chronic fatigue syndrome.
American Indian tribes used it widely. Smoke or steam from the
roots was inhaled or root preparations drunk for colds or influenza, for sinus, nasal, or lung congestion, for sore throats, hay
fever, asthma, bronchitis, pneumonia, tuberculosis, headaches,
and dizziness. Roots were used as a tonic and appetite stimulant
and to promote weight gain in debilitated persons. Externally, a
wash of pounded roots was used on sores, acne, burns, bruises,
sprains, cuts, wounds, infected compound fractures, broken
bones, sore backs, areas of rheumatic and arthritic pain, and dandruff. Root oil was used to treat sore or infected eyes. Laboratory
tests show strong antibacterial activity in the essential oil. **WARNING:**
Preparations can cause skin rashes in susceptible individuals.
Proper identification is essential; do not confuse with fatally toxic
members of the parsley family.

FLOWERS SMALL IN UMBELS;
COMPOUND, FINELY DISSECTED LEAVES
ALTERNATE ON STEM

DILL   **Leaves, seeds**

Anethum graveolens L .   Parsley Family

Smooth, branched annual, often glaucous, 2–4 ft. Leaves finely dissected into linear segments *with characteristic fragrance* (the flavoring for dill pickles). Flowers in umbel, with 30–40 spreading rays, to 6 in.; individual flowers yellowish; June–Sept. Fruits to ⅜ in. long, half as wide, also with *characteristic dill fragrance*; late summer–autumn. **WHERE FOUND:** Garden soils. Occasional throughout the U.S. Alien (s. Europe). **USES:** Leaves, called dill weed, mostly used for flavoring, considered digestive, carminative; a folk medicine for conditions of the gastrointestinal and urinary tract and to reduce spasms. Contains numerous bioactive compounds. Seeds (fruit) formerly widely used as a carminative and stomachic. Research confirms antispasmodic and antibacterial activity. Approved in Germany as a tea for dyspepsia. **WARNING:** Proper identification essential. Do not confuse with fatally toxic members of the parsley family.

Dill (Anethum graveolens) *leaves have a distinctive fragrance.*

Fennel (Foeniculum vulgare) *is a common weed in California.*

FENNEL, SWEET FENNEL

Seeds

Foeniculum vulgare P. Mill.

Parsley Family

⚠ Strong anise or licorice-scented perennial, to 6 ft. Stems solid, ridged. Leaves feathery, finely dissected into threadlike segments; bases widely sheathing. Flowers in umbellets arranged in flat-topped umbels; May–Sept. Oblong fruits flattened, prominently ribbed, smell like licorice when crushed. **WHERE FOUND:** Disturbed sites, roadsides, often forming dense colonies. Common escape, Calif. to B.C., Nev., Utah, Ariz., N.M., Tex.; central and eastern U.S. Alien (Europe). **USES:** Fennel seed is an ancient remedy and is still widely used in India, China, Europe, North America, and elsewhere as a pleasant-tasting digestive aid and to relieve gas, regulate menstruation, and stimulate the flow of mother's milk. Seeds chewed for upset stomach, indigestion, and heartburn. Tea from the seeds used for children's colic and flatulence. **WARNING:** Don't confuse this licorice-scented, yellow-flowered plant with the similar-looking Poison Hemlock, *Conium maculatum* L., which grows in colonies in the same coastal habitats as fennel. *Conium* has white-flowered umbels, purple streaks on the stems, and is rank-smelling.

FOOTHILL LOMATIUM, BLADDER PARSNIPS

Lomatium utriculatum

Plant, root

(Nutt. ex Torr. & Gray) Coult. & Rose

Parsley Family

⚠🖐 Perennial from long, slender taproot; to 2 ft. Stems leafy, softly hairy or hairless, purplish at base. Leaves alternate, dissected into many narrowly linear segments; petiole widely sheathing from leaf segments to stem. Flowers in small, dense umbellets arranged in umbels; Feb.–June. Bracts below umbellets obovate, green to purplish; margins papery. Celery-scented oblong to oval fruits flat, hairless, prominently ribbed; margins with broad, thin wings. **WHERE FOUND:** Dry, open, grassy or rocky slopes, meadows, woodlands. Along coast ranges of Calif. to B.C., west of the Sierra-Cascade crest. **USES:** Kawaiisu Indians used the plant to make a

The stems of Foothill Lomatium (Lomatium utriculatum) *are purple-tinted at the base.*

wash for swollen or broken limbs and the root to treat headaches and stomachaches. **WARNING:** Preparations can cause skin rashes in susceptible individuals. Proper plant identification is essential. Do not confuse with fatally toxic members of the parsley family.

WESTERN SWEET CICELY   Root, plant
Osmorhiza occidentalis (Nutt. ex Torr. & Gray) Torr.   Parsley Family
Stout perennial to 4 ft.; roots *licorice-scented*. Leaves alternate, 3-divided into *lance-shaped to oblong, toothed* leaflets. Flowers tiny, in umbellets arranged in larger, *open* umbel; Apr.–July. *Long, slender, hairless fruits, without tail at base.* **WHERE FOUND:** Open coniferous forests, oak woodlands. N. Calif. to B.C., Idaho, Nev., Utah; Mont. to Colo. **USES:** American Indian groups used root tea to treat gas pains, indigestion, stomachache, diarrhea, coughs, colds, fever, flu, pneumonia, whooping cough, eye and nose problems, as a cathartic, and to stimulate labor. Externally, root tea used to kill head lice; as a wash for treating skin rashes, eye problems, and sore breasts; as a feminine deodorant; and applied to snakebites, cuts, sores, swellings, and bruises. Referred to as "all medicine" by some tribes. The root was dried, cut into little pieces, and sucked for sore throats. The root was chewed and

Western Sweet Cicely (Osmorhiza occidentalis) *has licorice-scented roots.*

Poison Sanicle (Sanicula bipinnata) *has a sour-celery odor when crushed.*

packed near a bad tooth to kill the pain and reduce infection. *O. occidentalis* (Nutt. ex. Torr. & Gray) Torr. is more acrid and higher in essential oil than *O. chilensis* Hook & Arn.

POISON SANICLE
Sanicula bipinnata Hook. & Arn.

Root, leaves
Parsley Family

Perennial, to 2 ft; taproot slender. Smells faintly sour, celery-like. Stems leafy, slender. Leaves alternate, pinnately divided into well-separated, deeply lobed leaflets; petioles sheathing at base; margins coarsely toothed. Flowers few, in umbels; Apr.–June. Small, oval fruits covered in hooked bristles with swollen bases. **WHERE FOUND:** Common and abundant on shaded or open slopes, grass-lands, pine-oak woodlands, along coast ranges of Calif. **USES:** In spite of its name, the leaves were eaten as greens, and there are no records of poisonings. The boiled leaves were also used as a poultice for snakebites. **WARNING:** Of undetermined toxicity.

PACIFIC SANICLE
Sanicula crassicaulis Poepp. ex DC.

Root, leaves
Parsley Family

Faintly celery-scented perennial to 3 ft.; taproot stout. Stems leafy. Leaves alternate, deeply palmately lobed into 3–5 broad segments; petioles sheathing at base; margins with spine-tipped teeth. Flowers in compact umbels; Mar.–May. Round fruits covered in hooked bristles with swollen bases. **WHERE FOUND:** Moist to dry, open or shaded slopes, ra-vines, woodlands. Along Calif. coast ranges to B.C.; Baja Calif.; s. South America. **USES:** Though the roots were chewed and massaged into the skin to bring good fortune to gamblers, the plant was never eaten, because it was believed to be poisonous. It was also used as a poultice for snake-bites and wounds. **WARNING:** Potentially toxic.

Pacific Sanicle (Sanicula crassi-caulis) is faintly celery-scented.

HAIRY GOLDENASTER
Heterotheca villosa (Pursh) Shinners

Leaves, plant
Composite Family

Sprawling or erect perennial, to 4 ft.; highly variable. Stems and leaves bristly, with sticky glandular hairs above. Leaves flat, short-haired, lance-shaped to spoon-shaped; lower leaves clasping the stem. Flower heads few, at ends of branches; July–Aug. Bracts below head in 3–5 rows. Fruits conical or 3-angled. **WHERE FOUND:** Gravelly slopes, crevices in lava flows. Sw. desert mountains, n. and cen. high Sierra of Calif. to B.C.; every western state; n. Mexico. **USES:** The Ramah Navajo poulticed the leaves for ant bites, sore nose, and toothaches. The Cheyenne burned the plant to cleanse a house of evil spirits. They drank a tea of the tops when feeling ill and to improve sleep; flower tea taken for chest pains. The Ramah Navajo considered the plant a panacea and used it as an emetic and a ceremonial wash for sweat-lodge ceremonies, especially for indigestion and venereal diseases. A poultice of the cooked root was placed on toothaches. **RELATED SPECIES:** Extracts of the flowers of *Heterotheca inuloides* Cass., a Mexican species, have been shown to have significant anti-inflammatory, antioxidant, antimicrobial, and analgesic activity.

(Above) *Hairy Goldenaster* (Heterotheca villosa) *is highly variable in form.* (Right) *Threadleaf Groundsel* (Senecio flaccidus) *has a shrublike growth habit.*

Tansy Ragwort (Senecio jacobaea) *has finely divided, tansylike leaves.*

THREADLEAF GROUNDSEL
Leaves

Senecio flaccidus Less. var. *douglasii* (DC.) B. Turner & T. Barkley
[*S. douglasii* DC.]   Composite Family

⚠ Subshrub with shrubby appearance, persistently white-woolly, 1–5 ft. Leaves alternate, mostly linear, sometimes divided into threadlike segments, white-woolly throughout. Flower heads radiate, with 8–13 yellow ray flowers, bracts well developed; May–Aug. **WHERE FOUND:** Dry rocky or sandy soils. Colo. to Tex., west to Calif.; n. and cen. Mexico. **USES:** Costanoans drank plant tea to treat kidney ailments; used it externally as a wash for infected sores. The Kawaiisu used leaf tea as a strong laxative. Hopi used the related *S. flaccidus* var. *flaccidus* externally for rheumatism, sore muscles, pimples, and skin conditions. **WARNING:** Considered toxic. *Senecio* species contain liver-toxic pyrrolizidine alkaloids.

TANSY RAGWORT
Leaves, roots

Senecio jacobaea L.   Composite Family

⚠ Perennial, 3–5 ft. Leaves alternate, deeply dissected, fernlike, reduced above, with rank odor. Flowers yellow, daisylike, disk and rays yellow, 13 ray flowers; Aug.–Sept. **WHERE FOUND:** Disturbed sites, pastures, roadsides. B.C. to Calif., eastward. Alien (Europe). Noxious weed. **USES:** Used as a folk medicine in Europe. Leaves gargled for mouth sores or sore throat. Tea formerly used as a treatment for rheumatism, sciatica, and gout. Externally, leaf juice, considered cooling and astringent, was used as a wash on burns, sores, and ulcers. Leaf poulticed for swelling, inflammation, and bee stings. **WARNING:** Toxic to livestock. *Senecio* species contain liver-toxic pyrrolizidine alkaloids.

CALIFORNIA GOLDENROD, OREJA DE LIEBRE

Leaves, flowers

Solidago californica Nutt.

Composite Family

Densely soft-hairy perennial, to 4 ft. Leaves alternate, oblanceolate to oval, tapered at base; lower or basal leaves largest; margins toothed to entire. Flowers in many small heads in dense, narrow, mostly 1-sided branched sprays; ray flowers short; July–Oct. Bracts below head with papery margins. Fruits densely hairy with many white bristles at top. **WHERE FOUND:** Forest edges and clearings, grasslands, disturbed sites. Most of Calif. except cen. high Sierra, Ore.; Baja Calif. **USES:** Teas of goldenrod flowering tops have been used by different American Indian groups as a wash, poultice or powder for sores, wounds, burns and ulcers. A decoction held in the mouth was used as a toothache remedy. Flowers were chewed and the juice swallowed for sore throat. A hair rinse was used to prevent falling hair. The infusion was considered good for feminine hygiene. Modern studies of the saponin extracts of *Solidago* species show antitumor, anti-inflammatory, antifungal, analgesic, and diuretic activity. **WARNING:** Causes allergies, though most allergies attributed to goldenrods are due to ragweed pollen.

California Goldenrod (Solidago californica) *is densely soft-hairy.*

Canada Goldenrod (Solidago canadensis) *has small flowers in pyramid-shaped inflorescence.*

CANADA GOLDENROD
Leaves, flowers
Solidago canadensis L.
Composite Family

Sparsely rough-hairy perennial, to 5 ft. Leaves alternate, lance-shaped, 3-veined, tapering at base and tip; largest at midstem; margins coarsely to sharply toothed. Flowers in many small heads in dense, broadly pyramidal, 1-sided branched sprays; ray flowers very small; May–Nov. Lance-shaped bracts below head with papery margins. Fruits densely hairy with many white bristles at top. **WHERE FOUND:** Meadows, forest edges or openings, disturbed sites, roadsides. S. Calif. coast, n. Calif. to Alaska, Rocky Mts.; eastward. **USES:** American Indian groups used a poultice for boils, burns, sores, and ulcers. A tea was given to children suffering from flu or fever. The flowers were chewed, then poulticed externally for sore throat. A tea was taken for diarrhea and to relieve flu symptoms. It was considered helpful for general body aches and side pain. The leaf tea was used as a calming bath for babies, to help them sleep, and to treat "a child who does not talk or laugh." The plant tea was used to wash women just after childbirth. **RELATED SPECIES:** The European species *S. virgaurea* L. is still used for colds, flu, and urinary tract infections. Modern studies of the saponin extracts of *Solidago* species show antitumor, anti-inflammatory, antifungal, analgesic, and diuretic activity. The extract is especially potent against *Candida albicans*. **WARNING:** Causes allergies, though most allergies attributed to goldenrods are due to ragweed pollen.

COMPOSITES WITH PROMINENT OVERLAPPING BRACTS WITH STICKY AROMATIC "GUM"

GRINDELIA, GREAT VALLEY GUMWEED, GUMPLANT

Whole plant

Grindelia camporum Greene
[*G. robusta* Nutt.]

Composite Family

⚠ Sticky, gland-dotted perennial, to 4 ft. Stems whitish, appearing varnished. Leaves alternate, lance-shaped, oblong or spoon-shaped, base clasping stem; margins sharply toothed. Heads of numerous ray and disk flowers white-gummy in center before petals show; May–Oct. Thick, gummy bracts below head, widely spreading or strongly coiled; tips pointed. Fruit flat-awned at top. **WHERE FOUND:** Dry fields and plains, roadsides, streambanks, washes, sandy or alkaline soils. S. to n. coast ranges, n. mountains of Calif., Nev.; Baja Calif. **USES:** Eclectic physicians considered this species particularly effective for asthma. Also used for bronchitis, whooping cough, and other respiratory maladies, malaria, genitourinary-tract inflammation, vaginitis, and chronic and acute skin conditions. Costanoan Indians used a plant decoction on poison oak, boils, sores, wounds, and burns. Kawaiisu Indians put a decoction of leaves and flowers on sore parts of the body. **WARNING:** May concentrate high levels of selenium.

GRINDELIA, GUMWEED, GUMPLANT

Leaves, flowers, roots

Grindelia squarrosa (Pursh) Dunal

Composite Family

Sticky, gland-dotted biennial, to 3 ft. White to yellowish stems upright or low, spreading. Leaves alternate, oblong, strongly aromatic, base clasping stem; margins bluntly toothed. Numerous

Grindelia (Grindelia camporum) *has thick gummy bracts.*

Grindelia (Grindelia squarrosa) *has sticky bracts.*

heads of many ray and disk flowers with white-gummy centers before petals show; July–Sept. Gummy bracts below head pointed, strongly recurved. Fruits flat-awned at tip. **WHERE FOUND:** Dry fields, prairies, streamsides, roadsides, disturbed sites. Native from Mont. to N.M., Tex.; introduced in ne. Calif. to e. Wash., Idaho. **USES:** American Indian groups used Grindelia tops and flowering heads for respiratory, skin, genitourinary, and digestive ailments, including colds, coughs, pertussis, pneumonia, bronchitis, tuberculosis, and asthma. Also used for kidney pain and other kidney problems, edema, cystitis, to lessen and ease menstruation, as an abortifacient, to treat gonorrhea and syphilis, to relieve stomachache and colic, and for liver problems. A wash or poultice of the tops was used externally on scabs, cuts, sores, swellings, and other skin diseases, as a decoction for smallpox and measles, and as a wash or poultice on broken bones. Roots were also used to treat coughs. Gum was rubbed on the eyelids to treat snow blindness. Early 20th-century physicians prescribed it for asthma, coughs, and similar complaints; also for spleen congestion caused by malaria and the digestive consequences of malaria. Both *G. camporum* and *G. squarrosa* were official drugs in the *United States Pharmacopoeia* until 1960.

MISCELLANEOUS DAISYLIKE FLOWERS

CALENDULA, POT MARIGOLD
Calendula officinalis L.

Flowers, whole plant
Composite Family

Annual or short-lived perennial, to 1–2 ft. Leaves alternate, oblanceolate to spatula-shaped, soft-hairy. Flowers yellow-orange, daisylike, ray and disk flowers numerous and of same color; May–Nov. **WHERE FOUND:** Garden escape, sometimes persistent. Widely cultivated. Throughout. **USES:** Famous medicinal plant of European traditions. Flower tea used as a wash, poultice, ointment, or salve, used externally for slow-to-heal wounds, cuts, burns, bruises. Tea traditionally used as a gargle for sore throat or oral inflammations; also for gastric ul-

Calendula (Calendula officinalis) *is commonly grown as a garden annual. It is persistent in California.*

Blanket Flower (Gaillardia arista) *flowers often have a reddish tint at the base.*

cers, stomach ailments, and jaundice. Studies confirm anti-inflammatory, antiviral, and immunostimulant activity. Improves healing mechanisms at wound site and increases micro–blood vessels. Preparations widely used in modern Europe, particularly e. Europe, for skin and mucous membrane inflammations, hard-to-heal wounds, surgical wounds, mild burns, and sunburn. Approved in Germany for slow-healing wounds and ulcerations. **RELATED SPECIES:** Despite the name mari-gold, this plant should not be confused with garden marigolds, which are members of the genus *Tagetes*.

BLANKET FLOWER
Gaillardia arista Pursh

Plant, roots
Composite Family

Rough-hairy perennial, to 2 ft. Leaves, alternate, olive green, lance-shaped to linear, lobed to coarsely toothed. Showy heads with *domelike center* on long, slender stalks; ray flowers broad, 3-*lobed*, reddish brown at base; disk flowers dark purple to brown, *densely hairy at top*; May–Sept. **WHERE FOUND:** Open prairies, disturbed sites. Native from Ore. to B.C., N.D.; escaped ornamental from s. Calif. to Colo., Great Basin. **USES:** Blackfoot Indians used the plant to make an eyewash, nose drops, or a wash for nipples sore from nursing. The flower tea was used as a foot wash, and the roots to make a treatment for gastroenteritis or a poultice for skin problems. Okanagan-Colville Indians used the plant to treat kidney problems, as a poultice for backaches, and as a bath for venereal disease. Thompson Indians used plant preparations for cancer, tuberculosis, headache, and feeling unwell and to make a poultice for mumps. **RELATED SPECIES:** *G. pinnatifida* Torr. was used as a diuretic by the Hopi. *G. pulchella* Foug. was used by the western Keres externally to help wean infants and as an infusion to aid drumming skills.

Sneezeweed (Helenium autumnale) *has winged, angled stems.*

SNEEZEWEED
Leaves, flowers, roots, stems

Helenium autumnale L. Composite Family

Densely to sparsely hairy perennial, to 4 ft.; often forming colonies. Stems winged, angled. Leaves thick, dull green, lance-shaped to ovate, bases clasping and extending down stem; margins coarsely toothed to entire. Flowers in prominently rounded heads on short stalks in nearly flat-topped panicles; ray flowers 3-lobed, wedge-shaped, strongly reflexed, sometimes hard to see; disk flowers yellow; July–Sept. **WHERE FOUND:** Moist, open sites, fields, streambanks, wet ditches along roadsides, meadows, marsh edges. N. Calif. to B.C.; every western state. **USES:** As the common name implies, the primary use of dried flowers and leaves is as a snuff to induce sneezing and clear nasal passages and to treat congestive head colds, sinus congestion, and headache. Early 20th-century physicians used it as a tonic for chills, fever, and febrile diseases. Comanche Indians made a bath from the stems for treating fever. Roots were used in a compound to suppress menstruation after childbirth. **RELATED SPECIES:** *Helenium puberulum* DC., Rosilla, is used similarly and was considered helpful for treating venereal diseases. **WARNING:** *Helenium* species are toxic to cattle and contain hepatotoxic yet antitumor sesquiterpene lactones. Human safety unknown.

GOLDEN CROWNBEARD, GOLDWEED

Verbesina encelioides Leaves

(Cav.) Benth. & Hook. f. ex Gray Composite Family

Rough-hairy, grayish annual, to 4 ft; odor unpleasant. Leaves narrowly triangular to lance-shaped, 3-veined, tips pointed; lower leaves opposite, upper alternate; margins sharply toothed. Flower heads in flat-topped branched groups on long stalks; large ray flowers 3-toothed; May–Dec. **WHERE FOUND:** Open, sandy or rocky places, disturbed sites. Widespread weed in s. cen. coast of Calif.,

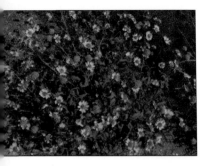

Golden Crownbeard (Verbesina encelioides) *is weedy in disturbed sites.*

Ariz., Rockies from Mont. to N.M., Tex.; n. and cen. Mexico. **USES:** American Indian groups used leaves as a wash for spider bites, snakebite, boils, and skin disease. Dried leaf tea used for stomach problems. The flowers chewed and swallowed as an emetic for stomach cramps. **WARNING:** Toxic. Causes lung edema and death when administered to mice or sheep.

LEAVES OPPOSITE; WITH YELLOW DAISY-LIKE RAY AND DISK FLOWERS

HEARTLEAF ARNICA
Arnica cordifolia Hook.

Roots, Flowers
Composite Family

Perennial, with few glands or short-hairy, to 20 in. Basal leaves coarsely toothed, *cordate at base,* in rosette on sterile plants, withering upon flowering; stem leaves in 2–4 pairs, opposite. Flowers in small, daisylike heads, 1–5 flower heads per plant, with 10–15 *pointed-tip* ray flowers, yellow throughout; base of flower receptacle generally long, white-hairy; May–Aug. **WHERE FOUND:** Common in high meadows, coniferous forests, 3500–10,000 ft., throughout western mountains. **USES:** American Indian groups chewed the root for sore throat and applied it to aching teeth. The plant was mashed and applied to swellings, bruises, and cuts. The roots were used as an aphrodisiac. An infusion was taken for tuberculosis. The plant was used for soreness in the eyes. **RELATED SPECIES:** The root of *A. latifolia* Bong. was used by American Indians for tuberculosis and as an aphrodisiac. The flowers of a number of other species of arnica from the Pacific states and Rocky Mts. are currently harvested to make oils and other medicinal products. The European arnica, *A. montana* L., is widely used, especially in Europe. Preparations are applied externally for reducing inflammation and pain of strains, sprains, and other injuries. Arnica is used internally in highly diluted homeopathic preparations to counter-

Heartleaf Arnica (Arnica cordifolia) *is found on high mountains.*

act shock and trauma and in other uses. When harvesting from the wild, pick flowers sparingly; never harvest rhizomes or roots, as this destroys the plant. **WARNING:** Except in homeopathic preparations, arnica is highly toxic if taken internally. Inflammation and irritation can result from the use of undiluted arnica preparations externally on open wounds.

FETID MARIGOLD
Leaves

Dyssodia papposa (Vent.) A. S. Hitchc.   Composite Family

Strongly ill-scented, multibranched annual, to 2 ft. Leaves and bracts below head covered in brownish oil glands. Leaves opposite, divided into many narrow, linear lobes. Heads on short stalks, densely clustered at branch tips; May–Sept. Papery, lance-shaped bracts below head. Fruits with bristle-tipped scales at top. **WHERE FOUND:** Roadsides, disturbed sites. Widespread weed throughout U.S.; every western state except Ore., Wash., Idaho. Native to Great Plains and Mexico. **USES:** American Indians drank an infusion of fresh or dried plants or used it as a rub for fever. A cold tea was taken internally if a red ant was swallowed, and a poultice of

Fetid Marigold (Dyssodia papposa) *has an unpleasant scent.*

Sanvitalia (Sanvitalia abertii) *has greenish yellow disk flowers.*

Wild Zinnia (Zinnia grandiflora) *is one of the showiest wildflowers of American deserts.*

chewed leaves was applied for ant bites. Leaves were inserted in the nostrils to cause nosebleed to alleviate headache. The plant was smoked for epileptic fits and inhaled for headaches. The pulverized leaves were used for breathing difficulties. **WARNING:** Potentially toxic.

SANVITALIA
Leaves

Sanvitalia abertii Gray   Composite Family

Rough annual with white, curly hairs, to 1 ft. Leaves opposite, linear to narrowly lance-shaped; margins entire. Flowers in small, round to short conical heads on slender stalks; leathery ray flowers notched, drying cream color; disk flowers greenish yellow; July–Oct. Fruits warty or angled with few short, stout awns at top. **WHERE FOUND:** Dry slopes, mesas, and washes. Desert mountains of se. Calif. to Tex.; Mexico. **USES:** The leaves were chewed to treat mouth sores, sore throats, fevers, headaches, and colds and to induce sweating. It was combined with other plants as a tea for menstrual pain and snakebite. A cold tea was applied externally to treat fever, headache, and skin sores. The Navajo considered it a life medicine or panacea.

WILD ZINNIA
Whole plant

Zinnia grandiflora Nutt.   Composite Family

Rough-hairy, multistemmed perennial, to 10 in. Leaves opposite, linear, sessile, 3-veined; margins entire. Flowers in showy heads on short stalks; ray flowers broad, reflexed, often deep orange-red at base; disk flowers red, sometimes green; May–Oct. **WHERE FOUND:** Dry, open places, grasslands, hills, roadsides, sagebrush scrub.

Ariz., Colo., N.M., Tex.; n. Mexico. **USES:** Preparations of the plant were used for stomachache and heartburn, as a strong laxative, for kidney problems, nose and throat problems, as a wash to control excessive sweating, and as a ceremonial emetic. American Indian groups also made an eyewash from the blossoms and inhaled smoke in sweat baths to control fever.

LEAVES OPPOSITE; YELLOW DAISYLIKE RAY AND DISK FLOWERS; COREOPSIS

GOLDEN TICKSEED   **Roots, plant**
Coreopsis tinctoria Nutt.   Composite Family

Single-stemmed, hairless annual, to 4 ft. Leaves opposite, divided into several linear lobes. Flowers in radiating heads of few ray flowers, spotted reddish brown at base; disk flowers reddish brown; June–Sept. Outer bracts below head much smaller; inner bracts membranous. Black fruits linear. **WHERE FOUND:** Moist, low sites, disturbed sites. Widespread native or garden escape from cen. coast of Calif. to every state but Nev., Utah. **USES:** The Cherokees infused the root to make a lotion and applied it to the body during ceremonial chanting. The Ramah Navajo considered the root a life medicine or panacea and used root tea for bloody diarrhea. A tea of the aboveground parts of the plant was drunk by pregnant women to increase the chances of having a female baby. The smoldering plant was used as a fumigant for sexual infections. **RELATED SPECIES:** An infusion of *C. leavenworthii* Torr. & Gray was a Seminole remedy for heat prostration. A stem decoction of *C. tripteris* L. was drunk by the Meskwaki to relieve internal pains and to stop internal bleeding.

Golden Tickseed (Coreopsis tinctoria) *has bicolored flowers.*

HEADS WITH DISK FLOWERS ONLY (NO PETALLIKE RAY FLOWERS); LEAVES ALTERNATE

HYMENOPAPPUS
Hymenopappus filifolius Hook.

Roots, plant
Composite Family

Aromatic perennial, to 3 ft. Angled stems and leaves hairless to densely woolly, minutely gland-dotted. Leaves mostly basal (sometimes absent), divided into many linear or threadlike segments. Flowers yellow to whitish, abruptly narrowed at base, in many-flowered heads on slender stalks in panicles; May–Oct. Bracts below head with rounded, membranous tips; margins papery. Densely hairy fruits with many membranous scales at top. **WHERE FOUND:** Dry, open habitats, rocky slopes, sometimes on limestone. Widespread east of the Sierra-Cascade crest to the Great Plains, from s. Calif. to Wash., every western state; Baja Calif., n. Mexico. **USES:** Zuni Indians spread lard on swollen glands and other swellings, then spit a poultice of chewed leaves as a covering. Hopi Indians chewed the root to treat pain caused by tooth decay. Ramah Navajo used plant tea as a drink and a lotion for wounds. Kayenta Navajo used a plant poultice on sores caused by bird infections and to treat illness caused by a lunar eclipse. Ramah Navajo used a plant tea to treat coughs.

PINEAPPLE-WEED
Matricaria discoidea DC.
[*Matricaria matricarioides* (Less.) Porter]

Leaves, flowers
Composite Family

Pineapple-scented annual; 4–16 in. Leaves *finely dissected; segments linear.* Flowers tiny, *without rays;* yellow "button" is a rayless composite flower; May–Oct. **WHERE FOUND:** Waste places, roadsides. Throughout N. America. Alien (Europe). **USES:** Numerous American Indian groups used tea of the pleasant-tasting, fragrant leaves and flowers to treat upset stomach, stomach pain, gas, colic, indigestion, diarrhea, constipation, convulsion in babies, colds, fevers, heart ailments, and menstrual cramps and to strengthen the blood and facili-

Hymenopappus (Hymenopappus filifolius) *has gland-dotted, variable leaves.*

Pineapple-weed (Matricaria discoidea) *often grows in poor, dry soils, even in the cracks of pavement.*

tate delivery of the placenta during childbirth. Once considered a cure-all and tonic; used in the Sun Dance ceremony and in sweat lodges for its fragrance; added to many medicines to make them taste good. Used externally for infected sores. **RELATED SPECIES:** Pineapple Weed has similar properties to German Chamomile, *M. recutita* L., and has been used as a substitute for it. **WARNING:** Some individuals may be allergic to this plant.

DESERT TURTLEBACK, VELVET TURTLEBACK

Plant, root

Psathyrotes ramosissima (Torr.) Gray — Composite Family

Velvety, white-woolly annual with strong turpentine odor; mat- or mound-forming; to 5 in. Stems becoming hairless, shiny. Leaves thick, alternate, round to broadly ovate; margins scalloped; Mar.–June. Outer bracts below head are spreading or recurved. Densely hairy fruits with many brown bristles at top. **WHERE FOUND:** Dry, open, sandy flats, slopes, washes, deserts, mainly in creosote bush scrub. S. Calif. to Nev., Utah, Ariz.; Baja Calif., n. Mexico. **USES:** Paiute and Shoshone Indians used plant for stomachache, constipation, diarrhea, and other gastrointestinal complaints, liver disorders, cough from tuberculosis, and venereal disease. Plant poulticed on sores, cuts, and swellings, snake and insect bites; mixed with fir or pine pitch for draining boils or removing slivers. Small pieces of dried root were chewed to relieve toothache. **RELATED SPECIES:** *P. annua* (Nutt.) Gray was used interchangeably for many of the same ailments, as well as urinary tract problems and in eyewashes.

COMMON TANSY

Whole plant

Tanacetum vulgare L. — Composite Family

⚠ *Strong-scented* perennial; 1–4 ft. Leaves *fernlike*. Flowers to ½ in. in flat terminal clusters; June– Sept. **WHERE FOUND:** Roadsides, fields.

(Above) *Desert Turtleback* (Psathyrotes ramosissima) *is a mat-forming annual with velvety leaves.* (Right) *Common tansy* (Tanacetum vulgare). *The leaves are fernlike, the flowers yellow buttons.*

Scattered throughout our area. Alien (Europe). USES: Traditionally, a weak, cold leaf tea was taken for dyspepsia, flatulence, jaundice, worms, suppressed menses, and weak kidneys, and was used externally as a wash for swelling, tumors, and inflammations; a spray or inhalant of tea used for sore throats. Experiments have confirmed that Tansy is antispasmodic and antiseptic. Leaves insecticidal. WARNING: Oil is **lethal**—½ ounce can kill in 2–4 hours. May cause dermatitis.

HEADS WITH RAY FLOWERS ONLY (NO DISK FLOWERS); LEAVES ALTERNATE

WILD LETTUCE, BITTER LETTUCE   Sap, leaves
Lactuca virosa L.   Composite Family

Large, stout biennial with abundant milky juice to 6 ft.; forms colonies. Basal leaves obovate, shallowly lobed; stem leaves alternate, oval to oblong, sharply toothed, bases widely clasping stems. Flowers in numerous small, elongate heads in open-branched groups; Aug.–Oct. WHERE FOUND: Dry, sandy or rocky areas, disturbed sites, roadsides. Cen. coast of Calif. Alien (Europe). USES: The dried milky sap of Wild Lettuce is a source of lactucarium, which was formerly an official drug in the U.S. and Europe. Early medical doctors prescribed Wild Lettuce for its purported sedative properties for insomnia, restlessness, nervousness, and irritable coughs, especially for children. Lactucarium, or "lettuce opium," had a minor wave of popularity as a recreational drug in the 1970s but was too weak to sustain a following. An extract of *L. virosa* has shown activity against *Candida albicans*. Recent pharmacological studies are scanty, but sesquiterpenes such as lactopicrin have been identified. **RELATED SPECIES:** *L. serriola* L. and *L. scariola* L. were used by American Indians groups for stomach problems with nausea, vomiting, and diarrhea. The roots of *L. spicata* L., Tall Lettuce, were decocted for heart problems, internal bleeding, abdominal and chest pain, vomiting, and diarrhea. **WARNING:** This and other *Lactuca* species may cause dermatitis or internal poisoning in large doses.

COMMON SOWTHISTLE

Leaves

Sonchus oleraceus L.

Composite Family

Hairless, milky-sapped annual from taproot, to 6 ft. Stout stems smooth or slightly ribbed. Leaves alternate, deeply pinnately lobed; lobes triangular, pointed; margins sharply toothed. Base of leaves clasping, with sharply pointed lobes, curved forward, resembling a sow's ear. Flower heads swollen at base, vase-shaped, sometimes woolly below; July–Oct. **WHERE FOUND:** Extremely common weed in disturbed sites. Alien (Europe). **USES:** The roots and leaves have been widely used in Europe as a folk remedy since before the time of Christ. Tea was used to bring on late or suppressed menstruation, increase mother's milk, improve loose bowels, eliminate worms, benefit the liver, strengthen the diges-

(Above) *Wild Lettuce* (Lactuca virosa) *stems have a milky juice.*
(Right) *Common Sowthistle* (Sonchus oleraceus) *is a common weed introduced from Europe.*

tion, and calm teething babies. Gum from the abundant milky sap has been used to aid opium withdrawal. The sap was drunk with water to cool the stomach and relieve diarrhea, to eliminate kidney stones, ease inflammation, and for piles. Flavonol glycosides, including a form of quercitin, have been extracted from *Sonchus* species. **RELATED SPECIES:** Other species, including S. *asper* (L.) Hill. and S. *arvensis* L. have been used similarly.

DANDELION-LIKE HEADS WITH RAY FLOWERS ONLY; LEAVES IN DISTINCT BASAL ROSETTES

LONGLEAF HAWKSBEARD
Whole plant

Crepis acuminata Nutt.
Composite Family

Woolly-haired perennial with milky sap, to 30 in. Basal rosette of gray-green leaves, deeply lobed in middle, lobes pointed; tip and bases long, tapered; stem leaves alternate. Flowers numerous, in small heads in loose flat-topped groups; May–Aug. Outer bracts below head much smaller, inner bracts lance-shaped, smooth, shiny. **WHERE FOUND:** Dry, open, rocky sites; lowlands and foothills to mid-elevations. Lower Calif. to Wash. (mainly east of Sierra-Cascade crest), every western state except Tex. **USES:** Shoshone Indians crushed either the seed or the whole plant and applied it as a poultice after childbirth to relieve sore or caked breasts and to induce milk flow. The powdered root was sprinkled in the eye to remove foreign objects or reduce inflammation.

(Left) *Longleaf Hawksbeard* (Crepis acuminata) *is a woolly-haired perennial with milky sap and grayish-green leaves.* (Above) *Dandelion* (Taraxacum officinale) *is one of the most familiar weeds.*

DANDELION

Roots, leaves, flowers

Taraxacum officinale G. H. Weber ex Wiggers Composite Family

Hairless perennial from stout taproot, to 2 ft. Milky sap. Basal rosette of oblong to oblanceolate leaves, deeply lobed and toothed. Familiar flowers in solitary head on hollow, leafless stems; Mar.–Oct. **WHERE FOUND:** Widespread weed of lawns, meadows, roadsides, disturbed sites throughout. Alien (Europe). **USES:** Dandelion root is still official in the *Chinese Pharmacopoeia*, and was formerly official in the *U.S. Pharmacopoeia* and many European pharmacopoeias. The herb was historically prescribed by physicians to treat liver disease and jaundice and to stimulate bile flow. It is mildly diuretic (not indicated when inflammation is present) and laxative; used for kidney disorders, stomachache, dyspepsia, low back pain, menstrual cramps, allergies, and arthritis. Dandelion is high in vitamins A and C, and the leaves are often eaten as a spring tonic herb. It is considered a blood tonic or blood purifier, useful for treating anemia and chronic skin diseases and for stimulating lactation. Dandelion leaf approved in Germany for treatment of loss of appetite and dyspepsia with a feeling of fullness and flatulence. Root approved for treatment of bile-flow disturbances, as a diuretic, to stimulate appetite and treat dyspepsia. **WARNING:** Contact dermatitis has been reported from handling plant, probably caused by latex in stems and leaves.

DAISYLIKE FLOWERS WITH DISTINCTIVE "CONES": BLACK-EYED SUSANS AND RELATIVES

PRAIRIE CONEFLOWER

Whole plant

Ratibida columnifera (Nutt.) Woot. & Standl. Composite Family

Rough-hairy perennial, to 4 ft. Leaves alternate, pinnately divided into linear to lance-shaped segments. Flowers in long, columnar heads on slender, long stalks; large, broad ray flowers sometimes purplish, spreading or reflexed; disk flowers purplish brown; June–Aug. **WHERE FOUND:** Dry, open places, disturbed sites, roadsides. Ariz. to Idaho, Mont. to N.M., Tex.; B.C. to Minn.; Mexico. **USES:** Cheyenne used a wash of the flowers to draw out venom and alleviate pain of rattlesnake bite and to treat poison ivy. Lakota used the plant tops to relieve headache and stomachache. The Zuni used it as an emetic. The Ramah Navajo used a cold tea to reduce fevers. **RELATED SPECIES:** The root of *R. pinnata* (Vent.) Barnh. was used by the Meskwaki to relieve toothaches; the Ramah Navajo made a tea of the root to heal birth injuries, and a leaf tea for coughs and fevers, gonorrhea, and syphilis.

BLACK-EYED SUSAN
Rudbeckia hirta L.

Root, flowers, leaves
Composite Family

Rough-hairy biennial or short-lived perennial, to 3 ft. Leaves alternate, oblanceolate to lance-shaped; margins entire to scalloped. Flower heads round; ray flowers spreading to reflexed; disk flowers dark purple; June–Oct. **WHERE FOUND:** Meadows, fields, disturbed sites, roadsides. Native to Great Plains, Tex., and eastern N. America. Introduced in Calif., Wash., Idaho, Utah, Wyo., Colo., N.M. **USES:** American Indian groups used the root to treat colds, worms, congestive heart disease, as a stimulating diuretic, and for gonorrhea and syphilis. Externally a wash was used for sores and snakebites, and the juice used for earaches. Flower tea was used to treat fevers and headache. Leaves were eaten as a spring tonic potherb to maintain health. Like *Echinacea*, it has been found to have immunostimulant activity. **RELATED SPECIES:** A Slovakian study demonstrated higher immunostimulatory activity for *R. fulgida* var. *speciosa* (Wenderoth) Perdue [*R. speciosa* Wenderoth] than for *Echinacea*. **WARNING:** Contact dermatitis from the plant has been reported.

GREEN-HEADED CONEFLOWER
Rudbeckia laciniata L.

Root, flowers, leaves
Composite Family

Coarsely hairy or hairless perennial, to 6½ ft. Large, alternate leaves deeply divided into 3–5 sharply toothed lobes. Flower

(Left) *Prairie Coneflower* (Ratibida columnifera). *Note the tall central cone.* (Above) *Black-eyed Susan* (Rudbeckia hirta) *has prominent dark brown disk flowers.*

Green-headed Coneflower (Rudbeckia laciniata) *has deeply divided leaves.*

heads rounded to elongated on long stalks; ray flowers reflexed; disk flower greenish yellow; June–Sept. **WHERE FOUND:** Moist meadows, streambanks, thickets. Wash., Idaho, Mont., Wyo., Utah, Colo., Ariz., N.M., Tex.; throughout eastern and cen. N. America. **USES:** Cherokee ate the cooked leaves as a spring tonic. Historically, physicians prescribed the herb for kidney infections, difficult urination, and other urinary problems. In Europe it was also used as a tonic.

LEAVES ALTERNATE; PLANTS WITH SUN-FLOWERLIKE FLOWERS

BALSAM ROOT, ARROWLEAF BALSAM ROOT
Whole plant
Balsamorhiza sagittata (Pursh) Nutt.   Composite Family

⚠ Resinous, aromatic perennial, to 30 in. Large basal leaves triangular to heart-shaped on long petioles, grayish-woolly below, softly hairy above; margins entire. Flowers large, on showy heads at stem tips with very reduced, alternate, lance-shaped leaves below; Apr.–July. Lance-shaped bracts below head woolly, outer ones longer; tips abruptly tapered, pointed. **WHERE FOUND:** Forest openings, meadows, valleys, slopes, at mid- to high elevations. Mostly east of the Sierra-Cascade crest from s. cen. and ne. Calif. to s. B.C., Nev., n. Ariz., Rocky Mts. from Mont. to s. Colo. **USES:** All parts of this resinous plant were used for medicine. Some American Indian groups made a tea from the whole plant for stomachache and applied it externally for pain and as an eyewash. Plant tea was poured on the head or the steam inhaled for headaches. Root tea was used during labor to facilitate delivery, to promote perspiration in treatment of rheumatism, for fever,

(Above) *Balsam Root* (Balsamorhiza sagittata) *has large, aromatic leaves.* (Right) *Common Sunflower* (Helianthus annuus), *native to the United States, is cultivated worldwide.*

whooping cough, tuberculosis, and as a cathartic and diuretic. Externally, the root was applied to wounds, cuts, and bruises. The root was chewed for sore mouth and throat and toothache and applied to sores, blisters, and arrow or gunshot wounds. Dried root powder applied to swellings, syphilitic sores, boils, and insect bites. The root was burned and the smoke used to disinfect a sickroom or inhaled for body aches. Leaves poulticed to burns. Leaf tea was used as a wash for poison ivy. The seeds were eaten to relieve dysentery. Eating large quantities of the young shoots was said to have a sedative effect. Antibacterial and antifungal compounds have been isolated from this plant. **WARNING:** The roots are acrid and nauseating when eaten fresh or when a quantity of the tea is drunk.

COMMON SUNFLOWER
Flowers, leaves, seeds, stems, roots
Helianthus annuus L.
Composite Family

Rough-hairy annual, to 10 ft. Stout stems reddish. Leaves widely ovate, alternate, on long petioles, 3-veined from base; bases heart-shaped; margins coarsely toothed. Familiar flowers in large, showy heads with red-brown disk flowers on long stalks; Feb.–Oct. **WHERE FOUND:** Prairies, valleys, foothills, disturbed sites, roadsides. Widespread across N. America. **USES:** Historically, physicians and American Indian groups used a flower tincture to treat lung disease. Physicians also used the seed oil to treat cough, dysentery, and bladder and kidney problems, and the stem pith as a diuretic and treatment for fever and inflammation. Indian groups used the flowers for chest pains, a leaf tea for fever, and root tea for rheumatism. Externally, leaf poulticed for snakebite and spider bites, sores and swellings. The plant juice was used to treat cuts. Seeds eaten to stimulate appetite. Modern studies have demonstrated anti-inflammatory and immune-cell-modulating effects of terpenoid extracts. **WARNING:** Pollen or plant extracts may cause allergic reactions.

NARROWLEAF MULES EARS
Wyethia angustifolia (DC.) Nutt.

Root, leaves
Composite Family

⚠ Rough-hairy perennial, to 3 ft. Basal leaves long, lance-shaped, on long petioles, tapering at base and tip; margins toothed, sometimes without teeth. Smaller stem leaves alternate, lance-shaped, not stalked. Large, showy flower heads solitary on long, slender stalks; ray flowers many; Apr.–Aug. Bracts below head purplish at base; margins hairy. Fruits angled, hairy at top with few awn-tipped scales. **WHERE FOUND:** Dry, open, grassy slopes, meadows, low to mid-elevations. S. to n. coast ranges, n. mountain ranges of Calif. to Wash. **USES:** A leaf decoction was used to produce a sweat and in a bath for fevers. The froth made from pounding the roots was used as a poultice for lung problems or to drain blisters. A decoction of the roots was taken internally as an emetic. **WARNING:** Of undefined safety.

(Above) *Narrowleaf Mules Ears* (Wyethia angustifolia) *has sunflowerlike flowers.* (Right) *Mountain Mules Ears* (Wyethia mollis) *has fine-hairy leaves.*

MOUNTAIN MULES EARS, WOOLY WYETHIA

Root, leaves

Wyethia mollis Gray

Composite Family

⚠ White-woolly perennial becoming green and hairless with age; to 3 ft. Basal leaves broadly oblong on short, thick petioles; bases rounded; margins entire. Smaller stem leaves alternate, ovate, on short petioles. Flowers in large, showy heads on short stalks; ray flowers few; May–Aug. Bracts below head few, leaflike. **WHERE FOUND:** Open forest, dry rocky or wooded slopes, ridges, lower montane coniferous forests. N. Calif. to s. Ore., Nev. **USES:** Root tea was used as a blood tonic and to treat venereal disease and tuberculosis. In concentrated form, it worked as both an emetic and a cathartic. Root poultice used for swelling, leaf poultice for broken bones and sprains. A leaf tea was taken for stomachache. **WARNING:** Of undefined safety.

MISCELLANEOUS ORANGE FLOWERS

SCARLET PIMPERNEL

Whole plant

Anagallis arvensis L.

Primrose Family

Hairless, *low-spreading* annual, to 1 ft. Leaves opposite, ovate to oval, sessile; margins entire. Flowers small, *flat, salmon*, scarlet, ☠ or sometimes blue, *solitary on slender stalks* from leaf axils; ⚠ Mar.–Sept. **WHERE FOUND:** Disturbed places, gardens. Throughout N. America except Wyo., Colo. Alien (Europe). **USES:** Historically, herbalists used plant internally for rheumatism, externally for skin ulcers. In Europe it was traditionally used to treat intestinal obstruction, tuberculosis, edema, epilepsy, and mania. In India

Scarlet Pimpernel (Anagallis arvensis) *is often a weed in lawns.*

Safflower (Carthamus tinctorius) *is widely cultivated for its edible oil.*

the plant has a long history of use as an expectorant and diaphoretic and to treat wounds. It is valued especially for easing mania and other psychological conditions. Saponin glycosides from the plant inhibit herpes and the replication of polio virus replication and can kill intestinal worms. **WARNING:** Can be quite toxic in any but small doses. Poisonous to horses and dogs.

SAFFLOWER
Carthamus tinctorius L.

Flowers
Composite Family

Hairless annual to 3 ft. Leaves alternate, *narrowly ovate with spine-tipped teeth* clasping stem. Flowers in *urn-shaped*, orange to reddish, heads in *flat-topped clusters*; June–Oct. **WHERE FOUND:** Disturbed places, roadsides. Escaped in warm areas. Calif., Wash., Idaho, Utah, Colo., N.M. Alien (Mediterranean). **USES:** American Indians used flower tea to treat constipation and to increase sweating. Nineteenth-century physicians used an alcoholic extract for measles, scarlet fever, and other eruptive diseases and to induce menses. In Chinese medicine the herb is prescribed in teas and tablets, along with other herbs, for blood stasis, abdominal pain, and blocked menstruation. Seeds are the commercial source of safflower oil, grown as an agricultural crop in Calif.

WESTERN WALLFLOWER
Erysimum capitatum (Dougl. *ex* Hook.) Greene

Whole plant
Mustard Family

Gray-haired, short-lived perennial, to 3 ft. Leaves alternate, *narrowly oblanceolate to lance-shaped*; coarsely toothed to entire. Flowers *orange* to yellow flowers in dense racemes at stem tips; stamens 6; Mar.–Aug. **WHERE FOUND:** Dry, stony areas, mostly inland. Throughout western N. America; eastward. **USES:** American Indians used the crushed leaves as an inhalant for headaches. Powdered pods were used as a snuff for nasal

Western Wallflower (Erysimum capitatum) *has yellow to orange flowers.*

congestion. The whole plant was chewed and blown over pregnant women to facilitate labor. The root was heated and placed over an aching tooth. A poultice of chewed leaves was applied to swellings. The plant was taken for advanced cases of tuberculosis. A whole plant tea was used for muscle aches. Both flowers and fruit were eaten to induce vomiting in cases of stomachache. **RELATED SPECIES:** Other western species were used similarly. *E. officinale* L. is a folk remedy in Europe for relief of coughs and mucous congestion.

CALIFORNIA POPPY
Whole plant

Eschscholzia californica Cham.
Poppy Family

Hairless annual or perennial with whitish film, to 2 ft. Leaves mostly basal, *deeply dissected into many linear lobes*; margins entire. Flowers *atop flattened rim*, on long stalks; petals 4, *shiny*; sepals fused into cap, falling off at flowering; *stamens many*; Feb.–Nov. Fruit *long, slender*. **WHERE FOUND:** Grasslands, hillsides, open areas, disturbed sites. S. Calif. to Wash.; every western state except Mont.; Baja Calif. Widely cultivated elsewhere. **USES:** Pomo Indians rubbed the mashed seedpod or a decoction of it on a nursing mother's breast to dry up her milk. The plant was given to babies as a sedative and placed under the bed for better sleep. Other tribes decocted the flowers and rubbed it in the hair to kill lice. The root juice was taken for stomachaches and tuberculosis, used as a narcotic to temporarily stun companions when gambling, and as a wash for weeping sores, and, interchangeably with crushed

seedpods, to help stop milk flow. Modern herbalists recommend extracts of the herb to ease anxiety and sleeplessness and for hyperactive children. Science has identified sedative but nonnarcotic alkaloids in the plant, especially highest in the root.

California Poppy (Eschscholzia californica) is the floral symbol and state flower of California.

PEYOTE
Whole plant
Lophophora williamsii (Lem. ex Salm.-Dyck) Coult.   Cactus Family

Short (to 2 in.), cylindrical, *spineless* cactus, widening above, with long *tufts of white hairs*. Flowers small, with separate pink petals with white margins on apex of new growth. Fruit red, fleshy. **WHERE FOUND:** Limestone soils in desert and dry scrubby areas. Lower N.M., Tex. Rare. **USES:** A divinatory plant of the Aztecs, peyote is used today as a sacrament in religious and ceremonial rituals to produce visions and to give practitioners and patients insight into the causes of disease. American Indian groups used peyote to treat fevers, colds, influenza, tuberculosis, scarlet fever, pneumonia, gastrointestinal problems, and venereal disease. Some considered it a panacea. Externally it has been used to treat cuts, bruises, and rheumatic aches, and as a hair tonic. **WARNING:** A strong hallucinogen and nervous-system stimulant. Causes nausea, vomiting, and hallucinations. Too rare to harvest; endangered.

BEAVERTAIL PRICKLYPEAR CACTUS
Whole plant
Opuntia basilaris Engelm. & Bigelow   Cactus Family

Flat stems jointed, clumped from base; low-spreading or upright, to 20 in. Joints broadly obovate, *often purple-tinged*, *covered with small, round clusters of minute, thin, brown spines*. Flowers rose, purple, or pink, clustered at joint tips with numerous petals and stamens; Mar.–June. **WHERE FOUND:** Deserts, arid mountain slopes, chaparral, pinyon-juniper woodland, creosote bush scrub. Se. deserts of Calif., Nev., Utah, Ariz.; Mexico. **USES:** Shoshone Indi-

Peyote (Lophophora williamsii), *a rare spineless cactus, is shown here in a botanical garden.*

Close-up of a Peyote flower.

Beavertail Pricklypear Cactus (Opuntia basilaris) *often has purple-tinted joints.*

ans used the fresh pulp as a dressing on cuts and wounds to allay pain and encourage healing. Rubbed on the skin, the fuzzy spines were used to remove warts or moles. The juice or flower tea was used to treat diabetes and urethritis. **RELATED SPECIES:** Numerous species of *Opuntia* were used to treat skin problems, infections, burns, cuts, aches, pain and swelling, as laxatives, styptics, and labor promoters. The Mexican *O. streptacantha* Lem. has blood sugar–lowering and cholesterol-lowering effects in laboratory tests and human studies; used to treat diabetes in Mexico. The fleshy stems of *O. dillenii* (Ker.-Gawl.) Haw. are soaked in water or baked and applied to deep abscesses on the feet and inflamed skin. Fresh leaves of *O. ficus-indica* (L.) P. Mill. are cooked with pork and eaten as a tonic or cut and applied externally for abscesses.

MISCELLANEOUS REDDISH-STEMMED PLANTS

SPOTTED CORALROOT
Corallorhiza maculata (Raf.) Raf.

Whole plant
Orchid Family

Red-brown to purplish stems, *lacking chlorophyll,* unbranched, upright to 8–20 in. Leaves sheathing, scalelike. Flowers grayish to dull maroon, 5 *petals, red-spotted;* May–Aug. **WHERE FOUND:** Rich humus in moist to fairly dry, shaded coniferous or aspen forests. S. Calif. to Alaska, every western state; eastern N. America. **USES:** Dried-stalk tea used by several American Indian groups to strengthen the blood of pneumonia patients. Plant tea used as a wash for ringworm or skin problems. Tea from the whole dried plant used for colds and to induce profuse sweating to break a fever. **RELATED SPECIES:** The rhizome of *C. odontorhiza* (Willd.) Nutt., indigenous to western N. America and known as Crawley Root by the Eclectic physicians, was prescribed for serious lung ailments,

(Left) *Spotted Coralroot* (Corallorrhiza maculata) *lacks chlorophyll.* (Above) *Snowplant* (Sarcodes sanguinea) *is bright red throughout.*

such as tuberculosis, accompanied by spitting of blood and general weakness. **COMMENT:** This widely scattered species is rarely abundant enough to harvest, and the growth of saprophytic plants is easily disrupted. It should not be harvested.

SNOWPLANT

Sarcodes sanguinea Torr.

Whole plant

Heath Family

Entire plant bright red, fleshy; thick, unbranched stems to 16 in., solitary or clustered. Leaves scalelike, mostly basal. Flowers bell-shaped, 5-parted; May–July. **WHERE FOUND:** Mixed or coniferous montane forests. High Sierra of Calif. to sw. Ore., Nev.; n. Baja Calif. Parasitic on conifers via mycorrhizal associations. **USES:** A tea of the plant was used to strengthen patients with pneumonia. Tea of dried powdered plant used as a wash on canker sores and ulcers to relieve itching; also used for sore mouth and toothache.

MISCELLANEOUS SPURRED FLOWERS

CRIMSON COLUMBINE

Aquilegia formosa Fisch. *ex* DC.

Whole plant

Buttercup Family

Hairless perennial with whitish film, to 3 ft. Leaves alternate, mainly basal, *pinnately 3-divided* into lobed segments; tips are rounded. *Nodding*, showy flowers with 5 *tubular petal spurs* and 5 spreading sepals; yellow at spur openings; *stamens many, well exserted*; Apr.–Aug. **WHERE FOUND:** Moist, shady forests, streambanks. S. Calif. to Alaska; Idaho, Nev., Utah; w. Rockies from

(Left) *Crimson Columbine* (Aquilegia formosa) *has nodding flowers with five tubular spurs.* (Above) *Pacific Bleeding Heart* (Dicentra formosa) *has fernlike leaves.*

Mont. to Wyo. **USES:** Roots or leaves were chewed by American Indians to treat coughs and sore throat; applied to bee stings. A root tea was used for coughs, stomachache, and diarrhea and to induce vomiting. Root and leaf tea drunk for dizziness. Fresh roots mashed and massaged into aching joints affected by rheumatism. Roots were smeared on runner's legs to increase stamina. Whole-plant tea taken for venereal disease. Seeds chewed for stomachache; mashed and rubbed into the hair to prevent lice. Poultice of chewed leaves or milky pulp from scraped roots applied to sores. **RELATED SPECIES:** *A. canadensis* L., Columbine, was used by American Indian groups for heart and kidney troubles and as a witchcraft medicine, as well as for uses described above. **WARNING:** Plant contains toxic alkaloids; potentially poisonous.

PACIFIC BLEEDING HEART   **Leaves, roots**
Dicentra formosa (Haw.) Walp.   Poppy Family

Hairless perennial, to 1 ½ ft. Leaves basal, deeply dissected, *fernlike*, on long petioles; margins toothed. Flowers *nodding, heart-shaped,* deep to pale pink; *outer 2 petal tips spreading*; inner petals fused at tip, *crested*; stamens 6, in 2 sets; Mar.–July. **WHERE FOUND:** Moist, shady forests, streambanks. Cen. and n. coast ranges, n. Sierra and Cascades of Calif. to B.C., w. of Cascade-Sierra crest. **USES:** American Indian groups chewed the raw root to alleviate toothache; tea of pounded roots taken for worms. Crushed plant tea used as a rinse to make hair grow. **RELATED SPECIES:** Early 20th-century physicians used preparations from the tubers of *D. canadensis* (Goldie) Walp. from eastern N. America for menstrual problems, syphilis, and diarrhea. **WARNING:** May contain alkaloids with CNS-depressant activity; potentially poisonous; may also cause skin rash.

FLOWERS 3-PARTED

LONG-TAILED WILD GINGER
Asarum caudatum Lindl.

Whole plant, root

Birthwort Family

Aromatic, *mat-forming* perennial, to 6 in. Leaves shiny, *dark glossy green*, *heart-shaped*; margins entire. Flowers solitary, maroon, *borne at ground level*; sepals 3, with *long tapered tails*; Apr.–July. **WHERE FOUND:** Moist, shaded redwood and mixed conifer forests. N. coast and Klamath ranges of Calif. to B.C., Idaho, Mont. **USES:** American Indians applied warmed fresh leaves to relieve toothache and used them as a poultice to bring boils to a head. The entire plant or the stems were placed in a baby's bed for illness and as a calmative. Strong leaf tea used as a wash for sores. Leaf poulticed to newborn's navel to prevent infection. Plant tea used as a wash for headache, intestinal pain, and knee pain. Root tea drunk for stomach ailments, indigestion, colic, colds, and constipation. Plant extracts have antifungal properties. **WARNING:** Members of this genus contain varying amounts of the mutagenic terpene beta-asarone, as well as the nephrotoxic and mutagenic compound aristolochic acid. Internal use should be avoided.

Long-tailed Wild Ginger (Asarum caudatum) *flowers are found at ground level beneath the heart-shaped leaves.*

Giant Trillium (Trillium chloropetalum) *has three-divided, mottled leaves.*

GIANT TRILLIUM, GIANT WAKEROBIN

Root, leaves

Trillium chloropetalum (Torr.) T. J. Howell — Lily Family

⚠️ Hairless perennial to 2½ ft. *Leaves 3-divided, ovate, whorled,* sessile, *mottled* with dark blotches. Flowers showy, aromatic, sitting *directly above leaves*; petals maroon to greenish yellow, upright; Feb.–July. **WHERE FOUND:** Moist, shaded woods, edges of redwood forests. N. cen. coast ranges, Cascades of Calif. to w. Wash.; west of Cascade-Sierra crest. **USES:** Members of the genus *Trillium* from Europe and Asia have long been used to check bleeding and excessive mucous discharge and to treat skin afflictions. Roots used by American Indian groups as a uterine stimulant, a warm poultice for chest pain, for stiff neck, sore throat, toothache, cuts; combined with bruised leaves as a treatment for boils. **WARNING:** The fresh rhizome is intensely acrid and can cause nausea and vomiting when taken internally. These properties are reduced in the dried root.

FLOWERS 4-PARTED

FIREWEED

Leaves, roots

Chamerion angustifolium (L.) Holub. — Evening-primrose Family
[*Epilobium angustifolium* L.]

Stout perennial forming thickets, to 7 ft. Leaves *alternate*, lance-shaped, on purplish red stems, distinctly veined below; margins entire. Flowers rose-pink, in elongated racemes at stem tips; spreading petal lobes *above slender ovary; exserted stigma, lobes 4, becoming recoiled; stamens 8*; June–Sept. **WHERE FOUND:** Moist to dry, disturbed or burned sites. Throughout N. America; Eurasia. **USES:** Menominee Indians used root tea as a wash for swellings. A poul-

Fireweed (Chamerion angusti-folium) *is a common weed after fires.*

tice of roasted, mashed roots was applied to boils; leaf poultice used for bruises or to remove a sliver. Root tea used for coughs. Fireweed contains a potent anti-inflammatory flavonoid and is antibacterial. A tea or alcoholic tincture was used by early 20th-century physicians to treat diarrhea. **RELATED SPECIES:** *E. palustre* L., common throughout western N. America, was used interchangeably.

FLOWERS PEALIKE

RED CLOVER
Trifolium pratense L.

Flowers, leaves
Pea Family

⚠ Hairy perennial, to 2 ft. Leaves divided into 3 *oval, finely toothed leaflets with whitish crescent in the center.* Flowers red to pink, pealike, in dense *oval head;* Apr.–Oct. **WHERE FOUND:** Disturbed sites, fields, lawns. Widespread weed and cultivated forage crop throughout N. America. Alien (Europe). **USES:** Used in Asia, Europe, and N. America to treat spasmodic and persistent coughs, including whooping cough; externally as a wash or poultice for athlete's foot, arthritic pain, psoriasis, eczema, deep burns, rashes, and hardened breasts in lactation. Red Clover is said to stimulate liver and gall bladder activity, increase the appetite, and aid healing of ulcers and burns. It was used for kidney disease, urinary tract infections, and as a blood purifier. Widely used as a folk cancer remedy. Recent laboratory and human studies show that it contains phytoestrogenic isoflavones, including genistein, daidzein, formononetin, and biochanin A, among others, that act as estrogen regulators. Red Clover products are widely promoted to ease symptoms of menopause such as hot flashes, and to maintain bone strength. Other factors considered, people whose diets are high in isoflavones have less cancer and heart disease, and live longer than those whose diets are low in them. Standardized extracts of Red Clover, produced in Australia, are now sold in the U.S. One tablet contains 40 mg of phytoestro-

Red Clover (Trifolium pratense) *is a familiar field weed throughout North America.*

gens, eight times the amount in the typical American diet. **WARN-ING:** Red Clover contains coumarins, which may interact with prescription blood thinners such as warfarin to reduce clotting time.

FLOWERS 5-PARTED; PETALS SEPARATE; LEAVES OPPOSITE

SHOWY MILKWEED
Asclepias speciosa Torr.

Whole plant
Milkweed Family

⚠ White-velvety perennial with *milky sap*, to 4 ft. Leaves *opposite*, ovate to oblong; margins entire. Flowers rose-purple in woolly umbels; *petals reflexed; tapered prongs rising from center with short, incurved horns below*; May–Aug. Densely hairy, *soft-spined pods* with many hairy seeds. **WHERE FOUND:** Moist, dry, or disturbed sites, fields, roadsides. Throughout western N. America; Great Plains. **USES:** Tea of plant tops historically used as an eyewash for blindness and snow blindness. Root tea used for headaches, coughs, bloody diarrhea, to bring out measles rash, and for general debility; in small doses for venereal disease. Milky stem latex applied to warts, corns, calluses, and skin sores. Ground seeds were used as a disinfectant for skin sores. Seed tea used to draw out the poison from snakebites. **WARNING:** Though this species is probably less toxic than many *Asclepias* spp., the root is considered toxic. The young pods and shoots were eaten as a vegetable, but caution is still advised because of the toxic nature of many species.

Showy Milkweed (Asclepias speciosa) *flowers are in woolly umbels.*

GREAT BASIN CENTAURY, DESERT CENTAURY

Leaves, stems

Centaurium exaltatum (Griseb.) W. Wight ex Piper   Gentian Family

Hairless, sparingly branched annual, to 18 in. Leaves slender to lance-shaped with an acute tip. Flowers whitish to rose-pink, tubular with 5 small spreading petals, in *flat-topped clusters*; May–Aug. Whole plant *intensely bitter*. **WHERE FOUND:** Damp, scrubby places, hanging gardens, sometimes saline seeps, below 6000 ft., along coast and edge of deserts, s. to ne. Calif. All western states except Ariz. **USES:** The Miwok Indians made a decoction of stems and leaves for internal pains, stomachaches, toothaches, and consumption. **RELATED SPECIES:** American Indian groups used flowers and leaf tea of California Centaury, *C. venustum* (Gray) B. L. Robins., to reduce fevers. In Europe, *C. umbellatum* auct. non Gilib. is used as a pure bitter digestive tonic to be taken regularly for months, or even years, before meals to increase production of hydrochloric acid, pepsin, and other digestive enzymes. Centaury is prescribed by herbalists for heartburn, weak stomach, and nausea. Many *Centaurium* species contain bitter compounds known as secoiridoids, such as sweroside, and are used similarly.

REDSTEM STORKSBILL

Leaves, roots

Erodium cicutarium (L.) L'Her. ex Ait.   Geranium Family

Slender, sprawling annual with sparse long, glandular hairs. Leaves pinnately compound, long-stalked, with small *lance-shaped*

Most species of Centaurium *such as Great Basin Centaury (*Centaurium exaltatum*) and California Centaury (*C. venustum*), pictured here, are used for similar purposes.*

*The petals of Redstem Storksbill (*Erodium cicutarium*) have two spots.*

glands at the base; leaflets pinnately cut to margin. Flowers small, rose-lavender, with 5 separate 2-*spotted petals*, which fall quickly; Feb.–Mar. **USES:** Costanoan Indians drank leaf tea for typhoid fever. Jemez women ate the roots to increase milk production. Navajo poulticed the plant for wild animal bites and infected wounds. Zuni applied the masticated root to sores and rashes, drank root tea for stomachaches. Plant tea a European folk remedy to relieve water retention and excessive menstrual bleeding, and to treat dysentery.

FLOWERS 5-PARTED; LEAVES ALTERNATE

CAROLINA GERANIUM
Geranium carolinianum L.

Whole plant
Geranium Family

Short-haired annual, to 2 ft. Leaves alternate, *deeply 5-cleft; segments lobed, tips rounded.* Flowers *small*, rose-pink to white, 5-parted, on *short stalks in dense umbels; petals notched; sepals awn-tipped;* stamens 10; Apr.–Oct. **WHERE FOUND:** Open, shaded, or moist sites. Coast ranges, n. Sierra of Calif., to every western state except Colo. Throughout N. America. **USES:** High in tannins, which have antibacterial, antiviral, and astringent properties, most wild *Geranium* spp. have been used interchangeably as folk remedies to treat inflamed mucous membranes and externally to stop bleeding. Tea used as a gargle for sore throats, aphthous stomatitis, thrush, and pyorrhea, and to treat gastric ulcers, diarrhea, bleeding, nosebleed, hemorrhoids, bloody urine, kidney inflammation, excess menstruation, wounds, children's rashes, diabetes, leukorrhea, acne, and conjunctivitis. **RELATED SPECIES:** *G. atropurpureum* Heller, Western Purple Cranesbill, was used by the Ramah Navajo as a panacea. *G. caespitosum* James, Pineywoods Geranium, was made into a paste by the western Keres and applied to sores. *G. lentum* Woot. & Standl. was applied to any in-

Carolina Geranium (Geranium carolinianum) *leaves are deeply divided.*

jury. *G. maculatum* L., Wild Geranium, from eastern N. America, was a favorite folk remedy; prescribed by early 20th-century physicians for diarrhea, vaginitis, and other uses.

RICHARDSON'S GERANIUM
Roots, leaves
Geranium richardsonii Fisch. & Trautv.   Geranium Family
Perennial, to 3 ft. Leaves alternate, palmately cleft into *5–7 broad lobes; tips coarsely toothed.* Flower stalks with *red to purple gland-tipped hairs.* Large, white to pinkish flowers with *purple veins;* petals *rounded, hairy at base;* sepals waned; stamens 10; May–Aug. Slender fruit stiff-haired, *base coiling upward to release seed.* **WHERE FOUND:** Moist sites, meadows at mid elevation. E. Calif. to e. B.C. All western states except Tex.; n. Mexico. **USES:** Cheyenne Indians rubbed the leaves on the nose, snuffed the powdered leaves or root tea, and drank the tea to treat nosebleed. The Ramah Navajo considered the plant a life medicine.

CHEESEWEED, LITTLE MALLOW
Whole plant
Malva parviflora L.   Mallow Family
Weedy annual, to 3 ft. Leaves alternate, shallowly palmately 5–7-lobed; margins scalloped. Flowers small, pink to white, with 3 *linear bractlets below sepals;* petals notched, *hairless at base; stamens many, fused into tube; stigma tips linear;* year-round. Round fruit splitting into several *cheese- or pie-wedge* pieces. **WHERE FOUND:** Disturbed sites, roadsides, fields, gardens. Widespread from Calif. to East Coast; every western state. Native to Eurasia. **USES:** Mallow leaf and root tea used in Europe, Americas, and Asia to treat coughs, colds, sore throat, tonsillitis, laryngitis, bronchitis,

Richardson's Geranium (Geranium richardsonii) leaves are deeply divided and toothed.

Cheeseweed (Malva spp.) are used interchangeably. Malva neglecta is pictured here.

asthma, emphysema, gastritis, ulcers, enteritis, colitis (as a warm enema), and kidney and bladder infections. Externally, poultices and washes used to soothe acne, boils, sores, wounds, rashes, dandruff, and other skin irritations. High vitamin-A content and abundant mucilage may explain some of its uses. **RELATED SPECIES:** Mallows such as *M. sylvestris* L. and *M. neglecta* Wallr. are used interchangeably. Chinese doctors prescribe a seed tea of *M. verticillata* L. to treat painful urination, edema, swollen breasts, and breast abscess, to increase milk production, and as a lubricant for constipation.

REDWOOD SORREL, OREGON OXALIS
Plant, root
Oxalis oregana Nutt.
Oxalis Family

Perennial with long, brownish hairs, to 1 ft. Leaves *basal*, divided into 3 *heart-shaped leaflets*, purplish below, often drooping from center, *sour-tasting*. Flowers *solitary*, deep pink to white, purple-veined; Feb.–Sept. **WHERE FOUND:** Moist, shady redwood, mixed conifer forests. Cen. coast ranges of Calif. to w. Wash. **USES:** Plant used as a poultice on sores, boils, and swelling; to draw out infection; and as a wash for rheumatism. In conjunction with a magic charm, the plant was used to stimulate the appetite. Juice from chewed root used to treat sore eyes. **WARNING:** Potentially toxic because of high oxalic acid content.

(Above) *The sour-tasting leaves of Redwood Sorrel* (Oxalis oregana) *contain oxalic acid.* (Right) *Copper Globemallow* (Sphaeralcea angustifolia) *has a solitary purple-veined flower.*

COPPER GLOBEMALLOW, YERBA DEL NEGRO

Leaves, flowers, root

Sphaeralcea angustifolia (Cav.) G. Don.
Mallow Family

Gray-haired perennial, woody at base, to 6 ft. Leaves alternate, *lance-shaped to linear*; margins scalloped. Flowers red-orange, in small clusters from leaf axils; Aug.–Oct. **WHERE FOUND:** Sandy desert washes. San Diego Co., Calif., to Nev., Ariz., Colo., N.M., Tex.; n. Mexico. **USES:** Several *Sphaeralcea* species were used interchangeably. The plant contains abundant mucilage, with soothing properties. Externally, the root was mashed or chewed and poulticed or sprinkled as a powder on sores, swellings, wounds, and snakebites. Wilted leaves were bound to arthritic joints and swollen areas. Leaf tea used as an eyewash and for treating colds, coughs, influenza, upset stomach, stomachache, diarrhea, bloody stools, and constipation. Stems chewed for gastrointestinal complaints. Root tea taken to treat broken bones, headache, as an appetite stimulant, to prevent pregnancy, and for internal injury and bleeding. It was often mixed with other medicines to make them more palatable. **RELATED SPECIES:** S. *angustifolia* (Cav.) G. Don, Copper Globemallow, and S. *munroana* (Dougl. ex Lindl.) Spach ex Gray were used for similar ailments by Indian groups of western N. America.

FLOWERS 5-PARTED; PETALS FUSED: TUBULAR OR BELL-SHAPED; LEAVES OPPOSITE

SPREADING DOGBANE

Whole plant

Apocynum androsaemifolium L.
Dogbane Family

Widely branched perennial with *milky sap*, to 1–4 ft. Leaves opposite, ovate, *drooping*, on reddish, smooth stems. Flowers are drooping pink bells, *rose-striped within*, in leaf axils *and terminal*; petal lobes *spreading to recurved*; May–Sept. *Paired pods long, slender*. **WHERE FOUND:** Dry, open slopes or woods. Throughout N. America. **USES:** American Indian groups used root for syphilis, coated tongue, dropsy, and headache. For headaches the roots were either chewed, inhaled as steam, applied as a poultice, or made into a tea. Root tea used for heart palpitations and liver problems, taken internally, or sprinkled on the chest for convulsions; also as a worm remedy, to relieve stomach cramps, and to expel placenta; taken weekly as a contraceptive. Roots used by European settlers as a tonic or as a strong laxative and to induce sweating. The dried, powdered root was given for dizziness and insanity. Milky juice from the plant applied to warts. Leaves were chewed and swallowed or the dried leaves smoked as an aphrodisiac. Historically, physicians used root for heart irregularities and liver ailments, among other uses. **WARNING:** The plant contains cardiac glycosides such as strophanthin that stimulate heart function and can be toxic even in moderate doses.

MADAGASCAR PERIWINKLE
Catharanthus roseus (L.) G. Don.
[*Vinca rosea* L.]

Whole plant
Dogbane Family

Erect-stemmed perennial, often grown as an annual, 1–2 ft. Leaves opposite, elliptical, or oblong to lance-shaped, 1–2 in. long, glossy, entire. Flowers rose-pink to white, 5-parted, thin tube about 1 in. long, 1 ½ in. across; summer. **WHERE FOUND:** Widely cultivated as an ornamental in warmer regions, escaped and naturalized in tropical regions throughout the world. Alien (India to Madagascar). **USES:** Though toxic, the plant is the source of so-called vinca alkaloids, such as vincristine and vinblastine, which are important drugs used in chemotherapy for the treatment of childhood leukemia, Hodgkin's disease, and other forms of cancer. Anticancer activity was serendipitously discovered in the early 1960s by researchers who were following leads on its potential antidiabetic activity, based on its historical use in herbal medicine for treating diabetes. **WARNING:** Despite the importance of alkaloids extracted from the plant for chemotherapy, all plant parts are toxic to livestock and humans.

Spreading Dogbane (Apocynum androsaemifolium) *has rose-striped flowers.*

(Left) *Madagascar Periwinkle* (Catharanthus roseus) *is an important source of alkaloids used in chemotherapy.* (Above) *Desert Four o' Clock* (Mirabilis multiflora) *is covered with long, sticky hairs.*

DESERT FOUR O'CLOCK, MARAVILLA   Root
Mirabilis multiflora (Torr.) Gray   Four o'clock Family

⚠ Upright, *sticky* perennial covered in long hairs, to 3 ft. Leaves opposite, *heart-shaped* to ovate, fleshy; margins entire. Flowers rose-purple, long-tubular, *in 5-lobed, bell-shaped cup*; stamens 5, exserted; opens in evening; Apr.–Aug. **WHERE FOUND:** Deserts; dry rocky or sandy places. S. Calif. to w. Colo., Ariz., N.M., Tex.; Baja Calif. **USES:** American Indian shamans chewed the root for its psychoactive effects and as a diagnostic drug. Root was used as an appetite suppressant to lessen food intake and alleviate hunger. Taken internally or rubbed on the belly after overeating, it was used to treat indigestion, stomach pain, mouth diseases, rheumatism, swellings, and edema. The Tewa drank a tea of the ground root to relieve swelling with water retention. **RELATED SPECIES:** A leaf tea of *Mirabilis californica* Gray, Wishbone Bush, was used as a purgative and to treat measles. **WARNING:** Potentially toxic.

LONGLEAF PHLOX   Roots, plant
Phlox longifolia Nutt.   Phlox Family

Glandular, hairy perennial, to 16 in. Leaves opposite, *very narrow*, sessile; margins entire. Flowers sweet-scented, pink to white, tubular with broad, spreading petals; sepal tube ribbed, *membranes between ribs bulged at base*; stamens 5, *unequal, attached at different levels within petal tube*; Apr.–July. **WHERE FOUND:**

Longleaf Phlox (Phlox longifolia)
is a glandular-hairy perennial.

Dry, open, often rocky sites, sagebrush, pinyon-juniper, ponderosa pine, aspen communities. Mono Co., Calif., to every western state except Tex. **USES:** Root tea used to alleviate stomach pains in children and babies, to treat diarrhea and venereal disease, as a laxative, and rubbed on the body for colds and aches. A leaf or whole plant preparation used for boils externally or stomach complaints internally. **RELATED SPECIES:** Several western *Phlox* spp. were used in traditional medicine. Ramah Navajo used a tea of *P. stansburyi* (Torr.) Heller to regulate the menses. Havasupai decocted the pounded roots of *P. austromontana* Coville, Desert Phlox, and rubbed it on the body for muscle aches and colds. The crushed roots were given to babies to ease stomachache. *P. longifolia* Nutt. used for similar purposes and also for anemia, as an eyewash, and for sexually transmitted diseases. Navajo used the crushed plant to dress burns, as a cleansing laxative and diuretic, for easing childbirth, and for toothaches.

FLOWERS 5-PARTED; PETALS FUSED, TUBULAR OR BELL-SHAPED; LEAVES ALTERNATE

DESERT TRUMPET, SKY ROCKETS, SCARLET GILLI
Ipomopsis aggregata (Pursh) V. Grant   **Plant, roots**
[*Gilia aggregata* (Pursh) Spreng.]   Phlox Family

 Sticky, short-lived perennial with white hairs, to 3 ft. Leaves alternate, *pinnately dissected into linear lobes.* Flowers numerous, *long-tubular, star-shaped,* in *one-sided* racemes; petals *yellow-mottled;* Apr.–Sept. **WHERE FOUND:** Dry, rocky, open sites. Cen. and n. Calif. to B.C., all western states; n. Mexico. **USES:** Both the plant and the root used as an emetic. Plant tea used as a wash on the bodies of hunters to bring good luck; as a face and hair wash by young girls, for scabies, gonorrhea, syphilis, and spider bites, and

Desert Trumpet (Ipomopsis aggregata) *has showy, star-shaped flowers.*

as an eyewash; poulticed for rheumatic aches. Plant tea also taken as a blood tonic, a postpartum tonic, for stomach problems. The root was used to treat constipation, colds, and high fevers. Studies show antiviral activity against parainfluenza virus type 3 and cytotoxic activity by components of *Ipomopsis*. **WARNING:** Of unknown safety.

FLOWERS 5-PARTED; PETALS FUSED, FLATTENED

PIPSISSEWA
Chimaphila umbellata (L.) W.P.C. Bart.

Leaves
Wintergreen Family

 Evergreen perennial, 6–12 in.; often an *extensive ground cover*. Leaves w*horled*, lance-shaped, *leathery*, toothed above middle. Flowers *flat*, pink to red, *nodding* in densely glandular racemes; June–Aug. **WHERE FOUND:** Dry coniferous forests. N. Calif. to B.C.; all western states except Tex., to eastern N. America. **USES:** Widely used by American Indians, Pipsissewa is still an important remedy for urinary tract infections in modern herbal practice because of its soothing and mildly antiseptic qualities. American Indian tribes made a leaf tea as a spring tonic, to reduce fevers, for bladder stones, stomach disorders, tuberculosis, long-lasting colds, head colds, backache, gonorrhea, chest pain, and rheumatism. Also as a diuretic and as an antispasmodic for nervous disorders, including epilepsy, for pain, and for fever connected with heart conditions. Externally, plant tea used as a wash for sores and blisters, liniment for sore muscles, poulticed for swelling, especially of the legs and feet. Whole plant tea used as a blood purifier and

(Left) *Pipsissewa* (Chimaphila umbellata) *has waxy flowers.*
(Above) *A close-up of the Pipsissewa flower.*

appetite stimulant. The herb was formerly official in the *U.S. Pharmacopoeia*. Historically prescribed by physicians as a diuretic, astringent, and urinary tract disinfectant, especially for chronic bladder infections with burning urination, also for prostate inflammation. A fluid extract made from the leaf contains antibacterial quinones, such as arbutin, and naphthaquinones, such as renifolin and chimaphilin. Diuretic, astringent, urinary antiseptic, and antibacterial activity has been confirmed. **WARNING:** Leaves poulticed on skin may induce redness, blisters, and peeling. Arbutin hydrolyzes to the **toxic** urinary antiseptic hydroquinone.

LIVERLEAF WINTERGREEN, BOG WINTERGREEN
Leaves, roots
Pyrola asarifolia Michx.
Wintergreen Family

Evergreen perennial, to 1½ ft. Leaves leathery, *basal*, ovate to round, purple below; margins entire to toothed. Flowers, red to pink, *nodding*, on *elongated racemes*; June–Sept. **WHERE FOUND:** Moist to dry forests, wetlands. S. mountains, n. coast ranges, n. high Sierra of Calif. to Alaska; all other western states except Ariz., Tex. to eastern N. America. **USES:** American Indian groups used leaves as a tonic and to treat liver and kidney problems, gonorrhea, and blood in the sputum. Hyperactive children were steamed with plant tea to calm them down. Contains arbutin, a proven diuretic and antibacterial agent that breaks down into

Liverleaf Wintergreen (Pyrola asarifolia) is a small evergreen perennial with leathery leaves.

toxic hydroquinone when metabolized. Arbutin is found in many members of the wintergreen family. **RELATED SPECIES:** Another western species, *P. picta* Sm., White-veined Wintergreen, was used by the Karok to wash children who were not feeling well.

PETALS FUSED; FLOWERS 2-LIPPED (BILABIATE); FLOWERS IN WHORLS; LEAVES OPPOSITE, MOSTLY AROMATIC (MINT FAMILY)

NETTLELEAF HORSEMINT
Leaves

Agastache urticifolia (Benth.) Kuntze

Mint Family

Strongly aromatic perennial, to 5 ft. Leaves opposite, *triangular to ovate,* on square stems; margins toothed. *Flowers in dense, oblong spikes,* rose-purple (or whitish) flowers; June–Sept. **WHERE FOUND:** Woodlands, moist areas, open slopes. Cen. and n. Calif. to B.C., Idaho, Nev., Utah; w. Rockies from Mont. to Colo. **USES:** American Indian groups used leaf tea for indigestion, stomach pains, colds, measles, rheumatism, and as a laxative. A poultice of mashed leaves was applied to swellings. The leaves were placed in babies' blankets to treat fever. An im-

Nettleleaf Horsemint (Agastache urticifolia) flowers range from white to pink.

portant food, fiber, and dye plant. **RELATED SPECIES:** Cherokee used a wash of *A. nepetoides* (L.) Kuntze to relieve itching of poison ivy rash. Ramah Navajo used tea of *A. neomexicana* [*A. pallidiflora* ssp. *neomexicana* var. *neomexicana* (Briq.) R. W. Sanders] to ease bad coughs. A tea of *A. foeniculum* (Pursh) Kuntze, Anise Hyssop, was used for coughs and to strengthen a weak or dispirited heart. The root tea was used for coughs and colds. *A. rugosa* (Fisch. & Mey.) is the Chinese drug huo xiang, used in prescriptions to ease nausea, vomiting, reduced appetite, or a feeling of distension or abdominal fullness, especially due to digestive weakness and water retention.

MOTHERWORT
Leaves

Leonurus cardiaca L.

Mint Family

Square-stemmed perennial, to 5 ft. Leaves opposite, with 3–5 *pointed lobes, lower leaves becoming more deeply cleft.* Flowers small, pink to white, in *dense whorls above leaf nodes; upper lip furry*; May–Sept. **WHERE FOUND:** Disturbed sites. Occasional weed throughout N. America. **USES:** As the name implies, Motherwort was used for women's problems, including amenorrhea, suppressed menstruation, and dysmenorrhea. It was used as a calmative for nervous problems, delirium tremens, restlessness, wakefulness, chorea, convulsions, headache, stomachache, poor digestion, and general debility. Said to be a mild heart tonic. Currently used in Europe for heart irregularities and nervous conditions. Extracts approved in Germany for nervous heart conditions and in the supportive treatment of hyperthyroidism. Research confirms antispasmodic, hypotensive, sedative, cardiotonic, diuretic, antioxidant, immunostimulating, and cancer-preventative activity. **RELATED SPECIES:** *L. artemisia* (Sweet) S. Y Hu (*L. heterophyllus* Sweet) is used in Asia for gynecological problems and to reduce masses due to "blood stagnation." *Leonu-*

Motherwort (Leonurus cardiaca) is often found around farm yards.

Mountain Monardella
(Monardella odoratissima) *is
strongly aromatic.*

Monardella villosa *has beautiful
deep pink flowers.*

rus species contain alkaloids and other compounds with proven
sedative, hypotensive, and heart-regulating effects in laboratory
tests and in humans. **WARNING:** May cause dermatitis in susceptible
individuals. Avoid use during pregnancy and lactation.

MOUNTAIN MONARDELLA, COYOTE MINT

Monardella odoratissima Benth.

Whole plant
Mint Family

Strongly aromatic, mostly hairy, clumping perennial, to 2 ft.
Stems square. Leaves opposite, lance-shaped to ovate, purple-
tinged; margins entire. Flowers slightly two-lipped, red-purple to
whitish, in *flat, solitary head* with cuplike series of bracts below;
petal *lobes slender*; sepal lobes woolly; stamens 4; May–Sept.
Outer bracts reflexed or spreading; middle bracts papery. **WHERE
FOUND:** Dry, open sites, rocky slopes. S. Sierra, desert mountains,
Cascades of Calif., to every western state except Tex. **USES:** The
pleasantly fragrant, minty flowering tops and leaves were made
into tea to treat indigestion, gas pain, upset stomach, colds,
fevers, as a cleansing sweat medicine, blood tonic, general tonic,
and laxative; externally, used as a wash for sore or inflamed eyes.
RELATED SPECIES: Native Americans used the flowering tops of
Monardella villosa Benth., Coyote Mint, as a poultice for cuts on
the back to draw out bad blood, and to treat pneumonia, respiratory problems, and stomachache.

CALIFORNIA HEDGENETTLE

Stachys bullata Benth.

Whole plant
Mint Family

Coarse-haired aromatic perennial, often glandular, to 3 ft. Leaves
opposite, ovate to oblong on square stems; margins toothed.

California Hedgenettle (Stachys bullata) *has a bitter-aromatic fragrance.*

Flowers pink, *unspotted*, in *separated whorls of 6*, above hairy bracts; bottom of corolla tube without small pouch; *ring of hairs at base inside flower tube produces small pouch; stamens 4, lying under upper lip*; Apr.–Sept. **WHERE FOUND:** Dry coastal slopes, oak woodlands. S. and cen. coast ranges of Calif. **USES:** American Indians drank leaf tea or applied plant as a poultice for skin infections, boils, swelling, joint pain, sore throat, earache, headache, stomachache, colic, coughs, and colds. In Chinese herbal medicine it is prescribed for hematuria, jaundice, and bacterial dysentery. **RELATED SPECIES:** The closely related European species, *S. palustris* L. and *S. sylvatica* L., Woundwort, were poulticed to stop bleeding and promote healing of even the most serious wounds. Tea used to relieve pain and inflammation of gout, cramps, and internal bleeding. *S. palustris* L. is also a common wild plant in western N. America. In Asia a tea of the stalks and leaves of *S. aspera* Michx. is drunk to relieve gas and used as a deodorant; used interchangeably with the tubers of *S. sieboldii* Miq. in hot wine to cure colds and flu.

FLOWERS IN RACEMES, PANICLES, OR HEADS (OTHER THAN COMPOSITES)

CARDINAL FLOWER
Lobelia cardinalis L.

Root, leaves
Bluebell Family

One of our most showy wildflowers. Perennial; 2–3 ft. Leaves oval to lance-shaped, toothed. Flowers vibrant scarlet (rarely white), in brilliant spikes; July–Sept. **WHERE FOUND:** Moist soil, streambanks. S. Calif. to Tex., common in eastern N. America. **USES:** American Indian groups used root tea for stomachaches, syphilis, typhoid, worms, as an ingredient in love potions. Leaf tea used for colds, croup, nosebleeds, fevers, headaches, rheumatism. It was once thought to help cramps and expel worms and to act as a nerve tonic. **WARNING:** Potentially toxic; degree of toxicity unknown.

ELEPHANT'S-HEAD LOUSEWORT, INDIAN WARRIOR

Pedicularis groenlandica Retz.

Leaves

Figwort Family

Hairless perennial, to 3 ft. Leaves mostly basal, *pinnately divided into oblong, toothed segments,* fernlike. Flower fancy, pink to reddish purple with *top petal elongated and upcurved into elephant trunk, lower petal earlike,* in dense spikes; June–Aug. **WHERE FOUND:** Wet meadows, streamsides at mid- to high elevation. S. and n. Sierra, Cascades of Calif. to s. Alaska. Every western state except Tex. **USES:** An infusion of the leaves and stems has expectorant and antitussive properties. The name Lousewort refers to its use to rid animals of lice. The Washo used a poultice of the plant on cuts, sores, and swellings, and drank a decoction of the leaves as a general tonic. The roots were a popular remedy with many tribes of western N. America, especially as an infusion for relieving stomach pain, ulcers, and blood in the stools and as an ingredient in

Cardinal Flower (Lobelia cardinalis) *is one of the showiest wildflowers.*

Elephant's-head Lousewort (Pedicularis groenlandica) *has an upcurved petal resembling an elephant's trunk.*

cough medicines, for sore throats, as a blood tonic, as a cleansing purgative for stomachaches during menses; externally as a poultice for swellings. The root was mashed or cooked and added to food as a love charm. **RELATED SPECIES:** Several species are used in Chinese medicine, including *P. lasiophrys* and *P. striata*. Antioxidant phenylpropanoids have been extracted from *Pedicularis* species. In India the leaves of *P. pectinata* Wall. are considered diuretic and are used to stop spitting of blood.

CALIFORNIA FIGWORT
Scrophularia californica Cham. & Schlecht.

Leaves, root
Figwort Family

Finely glandular perennial, to 5 ft. Leaves opposite, triangular, on *square stems.* Flowers small, *urn-shaped,* maroon above, yellowish green below; lower lip small, recurved; Feb.–Aug. **WHERE FOUND:** Moist places, roadside ditches. Cen. coast ranges, n. Sierra, Klamath Range of Calif. to s. B.C. **USES:** American Indian groups poulticed leaves or applied fresh plant juice to boils, bacterial infections, fungal infections, burns, wounds, hives, scabies, swelling, cradle cap, and rashes. Root tea used for suppressed or irregular menses and cramping and to decrease postpartum bleeding. Whole plant was used for treating congestive heart disease. **RELATED SPECIES:** A poultice of the fresh herb of the European species *S. aquatica* L. used as a folk remedy to heal wounds, ulcers, and sores. A poultice, ointment, or wash of *S. nodosa* L. of eastern N. America and Europe was a folk remedy for abscesses, wounds, ringworm, scabies, rashes, painful swellings, enlarged lymph nodes, sore breasts, sprains, burns, and inflammation; also used as a diuretic tea, for liver conditions, and to stimulate the menses or relieve menstrual pain. The Chinese *S. ningpoensis* Hemsl. is prescribed by Chinese herbalists for severe infections with fever, to counteract a toxic

California Figwort (Scrophularia californica) *has a protruding upper petal.*

state of the blood with constipation, and for irritability, red or swollen eyes, sore throat, and swollen lymph nodes. Research confirms anti-inflammatory, antimicrobial, and blood pressure–lowering effects. Anti-inflammatory phenylpropanoids have been isolated from many species of *Scrophularia*.

MISCELLANEOUS FLOWERS IN RACEMES OR SOLITARY IN THE LEAF AXILS

HYSSOP LOOSESTRIFE
Whole plant
Lythrum hyssopifolia L.
Loosestrife Family

Hairless, pale green annual or biennial; to 2 ft. Leaves oval to oblong, *mostly alternate*, stalkless, on *angled stems*; margins without teeth. Flowers tiny, pink to rose, *stalkless, solitary* in leaf axils; Apr.–Oct. **WHERE FOUND:** Marshes, pond margins, moist areas. Coast ranges and n. Sierra of Calif., Ore., Wash., northeastern N. America. Alien (Europe). **USES:** Considered astringent, demulcent, and a blood purifier. Plant once used for treating mucous membrane or skin afflictions, sore throat, diarrhea, skin ulcers, or rashes.

Hyssop Loosestrife (Lythrum hyssopifolia) *has tiny pink to rose, stalkless flowers in the leaf axils.*

Lady's Thumb (Polygonum persicaria) *has a purplish triangular blotch in the middle of the leaf.*

LADY'S THUMB, HEART'S EASE
Polygonum persicaria L.

Leaves
Buckwheat Family

Annual; branched, reddish stems, to 2 ft. Nodes swollen. Leaves narrowly lance-shaped, alternate, on short petioles, *often with purplish, triangular blotch in middle*; gland-dotted below. Brownish, papery sheaths surrounding stem at *swollen leaf base*, sparsely hairy with weak-bristled margin. Flowers deep pink, in dense, oblong spikes; May–Nov. **WHERE FOUND:** Moist or wet, disturbed sites throughout. Alien (Europe). **USES:** Used in Europe to treat arthritis, respiratory problems, diarrhea, jaundice, chronic eczema, inflammation, stomachache, and sore throat. Externally, juice applied to wounds, bruises, and cuts. American Indians adopted the leaf tea for heart troubles, stomachaches, and as a diuretic for kidney stones. The whole herb was poulticed for pain, rubbed on poison ivy rash, and on horses' backs to keep flies away. **WARNING:** Fresh juice can be irritating, especially to mucous membranes.

FLOWERS WITH MANY PETALS

BITTERROOT
Lewisia rediviva Pursh

Root
Purslane Family

Small, tufted perennial, to 4 in. Leaves *basal, fleshy*, linear; tips blunt. Flowers *showy*, rose to white, solitary at ground level; short flower stalks with *linear, papery bracts at middle*; Mar.–July. **WHERE FOUND:** Open, rocky or sandy soils, rock crevices. Cen. coast ranges of Calif. to B.C., Idaho, Nev., Utah, Ariz.; w. Rockies from Mont. to Colo. **USES:** Northwest Indians ate the roots for sore throat, poi-

Bitterroot (Lewisia rediviva) *has showy, pink to white flowers and fleshy leaves.*

Western Peony (Paeonia brownii) *has deeply dissected leaves with rounded tips.*

son oak rash, diabetes, and as a general strengthening tonic. Root tea was used for heart and pleurisy pain and as a blood purifier. Externally, root poulticed to sores.

WESTERN PEONY
Root, plant

Paeonia brownii Dougl. ex Hook.

Peony Family

Single-stemmed perennial to 1 ½ ft. Leaves large, alternate, *deeply dissected, fleshy*, with whitish film; *tips rounded*. Flowers *round, nodding,* maroon to bronze, with yellow to green margins on downcurved stalks; *stamens many*; Apr.–July. **WHERE FOUND:** Open, dry mountain slopes, scrublands, sagebrush. N. Calif. to B.C., Idaho, Nev., Utah; w. Rockies from Mont. to Wyo. **USES:** American Indian groups used root tea to treat nausea, stomachache, indigestion, constipation, diarrhea, coughs, sore throat, colds, pneumonia, tuberculosis, heart trouble, chest pains, kidney problems, venereal disease, and sore eyes; also used to fatten people and horses and as a wash to relieve headache. Powdered root poulticed on burns, cuts, wounds, and sores. Crushed roots poulticed on boils or deep wounds. **RELATED SPECIES:** The sliced and baked roots of *P. california* Nutt. were eaten by the Diegueño for indigestion. Chinese herbalists prescribe *P. suffruticosa* Andr. for immune-system enhancement, cardiovascular problems, painful or too profuse menstrual bleeding, high blood pressure, and abscesses or draining sores. Research shows the roots to have antibacterial and hypotensive properties.

FLOWERS SMALL IN HEADS (COMPOSITES); TUBULAR AND RAY FLOWERS

PEREZIA, DUMERELIA, TRIXIS
Whole plant

Acourtia microcephala DC.

Composite Family

Rough-haired, glandular perennial, to 5 ft. Stems grooved, leafy. Leaves large, alternate, oblong to oval, clasping stem; margins finely toothed. Flowers pink-purple to white, *2-lipped*, in oblong heads; *inner lip deeply 2-lobed, coiled*; outer lip 3-notched; June–Aug. **WHERE FOUND:** Dry, shrubby slopes; burned areas. cen. to s. Calif. to nw. Baja Calif. **USES:** Cahuilla Indians decocted the plant for use as a cathartic, a swift remedy for diarrhea. **RELATED SPECIES:** The root of *Perezia wrightii* [*A. wrightii* (Gray) Reveal & King] was used by the Navajo as a tea to ease difficult labor and as a postpartum remedy. The root of *A. formosa* Don. is used in Mexico as a purgative for treating cholera and other ailments; *A. moschata* DC. is used as a digestive aid.

Perezia (Acourtia microcephala) *has large leaves that clasp the stem.*

SPREADING FLEABANE
Whole plant

Erigeron divergens Torr. & Gray
Composite Family

 Taprooted annual or short-lived perennial with *dense, short, spreading hairs*; to 2 ft. Leaves alternate, *narrowly oblanceolate*; basal rosette; margins entire. Flowers in flat, *finely glandular heads* with many slender pink, blue, or white ray flowers; disk flowers whitish; Mar.–Nov. **WHERE FOUND:** Many habitats at mid-elevation. Mountains of lower and upper Calif. to B.C., every western state; Baja Calif. Mainly east of Sierra-Cascade crest. **USES:** A tea was taken for snakebites and to facilitate childbirth; cold tea used internally and externally for "lightning infection" and applied externally as an eyewash. The plant used as a snuff for headaches. Zuni Indians used flower tea for stomachache. The root was chewed and the juice applied to sore eyes. The Navajo used tea externally and internally to stop nosebleeds and spitting of blood. The crushed leaves poulticed for spider bites and bleeding. **WARNING:** May cause contact dermatitis.

DAISY FLEABANE
Whole plant

Erigeron philadelphicus L.
Composite Family

Fibrous-rooted perennial with *long, spreading hairs*, to 3 ft. Leaves alternate, oblanceolate; *stem leaves clasping*; margins coarsely toothed. Small, flat heads of numerous *(more than 100)*, *very slender*, pink to white ray flowers; disk flowers yellow; Mar.–July. **WHERE FOUND:** Moist, open sites. Widespread throughout

Spreading Fleabane (Erigeron divergens). *The crushed leaves were used for spider bites.*

Daisy Fleabane (Erigeron philadelphicus) *has white to pink-violet-tinted ray flowers.*

N. America. **USES:** American Indian groups used plant tea to treat spitting of blood, water retention, stomachache, suppressed menstruation, coughs, chronic diarrhea, chronic phlegm, headache, fevers, and epilepsy. Root tea taken for kidney and menstrual problems. The root was either chewed or infused to treat colds by inducing sweating. Externally, plant was boiled and used as a wash for poison ivy and itchy rashes and mixed with tallow to use on sores. Several tribes snuffed the dried and powdered flowers to ease sick headaches or to induce sneezing to ease mucous congestion during colds. **WARNING:** May cause contact dermatitis.

TUBULAR FLOWERS ONLY (COMPOSITES)

GREATER BURDOCK
Arctium lappa L.

Whole plant
Sunflower Family

Biennial, to 2–9 ft. Leaves large, *rhubarb*like, widely *ovate*, on long petioles; white-woolly below; margins scalloped. *Stalk* solid, celerylike—*grooved* above. Flowers red-purple, *enclosed in bur-rlike head with hooked spines; heads on long stalks* in flat-topped clusters; June–Oct. Seedpods (familiar burs) stick to clothing. **WHERE FOUND:** Disturbed sites. Widespread weed throughout N.

America; Ore., Wash., eastward. Alien (Europe). **USES:** Root tea widely used in folk medicine as a blood purifier and diuretic, to stimulate bile secretion, digestion, and sweating in cases of gout, rheumatism, catarrh, venereal disease, and leprosy. American Indian groups adopted this alien to treat rheumatism, urinary calculi, scurvy, and female weakness. Tea of flower buds used as a wash for sores. Leaves chewed to relieve stomachache and cramps. An extract of the seeds was highly touted as a diuretic for kidney disease. The plant has a long history of use in Asia, Europe, and the Americas, both internally and externally, for skin diseases, especially psoriasis. Fruit (seeds) used in Chinese medicine (niu bang zi) for fever, coughs, sore throat, mumps, and early stages of measles. In Japan the root, called gobo, is an important strengthening tonic often cooked as food. Research has shown that root preparations stimulate liver and bile function and deactivate some cancer-causing chemicals. Burdock fruit extracts reduce blood sugar levels in laboratory experiments. The root extract contains antitumor sesquiterpene lactones and antibacterial polyacetylenes. **WARNING:** Leaf hairs may irritate skin. Do not confuse leaves with the toxic leaves of Rhubarb.

COMMON BURDOCK

Root, seeds, leaves

Arctium minus Bernh.   Composite Family

 Smaller than *A. lappa* (above); 2–5 ft. Leaf stems *hollow, not furrowed*. Flowers smaller, to 1¼ in. across, *without stalks or short stalked*; July–Oct. **WHERE FOUND:** Waste places. Most of our area. Alien (Europe). **USES:** Same as for *A. lappa*. Used extensively by American Indians.

Greater Burdock (Arctium lappa) lappa *has flowers in a more or less flat-topped cluster.*

The hooked barbs on the fruit of Greater Burdock cling to clothing.

(Above) *Common Burdock* (Arctium minus) *has flower heads arranged in a loose raceme.* (Right) *Cobweb Thistle* (Cirsium occidentale) *has spiny bracts covered with cobwebby hairs.*

COBWEB THISTLE
Stems

Cirsium occidentale (Nutt.) Jepson Composite Family

Variable, herbaceous, spiny-stemmed biennial, 2–4 ft. Leaves alternate, lance-shaped, densely gray-hairy beneath, margins wavy, with numerous spines. Flowers reddish violet, bracts of each flower covered *with dense, cobwebby hairs*; May–July. **WHERE FOUND:** Dry open ground. S. Ore. to sw. Idaho, w. Nev., Calif. **USES:** Stalks and stems considered cooling, diuretic. Widely used by native groups of the West as a food source. The Kawaiisu skinned the early spring stems and ate them raw. **RELATED SPECIES:** The weedy Japanese thistle *Cirsium japonicum* DC. contains anti-inflammatory and antihemorrhagic constituents; used in Asian medicine to stop bleeding.

YELLOWSPINE THISTLE
Whole plant

Cirsium ochrocentrum Gray Composite Family

White, *woolly-haired* perennial, *spreading vigorously by creeping rootstocks*; to 3 ft. Leaves crowded, alternate, oblong, *deeply pinnately lobed*; *margins with stout, yellowish spines* (to ½ in.); upper leaves green. Flowers *in large heads*, red (varying to pink, pale lavender, or white), solitary on short stalks; Apr.–Sept. **WHERE FOUND:** Dry slopes, prairies, disturbed areas, roadsides. W. Colo., cen. Ariz., N.M., Tex. to Great Plains. Noxious weed elsewhere, Utah to Calif. **USES:** American Indian groups soaked plant overnight in a

Yellowspine Thistle (Cirsium ochrocentrum) *is covered with white woolly hairs.*

Dotted Blazing-Star (Liatris punctata) *has long narrow leaves.*

vessel of cold water, then drank the cold tea morning, noon, and night to treat syphilis. Zunis infused fresh or dried root for diabetes. Root tea taken by men and women as a contraceptive. The Kiowa used flower tea as a wash for burns and sores.

DOTTED BLAZING-STAR

Root

Liatris punctata Hook.

Composite Family

Hairless perennial, to 30 in. Leaves alternate, linear, *strongly dotted*; margins entire, hairy. Flowers in *numerous narrow* heads of *few* rose-purple flowers (rarely white) in *spikes*; Aug.–Oct. **WHERE FOUND:** Dry plains and slopes. Eastern slope of the Rockies; Mont. to Colo., Tex., Ariz. **USES:** Blackfoot Indians took roots for stomachaches and applied roots to swellings. Comanche swallowed root juice to treat swollen testicles. Meskwaki used root tea to treat itch, gonorrhea, bloody urine, and bladder problems in women. **RELATED SPECIES:** Several *Liatris* species, including *L. spicata* (L.) Willd., Dense Gayfeather, *L. scariosa* (L.) Willd., Devil's Bite, and *L. laxa* Small, Rattlesnake Master, were used similarly for their diuretic, tonic, and stimulant properties.

RUSH SKELETON WEED
Stems, leaves, root

Lygodesmia juncea (Pursh) D. Don ex Hook.
Composite Family

Hairless, multibranched perennial, to 2 ft. Sap milky. Leaves alternate, *linear, stiff,* on *grooved stems*; reduced to scales above. Flowers in solitary, *oblong heads of 5* pink flowers (sometimes white) *at branch tips*; June–Sept. **WHERE FOUND:** Dry, open sites; sandy soils. Widespread in Great Plains; occasional westward, except Calif. **USES:** American Indian groups used stem tea as a mood enhancer or tranquilizer for pregnant women or new mothers to ensure good sleep, improve baby's health, and increase milk flow; also to treat burning coughs and heartburn. Tea of plant tops used both to induce and to stop vomiting and as a laxative and antidiarrheal. Leaves were used to treat smallpox. The plant fuzz was used on boils and running sores, to relieve toothache and kidney problems, and as a general tonic for children. The plant was used to make an eyewash for sore eyes. Root tea was used in a tonic formula.

Rush Skeleton Weed (Lygodesmia juncea) *has stiff leaves on grooved stems.*

COMMON CAMAS

Bulbs

Camassia quamash (Pursh) Greene — Lily Family

 Herbaceous, slender-stalked perennial, 4–8 in. tall, with oval to globe-shaped bulb usually covered in a black sheath. Leaves mostly basal, linear, shorter than flower stalk, paler above. Flowers in few- to many-flowered racemes, blue-violet, 6-parted; petals twisted over ovary after flowering; May–June. **WHERE FOUND:** Mountain meadows. B.C. to Mont., Utah, s. to coast ranges of n. Calif. **USES:** Bulb—roasted, in soups, steamed, or boiled—widely used as a food source by native groups of the Pacific Northwest. Blackfoot used tea of bulbs to induce labor. Tea of leaves taken to lessen bleeding after childbirth and to help expel the placenta. **WARNING:** Do not confuse with other toxic members of the lily family such as Death Camas (*Zigadenus* spp.)

ROCKY MOUNTAIN IRIS, BLUE FLAG

Roots

Iris missouriensis Nutt. — Iris Family

Hairless perennial from *thick rhizome*, to 3 ft. Leaves narrow (to ¾ in.), basal, grasslike, *flattened into one plane (fanlike)*, clasping, often purplish at base. Flowers showy, 2 per stem, *with short petal tube sitting above oblong ovary on long stalks*; purple petals upright; lighter-colored sepals petallike, drooping, with *central yellow stripe and dark purple veins*, each with shorter, forked, petallike stigma above covering a single stamen; May–July. **WHERE FOUND:**

(Left) *Common Camas* (Camassia quamash) *has brilliant blue flowers.* (Above) *Common Camas occurs in moist meadows.*

Moist flats, meadows, streambanks. Every western state except Tex.; B.C., n. Mexico. **USES:** Many iris species used as emetics, purgatives, and diuretics, to stimulate bile flow, salivary, and other digestive secretions, and for digestive problems. American Indian groups used root tea for gastric distress, stomachache, kidney and bladder problems, and gonorrhea. Externally, poulticed on sores, bruises, venereal lesions, aches and pains; a piece of root used in the cavity of an aching tooth or on gum near tooth. Some medicine men were said to add the root to a smoking mixture to induce extreme nausea so that they could charge a hefty fee for a cure. Paste of the ground seed applied to sores and burns. **WARNING:** Contains an acrid, nauseating principle. Can cause inflammation of eyes, throat, and headache. Iridin, another component, is toxic to humans and livestock. May irritate the gastrointestinal tract.

CALIFORNIA BLUE-EYED GRASS
Root, leaves
Sisyrinchium bellum S. Wats.
Iris Family

Hairless, *branching* perennial to 2 ft. Leaves linear, grasslike, basal, *flattened in one plane, fanlike.* Flowers dark blue with yellow center in umbellike clusters; petals 6, spreading, bristle-tipped, *sitting at top of ovary; stamens 3, fused.* Bracts below flower with *papery margins;* Feb.–July. **WHERE FOUND:** Moist, open, grassy places. Most of Calif., except cen. Sierra to Ore. **USES:** Herb formerly used to treat fevers, chills, and asthma. Root tea taken for upset stomach, stomachaches, heartburn, ulcers, and as a laxa-

(Left) *Rocky Mountain Iris* (Iris missouriensis) *is a common showy Iris in western states.* (Above) *California Blue-Eyed Grass* (Sisyrinchium bellum) *roots were used for upset stomach.*

tive. **RELATED SPECIES:** Other closely related species, such as *S. albidum* Raf., *S. campestre* Bickn., and *S. angustifolium* P. Mill., were also used for stomach ailments and for both constipation and diarrhea. Blue-eyed grass was carried as a charm to ward off snakes. **WARNING:** Of unknown safety.

FLOWERS 4-PARTED

ROCKY MOUNTAIN BEEPLANT
Cleome serrulata Pursh

Whole plant
Caper Family

Hairless annual, to 3 ft. Leaves alternate, *palmately divided into 3 oblong leaflets*; margins entire. Flowers purple, on *dense, elongated* racemes; sepals fused; *stamens 6, well exserted*, purple with green anthers; May–Sept. **WHERE FOUND:** Sagebrush scrub, juniper woodland. San Diego Co., Calif.; Rockies; throughout western N. America. **USES:** American Indian groups mixed ground plant with water or made tea for stomach disorders. Fresh plants wrapped in cloth, then applied to the abdomen for the same purpose. Whole plant tea a fever remedy. Leaves soaked in cold water were used as a body deodorant. Ramah Navajo considered the seeds an important part of cleansing ceremonies to purify the blood and clear the voice. **RELATED SPECIES:** The seeds and whole plant of *C. viscosa* L. are widely used in Asia as a poultice for rheumatism and painful joints and as a condiment to improve digestion, relieve gas pains, and to discourage intestinal worms.

Rocky Mountain Beeplant
(Cleome serrulata) *has palmately divided leaves.*

PURPLE LOOSESTRIFE
Plant

Lythrum salicaria L.
Loosestrife Family

Erect, simple or multibranched perennial, to 3 ft. Densely hairy *above*. Leaves *clasping* or short-stalked, opposite or in 3s; narrow to more lance-shaped toward plant base, entire. Flowers several in spikes, clustered above upper leaves, with 4–6 bright purple separate petals and 8–10 stamens; July–Oct. **WHERE FOUND:** Naturalized sparingly in western states except Ariz., N.M.; eastward, an invasive weed in swampy meadows, often forming large stands and blanketing moist meadows in a sea of color. Alien (Europe). **USES:** Historically used to treat chronic diarrhea and dysentery, vaginal yeast infections, fevers, liver ailments, constipation, and spitting of blood. Externally, plant used as a wash, poultice, or salve ingredient for wounds, sores, and sore eyes. Tea gargled for an infected throat. Research confirms that extracts stop bleeding and have some antibacterial activity.

WILD RADISH
Plant, seeds

Raphanus sativus L.
Mustard Family

Rough-hairy, annual or biennial, to 1–4 ft. Leaves alternate, *pinnately lobed, end segment large, rounded*; margins toothed. Flowers purplish (or white, yellowish, rose, or salmon), *with dark veins*, in elongated, highly branched racemes; *petals with tapered base; stamens* 6; Feb.–July. **WHERE FOUND:** Disturbed sites, fields,

(Left) *Purple Loosestrife* (Lythrum salicaria) *is an invasive weed from Europe.* (Above) *Wild Radish* (Raphanus sativus) *flowers range from white to pink, rose, and violet.*

American Speedwell (Veronica americana). *Note the dark lines on petals.*

roadsides. Widespread weed throughout U.S. Alien (Europe). **USES:** In Europe and Asia juice from root used to treat coughs, chronic bronchitis, kidney stones, digestive upset, gall bladder problems, gas, diarrhea, headaches, and insomnia. In China root is crushed and poulticed for rheumatic pains, burns, bruises, scalds, and foot infections. Root contains diastase, an enzyme that assists in starch digestion, accounting for use of the root as a digestive aid with food. Root tea, harvested after seeds ripen, is drunk for dysentery, cooked with pork to stop coughing and relieve dropsy. Dried flower and seed tea used for diarrhea. Leaf tea used to bathe lower back to ease pain. Chinese herbalists prescribe seed tea and extracts in pills to promote good digestion, improve appetite, relieve food stagnation with a feeling of fullness, to treat pain, distention, and coughs with excessive phlegm and wheezing. Chemical compounds in radish seed show strong inhibitory effects against pathogenic bacteria and fungi. Experimentally shown to be diuretic and to reduce stones of urinary tract. **WARNING:** Large amounts may irritate digestive system.

AMERICAN SPEEDWELL, AMERICAN BROOKLIME
Leaves

Veronica americana Schwein. ex Benth.
Figwort Family

Hairless, low-spreading perennial to 2 ft., rooting at nodes. Leaves opposite, oval to lance-shaped, on short petioles; margins scalloped. Flowers flat, blue with *dark lines, bearing 2 stamens, in open racemes from leaf axils*; May–Sept. **WHERE FOUND:** Wet places, marshes, streambanks, seeps. Calif. to Alaska, widespread in N. America. **USES:** Formerly used for skin problems, urinary tract disorders, to promote menstruation, and to prevent scurvy. The common name Speedwell is from a European tradition of giving a blue bouquet to travelers to speed them well on their way. **RELATED SPECIES:** Common speedwell, *V. officinalis* L., a European alien, was formerly recognized in pharmacopoeias for a wide range of ailments, particularly coughs, asthma, lung diseases, gout, rheumatism, and jaundice. Considered an expectorant, diuretic, and tonic.

Persian Self-heal (Veronica persica) *flowers have purple lines and white centers.*

PERSIAN SELF-HEAL
Veronica persica Poir.

Leaves
Figwort Family

Long-haired annual, to 2 ft. Stems often low, spreading. Leaves opposite, ovate, on short stalks; margins scalloped to toothed. Flowers flat, blue with *purple lines and white center, solitary on long stalks from leaf axil*; Feb.–June. **WHERE FOUND:** Weed of lawns, fields, gardens. Widespread throughout N. America. Alien (Asia, Europe). **USES:** An introduced species with little known history of native use. In Chinese tradition *Veronica* species were used as expectorants, restoratives, tonics, and diuretics, to heal bones and ligaments, to regulate menses, and to treat coughs and urinary inflammation.

FLOWERS 5-PARTED; PETALS SEPARATE OR APPARENTLY SO

BORAGE
Borago officinalis L.

Leaves, flowers, seeds
Borage Family

Coarse annual, 1–4 ft. Stems succulent, hollow. Leaves have cucumber fragrance when crushed; rough-hairy lower leaves broadly ovate and stalked, upper leaves sessile. Flowers a brilliant blue star with prominent black anthers forming a conelike structure, to 1 in. across; drooping downward; June–Sept. **WHERE FOUND:** Near gardens, sometimes escaped casual weed. Alien (Europe). Occasional. **USES:** Cooling and diuretic leaf tea formerly used for fevers, jaundice, rheumatism. Externally, a poultice used for wounds as an anti-inflammatory. Flowers edible. Seed oil a rich source of gamma-linolenic acid (as in Evening Primrose, p. 100). Such oils are said to alleviate imbalances and abnormalities of essential fatty acids in prostaglandin production. A small clinical study showed Borage seed oil reduced stress by lowering systolic blood pressure and heart rate. **WARNING:** Like Comfrey leaves, Borage leaves (but not the seed oil or flowers) contain liver-toxic and carcinogenic pyrrolizidine alkaloids. Risk of using leaves outweighs benefits.

PRAIRIE FLAX
Whole plant
Linum lewisii Pursh
Flax Family

Hairless, *slender-stemmed* perennial, to 2½ ft. Leaves alternate, linear, sessile, entire; tips pointed. Flowers light blue in one-sided racemes, nodding in bud; *stamens 5, styles 5;* May–Sept. *Round fruit* 10-*seeded;* flat, brownish seeds *teardrop-shaped, shiny, sticky when wet.* **WHERE FOUND:** Dry, open slopes and ridges; montane meadows. Calif. to Alaska, every western state; Midwest, n. Mexico. **USES:** Native American groups used plant as a poultice on bruises and swellings and for goiter or gallbladder problems. Tea used for gas, heartburn, stomach upset, and headaches. Externally, tea used as a wash for hair loss. **RELATED SPECIES:** Seeds of European

Borage (Borago officinalis) is found in gardens and escaped.

Prairie Flax (Linum lewisii). Note the light blue flowers nodding in bud.

Flax, *L. usitatissimum* L., are used for their demulcent and emollient properties to treat inflammatory conditions of the mucous membranes of the respiratory, digestive, and urinary tracts. Flax seeds contain lignans, weak estrogens with reported cardiovascular and cancer-protective effects. **WARNING:** Do not use green plant parts or roots internally, as they may contain cyanidelike compounds.

FLOWERS 5-PARTED; PETALS FUSED, TUBULAR; LEAVES OPPOSITE

MARSH GENTIAN
Gentiana affinis Griseb.

Whole plant
Gentian Family

Perennial, to 20 in. Leaves opposite, lance-shaped to oval, sessile; margins entire, *minutely hairy-fringed*. Flowers narrowly bell-shaped, *intensely* blue, *pleated*, densely clustered at stem tips; sepal *lobes linear*, fringed with hairs; petal lobes often dotted green, with *2 smaller, bristle-tipped lobes between*; June–Sept. **WHERE FOUND:** Moist meadows, streambanks, rocky slopes, serpentine areas; from mid to alpine elevations. N. coast ranges of Calif. to B.C., Rockies; all western states. **USES:** Navajo used the plant as a stimulant for fainting, an antidote to witchcraft, and to make a snuff for treating headaches. **RELATED SPECIES:** Numerous species of Gentian are used as folk and official remedies throughout the world. In Europe Yellow Gentian, *G. lutea* L., is added to many digestive tonics. Bitter secoiridoid glycosides are found in all

(Above) *Rocky Mountain Gentian* (Gentiana calycosa) *has intensely blue, upright, bell-shaped flowers.* (Right) *Phacelia* (Phacelia *spp.*) *flowers are in a coiled raceme.*

species and have proven stimulating effects on gastric secretions. In western N. America, Rocky Mountain Gentian (*G. calycosa*) Griseb. and *Gentianopsis crinita* (Froel. [*G. crinita* (Froel.) Ma] were used as digestive stimulants. In China *G. scabra* Bge. is prescribed for clearing infections of the urinary and digestive tracts and for headaches associated with liver irritation.

CALIFORNIA COAST PHACELIA, SCORPIONWEED
Root, Leaf juice

Phacelia californica Cham.   Waterleaf Family

Branched, *very bristly* perennial to 2 feet. Leaves entire, to *5- or 7-lobed*; lobes ovate, acute. Flowers lavender bell-shaped, 5-lobed, in dense, *coiled* racemes with long stamens; Apr.–July. **WHERE FOUND:** Rocky bluffs, canyons, roadsides. N. cen. coast ranges and s. and n. Sierra, Calif., to s. Ore. *Phacelia* is a large and varied genus in western N. America, with over 90 species in Calif. alone. Hybrids make exact identity difficult. **USES:** The Costanoans used a decoction of the root to reduce fevers. The Kawaiisu infused the root for colds, coughs, stomach problems, and general feeling of illness. The Pomo and Kashaya rubbed the crushed leaf juice on cold sores and impetigo. **RELATED SPECIES:** The Western Keres washed swellings with root tea of *P. crenulata* var. *corrugata* (A. Nels.) Brand, Cleft-leaf Wild Heliotrope. The Thompson Indians drank a tea of *P. hastata* Dougl. ex Lehm. to regulate menses. The Shuswap used tea of *P. linearis* (Pursh) Holz. for bad colds. Zuni made a paste of powdered leaves of *P. neomexica* Thurb. ex Torr. and poulticed it on rashes. The Kawaiisu used a root tea of *P. ramosissima* Dougl. ex. Lehm. as a cleansing purgative and to treat gonorrhea.

GREATER PERIWINKLE, PERIWINKLE
Whole plant

Vinca major L.   Dogbane Family

Evergreen perennial, *sprawling*, somewhat viny, rooting at nodes; to 2 ft. *Leaves opposite*, ovate, rounded at base. Flowers *pinwheel-like*, blue to violet, rarely white, solitary in leaf axils; petal lobes flattened; calyx lobes linear, *minutely hairy, longer than narrow part of corolla tube*; Mar.–July. **WHERE FOUND:** Widely cultivated ornamental throughout N. America. Escaped into shady places from Calif. to s. U.S. Alien (Europe). **USES:** Used by European herbalists for bleeding, excess menstruation, hemorrhoids, bedwetting, as a gargle for sore throat, and as a sedative tea. **WARNING:** The related Madagascar Periwinkle, *Catharanthus roseus* (L.) G. Don, is source of vincristine, vinblastine, and other cancer chemotherapy drugs. Vinca species contain many of the same or similar toxic alkaloids; internal use should be only under the advice of a qualified health practitioner.

(Above) *Greater Periwinkle*
(Vinca major) *is an evergreen*
creeper with spiraling blue flow-
ers. (Right) *Lesser Periwinkle*
(Vinca minor) *is glabrous (without*
hairs) and generally smaller than
Greater Periwinkle.

LESSER PERIWINKLE, COMMON PERIWINKLE

Whole plant

Vinca minor L.   Dogbane Family

 Trailing evergreen with very slender stems. Leaves opposite, entire, elliptical, *not ciliate*. Flower blue, to ¾ in. across, tube about
½ in. long. Calyx lobes obtuse, glabrous (without hairs), *equal to
or shorter than narrow part of corolla tube*; Feb.-May. **WHERE FOUND:**
Escaped or persistent after cultivation. Alien (Eurasia). Naturalized throughout Northern Hemisphere. **USES:** The flowers and
leaves are used by European herbalists for headaches, to relieve
painful digestion, gas, hypertension, dizziness, memory problems,
ringing in the ears, and other hearing problems. **WARNING:** Contains
toxic vinca alkaloids, some of which have anticancer activity.
More toxic than *V. major*.

BLUE VERVAIN

Root, leaves

Verbena hastata L.   Vervain Family

Rough-haired perennial, to 2–4 ft. Leaves opposite, mostly *lance-
shaped*, on square stems; tips pointed; margins sharply toothed.
Flowers tiny, blue to violet, short-tubular, *densely clustered in
slender, branching, pencillike spikes*; June–Sept. **WHERE FOUND:**
Moist, low places, ditches, fields. N. Calif. to s. B.C., every state;
widespread throughout N. America. **USES:** Species of *Verbena* are
used in both European and Native American traditions, often for

Blue Vervain (Verbena hastata)
blooms in late summer.

similar conditions. American Indians and herbalists use leaf tea as a female tonic for convalescence, general debility, and anorexia; also for colds, coughs, fevers, bowel complaints, dysentery, stomach cramps; it is emetic in large doses. Used historically by physicians to promote sweating in fevers and colds, also in coughs, colic, stomach cramping, to expel worms, for repressed menstruation, breast complaints, and urinary tract disorders. A particularly valuable use reported by the Iroquois was "to make an obnoxious person leave." Root considered stronger than leaves.

FLOWERS 5-PARTED; PETALS FUSED, TUBULAR; LEAVES ALTERNATE

BLUEBELL, HAREBELL
Plant, root
Campanula rotundifolia L.
Bellflower Family

Hairless perennial to 2½ ft. Leaves basal, round to oval, coarsely toothed, stalked; alternate stem leaves *linear to lance-shaped,* entire, *sessile.* Flowers showy, bell-shaped, purplish blue, nodding, in racemes; June–Sept. **WHERE FOUND:** Moist, grassy slopes, mountain meadows. N. Calif. to Alaska; every western state except Nev.; Northeastern N. America; Eurasia. **USES:** American Indians used plant tea as a wash for sore eyes. A root tea was used for ear drops. The root was chewed for heart problems. The plant was used as a protecting fumigant for a variety of illnesses. It was rubbed on the body of those bothered by witches.

SKUNKWEED
Plant, root
Navarretia squarrosa (Eschsch.) Hook. & Arn.
Phlox Family

Sticky, spiny annual, to 2 ft. Strongly *skunk-scented.* Leaves alternate, *pinnately dissected into narrow, spine-tipped lobes.* Flowers

Bluebell, Harebell (Campanula rotundifolia) *has small leaves rounded at the base.*

Skunkweed (Navarretia squarrosa) *has a strong skunky scent.*

deep blue, narrowly tubular, in *dense, spiny, headlike clusters*; petal lobes spreading; sepal tube sharply 5-pointed; *stamens 5, included in petal tube; stigma 3-parted*; June–Sept. **WHERE FOUND:** Dry to moist open slopes, meadows, fields, gravelly flats. West of Cascade-Sierra crest from cen. coast ranges of Calif. to s. B.C. **USES:** Skunkweed was used as a tonic and laxative and to treat fevers. Leaf or root tea used as a wash for swellings or sore eyes. California herbalists use a tincture of the fresh plant to allay symptoms of asthma.

FLOWERS 5-PARTED; PETALS FUSED

PACIFIC HOUNDS-TONGUE   Roots
Cynoglossum grande Dougl. *ex* Lehm.   Borage Family

Perennial, to 3 ft. Stems hairless. *Leaves large, ovate, to 1 ft. long, mostly basal, rough-haired, on long petioles*; margins entire. Flowers blue, *flat*, along *coiled branches* at top of long stalk, with *inner ring of white "teeth"*; similar to forget-me-not; Mar.–July. Nutlets covered in *barbed prickles*. **WHERE FOUND:** Open or shaded forests. Along cen. and n. coast ranges of Calif. to B.C. **USES:** American Indian groups used root tea to treat gonorrhea and other venereal

Pacific Hounds-tongue (Cynoglossum grande) has flat blue flowers.

Pacific Hounds-tongue is one of the showiest North American members of the genus.

diseases. Grated roots were used to draw out inflammation from burns and scalds and to relieve stomachaches. **RELATED SPECIES:** European Hound's-tongue, *C. officinale* L., was formerly a folk remedy for mucous congestion of the respiratory tract and other uses. Herbalists also used the root externally as a substitute for comfrey to help heal burns, rashes, and wounds. **WARNING:** The root contains liver-toxic pyrrolizidine alkaloids. Avoid internal use.

JIMSONWEED, THORNAPPLE
Datura stramonium L.

Leaves, seeds
Nightshade Family

 Flowers white to purplish. See p. 52.

BULL NETTLE
Solanum elaeagnifolium Cav.

Root, leaves, berries
Nightshade Family

Gray or silvery-haired, short-spined perennial, to 3 ft.; often forming colonies. Hairs flat, dense, *branched from center.* Leaves alternate, oblong to lance-shaped; margins entire. Flowers purple to blue, star-shaped, with 5 *stamens upright in center in small clusters at end of leafy stalks*; Apr.–Sept. *Berry* orange, reddish, or yellow. **WHERE FOUND:** Dry, disturbed places, roadsides. Widespread

Bull Nettle (Solanum elaeagni-folium) *is heavily armed with short spines.*

Comfrey (Symphytum *spp.*) *is often persistent in old garden sites.*

weed from Calif., Wash., Nev., Utah, Ariz., Rocky Mts. from Colo. to N.M., Tex. Native to cen. U.S. and Mexico. **USES:** Leaves were used for sore eyes and for nose and throat problems. The ground dried berries were used to treat colds; raw seedpods used as a laxative. A piece of fresh root was chewed and placed on an aching tooth. **WARNING: Toxic.** Contains steroids, toxic alkaloids, and glucosides. Will cause vomiting, vertigo, convulsions, weakened heart, paralysis. Green berries can cause diarrhea, dilated pupils, nausea, and vomiting.

COMFREY   **Leaves, root**
Symphytum officinale L.   Borage Family
Large-rooted perennial; 1–3 ft. Leaves large, to 1 ft. or more long, *rough-hairy*; broadly oval to lance-shaped. Bell-like flowers in furled clusters, purple-blue, pink, or white; May–Sept. **WHERE FOUND:** Escaped. Alien. Often cultivated; persistent. **USES:** Although *S. officinale* is listed as the species used medicinally in most herb books, many of the 25 species of *Symphytum* are cultivated in American gardens. Comfrey was popular as a medicinal plant in the 1970s and early 80s, but studies showing toxic pyrrolizidine

alkaloids, especially in the root, have halted the love affair. Studies have shown that leaves harvested during the blooming period are low in alkaloid content. Root tea and the weaker leaf tea were formerly used as a tonic, astringent, and demulcent, for diarrhea, dysentery, bronchial irritation, coughs, vomiting of blood; leaves and root were poulticed to knit bones and promote healing of bruises, wounds, ulcers, and sore breasts. Contains allantoin, which promotes healing. In Germany external application of the leaf is approved for bruises and sprains; root poultice approved for bruising, pulled muscles and ligaments, and sprains. **RELATED SPECIES:** The most widely grown species is Russian Comfrey, S. × *uplandicum* Nyman (pro. sp.), a hybrid bred as a fodder crop, which is higher in toxic alkaloids than *S. officinale*. **WARNING:** Use of the root is discouraged because of high levels of liver-toxic pyrrolizidine alkaloids. In Germany, external use of the leaf is limited to 4 to 6 weeks each year. There is also a danger that the leaves of Comfrey (*Symphytum*) may be confused with the first-year leaf rosettes of Foxglove (*Digitalis*), with **fatal results.** Consult an expert on identification before using.

FLOWERS 5-PARTED; PETALS FUSED, 2-LIPPED; LEAVES CROWDED, STEMS PURPLISH

CALIFORNIA BROOMRAPE, CANCER ROOT　Whole plant
Orobanche californica Cham. & Schlect.　　　Broomrape Family

Stems solitary or clustered, to 12 in. Tubular flowers, purplish to pink or white, 2-lipped, crowded into short, flat-topped clusters; Aug.–Sept. *Petals dark-veined, lobes widely spreading.* **WHERE FOUND:** Generally dry, rocky, or sandy soils, coastal bluffs, moist meadows, stream margins. Cen. coast ranges of Calif. to B.C., Baja Calif. Parasitic on herbs, generally of the composite family (for example, *Grindelia, Eri-geron, Aster, Artemisia*). **USES:** Paiute Indians used a decoction of the plant to treat colds, pneumonia, and other respiratory problems. **RELATED SPECIES:** *O. uniflora*

California Broomrape (Orobanche californica) *has dark-veined petals.*

Clustered Broomrape (Orobanche fasciculata) *has sticky, purplish to yellow stems.*

L., Naked Broomrape, was used by some tribes externally for treating ulcers and cancerous growths and internally for bowel problems. Said to be analogous to *Conopholis americana* (L.) Wallr. f. [*O. americana* L.] of eastern N. America, used historically by late-19th-century physicians to stop bleeding of bowels and uterus, and for diarrhea. Externally, used to treat skin infections caused by *Streptococcus*, as a poultice or wash for wounds, ulcers, and herpes lesions. The name Cancer Root comes from herbalists' use of eastern N. American and European species as a powder on ulcerated cutaneous cancers.

CLUSTERED BROOMRAPE
Orobanche fasciculata Nutt.

Plant, root, seed
Broomrape Family

Sticky stems, purplish or yellow, solitary or clustered, to 8 in. Tubular, curving flowers 2-lipped, on elongated stalks in somewhat flat-topped clusters; petals yellow to dull red or purple; *top lip upright*; bottom lip spreading, dark-veined with yellow patches; Apr.–July. **WHERE FOUND:** Dry, open areas, sagebrush scrub, pinyon-juniper woodland. Calif. to Alaska, all western states; Midwest, n. Mexico. Parasitic on shrubs (*Artemisia, Eriodictyon, Eriogonum*). **USES:** American Indian groups used the powdered or chewed plant on hemorrhoids, wounds, and open sores. Plant tea used to treat toothache and to kill lice. Stem tea, plant juice, or powdered seeds used to relieve joint pain, swollen spleen, and to flush the urinary system. Montana Indians used specimens parasitic on Sweet Sage roots to treat cancer. Keres Indians ate the root to treat respiratory conditions. Some tribes believed picking it or keeping it in one's house would bring bad luck.

FLOWERS 5-PARTED; PETALS FUSED, 2-LIPPED (BILABIATE); FLOWERS IN WHORLED FLOWER HEADS; STRONGLY AROMATIC

MOCK PENNYROYAL
Hedeoma drummondii Benth.

Leaves, roots

Mint Family

Aromatic, *multibranched* perennial, woody at base, to 10 in. Leaves opposite, *narrowly oblong* on square stems. Flowers small, blue to purple, *clustered in leaf axils*; top petal lip short, straight; *sepal tube becoming inflated and closed in fruit*; stamens 2, scarcely exserted under upper lip; May–Aug. **WHERE FOUND:** Dry, open, rocky places. Se. desert mountains of Calif., Nev., Ariz., Utah, Rockies from Mont. to N.M., Tex.; n. Mexico. Great Plains states. **USES:** American Indian groups used leaf tea to treat fever, colds, congestion, coughs, influenza, whooping cough, headache, stomach pain, indigestion, constipation, dysentery, and suppressed menstruation. Navajo used plant as an analgesic. Leaf tea was used as a tonic and appetite stimulant. Root tea used for colds and put on the forehead for itching eyes. Leaves were held in the mouth to relieve toothache and as a poultice to relieve

Mock Pennyroyal (Hedeoma drummondii) *has a strongly aromatic fragrance.*

Wild Mint (Mentha canadensis) *grows in moist habitats.*

headache. Leaves rubbed on the body as an insect repellent. **RE-LATED SPECIES:** American Pennyroyal, *H. pulegioides* (L.) Pers., was used similarly. Early 20th-century physicians prescribed it for suppressed menses, especially with fatigue and back and limb pain. **WARNING:** Contact with essential oil (a popular insect repellent) can cause dermatitis. Essential oil contains strong liver toxins. Avoid internal use.

WILD MINT
Mentha canadensis L.

Whole plant
Mint Family

[*Mentha aquatica* L., *Mentha arvensis* L. var. *canadensis* (L.) Kuntze]

Aromatic, with fine backward-bending hairs, at least on stem angles, perennial, to 6–25 in. Stems square, *hairs denser on angles*. Leaves opposite, lance-shaped to oval, gland-dotted; margins sharply toothed. Flowers tiny, pale lavender to white, slightly 2-lipped, *in dense, widely separated whorls above leaves*; June–Oct. **WHERE FOUND:** Moist areas, streambanks, meadows. Widespread in northern N. America, extending s. to Calif., N.M., Tex.; not in Ariz., N.M. **USES:** American Indian groups used leaf tea to treat colds, influenza, coughs, sore throat, fevers, colic, gas, stomach pain, headaches, body aches, toothache, kidney problems, and nausea. Leaf poultice or steam bath used for pain and swelling, rheumatism, and arthritis. The fresh plant was strewn in dwellings to discourage bedbugs and other insects. Many mints (*Mentha* spp.) have similar uses as a stimulant, carminative, antispasmodic, anodyne, analgesic, and nerve tonic.

PEPPERMINT
Mentha × piperita L.

Whole plant
Mint Family

Aromatic, *hairless* perennial, spreading by creeping rhizomes, to 12–36 in. Stems square, *purplish*. Leaves opposite, lance-shaped to oval, *on short petioles*; margins toothed. Flowers pale violet or whitish, slightly 2-lipped, in *loose, interrupted terminal spikes*; July–frost. **WHERE FOUND:** Moist sites, streambanks, roadsides. Widely scattered in N. America; Calif. to B.C., Utah. Peppermint is a hybrid between Spearmint (*M. spicata* L.) and Watermint (*M. aquatica* L.). Native to Europe, it was first grown commercially in England about 1750 and is now commercially grown on a large scale in the Pacific Northwest, primarily for the essential oil. **USES:** Pleasantly flavored tea long used as a digestive stimulant, carminative, antispasmodic, and antinauseant to treat flatulence, nausea, stomach spasms, diarrhea (especially in children), sore throats, nervous tension, and insomnia. It is also beneficial as an inhalant for asthma and chronic bronchitis. Peppermint leaf is approved in Germany for use in muscle spasms of the gastroin-

Peppermint (Mentha × piperita) *leaves have a distinctive fragrance. Leaf veins are usually reddish.*

European Pennyroyal (Mentha pulegium) *is a European weed of moist soils.*

testinal tract as well as spasms of the gallbladder and bile ducts. The essential oil is used externally to treat neuralgia and myalgia. Peppermint oil is added to cough drops, breath mints, and digestive aids. Menthol, the chief constituent of peppermint oil, is an approved antitussive ingredient in cough drops (though most menthol used commercially is synthetic rather than extracted from peppermint oil itself). **WARNING:** Oil is **toxic** if taken internally; externally, may cause dermatitis. Infants should never be exposed to menthol-containing products, which can cause lung collapse. Do not use peppermint oil in cases of gallbladder or bile duct obstruction. Menthol may cause allergic reactions.

EUROPEAN PENNYROYAL
Whole plant

Mentha pulegium L.
Mint Family

Aromatic, grayish-haired perennial, to 2 ft. Leaves opposite, oval, on square stems; margins entire to finely toothed. Flowers lavender, *in dense whorls in leaf axils*; June–Oct. **WHERE FOUND:** Low, moist places, pastures, ditches. Coast ranges, n. Sierra of Calif. to B.C.; eastern U.S. Alien (Europe). **USES:** Herbalists use leaf tea to treat stomach cramps, flatulent colic, nausea, and suppressed menses. Has been used as a dangerous abortifacient. The species name *pulegium*, derived from the Latin *pulex* ("flea"), honors the use of the plant as a flea repellent for dogs since ancient times. Oil of European Pennyroyal has long been used in insect repellent formulations to deter mosquitoes, fleas, mites, and ticks from the skin and clothing. Pulegone does appear to repel ants and other insects that live in proximity to the plant. **WARNING:** Avoid ingestion of Pennyroyal oil, which is toxic; since 1980 at least sixteen cases of toxicity associated with pennyroyal ingestion have also been reported. Since 1897, four deaths from ingestion of pennyroyal products have been documented.

SPEARMINT
Mentha spicata L.

Leaves
Mint Family

Creeping perennial; 6–36 in. Leaves opposite; without *stalks* (or very short stalks); with a distinct *odor of spearmint*. Flowers, pale pink-violet, in slender, elongated spikes; June–frost. **WHERE FOUND:** Wet soil. Escaped in much of our area. Alien (Europe). Commercially cultivated on a large scale in Wash., Ore., and Idaho. **USES:** Once the primary mint used in medicine, in the late 18th century it was largely replaced by Peppermint. Spearmint and its essential oil are used as carminatives (to relieve gas) and to disguise the flavor of other medicines. Spearmint has been traditionally valued as a stomachic, antiseptic, and antispasmodic. The leaf tea has been used for stomachaches, diarrhea, nausea, colds, headaches, cramps, fevers, and is a folk cancer remedy. **WARNING:** Oil is **toxic** if taken internally; externally, causes dermatitis.

MINTLEAF BEEBALM,
OREGANA DE LA SIERRA
Monarda fistulosa ssp. *fistulosa* var. *menthifolia* (Graham) Fern.

Whole plant
Mint Family

Aromatic, finely hairy, upright perennial with creeping rhizome, to 3 ft. Leaves opposite, triangular to oval, on square stems; margins toothed. Bright lavender-purple, *narrowly tubular flowers in a single dense head at stem tip*; bracts below often purple-tinged; May–Sept. Up-

Spearmint (Mentha spicata) *leaves have a pleasant fragrance reminding some of mint chewing gum.*

(Above) *Beebalm* (Monarda fistulosa) *is a favorite plant of butterflies.* (Right) *Vinegar Weed* (Trichostema lanceolatum)

per lip slightly curved, bottom lip reflexed; *petals and sepal tips hairy; stamens 2, barely exserted.* Smooth nutlets 4, oval. **WHERE FOUND:** Open or lightly shaded dry or moist areas. Ore., Idaho, Utah, Ariz.; Rockies from Mont. to N.M., Tex.; throughout Canada, cen. and e. U.S.; n. Mexico. **USES:** American Indian groups rubbed mintleaf beebalm on the body or head and took it internally for fever and headaches; to treat sore throat and make a wash for sore eyes; and as a lotion or internally for gunshot or arrow wounds. The root was soaked in water boiled with some fat, and this tea was drunk for colds. A piece of the root was chewed and held in the mouth and was swallowed a little at a time. **RELATED SPECIES:** American Indian groups used Wild Oregano, *M. pectinata* Nutt., both taken internally and as a poultice, to treat headache, general aches and pains, cough, fever, and flu. *M. fistulosa* L., Wild Bergamot Beebalm, was used to treat a wide variety of ailments, including colds, congestion, flu, cough, fever, convulsions, abdominal pain, colic, gas, chest pain, headache, toothache, bleeding, suppressed menstruation, and acne.

VINEGAR WEED, TURPENTINE WEED, BLUECURLS

Leaves, flowers

Trichostema lanceolatum Benth.   Mint Family

Strong-scented, gray-haired, glandular annual, to 3 ft. Leaves opposite, lance-shaped; margins entire. Light blue flowers *abruptly bent upward*, in small racemes from leaf axils; Aug.–Oct. *Stamens*

4, long, and curving downward. Nutlets hairy. **WHERE FOUND:** Dry, open, often disturbed sites, meadows. Most of Calif. to Ore.; Baja Calif. **USES:** Preparations of the leaves and flowers of this strong-scented plant have been used internally by American Indians for headaches, colds, fever, urethra strictures, general infirmity, and stomachache, and externally as a wash or poultice for high fever, typhoid, malaria, headaches and other pain, smallpox, infected sores, and stomachache, and snorted up the nose for nosebleeds and headaches. Indian women would squat over a steaming pot of the simmering herbs to relieve uterine problems. Indians chewed leaves for toothache and rubbed leaves on the skin for pain, and on the face and chest for colds. Vinegar weed is also used as a bug repellent and as a beverage tea.

FLOWERS 5-PARTED; PETALS FUSED, 2-LIPPED (BILABIATE); FLOWERS IN WHORLED FLOWER HEADS; LEAVES NOT STRONGLY AROMATIC

GROUND IVY, GILL-OVER-THE-GROUND
Glechoma hederacea L.

Leaves
Mint Family

Creeping, ivylike perennial. Leaves scallop-edged, round to kidney-shaped; sometimes purple-tinted. Two-lipped violet flowers, in whorls of leaf axils; Mar.–July. **WHERE FOUND:** Roadsides, lawns. Throughout our area. Alien (Europe). **USES:** Traditionally, leaf tea used for lung ailments, asthma, jaundice, kidney ailments, and as a blood purifier. Externally, it was a folk remedy for cancer, backaches, bruises, and piles. Research confirms that it has anti-inflammatory, diuretic activity; experimentally, it has antitumor effects. **WARNING:** Reportedly **toxic** to horses, causing throat irritation and labored breathing. This effect has also

Ground Ivy (Glechoma hederacea) has rounded leaves with scalloped edges.

been reported in humans. In two cases reported to Foster, fresh leaves were steeped in ½ cup of hot water for ten minutes, then drunk. Five minutes later, symptoms of throat irritation and labored breathing appeared; the individuals had difficulty sleeping that night. Symptoms resolved in 24 hours.

SELF-HEAL, HEAL-ALL   **Whole plant**
Prunella vulgaris L.   Mint Family

Low-growing, occasionally long-stemmed perennial, to 3–12 in. Leaves opposite, lance-shaped to oval, on weak square stems; margins entire. Dark purple to blue (sometimes pink or white) flowers in *thick, oblong spikes*; May–Sept. **WHERE FOUND:** Moist places, disturbed sites, roadsides, lawns. Widespread throughout N. America. Alien (Eurasian). **USES:** Applied fresh as a poultice, self-heal was praised by Renaissance herbalists for healing wounds and stopping internal bleeding. Western herbal uses include as a gargle or mouth wash for sore throat, thrush, and gum diseases and as a tea for bleeding and diarrhea. Many American Indian groups adopted it for fevers, colds, coughs, shortness of breath, sore throats, diarrhea, stomach cramps, upset stomach, vomiting, venereal disease, diabetes, heart problems, mouth sores, and as a general tonic. Externally, used for acne, burns, sores, boils, cuts, bruises, hemorrhoids, backaches, and sore and stiff legs. Chinese herbalists prescribe it to relieve red and sore eyes, headaches, dizziness, swollen neck glands, and high blood

Self-heal (Prunella vulgaris) *is a common weed from Europe, often in lawns.*

Chia (Salvia columbariae) *seeds were a popular food.*

pressure. Extracts of the plant demonstrate potent antioxidant, blood pressure–lowering effects, and antibacterial effects in laboratory studies. **WARNING:** Avoid use during pregnancy.

CHIA   Seeds, leaves
Salvia columbariae Benth.   Mint Family
Stiff-haired *annual*, to 6–24 in. Leaves mostly basal, *pinnately dissected; segments often pinnately lobed again.* Small, pale to deep blue flowers, sometimes with white, blue-spotted tube, in dense whorls on tall, nearly leafless stalks; *ovate bracts below whorl spine-tipped*; Mar.–June. **WHERE FOUND:** Dry, open, often disturbed sites, hillsides, deserts. Coast ranges, s. and n. Sierra of Calif., Nev., sw. Utah, Ariz., N.M.; Baja Calif., n. Mexico. **USES:** Chia is a common name for several species of *Salvia* from Mexico and the western U.S. Leaf tea used for stomach problems and fever. The seeds are a well-known native food of the Southwest, still used today. American Indian groups mixed seeds with water for a refreshing drink and as sustenance to stave off hunger. Seed mush (which becomes mucilaginous in water) was poulticed for infections; used historically to treat gunshot wounds. To remove something from the eye, one seed was placed under the eyelid and allowed to slide over the eye, with its mucilage coat picking up stray particles. Mexicans simmered the seeds with a sweetener to make a drink for easing sore throat and fevers. Boiled milk with chia taken before bed has been used for insomnia. **RELATED SPECIES:** *Salvia*

hispanica L., also known as chia (and used interchangeably), was the subject of a study published in 2000 that found that hens fed up to 28 percent chia seeds in their diet produced eggs with significantly less cholesterol and higher levels of healthy omega-3 fatty acids compared with controls.

PEALIKE FLOWERS

LEATHER-ROOT
Roots
Hoita macrostachya (DC.) Rybd. Pea Family
Upright, gland-dotted, multibranched perennial, to 6½ ft. Leaves alternate, divided into 3 *ovate leaflets, the terminal one stalked*; margins entire. Purple flowers in *dense, oblong spike covered with black or white hairs*; May–Aug. Hairy pod remaining closed, single-seeded. **WHERE FOUND:** Moist sites, streamsides, meadows. Most of Calif.; Baja Calif. **Uses:** A tea of the root was used as a wash to treat skin wounds, ulcers, and sores. **RELATED SPECIES:** *H. orbicularis* (Lindl.) Rydb. was used to strengthen the blood and treat fevers.

ALFALFA
Leaves
Medicago sativa L. Pea Family
⚠ Hairless perennial, to 3 ft. Leaves alternate, divided into 3 *oblanceolate leaflets, cloverlike*; margins *coarsely toothed near tip*. Purple to blue flowers in *dense*, spikelike racemes; Apr.–Oct. *Pod coiled, not prickly*, several-seeded, remaining closed. **WHERE FOUND:**

(Above) *Leather-root* (Hoita macrostachya) *was used to treat fevers.* (Right) *Alfalfa* (Medicago sativa) *is widely cultivated and has naturalized near fields where it has been planted.*

Disturbed sites, agricultural areas, roadsides. Widespread escape from cultivated areas throughout U.S.; every state. Native to Eurasia. **USES:** Traditionally, Alfalfa is considered an appetite stimulant, mineral-rich, and diuretic, and is said to protect against urinary tract, cardiovascular, and intestinal problems with regular use. Costanoan Indians held heated leaves near the ear to treat earache. Keres Indians used leaves as a bedbug repellent. In South Africa Alfalfa tea is used to prevent diabetes. In Europe the herb is used to relieve water-retention and prostate problems. Alfalfa is a rich source of isoflavones, such as genistein, which are weak estrogens and may help protect humans against certain cancers, heart disease, and other ailments. It also contains coumarins and vitamin K, which can help normalize blood pressure and have a beneficial effect on the cardiovascular system, and cholesterol-lowering saponins. **WARNING:** Alfalfa saponins may cause breakdown of red blood cells, causing bloating in livestock (hence weight gain). Alfalfa sprouts have been reported to induce lupus (systemic lupus erythematosus) and to cause recurrence in patients in which the disease has become dormant, though evidence is not well-documented.

SCURF PEA
Root, leaves

Psoralidium tenuiflorum (Pursh) Rydb.
Pea Family

Upright, *black gland–dotted* perennial, to 4 ft. *Forming large clumps.* Leaves alternate, palmately divided into 3–5 *oblanceolate*

(Left) *Scurf Pea* (Psoralidium tenuiflorum) *forms large clumps.* (Above) *California Tea* (Rupertia physodes) *has pleasantly aromatic leaves.*

leaflets, hairless above, rough-hairy below; *tips rounded*; margins entire. Flowers violet to blue in open racemes; sepal tube densely glandular, *tearing along one side in fruit*; top petal pale, all petals often with dark spot; Apr.–Sept. Oval pod *hairless, glandular, not enclosed in sepals*. **WHERE FOUND:** Plains, prairies; desert scrub and sagebrush communities. Ariz., Utah, Rockies from Mont. to N.M., Tex., Great Plains, Midwest. **USES:** American Indian groups used root tea for headache, chronic constipation, and tuberculosis. Plant tea used to treat influenza, and tuberculosis. Leaves burned to repel mosquitoes. Members of the Dakota tribe made garlands of scurf pea as protection from the sun.

CALIFORNIA TEA, INDIAN BREADROOT
Rupertia physodes (Dougl. ex Hook.) J. Grimes
[*Psoralea physodes* Dougl. ex Hook.]

Leaves
Pea Family

Pleasant-scented creeping perennial, to 2 ft.; hairless on lower stem and leaves. Leaves on stalks with 3 gland-dotted ovate leaflets. Small purple-yellow *pealike* flowers in dense racemes, *black-hairy* and *sticky-glandular*. Pod small, compressed. **WHERE FOUND:** Open forested areas. S. Calif. to Vancouver I. B. C., mostly in coastal mountains; Idaho. **USES:** The leaves were used by California tribes and early European settlers as a tea substitute and digestive aid. **RELATED SPECIES:** The seeds, roots, and leaves of a number of species of this genus worldwide are used for medicine. Leaves of *P. bituminosa* L. were used in folk medicine as a tonic and stimulant and to induce menstruation. The root of *P. pentaphylla* L., a native of Mexico, was formerly official in the Mexican and Spanish pharmacopoeias, and was used to reduce fevers. Seeds of *P. corylifolia* L. are prescribed in Chinese medicine as a strengthening tonic for premature ejaculation, impotence, incontinence, abdominal pain, and shortness of breath. In laboratory tests, the seeds show anti-inflammatory and pain-relieving properties. *Psoralea* seeds are high in the phytoestrogens genistein and daidzein, and a laboratory test showed increased bone calcification in animals given seed extracts.

SMALL FLOWERS IN UMBELS

PURPLE SANICLE
Sanicula bipinnatifida Dougl. ex Hook.

Root, leaves
Parsley Family

Perennial, to 30 in.; *taproot stout, thickened*. Leaves alternate, pinnately lobed in 3–7 *narrow, coarsely toothed* segments. *Petioles winged, toothed, sheathing at base*. Flowers small, purple (sometimes yellowish) in dense umbels; Feb.–May. Ovate fruits covered in *rigid, hooked bristles*. **WHERE FOUND:** Dry, open sites, rocky slopes.

Purple Sanicle (Sanicula bipinnatifida) *has small purple flowers.*

Scattered in Calif., especially coast ranges, to s. B.C.; Baja Calif. Sierra plants often have yellow flowers. **USES:** Used as a poultice or as a wash for snakebite. **RELATED SPECIES:** Teas and extracts of *S. marilandica* L. (eastern N. America) were traditionally used for treating sore throat, gonorrhea, dysentery, and vaginal yeast infections; used externally as a wash for dermatitis. American Indian groups used a plant tea as an emetic to counteract poisons, diuretic for water retention, and kidney problems, and as a laxative. Root tea used to regulate the menses and ease pain for rheumatism, snakebites, and reducing fevers. Extracts of the European *S. europea* L. are used traditionally by herbalists topically to heal wounds and stop bleeding and internally to slow excessive menstrual bleeding, spitting of blood, or blood in stools. Extracts have been shown to have antiviral effects against strains of influenza, as well as antifungal activity. Other species of Sanicle have potent antioxidant activity.

MISCELLANEOUS PLANTS WITH VIOLET TO BLUE FLOWERS

COLOMBIAN MONKSHOOD, WOLFBANE
Leaves
Aconitum columbianum Nutt. Buttercup Family

Tuberous perennial, to 6½ ft. Leaves alternate, *palmately deeply divided* into 3–5 wedge-shaped segments; margins toothed. Showy, deep blue flowers, sometimes white or cream, in elongated racemes; *hoodlike sepal enclosing 2 small petals, not spurred*, sitting above other flower parts; June–Sept. **WHERE FOUND:** Streambanks, moist meadows at mid to subalpine elevation. Throughout western N. America, except Tex.; S.D., Minn.; B.C., Mexico. Scattered populations occur in Iowa, Wisc., Ohio, and N.Y. **USES:** American Indian groups wisely considered aconite too poisonous for medicinal use. **RELATED SPECIES:** Historically, physicians used the root of the European Monkshood, *Aconitum napellus* L., in small doses to treat inflammatory, infectious, and febrile disease in general. Other uses included rheumatism, neuralgia,

Columbian Monkshood (Aconitum columbianum) *is highly toxic.*

Foxglove (Digitalis purpurea) *is commonly cultivated and has naturalized in the Pacific Northwest.*

neurological diseases, skin disease, respiratory ailments, urinary tract disease, digestive tract troubles, and circulatory problems. The specially processed, alkaloid-free roots of Sichuan Aconite (*A. carmichaelii* Debeaux) are an important drug plant in traditional Chinese medicine, widely prescribed for restoring warmth and vigor to patients with a cold, enfeebled digestive system. However, toxic reactions are regularly reported. **WARNING:** This plant, especially the root, contains deadly poisonous alkaloids. Therapeutic dose is dangerously close to the lethal dose. Deadly poison.

FOXGLOVE   **Leaves**
Digitalis purpurea L.   Figwort Family

Biennial; 3–6 ft. Leaves in a basal rosette, ovate to lance-shaped, soft-hairy, toothed; to 1 ft. long. Flowers purple to white, *spotted thimbles*, 1 ¼ in. long, on spikes; *in summer of second year.* **WHERE FOUND:** Garden escape, naturalized in some areas. Pacific Northwest, occasional elsewhere in the West. Often cultivated as an ornamental for its showy purple or white flowers. Note: only second-year plants produce flowers. In the first year, only leaves in a basal rosette. **USES:** Dried leaves are a source of heart-tonic digitalis glycosides. Used in modern medicine to increase force of systolic contractions in congestive heart failure; lowers venous pressure in hypertensive heart ailments and elevates blood pressure in weak heart; diuretic, reduces edema. **WARNING: Lethally toxic**. First year's leaf growth (rosette) has been mistaken for Comfrey leaves (*Symphytum*, see p. 199), with fatal results. Therapeutic dose of *Digitalis* is dangerously close to the lethal dose. For use by physicians only.

FULLER'S TEASEL
Dipsacus fullonum L.

Leaves, roots
Teasel Family

Stout, *spiny* biennial, to 6 ft. Leaves opposite, broadly lance-shaped, clasping stem; margins entire to minutely toothed. Tiny lavender flowers in *dense, spiny, conelike heads* on long stalks; May–Sept. Heads with *linear, upright, or spreading bracts below*. **WHERE FOUND:** Moist, disturbed places, fields, roadsides. Widespread weed throughout N. America. Alien (Europe). **USES:** Traditionally, leaf tea used as a wash for acne. Roots have been used for at least 2000 years to treat warts, sores, and fistulas, to improve appetite, and to invigorate liver function. **RELATED SPECIES:** *D. fullonum* ssp. *sylvestris* (Huds.) Clapham (*D. sylvestris* Huds.), Common Teasel, from Wyo., Ariz., Utah, is used similarly. In China, the roots of *D. asper* Wall. or *D. japonicus* Miq. are prescribed for painful, stiff swollen joints and lower back pain.

(Left) *Fuller's Teasel (Dipsacus spp.) is characterized by spiny, conelike flower heads.* (Above) *The lower petals of Western Dog Violet (Viola adunca) are white-bearded.*

WESTERN DOG VIOLET, HOOKED SPUR VIOLET

Whole plant

Viola adunca Sm.   Violet Family

Perennial from slender rhizomes, to 1 ft. Leaves mostly basal, *heart-shaped to round*; margins scalloped. Paired bracts at base of petiole (stipules) *lance-shaped, toothed*. Flowers showy, deep purple, with *slender spur and dark purple lines on long stalks*; nodding in bud; Mar.–Aug. **WHERE FOUND:** Moist banks, meadow edges, forest openings. Widespread over northern N. America, in every western state except Tex. **USES:** American Indian groups used plant tea externally as a wash on sore and swollen joints, internally for stomach pain and, in children, for asthma. Flower poulticed to torso for internal pains. Violet species in general have a long history of use in treating lung, urinary tract, and skin ailments.

FLOWERS IN HEADS; RAY FLOWERS ONLY OR DAISYLIKE HEADS (COMPOSITE FAMILY)

CHICORY

Root, leaf

Cichorium intybus L.   Composite Family

Taprooted perennial with *milky sap*, to 4 ft. Leaves mostly basal, *deeply pinnately lobed into sharply pointed, toothed segments*. Showy, blue to violet flower heads sessile along upper stalks, *petals square-tipped*; June–Oct. **WHERE FOUND:** Disturbed sites, fields, roadsides. Widespread weed in N. America. Alien (Europe). **USES:** Cherokee used root tea as a nerve tonic. Root and leaves traditionally used as a simple bitter digestive stimulant, laxative, and diuretic. Herbalists commonly recommend root preparations to improve the appetite and digestion and to treat gallstones and liver disorders. In a controlled laboratory experiment with an-

Chicory (Cichorium intybus) has sky-blue to violet (rarely white) flowers.

imals, chicory extract improved lipid profiles, cholesterol ratios, and lipid and cholesterol excretion. Experimentally, the extract has been shown to be antioxidant. Roasted chicory root is commonly added to coffee substitutes because of its rich, slightly bitter flavor; also used to flavor French roast coffee. Root and leaves approved in Germany for treatment of loss of appetite and dyspepsia. **WARNING:** May cause rare allergic reactions.

NARROW-LEAVED PURPLE CONEFLOWER
Echinacea angustifolia DC.

Root, whole plant
Composite Family

Taprooted perennial, 6–20 in. Leaves lance-shaped, stiff-hairy. Flowers with prominent cone-shaped disk surrounded by pale to deep purple spreading rays, *rays about as long as width of disk* (to 1 ¼ in.); June–Sept. **WHERE FOUND:** Prairies. Tex., w. Okla., w. Kans., Neb., west to e. Colo., e. Mont., N.D.; Man., Sask. **USES:** Plains Indians used *Echinacea* for a greater range of medicinal purposes than any other plant group. Root (chewed or in tea) used for snakebites, spider bites, cancers, toothaches, burns, hard-to-heal sores and wounds, flu, and colds. Research confirms many traditional uses, plus cortisonelike activity and insecticidal, bactericidal, and immunostimulant properties. Considered a nonspecific immune-system stimulant. Widely used in Western phytomedicines, including extracts, salves, and tinctures, for wounds, herpes sores, canker sores, throat infections; as a preventative for influenza, colds. It is a folk remedy for brown recluse spider bites, a use that should be researched. Best known as a preventative for colds and flu if taken at onset of symptoms and to lessen severity and duration of upper respiratory tract infections. **WARNING:** Rare allergic reactions reported.

*Narrow-leaved Purple Coneflower (*Echinacea angustifolia*) is common on the western prairies.*

Salsify (Tragopogon porrifolius)
blooms early in the spring.

SALSIFY, GOAT'S BEARD   **Whole plant**
Tragopogon porrifolius L.   Composite Family
    Hairless biennial with milky sap, to 3 ft. Leaves alternate, *grasslike*, clasping stem. Flowers purple, *solitary on long stalks*; Apr.–Aug. *Sharply pointed bracts below head longer than flowers.* **WHERE FOUND:** Moist, disturbed places, fields. Widespread weed throughout U.S. Alien (Europe). **USES:** Navajo made a lotion or drink to be used by either people or horses after being bitten by a rabid coyote. The plant was also used as ceremonial emetic. In Europe the roots were stewed and eaten as a folk remedy to remove obstructions of the gallbladder and relieve jaundice. **RELATED SPECIES:** Cold root tea of *T. pratensis* L. was used as a wash on boils and as a gargle for throat ailments.

TUBULAR FLOWERS ONLY; NO RAY FLOWERS; THISTLES (COMPOSITE FAMILY)

WAVYLEAF THISTLE   **Whole plant**
Cirsium undulatum (Nutt.) Spreng.   Composite Family
    Stout, white-woolly perennial from taproot, to 4 ft. *Not creeping.* Leaves alternate, oblong, *shallowly pinnately lobed*; margins *spine-tipped*; upper leaf gray. Flowers violet-pinkish (to rose, pale lavender, or white) in solitary heads on *longer stalks*; June–Sept. Outer bracts below heads *lance-shaped, gradually tapered to small, reflexed spine; inner with wavy tips*; midvein glandular. Fruits with barbed bristles at tip. **WHERE FOUND:** Open sites, prairies,

Wavyleaf Thistle (Cirsium undulatum) *has shallowly lobed leaves.*

Cardoon (Cynara cardunculus) *is a noxious weed in California.*

slopes, disturbed places. Native from Minn. to N.M., Ariz., e. Ore.; B.C. Noxious weed in Calif. **USES:** The Navajo infused the root and used it as an eyewash. A cold infusion of the plant was taken for general discomfort. The root tea was used for stomach disorders. **RELATED SPECIES:** The Hopis used tea of Cainville Thistle, *C. calcareum* (M. E. Jones) Woot. & Standl., as a worm medicine, laxative, and to relieve throat irritation associated with colds; externally for itching. Ramah Navajo washed sore eyes with a root infusion. The Navajo used a tea of New Mexico Thistle, *C. neomexicanum* Gray, to ease chills and fevers. Ramah Navajo considered the root a life medicine, or panacea.

CARDOON, ARTICHOKE THISTLE
Leaves

Cynara cardunculus L.
Composite Family

Large, very spiny thistle, to 2–8 ft. tall. Leaves alternate, lower leaves to 3 ft. long, very spiny, upper surface with loose cobwebby hairs; densely woolly-hairy beneath. Flower heads somewhat globe-shaped, purplish blue, bracts spine-tipped; June-Sept. **WHERE FOUND:** Disturbed sites. Cultivated. Noxious weed in Calif. Alien (se. Europe). **USES:** Cardoon is cultivated for its edible roots and stems. A folk medicine used as a blood purifier and diuretic in the treatment of rheumatism, gout, and jaundice. Grown today primarily as a robust ornamental.

ARTICHOKE
Leaves

Cynara scolymus L. Composite Family

Robust, branched cultivated perennial, to 6 ft. Leaves unarmed or minutely spiny, densely gray-hairy. Flowers purple, in large thistle-like head, to 6 in. across, with thick, fleshy bracts; summer. Unopened flower head is the familiar artichoke of commerce. **WHERE FOUND:** Extensively cultivated commercially in Calif. Occasionally naturalized in the West. Alien (Europe). **USES:** Leaf and leaf extracts traditionally used in Europe for the treatment of dyspeptic complaints, especially when accompanied by bile secretion disorders; also as a diuretic. Cynarin, a bitter principle, is considered the active constituent. Leaf preparations are widely used for liver-protectant activity, diuretic effects, and cholesterol-reducing activity. Approved in Germany for dyspeptic complaints and to reduce cholesterol levels. Primarily used to stimulate bile flow for biliary tract disorders. **WARNING:** Contraindicated in cases of known allergies to the composite family; also in case of bile duct obstruction.

MILK THISTLE
Seeds, leaves

Silybum marianum (L.) Gaertn. Composite Family

Annual or biennial to 3–6 ft. Leaves alternate, dark green, *white-mottled along veins*; older leaves wavy, margins lobed with *sharp, spine-tipped teeth*. Flowers purple tufts; receptacle densely bristle-spined; Apr.–Sept. Shiny fruit *dark purple-and-brown–spotted*, with detaching ring of white bristles at tip. **WHERE FOUND:** Disturbed sites, pastures. Invasive weed in s. Calif. to B.C., Nev., Ariz., N.M., Tex.; occasional eastward. Alien (Mediterranean). **USES:** Milk Thistle is popular with herbalists but unpopular with farmers. Used for over 2000 years as a remedy for liver disease. Modern studies confirm that silymarin, a mixture of flavonoids in highest concentration in the seeds, has liver-protective, antioxidant, and regenerative effects. It is used to treat acute poisoning from deadly *Amanita* (death-cap) mushrooms. Additional research shows that it decreases insulin resistance in diabetics, improves lipid balance in people with liver disease, and protects against several forms of cancer. Numerous clinical studies confirm its safety and efficacy in treating hepatitis and cirrhosis and in protecting the liver from drugs and toxins. Approved in Germany and other countries for the supportive treatment of chronic inflammatory liver disorders such as hepatitis, cirrhosis, and fatty infiltration caused by alcohol or other toxins. It also helps to prevent liver damage in persons exposed to toxic chemicals.

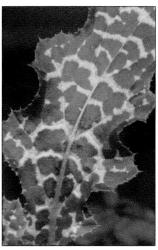

(Above) *Artichoke* (Cynara scolymus) *is grown as a vegetable and
has escaped from cultivation.*
(Right) *Milk Thistle* (Silybum
marianum). *Note the white mottled leaves.*

*Milk Thistle is widely naturalized
in California.*

CANNABIS, HEMP, MARIJUANA   Leaves, seeds, flowering tops
Cannabis sativa L.   Hemp Family

⚠ Annual weed; 5–14 ft. Leaves *palmate, with 5–7 lobes*. Leaflets lance-shaped, toothed. Flowers greenish, sticky; Aug.–Sept. **WHERE FOUND:** Escaped or cultivated (illegally) throughout our area. Alien (Eurasia). **USES:** The leaves are a well-known illicit psychoactive drug. Traditionally, the plant has had dozens of folk uses in cultures throughout the world. Chemical components in the leaves may be of use in relieving eye pressure in glaucoma. Widely used, mostly illegally, to relieve nausea in patients undergoing chemotherapy. Antibiotic for gram-positive bacteria. Though much maligned, it is potentially a very useful medicinal plant. Considered pain-relieving, anticonvulsant, nausea-relieving. An important fiber (hemp) and oilseed plant in many other countries, including Canada. **WARNING:** Not accepted socially or legally.

DURANGO ROOT   Roots
Datisca glomerata (K. Presl) Baill.   Datisca Family

⚠ *Stout*, hairless perennial, to 6 ft. Leaves alternate, *deeply pinnately lobed*; margins coarsely toothed. Small male and female flowers on separate plants, in *small clusters in leaf axils*; stamens with *large anthers* on very short stalks; styles 3, *threadlike, exserted*, deeply forked; May–Aug. **WHERE FOUND:** Along streams, washes. Calif. to w. Nev., Baja Calif. **USES:** American Indians made a pulverized root tea as a wash for sores and rheumatism. Tea also used for sore throat and swollen tonsils. **RELATED SPECIES:** *D. cannabina* L. is used in Iraq as a diuretic, expectorant, and purgative and to lower fevers. **WARNING:** *Datisca* species are reported to be toxic.

Cannabis (Cannabis sativa) *here seen with a sunflower growing legally in a cottage garden in the Swiss Alps.*

Durango Root (Datisca glomerata) *has deeply pinnately lobed leaves.*

Narrowleaf Plantain (Plantago lanceolata) *has narrow, ribbed leaves.*

NARROWLEAF PLANTAIN, ENGLISH PLANTAIN

Leaves, roots

Plantago lanceolata L.

Plantain Family

Long, lance-shaped leaves in basal rosettes, *prominently parallel-veined*; tips pointed, bases tapered; margins without teeth. Flowers tiny, in dense oval to elongated spikes at tips of long, leafless stalks; to 2 ft.; Apr.–Nov. **WHERE FOUND:** Disturbed sites, roadsides, lawns, fields. Widespread across N. America, introduced from Europe. **USES:** Plantain, one of the nine sacred herbs of the Anglo-Saxons, has an extensive history. Leaves in tea or chewed and swallowed (or the juice swallowed) for digestive tract problems such as diarrhea, irritable bowel syndrome, urinary tract infections, and respiratory infections. Externally, crushed, juicy leaves poulticed for skin inflammation. Considered an astringent, demulcent, and antiseptic. After the plant's introduction to North America, American Indian groups poulticed the leaves on burns, rashes, ulcers, blisters, insect stings, and bites. Internally, a tea was used for diarrhea and other bowel complaints and for earache. Small seeds used similarly to psyllium seed (also from *Plantago* species) as a bulk laxative. Extracts show antibacterial, anti-fungal, anti-inflammatory, pain-relieving, antioxidant, antiulcer,

(Left) *Common Plantain* (Plantago major) *is a common weed in lawns.* (Above) *Salad Burnet* (Sanguisorba *spp.*). *Asian, North American, and European species have highly astringent leaves.*

immunostimulating, diuretic, hypotensive, and hypoglycemic properties, among others. Compounds that contribute to wound healing activity are flavonoids, caffeic acid derivatives, polysaccharides, and alcohols present in the wax of the leaf surface. The potent but unstable antimicrobial iridoid glycoside aucubin is found in this and the following species. Both plants also contain abundant and soothing mucilage, as well as small amounts of the cell-growth stimulant allantoin.

COMMON PLANTAIN   **Leaves, roots**
Plantago major L.   Plantain Family

Hairless perennial, to 18 in. Leaves broadly oval, in *basal rosettes*, *prominent parallel veins* converging at base; tips bluntly pointed, bases rounded at thickened stalks; *margins wavy*. Flowers small, in dense, elongated spikes; Apr.–Oct. **WHERE FOUND:** Moist disturbed sites, roadsides, fields. Widespread weed throughout N. America. Alien (Europe). **USES:** Used interchangeably with *P. lanceolata*. Ancient Greeks and Romans used Plantain as an astringent, to heal wounds, and for asthma, fevers, and eye disorders. American Indian groups used a poultice for pain, swelling, wounds, cuts, sores, infections, blisters, insect bites and snakebites, and hemorrhoids. The juice or leaf infusion was used for sore eyes. Internally, leaf tea taken for diarrhea, ulcers, bloody urine, digestive upsets, and excess mucous discharge. The root was used for many similar complaints, as well as for fever, respiratory infections, and constipation. Extracts inhibit the biosynthesis of cyclooxygenase-2 prostaglandin. **RELATED SPECIES:** The nonprescription laxative drug psyllium is the seed and/or husks of *Plantago* species, which have been shown to lower cholesterol and glucose and reduce fat intake, in addition to their laxative effect.

SALAD BURNET
Sanguisorba officinalis L.

Leaves, root
Rose Family

Hairless perennial, to 5 ft. Leaves odd-pinnate; lower leaves larger, with up to 13 serrate oblong leaflets. Small flowers with *dark purple sepals* in elongated dense spikes; *stamens long, wavy;* Feb.–Apr. **WHERE FOUND:** Wet places, red fir forests. Nw. Calif. to Alaska. **USES:** In Europe traditionally tea used to treat colitis and diarrhea, to stop internal and external bleeding, and relieve nausea and dysentery. Externally, a wash used for eczema, burns, scalds, and infections. American soldiers in the Revolutionary War drank the tea before battles to lessen bleeding if wounded. Modern laboratory tests demonstrate hemostatic, antibacterial, and antifungal activity. In Asia the root is added to prescriptions used to treat blood in the stool and bleeding hemorrhoids, to slow excessive uterine bleeding, and topically for sores, ulcers, and burns. Powdered root used clinically for second- and third-degree burns. **WARNING:** Contains tannins, which are contraindicated for burns in Western medicine.

FLOWERS SMALL, INCONSPICUOUS; MISCELLANEOUS AQUATIC OR WETLAND PLANTS

WHORLED MARSH PENNYWORT
Hydrocotyle umbellata L.

Whole plant
Parsley Family

Spreading, low-growing perennial. Round leaves with wavy margin on slender stalks. Small flowers in umbels on stalks a little higher than leaves; Mar.–July. Small green *fruits smell like parsley when crushed.* **WHERE FOUND:** Along streams and marshes, swampy ground. S. Calif. coast. to eastern N. America; Mexico, s. Africa. **USES:** Seminole used plant tea to relieve coughs and shortness of breath and to strengthen respiratory tract. Roots used as sedative. **RELATED SPECIES:** Several species used in China, India, and elsewhere, notably *H. javanica* Thunb. and *H. sibthorpioides* Lam. The juice or crushed plant is poulticed for bruises, wounds, dog bites, and swellings. Tea used to reduce sinus congestion, benefit the vision, reduce inflammation of the ears, nose, and throat; also for dysentery, liver problems, and to relieve fevers after childbirth.

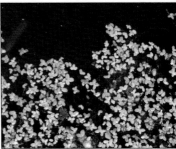

Whorled Marsh Pennywort (Hydrocotyle umbellata) has round leaves with a wavy margin.

Duckweed (Spirodela polyrrhiza) is a tiny plant forming large colonies.

DUCKWEED   **Whole plant**
Spirodela polyrrhiza (L.) Schleid.   Duckweed Family
    Minute floating plant, 5–10 mm. Typically in large colonies. *Plant body round to ovate, flat, symmetrical, 7–12-veined*; smooth, dark green above, reddish purple below. Rootlets 5–16; flowers rare. **WHERE FOUND:** Fresh, still waters, slow streams. Calif. to B.C., every state; worldwide. **USES:** In China a tea used for urinary tract infections with edema, congestive heart disease, measles, skin eruptions, and for treating body aches and fevers due to influenza. Studies show that duckweed has a fever-lowering effect. **WARNING:** May accumulate heavy metals and other toxins from polluted waters.

LARGE PLANTS; LEAVES TO 1 FT. LONG OR MORE

CASTORBEAN   **Seed oil**
Ricinus communis L.   Spurge Family
    Large herbaceous annual or perennial, 5–12 ft. Leaves large, palmately 5–11-lobed; margins sharply toothed. Female flowers above, male flowers in dense clusters at branch tips; May–Sept. *Spiny* fruit 3-parted, opening to release 3 mottled, smooth, shiny seeds. **WHERE FOUND:** Waste places, disturbed sites, roadsides. Escaped exotic from Eurasia; widely cultivated as an ornamental. Calif., Utah, Ariz., Tex. **Uses:** Castor oil famous since ancient Egyptian times as a purgative or laxative. Oil used as a laxative in food poisoning, taken before X-ray diagnosis of bowels. Also used to treat colic, diarrhea, dysentery, enteritis, acute constipation, and worms. Used externally for itching, ringworm, warts, dandruff, hair loss, hemorrhoids. The castor oil pack was popularized

Castorbean (Ricinus communis) *is a large-leaved tropical annual with green to red seed capsules.*

American White Hellebore (Veratrum viride), *with greenish flowers and pleated leaves.*

by the mystic Edgar Cayce to treat cancer, cysts, and tumors; it is still widely used as a folk cancer treatment. Leaf poultices used in Hawaii to treat headaches and children's fevers. In India a leaf poultice applied to boils and sores. The oil contains lectins with proven immune-stimulating properties that act orally or after absorption through the skin. In some African countries the seeds are used, perhaps dangerously, as an oral contraceptive. **WARNING:** The seeds are deadly poisonous. A single seed has caused fatalities in children. Do not use internally. The toxic principle, ricin, is not found in the refined oil. Avoid long-term use or use during pregnancy. Ricin, one of the most toxic known compounds, has been researched as an anticancer and anti-AIDS drug following bioengineering of the molecule.

AMERICAN WHITE OR FALSE HELLEBORE   Root, leaves
Veratrum viride Ait.   Lily Family

Stout, single-stemmed perennial from thick rhizome; to 7 ft. Leaves alternate, *large*, clasping, *pleated, with prominent parallel veins. Leaves emerge in early spring.* Star-shaped, musky-scented flowers in dense, open panicle, *lower branches drooping*; Apr.–Aug. **WHERE FOUND:** Wet, subalpine meadows, forest openings.

Nw. Calif. to Alaska, Idaho, Mont., Wyo., Utah; eastern N. America. **USES:** Traditionally, preparations of the toxic root were used to treat cough, sore throat, tonsillitis, bronchitis, pleurisy, early pneumonia, mastoiditis, fever, headaches, internal pains, nephritis, cystitis, hepatitis, peritonitis, gout, rheumatism, high blood pressure, heart disorders, irregular menstruation, and epilepsy; also as an emetic for stomach pain, to induce abortion and produce sterility, to treat puerperal infections, as a sedative, to treat insanity, and to commit suicide. Poultices or a wash of the root (sometimes leaves) used for aches and pains, bruises, sprains, fractures, swellings, skin infections, boils, rashes, itching, dandruff, sore throat, respiratory infections, and for growing hair. Powdered root has been used as a snuff to treat sinus infection headaches and to clear nasal passages. **WARNING:** Very toxic. Fatalities reported. Causes severe nausea and vomiting, bradycardia shock (due to alkaloids that act to sedate the heart muscles) and death. The plant's emetic properties probably prevent worse poisoning in many cases.

ORCHID FLOWERS
(3-PARTED WITH EXPANDED LOWER LIP)

STREAM ORCHID, GIANT HELLEBORINE   **Root**
Epipactis gigantea Dougl. ex Hook .   Orchid Family

Hairless perennial, *often forming clumps*; to 3 ft. Leaves alternate, *lance-shaped*, bases sheathing; margins entire. S*howy*, greenish to yellowish flowers with *dark purple to brown veins*, in loose, *one-sided raceme*; Apr.–Aug. Upper half of lip yellow, *tip grooved*. **WHERE FOUND:** Wet places, meadows, streambanks. Through- out w. N. America to the Rocky Mtns.; Baja Calif., n. Mexico. **USES:** American Indian groups used root as a general

Stream Orchid (Epipactis gigantea) *forms large clumps.*

tonic; also to treat mania and severe illness and as a mild relaxing tea. Used for purification of the "evil spirit of the north, or dark night," and in the puberty rites of young girls. **RELATED SPECIES:** In parts of Asia, crushed leaves and stems of *E. mairei* Schlecht. are poulticed to ease pain of burns and scalds. The plant contains abundant mucilage.

FLOWERS 4-PARTED

MONUMENT PLANT, GREEN GENTIAN
Swertia radiata (Kellogg) Kuntze
[*Frasera speciosa* Dougl. ex Griseb.]

Roots, leaves
Gentian Family

    Stout, thick-stemmed perennial, to 6 ft. *Large basal leaves* oblanceolate; stem leaves *whorled*; margins entire. Greenish yellow flowers purple-dotted, *each petal with 2 oblong, fringed nectary pits at base*; in dense panicles; June–Aug. **WHERE FOUND:** Mountain meadows, open forests. Throughout the West. **USES:** Historically used as a bitter digestive stimulant and tonic for stimulating appetite and digestion, especially in older people. American Indian groups also used it to ease diarrhea, colds, and asthma, as a tonic for general weakness, to fortify hunters, as a mild sedative, and to treat gonorrhea; externally, poulticed for headaches. **RELATED SPECIES:** *F. caroliniensis* Walt., American Columbo, used in digestive tonics; historically prescribed by physicians to cure persistent constipation. Asian species used similarly.

Monument Plant (Swertia radiata) *has greenish yellow, purple-dotted flowers.*

COYOTE TOBACCO
Leaves

Nicotiana attenuata Torr. ex. S. Wats. — Nightshade Family

 Malodorous, sparsely glandular annual; to 5 ft. Leaves alternate, lance-shaped, *on obvious petioles*; margins entire. *Slender*, trumpet-shaped flowers greenish to white, sometimes pink-tinged, in racemes; May–Nov. **WHERE FOUND:** Open, sandy areas; disturbed sites. Calif. to B.C., Idaho, Nev., Utah, Ariz.; Rockies from Mont. to N.M., Tex.; nw. Mexico. **USES:** American Indian groups smoked herb ceremonially and to induce visions. Culturally and economically, the various native tobacco species were among the most important plants. This species is one of the main sources of tobacco throughout western N. America. Medicinally, leaves poulticed for eczema, skin rashes, rheumatic swellings, coughs, toothache, dandruff, hair loss, cuts, and snakebite. Wash used to treat aches and pains, edema, hives, athlete's foot, and skin irritations. Smoked, often mixed with other herbs, to treat colds, asthma, tuberculosis, and headaches. Smoke blown in ear to treat earaches. Snuff used to treat nasal discharge or nosebleed. Weak tea has emetic and cathartic effects; used to treat measles, respiratory disease, and worms. **Related species:** *N. rustica* L., Aztec Tobacco, and *N. tabacum* L., Common Tobacco, used similarly. **Warning:** Contains nicotine, a toxic and highly addictive alkaloid.

FRINGECUP, PRAIRIE-CUPS
Whole plant

Tellima grandiflora (Pursh) Dougl. ex Lindl — Saxifrage Family

Coarse-haired perennial, to 3 ft. Leaves mostly *basal*, shallowly palmately lobed, *heart-shaped*; margins toothed. *Cup-shaped* flowers green, *becoming rose colored*, in long, *one-sided raceme*; petals *fringed*; Apr.–June. **WHERE FOUND:** Moist forests, streambanks, rocky sites. Cen. to n. coast ranges, Klamath Range of Calif., to s.

Coyote Tobacco (Nicotiana attenuata) has a rank, biting smell.

Fringecup (Tellima grandiflora) has rounded leaves.

Fringecup has strongly fringed petals.

Alaska, Idaho, Mont. **USES:** Plant tea used to stimulate depressed appetite. Reported to have been chewed to prevent dreaming of having sexual intercourse with the dead; said to have been used by forest elves to improve night vision.

SPURGE FAMILY

COPPERLEAF, YERBA DEL CANCER
Leaves

Acalypha lindheimeri Muell.-Arg.
Spurge Family

 Upright to low-spreading, multibranched perennial; to 16 in. Leaves alternate, lance-shaped; margins toothed. Small *male and female flowers in dense spike at stem tips, male flowers above female*, petals lacking; June–Sept. Bract below female flower ovate, deeply lobed; stigmas 3, *fringed, red*. **WHERE FOUND:** Dry sites. Ariz., N.M., Tex.; Mexico. **USES:** Weak tea is used by Hispanics to heal stomach and duodenal ulcers. **RELATED SPECIES:** *A. californica* Benth. from the Sonoran desert of Calif. is also called Yerba del Cancer. In India, leaves and flowers of *A. indica* L. used as laxative and for digestive problems; externally to stop bleeding of wounds. In Malaysia and China, dried leaves of five species used for diarrhea. **WARNING:** Do not use fresh plant internally; it can cause nausea and vomiting.

Copperleaf (Acalypha californica) has copper-colored stems.

Turkey Mullein (Croton setigerus) is gray-hairy throughout.

TURKEY MULLEIN, DOVE-WEED
Roots, leaves
Croton setigerus Hook.   Spurge Family

⚠ *Gray-green*, densely hairy annual, *forming low, rounded clumps*; *strong-scented*; to 8 in. Hairs *stiff, irritating*, multibranched or *star-shaped*. Leaves alternate, ovate, clustered at stem tips, *prominently 3-veined*. Minute male and female flowers without petals, in separate clusters; May–Oct. **WHERE FOUND:** Dry, open places, often in sandy or heavy soils; disturbed sites, along roads. Calif. to Wash., Idaho, Nev., Utah, Ariz. **USES:** American Indian groups used root tea for dysentery, bleeding diarrhea, headaches, fevers, and chills. Bruised-leaf poultice applied to chest as a counterirritant for internal pains. Added to baths to treat typhoid and other fevers. As a folk medicine, plant used to help heal liver ailments and dissolve gallstones. The abundant seeds are eaten by doves. **RELATED SPECIES:** The seeds of *C. tiglium* L. are the Chinese drug ba dou, included in prescriptions for constipation, fullness, and pain related to cold stagnation of the digestive organs; for water retention and mucus clogging the throat and contributing to wheezing and difficulty in breathing. **WARNING:** The seeds, considered toxic in Chinese medicine, are used in minute amounts with other ingredients. The herb is said to "chop through the gate and force open the door." The whole plant should be considered toxic.

TEXAS CROTON
Whole plant
Croton texensis (Klotzsch) Muell.-Arg.   Spurge Family

☠ *Grayish white*, hairy annual, to 3 ft. Hairs multibranched to *star-shaped*. Leaves alternate, lance-shaped to oblong, *yellowish green below*; margins entire. Small male and female flowers *on separate plants*; male flowers in *dense, terminal spikes*, female flowers *few*, *in clusters*; petals absent; May– Oct. **WHERE FOUND:** Dry prairies, plains, sandy soils; disturbed sites. Ariz., Utah, Wyo., Colo., N.M., Tex., to Great Plains; Mexico. **USES:** American Indian groups made plant tea for stomach disorders; also as a purgative, emetic, and diuretic. A leaf tea taken for gonorrhea or syphilis. Tea of whole ground plant mixed with salt taken for headaches and body aches. Seeds placed in the ears to improve hearing, ground seeds applied to open sores. Roots crushed and applied to hemorrhoids. **RELATED SPECIES:** The Cahuilla of s. Calif. used California Croton, *C. californicus* Muell.-Arg., in a hot stem and leaf tea in small doses to relieve congestion caused by colds. The bark of Cascarilla of the West Indies, *C. eleutena* (L.) Sw., is used in European herbalism as a stimulating digestive tonic to ease abdominal pain, gas, and diarrhea. **WARNING:** Most, if not all, *Croton* species are toxic and extremely caustic. Traditionally used only in minute doses.

PEPLYS, PETTY SPURGE   **Herb, sap**
Euphorbia peplus L.   Spurge Family

Hairless reddish green annual with *milky sap*, to 18 in. *Delicate*, obovate to round leaves alternate below, opposite above; margins entire. Small flower cup with *4 yellowish, crescent-shaped bracts along rim, each 2-horned*; Feb.–Aug. **WHERE FOUND:** Disturbed sites, gardens as a weed. Throughout N. America. Alien (Europe). **USES:** Known to the ancient Greek physicians Hippocrates and Galen as *peplis*, the herb or its milky sap was applied to the skin to elimi-

(Left) *Texas Croton* (Croton texensis) *is a gray-green, low-growing annual.* (Above) *Peplys* (Euphorbia peplus). *Note the cups surrounding each flower.*

Stillingia (Stillingia sylvatica) *has finely toothed, glandular leaves.*

nate warts. Leaf and stem tea used to ease mucous congestion in respiratory ailments. **WARNING:** Milky juice contains toxic and highly irritating diterpenes. Keep away from the eyes. Avoid internal use.

STILLINGIA, QUEEN'S-ROOT, QUEEN'S-DELIGHT
Root

Stillingia sylvatica Garden ex L.   Spurge Family

⚠ *Hairless* perennial with *milky sap*, to 3 ft. Leaves alternate, narrowly oval to (ob)lanceolate; margins *finely toothed, glandular.* Male and female flowers in dense spikes from *leaf axils*, male flowers above female; petals absent; bract below female flower *entire*; May–Aug. **WHERE FOUND:** Sandy soils, dunes, prairies, streambanks, disturbed sites. N.M. to se. Colo., Tex., southeastern U.S.; Mexico. **USES:** Stillingia was once listed in the *United States Pharmacopoeia* for treatment of secondary syphilis, glandular tuberculosis, skin diseases, and chronic hepatitis. Small doses of tincture were recommended; larger doses are emetic and cathartic. The fresh root is much more irritating and nauseating than the dried root. Historically, physicians prescribed Stillingia for chronic bronchitis, chronic coughs, laryngitis, croup, and chronic arthritis. American Indian groups used it for venereal disease, irregular periods, and diarrhea. Cold tea of crushed roots was used as an herbal Viagra. **WARNING:** Fresh root contains caustic milky juice. Avoid ingestion except on the advice (unlikely) of a physician.

SLENDER, MOSTLY TERMINAL FLOWER CLUSTERS OR IN LEAF AXILS; GOOSEFOOT AND BUCKWHEAT FAMILY

YARD KNOTWEED, PROSTRATE KNOTWEED

Root, leaves

Polygonum aviculare L. — Buckwheat Family

Bluish green, hairless annual. Slender, *wiry* stems low-growing to upright; to 4 ft. Leaves small, alternate, lance-shaped to oblong, with *silvery, papery, often torn sheath at base of petiole*; margins entire. Small clusters of green, white, or pink flowers in *leaf axils*; May–Nov. **WHERE FOUND:** Open, dry disturbed sites; saline soils. Widespread weed throughout N. America. Alien (Eurasia). **USES:** Traditionally used as an astringent for treating gastrointestinal tract disorders, diarrhea, and gastroenteritis. Also used for respiratory problems and to check internal bleeding. American Indian groups adopted it to treat urinary calculi, painful urination, blood in the urine, and stomachache; externally, poulticed for pain, cuts, swelling, and inflammation. Choctaw women drank a tea to prevent abortion. The Chinese treat painful urination as well as itching and worms with this species.

COMMON SMARTWEED, MILD WATER-PEPPER

Root, leaves

Polygonum hydropiper L. — Buckwheat Family

⚠️ Annual; branched, *reddish stems*, to 2 ft. *Nodes swollen*. Leaves lance-shaped, alternate, on short petioles; coarsely hairy on

(Above) *Yard Knotweed* (Polygonum aviculare) *is a weed once used to treat stomach problems.*
(Right) *Common Smartweed* (Polygonum hydropiper) *has stems with swollen nodes.*

Sheep Sorrel (Rumex acetosella) *produces reddish fruits. The plants often cover old infertile fields.*

midrib below. Brown, papery bracts surrounding stem at leaf base, coarsely hairy with stiff bristled margin. Small, greenish flowers with white or pale rose margins in nodding, elongated spikes at stem tips; June–Nov. **WHERE FOUND:** Moist or wet soils, marsh edges, shores. Widespread throughout N. America. Alien (Europe). **USES:** Traditionally used in Europe for colds and coughs, both as an extract and as a mustard plaster; externally, juice and extracts applied to various skin ailments, hemorrhoids, scabies, and sores. Tea gargled for toothache and laryngitis. Historically, physicians prescribed it for kidney stones, colds, and coughs. Externally, poulticed for chronic ulcers, hemorrhoids, inflammation of the skin, and flatulent colic. American Indian groups adopted it as a diuretic for urinary problems; externally, poulticed for pain, swelling, and headaches. Leaf tea a folk remedy for internal bleeding and menstrual or uterine disorders. Contains pungent compounds (hence the name Water-pepper). **WARNING:** May irritate the skin and is unpleasantly acrid when chewed fresh.

SHEEP SORREL   **Leaves, root**
Rumex acetosella L.   Buckwheat Family
Slender-stemmed, aggressive, hairless perennial from rhizome; to 4–12 in. Leaves mostly *basal, arrowhead-shaped*, slightly succulent, *sour-tasting*. Flowers tiny; greenish or red-tinted male and female flowers on separate plants, arranged in *whorled clusters on interrupted racemes;* Feb.–Sept. **WHERE FOUND:** Moist, disturbed areas, roadsides, lawns. Widespread weed throughout N. America. Alien (Europe). **USES:** American Indian groups used the leaves as a poultice to warts, bruises, and sores, and internally as a digestive tonic, diuretic, cooling herb, and liver cleanser, and for tuberculosis. An ingredient in an unproven alternative cancer remedy called essiac. The plant is rich in antioxidant and antimutagenic com-

pounds. The English botanist John Evelyn (1620–1706) wrote that sorrel is good for improving the appetite, cooling the liver, and strengthening the heart. **RELATED SPECIES:** *R. acetosella* is often substituted for the similar French Sorrel, *R. acetosa* L., used to treat fevers, bleeding, boils, wens, and skin tumors and as a diuretic.

YELLOW DOCK, CURLY DOCK
Root, leaves

Rumex crispus L.   Buckwheat Family

Stout, hairless perennial from *yellow taproot*; to 1–5 ft. Leaves alternate, lance-shaped to oblong; margins *strongly wavy*; papery sheath at base of petiole. Flowers green, on spikes; Jan.–Dec. Single-seeded fruit 3-angled, *enclosed by 3 papery, heart-shaped, veined bracts.* **WHERE FOUND:** Disturbed areas, fields, meadows. Widespread weed throughout N. America. Alien (Eurasia). **USES:** Traditionally, herbalists considered it a blood purifier and used it to treat chronic skin diseases, chronic enlarged lymph glands, for skin sores, rheumatism, liver ailments, sore throats, gall bladder ailments, diarrhea, dysentery, indigestion, constipation, jaundice, anemia, and other conditions. Roots were used internally in teas and tinctures; in ointments and salves. Used to treat skin ailments, including acne, eczema, scabies, mouth sores, chafed skin in infants, boils, ulcers, burns, itching, athlete's foot, bruises, muscle strains and pain, swelling, wounds, and cuts. Adopted by American Indian groups for similar uses. The root of *Rumex* species contains varying amounts of tannins and anthraquinone glycosides, the active compounds in stimulant laxatives. Depending upon variables such as harvest time and concentration of components, tannins may relieve diarrhea, while anthraquinones will induce a laxative effect. The levels of these compounds are usually insufficient to cause a laxative effect; rather, the root usually acts as a gentle bowel astringent, considered useful by herbalists in treating mild diarrhea or con-

Yellow Dock (Rumex crispus). *Note the crisp-edged leaves.*

stipation, often combined with other herbs. **WARNING:** This and other *Rumex* species contain varying amounts of oxalic acid; use should be avoided by those susceptible to kidney stones. Acute oxalate poisoning also reported in sheep.

CANAIGRE, DESERT DOCK, DESERT RHUBARB
Rumex hymenosepalus Torr.

Roots, leaves
Buckwheat Family

Stout, hairless perennial from *clustered tuberlike roots*; to 1–4 ft. Large, alternate leaves, lance-shaped to oblong, *fleshy*; margins wavy. Flowers in whorls on *dense, terminal panicle*; Dec.–May. **WHERE FOUND:** Dry, sandy places, deserts. Lower Calif. to Nev., Ariz., Utah, Wyo., Colo., N.M., w. Tex.; Baja Calif. **USES:** Southwest Indians used teas or chewed herb or root for diarrhea, sore throat, colds, and coughs. Externally, root tea used as a wash or poulticed to treat skin sores, sore gums, bites, and infected cuts. The Arapaho used a stem and leaf tea to wash sores. Some tribes considered this common desert plant a life medicine, or panacea. The root contains an average of 25 percent or more tannins, and the plant was investigated as a possible commercial source of tannins. In 1896 a bulletin of the Texas Agricultural Experiment Station (at what is now Texas A & M University) promoted Canaigre as a plant to be used in tanning, but an industry never developed. Enterprising but unethical entrepreneurs attempted to market the root in the late 1970s as "Wild Red American Ginseng" or "Wild Red Desert Ginseng." Fortunately, this fraud did not persist in the marketplace. **WARNING:** Contains extremely high levels of tannins. **May cause poisoning** due to high oxalic acid and tannin content.

Canaigre (Rumex hymenosepalus) *is common in southwestern deserts.*

Broad Bitter Dock (Rumex obtusifolius) *leaves have a heart-shaped base.*

BROAD BITTER DOCK
Rumex obtusifolius L.

Roots, leaves
Buckwheat Family

Stout, hairless perennial, to 2–5 ft. Large, alternate leaves lance-shaped to ovate; *base rounded to heart-shaped; margins flat to slightly wavy.* Flowers in loose whorls on open, highly branched interrupted panicle; June–Dec. Single-seeded fruit 3-angled, enclosed by 3 papery, veined bracts; *each bract with toothed margin.* **WHERE FOUND:** Moist areas. Widespread throughout N. America. Native to w. Europe. Hybridizes with *R. crispus.* **USES:** Bitter Dock used historically as substitute for Yellow Dock. It was used externally and internally to treat skin diseases, respiratory conditions, and lymph swellings said to be due to "bad blood." Delaware and Iroquois Indians used it as a tonic and blood purifier. It was also used for children's skin eruptions, whooping cough, jaundice, and as a contraceptive. **WARNING:** This and other *Rumex* species contain varying amounts of oxalic acid; use should be avoided by those susceptible to kidney stones.

SLENDER, MOSTLY TERMINAL FLOWER CLUSTERS OR IN LEAF AXILS; GOOSEFOOT AND BUCKWHEAT FAMILIES

MEXICAN TEA, AMERICAN WORMSEED, EPAZOTE
Chenopodium ambrosioides L.

Seeds, leaves
Goosefoot Family

Sharply aromatic, *mealy-glandular* annual or perennial, 3–5 ft. Leaves alternate, lance-shaped to oblong; margins usually *wavy or scalloped*, much reduced upward. Tiny flowers in *compact, rounded clusters at leaf base*; June–Dec. **WHERE FOUND:** Waste places. Throughout U.S. except Idaho, Mont., Wyo. Native to American tropics. **USES:** Still a popular remedy throughout Latin America,

Mexican Tea (Chenopodium ambrosioides) *has deeply lobed, strongly aromatic leaves.*

the leaf is taken in minute amounts during fasting, as a spring tonic, and for fever. Weak leaf tea occasionally used for chronic digestive problems such as weak, painful digestion with nausea, bloating, and pain. Externally, leaves poulticed for swelling, headaches, and rheumatism. The stewed seeds were also used to expel worms. In Mexican cooking a few leaves are added to beans during cooking to increase digestibility and lessen production of gas. Traditionally, seed tincture used against roundworms, hookworms, and small tapeworms, in conjunction with lubricant laxative such as castor oil. Until the late 20th century, physicians prescribed preparations of seed oil for roundworms, hookworms, dwarf (not large) tapeworms, intestinal amoeba. Now largely replaced by synthetic drugs. **WARNING:** The seeds contain an oil with toxic compounds such as ascaridole. Seeds and especially seed oil **highly toxic**; fatalities reported. Never use Epazote seed except under medical advice. May cause dermatitis or an allergic reaction. Foster has experienced vertigo from contact with essential oil released during harvest.

TUMBLEWEED, RUSSIAN THISTLE

Salsola tragus L.
[*S. kali* spp. *tragus* (L.) Allen]

Whole plant
Goosefoot Family

The familiar tumbleweed of Western movies. Multibranched annual *forming rounded bush*; to 2–4 ft. *Linear, spine-tipped* leaves alternate, becoming rigid. Flowers *solitary in leaf axils*; July–Oct. Plant breaks apart from root mass at maturity and is *blown around by the wind*, hence the common name. **WHERE FOUND:** Dis-

(Left) *Tumbleweed* (Salsola tragus). *Note the papery bracts.*
(Above) *Tumbleweed* (Salsola tragus) *is familiar from Western movies.*

turbed sites, dry habitats. Throughout U.S., especially deserts. Noxious weed native to Eurasia. **USES:** Historically, this was one of a number of plants burned to make a carbonate of soda called barilla from the ash. As a European folk remedy, the plant was used as a worm remedy, laxative, and diuretic. Experimentally, extracts or compounds from it lower blood pressure and have smooth muscle–relaxing effects. **RELATED SPECIES:** *S. collina* Pall. is used for hypertension and headaches in China. Science confirms tranquilizing effects.

FLOWERS IN AXILS; PLANTS WITH STINGING OR BRISTLY HAIRS

STINGING NETTLE
Urtica dioica L.

Leaves, root, stems
Nettle Family

Perennial with *stiff, stinging hairs, forming thickets;* 12–50 in. *Leaves opposite,* mostly ovate, on *angled stems;* margins coarsely toothed. Flowers tiny, greenish, in drooping clusters; Apr.–Sept. Genetic material from N. America, designated *U. dioica* ssp. *gracilis* (Ait.) Seland., with six varieties, differs from the European *U. dioica* ssp. *dioica* in that the American material has male and female flowers on separate plants. **WHERE FOUND:** Moist areas, disturbed sites. Lab. to Alaska, southward. European subspecies occasionally naturalized in our range. **USES:** Nettle tea has been used in Europe for centuries as a diuretic for kidney inflammation, water retention, and chronic bladder infections; to allay excess menstruation, nosebleeds, hemorrhoids, and digestive tract bleeding; and as a spring blood tonic. Nettle herb beer an old folk remedy for easing gout and rheumatic pains. Historically, physicians prescribed nettle herb juice, tea, or tincture to stop internal bleeding and to cure persistent bladder infections, chronic diarrhea, and eczema. Root tea used for hives, itch, dysentery, urinary retention, as a hair tonic, and as a general tonic. Fresh leaf juice applied to skin for sores, infections, rashes, and warts, and to the scalp to prevent hair loss. The whole plant is still decocted and mixed with vinegar as a restorative hair rinse. The fresh plant is commonly used in Latin America as a counterirritant on stiff and sore joints and muscles, sciatica, and bruises. The patient is flogged with the fresh plants, presumably setting up an immune reaction that relieves symptoms of the original ailment. Leaf poulticed for arthritis, skin inflammation, sores, and heat rash. Leaves approved in Germany for supportive treatment of rheumatism and kidney infections. Root preparations approved for symptomatic relief of urinary difficulties associated with early stages of benign prostatic hyperplasia, which affects a majority of men over 50. Laboratory and human studies show the herb extract is di-

Stinging Nettle (Urtica dioica) *is seldom noticed until one touches the plant.*

Field Nettle (Urtica urens) *is a much smaller plant in all respects.*

Cocklebur (Xanthium strumarium) *has characteristic burrs on seedpods.*

uretic and hemostatic and has a mild blood sugar–lowering effect. Some physicians advocate nettle as a natural antihistamine for relieving symptoms of hay fever, though one clinical study shows no statistical significance compared with a placebo. **RELATED SPECIES:** The small field nettle, *U. urens* L., a common weed, though weaker than *U. dioica*, is used similarly. **WARNING:** Fresh plants **sting.** Dried plant (used in tea) does not sting.

COCKLEBUR
Xanthium strumarium L.

Roots, leaves, burs, seeds
Composite Family

Stout annual weed, 2–5 ft. Leaves alternate, *triangular,* on long stalks; margins coarsely toothed. Flowers inconspicuous, green. Fruits oval, with *crowded hooked prickles*; Sept.–Nov. **WHERE FOUND:** Disturbed areas. Cosmopolitan weed throughout N. America and elsewhere. **USES:** Chinese, American Indian, and European traditions used herb for treating urinary disorders, skin problems, and to reduce pain. American Indian groups also used root for fever and as a uterine stimulant for placental delivery. Plant used to treat rheumatism, kidney disease, cystitis, gonorrhea, vomiting, diarrhea, and tuberculosis. A poultice or tea of seeds used on sores and wounds. The Chinese also used it for ear problems, headaches, and to lower blood sugar. Modern studies show antibacterial, cytotoxic, and trypanocidal effects of extracts. **WARNING:** Large dose or chronic use can be toxic to the liver. Toxic to, and mostly avoided by, grazing animals.

FLOWERS IN TERMINAL CLUSTERS; LEAVES MOSTLY SILVER-HAIRY, AT LEAST BENEATH; ARTEMISIAS

ANNUAL WORMWOOD, SWEET ANNIE

Leaves, seeds

Artemisia annua L. — Composite Family

Sweet-scented, bushy annual; 1–9 ft. Leaves 3-divided, *fernlike* segments oblong to lance-shaped, sharp-toothed or cleft. Tiny, green-yellow flowers, in clusters; July–Oct. **WHERE FOUND:** Waste ground. Throughout. Alien (Asia). **USES:** In Asia, leaf tea used for colds, flu, malarial fevers, dysentery, diarrhea. Externally, poulticed on abscesses and boils. A famous remedy in China for chlorquinine-resistant malaria. The active component currently used in tropical areas of the world for some forms of malaria, which is still a serious disease. Contains a half dozen or more antiviral compounds, some proven synergetic. **WARNING:** May cause allergic reactions or dermatitis.

CALIFORNIA MUGWORT

Whole plant

Artemisia douglasiana Bess. — Composite Family

Aromatic, branching perennial to 5 ft. Leaves alternate, lance-shaped to oval, gray-green and hairless above, densely white-woolly beneath; margins entire or with 3–5 shallow, irregular, pointed lobes near tip. Flowers greenish yellow, in numerous small, nodding heads; June–Oct. **WHERE FOUND:** Open to shady sites, fields, forest edges, streambanks. Calif. to e. Wash., n. Idaho, w. Nev.; Baja Calif. **USES:** American Indians burned the plant over a fire and inhaled the fumes to treat the flu. The strongly aromatic green leaves were poulticed, and tea used

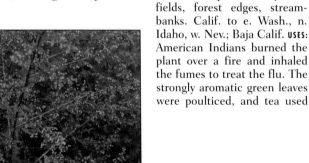

Annual Wormwood (Artemisia annua) has finely divided aromatic leaves.

as a wash or liniment with alcohol for rheumatism, arthritis, back pain, headaches. Heated leaves were held over the ear for earache and placed on an infant's severed umbilical cord. Smoke from burning plant inhaled for flu symptoms. The Paiutes placed branches over a bed of ashes and slept on them to treat colds and fever. Plant tea used for urinary problems, asthma, stomachache, cramps from diarrhea, suppressed or excessive menses, menstrual cramps, rheumatism, to keep young girls from premature aging, used as a hair wash to prevent balding, as a wash for itching sores, and used in steam baths for difficult labor. A fresh leaf infusion was given to children for pinworms. Used today by California herbalists to ease the pain of gallbladder stones and spasms. This species was an important magic plant to a number of American Indian tribes, used to enhance dreaming, worn to keep ghosts away and to avoid thinking of and affording protection from the dead. **WARNING:** This and other *Artemisia* species contain the neurotoxic and mutagenic compound thujone in varying amounts. Probably more is extracted in alcohol than in water, so weak teas are safer than tinctures. Traditionally, most *Artemisia* preparations were made with water.

California Mugwort (Artemisia douglasiana) *is used as a moxa, much as Common Mugwort (page 247)* (A. vulgaris) *is.*

Tarragon (Artemisia dracunculus) *is a common fragrance herb used in cooking.*

TARRAGON

Artemisia dracunculus L.

Whole plant
Composite Family

Branching perennial, to 5 ft.; scent of anise or odorless. Leaves alternate, linear, bright green, hairless; margins entire. Flowers greenish in small, nodding heads; July–Oct. **WHERE FOUND:** Open, dry sites, meadows, disturbed sites. Calif. to Alaska, every western state; Baja Calif., n. Mexico, Eurasia. **USES:** American Indian groups used a root tea for colds, dysentery, diarrhea, headaches, difficult childbirth, urinary disorders, and infant colic. Taken to promote appetite. Externally, used as a wash for arthritis, swellings, bruises, rheumatism, and for itching from chickenpox. Powdered leaves sprinkled on open sores. Fresh leaves mashed, moistened, and applied to forehead for headaches; placed in steam baths for rheumatic or arthritic pain; also used in diapers or as a diaper to alleviate diaper rash or raw skin. Sometimes substituted for the cooking herb French Tarragon, grown commercially in California, which does not produce viable seed and must be propagated vegetatively. French Tarragon smells strongly of anise; Wild Tarragon is often odorless and flavorless. **WARNING:** Relatively rare allergic reactions may result from use.

WESTERN MUGWORT, WHITE SAGE, CUDWEED

Artemisia ludoviciana Nutt.

Leaves, stems
Composite Family

Aromatic, branched perennial to 3 ft. Stems and both sides of leaves *densely white-woolly*. Leaves alternate, linear to narrowly lance-shaped; margins entire, toothed, or deeply lobed. Flowers greenish yellow in nodding heads on dense, elongated, narrow or open panicles; July–Oct. **WHERE FOUND:** Dry, open sites, disturbed sites; sandy to rocky soils. Every western state; n. Mexico. **USES:** Much used by American Indians as an astringent, to induce sweating, and to curb pain and diarrhea. Leaf tea was used for diarrhea, indigestion, tonsillitis, chest and throat constriction, colds, fever, flu, gastrointestinal disorders, and sore throat. A strong tea was given to women to facilitate labor. Externally, as a wash for eczema, bruising, itching, arthritis, and body odor. American Indians stuffed crushed leaves into the nostrils to allay nosebleed and into moccasins as a foot deodorant. Leaf snuff also used for nosebleeds, sinus attacks, headache, and sinus headache. Leaf poultice or tincture used on long-standing sores, cuts, blisters, broken bones, insect bites, and spider bites; rubbed on swollen areas and on boils to burst them. The leaves were chewed for colds and for children's respiratory disorders. **WARNING:** May cause allergic reactions or contact dermatitis.

Western Mugwort (Artemisia ludoviciana) *leaves and stems are densely white-woolly.*

Common Mugwort (Artemisia vulgaris) *has deeply cut leaves that are silver-woolly beneath.*

COMMON MUGWORT

Leaves

Artemisia vulgaris L.   Composite Family

Aromatic; 2–4 ft. Leaves *deeply cut, silvery-woolly beneath.* Flowerheads erect; July–Aug. **WHERE FOUND:** Waste ground. S. Canada to Ga.; Kans., Mich.; occasional westward. Alien weed (Eurasia). **USES:** Leaf tea used as a diuretic, to induce sweating, check menstrual irregularity, promote appetite, and as a nerve tonic. Used for bronchitis, colds, colic, epilepsy, fevers, kidney ailments, sciatica. Experimentally, mugwort lowers blood sugar and is antibacterial and antifungal. Dried, finely shredded leaves are rolled into cigar-shaped tube as a "burning stick" (moxa), famous in Chinese medicine, to stimulate acupuncture points, treat rheumatism. Once lighted and smoldering, the sticks are used to warm different energy centers of the body to ease pain syndromes and diseases. Application of heat and interaction of the skin surface with volatile essential oil components may stimulate an immune and nervous system response. Moxa treatments have been clinically shown to lower incidence of breach birth presentations. **WARNING:** May cause dermatitis. Reported to cause abortion and allergic reactions.

WESTERN RAGWEED, YERBA SAPO

Whole plant

Ambrosia psilostachya DC.

Composite Family

Aromatic perennial, to 5 ft. Straw-colored stems rough- or soft-hairy, glandular. Leaves opposite, deeply pinnately lobed, hairy; lobes coarsely toothed or entire. Male flowers in separate heads on long, nodding racemes, each head surrounded by shallow cup. Solitary female flower in leaf axils below racemes; July–Nov. **WHERE FOUND:** Common weed of roadsides, disturbed sites, fields. W. Calif. to Wash., every western state; eastern N. America, n. Mexico. **USES:** American Indian groups heated the leaves and applied them to aching joints. Steeped leaves were placed as a poultice over sore eyes. Leaf tea used as a wash for sores and dandruff. Tea from ground leaves and stems used for colds, bowel cramping, constipation, bloody stools. Tea taken during difficult labor. **WARNING:** Ragweed pollen famously causes late summer allergies. Ingesting or touching plant may cause allergic reactions. Pollen from the genus *Ambrosia* is responsible for approximately 90 percent of pollen-induced allergies in the U.S. Goldenrods (*Solidago* species) are often implicated by association because they bloom at the same times as the inconspicuous green flowers of ragweeds.

Western Ragweed (Ambrosia psilostachya) *has pinnately divided leaves.*

HORSEWEED, CANADA FLEABANE
Conyza canadensis (L.) Cronq.
[*Erigeron canadensis* L.]

Whole plant
Composite Family

Bristly annual or biennial weed, 1–7 ft. Leaves alternate, *narrowly lance-shaped, numerous*; margins entire. Tiny greenish white flowers (to ¼ in.) on many branches from leaf axils; disk flowers yellow; June–Nov. **WHERE FOUND:** Disturbed sites, fields, roadsides. Prolific weed throughout N. America. **USES:** Cahuilla Indians and other tribes used a leaf tea for diarrhea, postpartum bleeding, as a female remedy, and to ease stomach pain. Fresh leaves and stems were pounded to a juicy mass, poulticed to sore joints, sprains, backaches, injuries, and sunburns, and to remove liver spots or blotches on the skin. Also used externally for acne and applied to snakebites while drinking a tea internally. The plant was simmered and the steam inhaled to open the sinuses and relieve sore throat and cough from common cold. In India the plant is a popular folk medicine for diarrhea and dysentery, postpartum bleeding, kidney and bladder ailments such as urinary calculi and dropsy; used externally for ringworm and eczema. Extracts have demonstrated anti-inflammatory activity in rats. **WARNING:** May cause contact dermatitis.

Horseweed (Conyza canadensis) *is weedy, with inconspicuous greenish flowers*

COMMON JUNIPER

Berries, leaves, bark

Juniperus communis L.

Cypress Family

Mostly *low shrubs* or small trees, to 2–20 ft. Bark reddish brown, shredding off in papery peels. Blue-green leaves *needlelike or awl-like, spreading* on thin, flexible branches. Spicy, aromatic berry-like seed cones numerous, *bright blue to black with a thin, waxy coat*; sticky when crushed. **WHERE FOUND:** Rocky or wooded slopes, forests. Circumboreal in Northern Hemisphere. The most widespread Juniper, occurring in Europe, Asia, and North America; throughout except Tex. **USES:** American Indian groups used preparations for colds, coughs, sore throat, fevers, tuberculosis, kidney and other urinary tract disorders, stomachache, and gastrointestinal problems. Twig tea used for venereal disease, high blood pressure, and as a wash for sore eyes. Boughs often used as fumigant in sweat lodges. Tea of boughs and cones used as a sedative. Bark or fruit poulticed to wounds as an antiseptic. Branch and wood tea was used for postpartum illness, menstrual problems, and teething. Historically, physicians used berries and leafy branches as a gentle stimulant, diuretic, and carminative for skin diseases, digestive and urinary tract problems such as cystitis and gout, and rheumatic pains, and in a vapor bath for bronchial disease. Often combined with more powerful diuretics for edema. Juniper berries, used to flavor gin, are one of the most widely used herbal diuretics. Approved in Germany in teas for stomach complaints and to stimulate appetite. The essential oil has anti-inflammatory, diuretic, spasm-reducing, and intestinal antiseptic activity in laboratory studies. **WARNING:** Excessive use can cause digestive and urinary tract irritation. In Germany, use limited to four weeks. Avoid during pregnancy. Oil may cause blistering on skin.

Common Juniper (Juniperus communis) *berries are used to flavor gin.*

PARASITIC SHRUBS IN TREES: MISTLETOES

*Juniper Mistletoe (*Phoradendron juniperinum*) is found growing in junipers and Incense Cedar.*

JUNIPER MISTLETOE

Plant, berries

Phoradendron juniperinum Engelm. ex Gray — Mistletoe Family

Hairless forked stems square, yellow-green, emerging from host to 15 in. Leaves opposite, reduced to scales. Tiny greenish flowers, 2 per spike; June–Sept. Round, sticky berries white to pinkish or straw-colored. **WHERE FOUND:** *Parasitic on juniper and incense cedar*; pinyon-juniper woodland, ponderosa pine forests. Desert mountains of s. and high Sierra of Calif. to s. Ore., Nev., Utah, Ariz., Colo., N.M., Tex.; Baja Calif., Mexico. **USES:** Juniper mistletoe was a popular remedy with several tribes. The plant was used to protect one against "bad medicine of wizards," especially when related to stomach ailments. Taken as a cold infusion, it was used for digestive problems due to overeating and for children's diarrhea. When taken in quantity, the plant worked as a cleansing purgative. The crushed plant was used externally for rheumatism and warts. An infusion of the plant was drunk to help women relax during childbirth, and an infusion of the twigs, sometimes with other herbs, was used to stop postpartum bleeding. **WARNING:** Deaths of children have been attributed to eating the berries. All American species of mistletoe should be considered potentially toxic. Not for long-term use; avoid large doses.

American Mistletoe (Phoradendron leucarpum) *is easily seen
after the leaves of its host tree
drop in autumn.*

*American Mistletoe has thick, op-
posite leaves.*

AMERICAN MISTLETOE
Leaves, branches

Phoradendron leucarpum (Raf.) Reveal & M. C. Johnston
[*P. flavescens* Nutt. ex Engelm.]   Mistletoe Family

Stout, jointed stems, sparsely gray-hairy, to 24 in. Leaves thick, opposite, oval to obovate, green to yellowish; margins entire. Several tiny, yellowish green flowers in short spikes. Oval, *sticky berries translucent white* to pinkish. **WHERE FOUND:** Parasitic on deciduous trees, such as oak, sycamore, willow, poplar, ash, walnut. N.M., Tex. and eastward; Mexico. **USES:** Eclectic physicians used leaf preparations as an emetic and nerve tonic to treat epilepsy, convulsions, hysteria, delirium, nervous debility, heart problems, uterine bleeding, menstrual problems, and worms. American Indian groups used it for similar purposes and to induce abortion, for rheumatic pains, headache, toothache, lung problems, and general weakness. **WARNING:** Berries can be deadly; leaves and stems potentially toxic.

EUROPEAN MISTLETOE
Whole plant

Viscum album L.   Mistletoe Family

Smooth, evergreen, parasitic shrub, with rounded green stems up to 20 in. long. Leaves opposite, narrow-obovate, arching, 2–3 in. long, about ½ in. wide. Flowers inconspicuous, 3–5; Feb.–Mar. Fruit translucent white, fleshy, small berry. **WHERE FOUND:** Parasitic on alder, apple trees, birch, elm, maple, poplar, willow, and other deciduous trees. Native to Eurasia; introduced to Calif. by Luther Burbank around 1900; naturalized in Sonoma Co., Calif. Increasing from seed dispersal by birds. **USES:** Druids and Celts revered

European Mistletoe (Viscum album), *native to Europe, has naturalized near Santa Rosa, California.*

mistletoe for its miraculous properties, including protection from poisoning and witchcraft. An important herb in European tradition, historically and today. Preparations of the dried leaves, including tea and tinctures, traditionally used for the treatment of high blood pressure, arteriosclerosis, hypertensive headache, and other health problems. Hypotensive and immunostimulatory activity are confirmed by research. Mistletoe has been approved in Germany and elsewhere for localized treatment of joint inflammations (as an injection) and in oral forms for supportive treatment of malignant tumors through stimulation of the immune system. Controversial alternative cancer treatment in Europe. **WARNING:** Contains potentially toxic lectins. The herb or its preparations are not used in cases of protein hypersensitivity or chronic infections such as tuberculosis or during pregnancy. May cause high fever with chills, headaches, angina, circulatory disturbances, and allergic reactions when used in an injection. Use only under medical advice. Berries are considered highly poisonous.

LEAVES IN BASAL ROSETTE, SWORDLIKE OR SUCCULENT; AGAVES AND YUCCAS

CENTURY PLANT AGAVE
Agave spp.

Whole plant
Agave Family

More than two dozen species of *Agave* occur in the western U.S. Flowering stalks more or less woody, to 12 ft. or more. Leaves numerous, succulent, overlapping, forming a broad basal rosette. Flowers, usually white, mostly tubular or funnel-shaped, in stout scapes, either racemes or broad candelabralike panicles. Fruit a thick-walled capsule with many seeds. **WHERE FOUND:** Dry soils, desert, mountains. Western U.S. **USES:** Many species were traditionally used without regard to species identity. Large-paniceled species are commonly referred to as Century Plant or Mescal. Smaller species are called Lechuguilla and Amole. A mash of the

*Century Plant (Agave spp.) has
succulent leaves in a basal rosette.*

*The flowers of Century Plant
grow in a candelabra-like panicle.*

stalks of some species is made into the intoxicating drinks mescal
and tequila. Leaves, flower buds, and central crowns of Agave
were one of the most important food sources of native groups of
the Southwest. The juice of several species was used as a laxative,
for menstrual difficulties, and as a diuretic. Traditionally, tincture
of fresh leaf has been used to treat indigestion. Root tincture
once used as an antispasmodic to relieve gas or digestive tract
spasms. **WARNING:** Fresh juice may cause contact dermatitis. Ingestion of leaves has been reported to be toxic to livestock.

*Banana Yucca (Yucca baccata) is
an important food, medicine, and
fiber plant.*

BANANA YUCCA

Root, leaves

Yucca baccata Torr.

Agave Family

Stemless; basal rosette of rigid, *swordlike leaves* to 3 ft. long and 2 ½ in. wide. Leaves dark green to blue-green, *spine-tipped*, folded along midvein; *margins shredding into coarse, wiry fibers*. Large, nodding, bell-shaped flowers in dense panicles, *mostly remaining below leaves*; 6 fleshy petals, reddish brown outside, white to cream inside; Apr.–June. **WHERE FOUND:** Dry desert areas, sandy or rocky slopes and mesas; pinyon-juniper and Joshua tree woodland. Se. Calif. to Ariz., s. Nev., s. Utah, Colo., Tex.; nw. Mexico. **USES:** An important food and fiber plant for American Indian groups of the Southwest. Leaf tea used to treat vomiting or heartburn. Fruit eaten to make childbirth easier. Crushed root poultice on chest to treat sunstroke. Juice or foam of root was used to treat cataracts or blindness. Demonstrated anti-inflammatory properties make Yucca a popular modern herbal treatment for arthritis. **WARNING:** Saponins in root are potentially toxic.

MOJAVE YUCCA

Roots

Yucca schidigera Roezl ex Ortgies

Agave Family

Shrubby or treelike yucca, 3–15 ft. Leaves mostly in basal rosette, stiff, linear, swordlike, spine-tipped, yellowish to blue-green, mar-

Mojave Yucca (Yucca schidigera) is one of several yuccas with threadlike fibers on the leaf margins.

Mojave Yucca eventually arises from a trunk.

gins with shredding fibers. Flower stalk heavy, to 5 ft.; flowers cream-colored. **WHERE FOUND:** Mojave and Sonoran deserts, chaparral, creosote-bush scrub. S. Calif., Nev., Ariz.; n. Baja Calif. **USES:** American Indian groups used this species primarily as a food and fiber source. Fruits were eaten raw or cooked and were made into a beverage. Leaves used as a fiber for brushes, cordage, clothing, and brooms. Root also scraped and used for soap. Root adopted and popularized by early settlers as an anti-inflammatory, especially for rheumatism and arthritis. Also valued for the treatment of diabetes and digestive disorders. Antimutagenic, anti-inflammatory, antifungal, and antiarthritic properties suggested by laboratory studies. Controversial studies published in the late 1970s suggested that yucca extracts were safe and effective in treating various arthritic symptoms, such as pain, swelling, and stiffness. These studies, which did not stand up to scientific scrutiny, resulted in widespread use of root preparations for arthritic conditions. **WARNING:** Saponins in root are potentially toxic.

MISCELLANEOUS DESERT SHRUBS

MORMON TEA
Ephedra nevadensis S. Wats.

Leaves, stems, twigs
Ephedra Family

Round stems *grooved, jointed*, rigid; to 5 ft. Young branches *pale green*, covered with *whitish film*, becoming yellow to gray. Small, brownish, scalelike leaves fused into sheath around stem; *leaf bases gray*. Male and female cones on separate plants, clustered at nodes; Mar.–Apr. Bracts of pollen cone yellowish; bracts of seed cone with light brown to *yellow-green* center; seeds 2 per bract. **WHERE FOUND:** Dry, rocky slopes, deserts. S. and e. Calif. to Utah, Tex. **USES:** American Indians drank twig tea for stomach troubles, rheumatism, colds, gonorrhea, syphilis, kidney ailments, delayed menses; also as a blood

Mormon Tea (Ephedra nevadensis) *was once famously used to make tea drunk by teamsters.*

purifier and healthful, cleansing tea. Considered diuretic. Navajo and other Southwest tribes sipped a sweetened tea to ease coughs. Externally, poultice of powdered twigs and branches applied to sores. Among the Cahuilla the tea was considered bad for the system if taken for too long.

GREEN EPHEDRA
Leaves, stems, twigs

Ephedra viridis Coville
Ephedra Family

Densely branched, mostly evergreen shrub (turning yellowish with age) to 5 ft. Branches without thornlike tip. Leaves opposite, scalelike, 2 per stem node, persistent, turning brown, not photosynthetic. Male and female cones generally on separate plants. Seed cones generally without or with very short stalk, 2–6 per node; Mar.–Apr. **WHERE FOUND:** Dry rocky slopes, canyons, creosote bush scrub, pinyon/juniper woodlands. W. Colo. south to nw. N. M., n. Ariz., to e. Calif. **USES:** This, like most of the 12 North American *Ephedra* species were used similarly to Mormon Tea (above). Some tribes used tea for easing bowel complaints, children's diarrhea, anemia, and backaches. A number of European and Asian species of *Ephedra* contain ephedrine, pseudoephedrine, and related alkaloids that stimulate the central nervous system. **RELATED SPECIES:** Chinese *Ephedra* spp., such as *E. sinica* Staph., are sold collectively under the name ma huang. Extracts of species containing ephedrine, related compounds, and their purified alkaloids are widely used today in preparations to relieve temporary symptoms of asthma, hay fever accompanied by nasal congestion, coughs, colds (without fever), and recently in weight-loss and "energy" products. North American species contain little, if any, of the stimulant ephedra alkaloids. **WARNING:** Ephedra alkaloids may cause heart palpitations, high blood pressure, nervousness. The herb may potentiate monoamine oxidase inhibitors. Avoid use for anorexia and glaucoma. May stimulate the thyroid. Alkaloid-containing species should be used for weight loss or "energy" only on the advice of a qualified health care practitioner—and the practitioner's qualifications may be questionable if he or she gives such advice.

Green Ephedra (Ephedra viridis) *is one of 12 North American species of this genus.*

OCOTILLO, CANDLEWOOD
Fouquieria splendens Engelm.

Bark, roots, flowers
Ocotillo Family

Spiny stems upright or arching, to 25 ft. Branching from base. *Bark gray-green with dark furrows.* Succulent, *spoon-shaped leaves present during wet periods.* Showy, bright red flowers in dense sprays at branch tips; flowers tubular, 5-parted, with many sta-

mens exserted past petals; Mar.–July. **WHERE FOUND:** Dry, rocky soils, desert. S. Calif. to sw. Tex.; Baja Calif., cen. Mexico. **USES:** Hualapai Indians used roots to make a soothing bath for sore feet. Apache used root tea internally and as a bath to treat fatigue and tired, swollen limbs. Cahuilla used root tea to treat productive coughs in the elderly. Mahuna Indians used tea as a blood purifier and tonic. Herbalists use the bark for treating pelvic congestion, hemorrhoids, benign prostatic hypertrophy, urinary urgency, and lymphatic stasis and cancer.

(Top, left, above) *Ocotillo* (Fouquieria splendens) *is common in southwestern deserts. It has spines at the base of its tufts of leaves and bright red flowers.*

CHAPARRAL, CREOSOTE BUSH

Leaves, gum

Larrea tridentata (DC.) Cov.

Caltrop Family

⚠ Long-lived, resinous, bushy evergreen with strong *creosote* odor; to 13 ft. Stems upright to horizontal with black bands at swollen nodes. Leaves stalkless, divided into 2 thick, lance-shaped, leaflets fused at base; appearing as a simple, deeply 2-lobed leaf, margins smooth. Flowers yellow, solitary, with 5 spreading twisted petals and 10 stamens; Mar.–June. **WHERE FOUND:** Desert scrub; *dominant shrub throughout N. American deserts.* Se. Calif., east to sw. Utah, Ariz., N.M., w. Tex.; cen. Mexico. Over time a single plant may form a large circle of clonal offshoot plants; clones may live to 10,000 years. **USES:** Formerly a panacea of the Indians of the Southwest. Long used by Mormons as a folk cancer remedy. Popularized as an alternative cancer remedy in the 1970s and 1980s. Clinical trials failed to confirm significant anticancer activity. American Indian groups used leaf, flower, or twig tea for respiratory, digestive tract, skin, rheumatic, and gynecological disorders. Leaf tea used for colds, coughs, tuberculosis, asthma, diarrhea, dysentery, cramps, upset stomach, delayed menstruation and menstrual cramps, and as a general tonic. Externally, a wash or poultice was used on wounds to prevent infections, relieve swollen limbs due to poor circulation, as a hair wash for dandruff, and as a disinfectant and deodorant for sores, wounds, insect bites and snakebite, umbilical stump inflammation, sore and aching joints

Chaparral (Larrea tridentata) is the dominant shrub of American deserts.

The yellow flowers of Chaparral.

Sticky Monkey Flower (Mimulus aurantiacus) *has sticky glandular hairs.*

and muscles. It is still touted by some herbal advocates as a treatment for the above conditions as well as for HIV and cancer. Chaparral does contain potent antimicrobial, antiviral, antioxidant, and hyperglycemic agents. The compound nordihydroguaiaretic acid (NDGA), extracted from the leaves, was formerly used by the food industry as an antioxidant to preserve oils. **WARNING:** Avoid use during pregnancy or with liver or kidney disease. By 1992 at least four cases of serious liver problems requiring hospitalization were attributed to Chaparral consumption, which may have been due to allergic reactions. Consult a qualified herbalist before use.

STICKY MONKEY FLOWER
Leaves, stems, flowers
Mimulus aurantiacus W. Curtis
Figwort Family
[*Diplacus aurantiacus* (W. Curtis) Jepson ssp. *aurantiacus*]
Multibranched evergreen, to 5 ft. Stems and leaves *sticky*, covered in fine, glandular hairs. Leaves narrowly lance-shaped to oblong, dark green, sessile; margins toothed, generally rolled under. Large, tubular flowers 2-lipped with 5 notched lobes; color varies from mostly yellow-orange to peach, salmon, white, buff, or red; Mar.–Aug. **WHERE FOUND:** Open, rocky sites, hillsides, cliffs, canyons, slopes, disturbed areas, chaparral, forest. Calif. to sw. Ore. **USES:** Costanoan Indians used plant tea to treat kidney and bladder problems. Stems, leaves, and flower tea used by Mahuna Indians to treat diarrhea. Pomo Indians used as an eyewash.

JOJOBA
Seed
Simmondsia chinensis (Link) Schneid.
Jojoba Family
Multibranched evergreen with slender, rigid branches; to 5–6 ft. *Leathery* leaves *upright in pairs*, ovate to lance-shaped, sometimes wider at tip than base, dull green-gray, tips rounded; margins en-

Jojoba (Simmondsia chinensis) *is the source of jojoba oil.*

Jojoba has upright leaves.

tire. Leaves move with sun to expose less surface to sunlight and thus save moisture. Tiny male and female flowers on separate shrubs; Feb.–May. *Nutlike* fruit 3-parted, opening to release a single seed. Large brown seed contains liquid wax. **WHERE FOUND:** Arid areas. S. Calif. and Ariz.; n. Mexico. **USES:** Jojoba has gained popularity, particularly in cosmetic products, because of the high-quality oil extracted from the seed. Actually a liquid wax rather than an oil, in its physical properties it resembles the oil of the endangered sperm whale, harvested nearly to extinction for its oil. Jojoba oil is used in skin and hair care products to lubricate the scalp and impart softness. Unsubstantiated claims include control of dandruff, hair loss, and graying of hair; it has been touted for the treatment of warts, acne, cracked skin, arthritis, and body aches. The Papago applied dried and powdered, or charred, nuts to sores to heal them. In Mexico men apply the oil to scalp to stimulate hair growth.

OPPOSITE DECIDUOUS LEAVES; FLESHY WHITE FRUITS

WESTERN DOGWOOD
Bark, twigs

Cornus sericea ssp. *occidentalis* (Torr. & Gray) Fosberg
[*C. occidentalis* (Torr. & Gray) Coville]   Dogwood Family

Deciduous shrub, to 15 ft. Branches *red to purple*, hairless. Leaves ovate to lance-shaped, with 4–7 pairs of veins that arc toward leaf tip, away from leaf margin; lower surface densely hairy; margins smooth. Flowers small, white, 4-parted, in flat-topped branched clusters; May–July. Fruit whitish, berrylike. **WHERE FOUND:** Moist habitats. S. Calif. to Alaska, Idaho, Mont., Nev. **USES:** American Indian groups used bitter bark tea as a digestive tonic; externally as a wash for sore eyes. The twigs were decocted and given to women after childbirth. Traditionally, the species and subspecies are used interchangeably. Bark tea was widely used by American Indian groups for coughs, colds, fevers, sinus congestion, liver problems, diarrhea, postpartum bleeding, and general weakness, especially in the elderly. Externally, bark preparations used for sore eyes, snow blindness, and eye infections. A wash from the bark tea used for rashes, ulcers, dandruff, and many other skin problems. Roasted or dried, the inner bark was used in many ceremonial smoking mixtures. **RELATED SPECIES:** The closely related *C. sericea* L., Red-Osier Dogwood, occurs throughout much of N. America. The complex botanical forms are hard to differentiate even for a trained botanist. The bark tea of Pacific dogwood, *Cornus nuttallii* Audubon ex Torr. & Gray, common in western mountains, was used by a number of tribes as an emetic, tonic, laxative, and blood purifier. Boughs used in sweat lodges as a healing steam.

SNOWBERRY
Symphoricarpos albus (L.) Blake

Berries, bark, leaves, root
Honeysuckle Family

Deciduous upright shrub, to 6 ft., spreading by rhizomes. Young stems slender, hollow, hairless. Leaves ovate (to 2 in.) with *highly*

Western Dogwood (Cornus sericea ssp. occidentalis) has smooth red to purple branches and white fruits.

Snowberry (Symphoricarpos albus) with white berries.

variable margins—from smooth to wavy or lobed. Leaf tips bluntly pointed, bases rounded. Flowers small, pink to white, arranged in terminal clusters, 5-parted, with petals fused into a bell shape; insides of petal lobes have dense, white hairs; May–July. Fruit a white berry with 2 seeds; *persistent* through winter. **WHERE FOUND:** Dry or moist open forests, streambanks, rocky or n.-facing slopes. S. Calif. to s. Alaska, east to Mont., south to N.M. Naturalized in eastern U.S. **USES:** An important eye medicine for many American Indian tribes. Tea of mashed berries, bark, or leaves was used as a wash for sore eyes. Mashed berry tea used to treat diarrhea, as a cleansing spring laxative, and to detoxify after poisoning. Externally applied to sores, warts, rashes, burns, sore throat, also as an underarm deodorant and as a restorative hair rinse. Leaf tea drunk for colds. Stem and root preparations used to treat skin sores, rashes, colds, urinary retention, stomachache, and menstrual problems. Leaf poultices were applied for headaches and skin rash. **RELATED SPECIES:** A number of tribes also used a bark or leaf tea of *S. occidentalis* Hook. or *S. orbiculatus* Moench, Coral Berry, to wash weak or inflamed eyes. A tea of *S. longiflorus* Gray was taken to ease indigestion and stomach pains. **WARNING:** Berries, strongly emetic and cathartic, contain high levels of toxic saponins. American Indians considered more than two or three berries taken internally to be poisonous. Fatalities reported from ingesting berries.

OPPOSITE DECIDUOUS LEAVES, MARGINS ENTIRE, FRUITS FLESHY

TWINBERRY HONEYSUCKLE

Bark, berries, leaves

Lonicera involucrata Banks ex Spreng.
Honeysuckle Family

⚠ Upright, not climbing; to 12 ft. Mature bark shredding; young branches 4-angled. Ovate to broadly lance-shaped leaves with short petioles, abruptly pointed tips, and round to tapered bases; upper surface without hairs, lower surface hairy. Tubular flowers yellow, some-

Twinberry Honeysuckle (Lonicera involucrata) *with yellowish red tubular flowers.*

Canada Buffaloberry (Shepherdia canadensis) *has bright red fruits.*

times tinged orange or red, arranged *in pairs* on slender stalks from leaf axils, with *reddish leafy* bracts beneath; Mar.–July. **WHERE FOUND:** Moist sites: forest, streambanks, thickets. All western states; Alaska south to n. Mexico; eastern N. America. **USES:** American Indian groups used bark decoction externally on burns, wounds, infections, sore glands, and skin sores, as a bath for painful legs and feet, and poulticed on breasts to stimulate milk flow. Chewed leaves poulticed for swellings, itch, boils, sores, gonorrheal sores, and sore mouth. Stem tea used for general weakness and paralysis. Plant tea used for broken bones, scabs, sores, coughs, sore throat, bladder problems; in sweat baths for arthritis and rheumatism. Berries considered laxative and emetic; also used for lung and stomach problems, and dandruff. Leaves or bark were used for coughs. **WARNING:** Potentially toxic, particularly the berries.

CANADA BUFFALOBERRY
Shepherdia canadensis (L.) Nutt.

Bark, root, twig, berries
Oleaster Family

Deciduous shrub, to 8 ft. Young branches with *silvery to brown fuzz* and *rust spots*; thornless. Leaves oval, lower surface with dense white hairs and rusty brown spots (scales); margins smooth. Very small, yellowish brown flowers appear as leaves emerge; Apr.–June. Bright red, berrylike fruit oval, single-seeded, with a "soapy" feel. **WHERE FOUND:** Moist woods or streambanks; Ore. to Alaska.; Mont. to N.M.; eastern N. America. **USES:** American Indian groups used various preparations for digestive troubles. Tea of twigs and branches (with leaves) used as a laxative and for high blood pressure, stomach cancer; used in sweat lodges for purification rituals. Bark tea used to treat diarrhea. Roots strongly laxative; also used for chronic cough and tuberculosis. Berries or their juice used for indigestion, gallstones, stomach ulcers or cancer, acne, boils, mosquito bites, and as an aid to women in labor. Root or bark tea used as a wash for arthritis, aches, acne, cuts, sores, syphilitic sores, dandruff, and broken bones. The fruits and leaves were used as a sedative, and the froth from whipping the berries was thought to make one sleepy. **WARNING:** Though whipped berries were used to make "Indian ice cream," large quantities are potentially toxic.

OPPOSITE, DECIDUOUS OR EVERGREEN, SIMPLE LEAVES; ENTIRE MARGINS; FRUITS DRY

WESTERN SWEETSHRUB, SPICE-BUSH   Bark
Calycanthus occidentalis Hook. & Arn.   Sweet-Shrub Family
⚠ Deciduous, to 13 ft. *Strongly aromatic, spicy or fruit-scented* when crushed or scratched. Leaves ovate with short petioles, gradually pointed tips, and rounded bases. Lower surface hairy, upper surface rough; margins entire. Large, solitary, red to maroon flowers (less than 2 in. across) with many thick, nearly succulent, *upward-curved* petals that become shorter toward center of flower; Mar.–July. **WHERE FOUND:** Moist, shady sites, canyons, streambanks. Calif. to s. Cascades. **USES:** Pomo Indians used aromatic bark tea for bad chest colds, especially to help eliminate phlegm, and for sore throat and stomach problems. **RELATED SPECIES:** Bark tea of Sweetshrub, *C. floridus* L., was used for hives and urinary tract disorders and as an eye medicine for people who were losing their sight. The oozing sap was applied to children's skin sores. The root was considered a strong emetic for cleansing. **WARNING:** Grazing cattle have been reported to have a toxic reaction to eating this plant.

BUTTONBUSH   Leaves, bark, roots
Cephalanthus occidentalis L.   Madder Family
⚠ Shrub, 9–20 ft. Opposite or whorled deciduous leaves *oblong-ovate*, hairless; margins entire. White flowers in *globe-shaped cluster* from leaf axils; June–Sept. **WHERE FOUND:** Streambanks, lake and pond edges. Calif., Ariz. N.M., Tex., to eastern N. America. **USES:** American Indian

Western Sweetshrub (Calycanthus occidentalis) *has spicy-fragrant leaves.*

groups used bark tea for hemorrhage, headache, menstrual problems, fever, weakness, and jaundice and as a wash for eye inflammation. Leaf tea drunk to check menstrual flow. Bark chewed for toothaches. A strong bark tea was taken for dysentery and to ease coughs. Root-bark tea used to lower fevers and as a tonic. Traditionally used as a tonic, diuretic and astringent and to promote sweating. Leaf tea used for fevers, coughs, kidney stones, malaria, palsy, pleurisy, and toothaches. Superficially resembles a small Cinchona bush (source of quinine), belongs to the same plant family, and has a folk reputation for relieving fever and malaria. **WARNING:** Contains the glucosides cephalanthin and cephalin. The leaves have caused **poisoning** in grazing animals.

SILK TASSEL, QUININE BUSH, BEAR BUSH   Leaves
Garrya flavescens S. Wats.   Silk Tassel Family

Evergreen, to 10 ft. Leathery leaves on short petioles; pairs rotated 90 degrees at each node. Oblong to oval, flat or wavy leaves, dull gray-green above, densely hairy beneath; margins smooth. Flowers small, cupped by fused, opposite bracts; clustered in long, hanging catkins, *persisting through winter*; Feb.–Apr. **WHERE FOUND:** Desert slopes, chaparral, pine-oak woodland, Calif. to Utah, Ariz., N.M.; n. Baja Calif. **USES:** Kawaiisu Indians used the leaves to treat colds, fever, stomachache, constipation, and gonorrhea. Research suggests it is a smooth muscle relaxant for treating intestinal, urethral, bladder, or menstrual cramping, based on

(Above) *Buttonbush* (Cephalanthus occidentalis) *sports globe-shaped flowers.* (Right) *The catkinlike flowers of Silk Tassel* (Garrya flavescens) *persist through winter.*

its water-soluble bitter alkaloid, garryine. **RELATED SPECIES:** The Pomo used the leaves of *G. elliptica* Dougl. ex Lindl. as a tea to bring on the menses. Leaves of *G. fremontii* Torr. decocted for gallbladder problems, to reduce fevers, as a substitute for quinine, and as a general digestive tonic. **WARNING:** Avoid use during pregnancy. Potentially toxic.

OPPOSITE, SIMPLE LEAVES; TOOTHED MARGINS; DRY FRUITS

WESTERN BURNING BUSH
Euonymus occidentalis Nutt. ex Torr.

Bark

Staff-Tree Family

Deciduous, to 20 ft. Slender branches, often climbing; twigs generally 4-angled. Ovate leaves finely toothed, tips pointed, bases tapered or rounded. Flowers, 1–5 from leaf axils, maroon to brownish purple, *finely dotted* and flattened; Apr.–June. Flattened fruit opening to reveal brown seeds surrounded by red pulp. **WHERE FOUND:** Shaded streambanks, moist woods, canyons. High mountains and cen. and n. coast. Ore., Wash. **USES:** The Winnebago used a decoction of the inner bark for uterine ailments. Traditionally, herbalists used it to treat liver problems, gallbladder pain not involving stones, fatty stools, and constipation resulting from impaired bile flow. Also said to have bronchodilating, expectorant, diuretic, and mild heart-stimulating properties. **RELATED SPECIES:** *E. atropurpurea* Jacq., Wahoo, is traditionally used as laxative for painful digestion, stagnant liver, lung problems, water retention, and gallbladder problems. The bark contains small amounts of heart-stimulating compounds. Strawberry Bush, *E. americana* L., was used similarly. **WARNING:** Avoid use during pregnancy. Do not ingest—fruits may cause vomiting, diarrhea, and unconsciousness.

Western Burning Bush (Euonymus occidentalis) *has distinctive red-brown flowers.*

YERBA REUMA, ALKALI HEATH

Whole plant

Frankenia salina (Molina) I. M. Johnston
Frankenia Family
[*F. grandifolia* Cham. & Schlecht.]

Mat-forming or upright, to 12 in. Stems often *rooting at swollen nodes*. Gray-green, leathery leaves oblanceolate to obovate; newer leaves clustered in leaf axils; margins entire, rolled under. Pink to rose, tubular flowers solitary, sessile in branch axils; May–Nov. **WHERE FOUND:** Salt marshes, coastal alkali flats, beaches. N. coast ranges and nw. Sierra of Calif. to s. Nev.; Baja Calif., Mexico, S. America. **USES:** Plant tea used as an astringent wash for skin infections, rashes, burns; gargled for sore throat or sore gums. Tea used as a douche for vaginitis or vulvitis; internally to treat dysentery, vomiting, or diarrhea. Historically, physicians used wash for vaginal yeast infections, gonorrhea, and excessive mucous discharge during colds.

WILD MOCK ORANGE

Branches, leaves

Philadelphus lewisii Pursh
Mock Orange Family

Deciduous, to 10 ft. Bark reddish brown, aging gray, peeling in narrow strips. Ovate leaves, 1–3 in., with 3 prominent veins from base, tips pointed, bases tapered; margins entire to coarsely toothed. Showy, white flowers very *sweet-smelling* with 4 (sometimes 5) petals and many stamens. Woody fruit oval, 4-chambered, releasing seeds through slits on top. **WHERE FOUND:** Forest openings, slopes, canyons. Calif., Ore., Wash., Idaho, Mont.; B.C. **USES:** A decoction of the branches used for soaking eczema or hemorrhoids, put on sore chest, or drunk morning and evening as

Yerba Reuma (Frankenia salina) *is a low-growing evergreen of salt marshes and alkaline soils.*

Wild Mock Orange (Philadelphus lewisii) *has showy tufts of white flowers.*

a cleansing laxative. A powder of the wood in pitch or bear grease, or lather from leaves rubbed on skin for sores and swellings. Leaf poultice also used for infected breasts. **RELATED SPECIES:** A decoction of the roots of *P. californicus* Benth. was drunk to reduce fevers.

OPPOSITE, AROMATIC LEAVES, STEMS MOSTLY SQUARE IN CROSS SECTION, FLOWERS IRREGULAR; MINT FAMILY

DESERT LAVENDER, BEE SAGE
Hyptis emoryi Torr.

Leaves, flowers
Mint Family

Aromatic, multibranched, upright to 9 ft. or spreading. Stems and leaves densely gray-hairy. Leaves ovate, blunt-tipped; margins scalloped. Purple flowers densely clustered in leaf axils at branch tips; flowers 2-lipped; upper lip 2-lobed, lower 3-lobed with reflexed, pouched central lobe; Jan.–May. **WHERE FOUND:** Sandy washes, canyons, desert scrubland. S. Calif. deserts to Ariz.; Baja Calif., nw. Mexico. **USES:** Cahuilla Indians took a leaf and blossom tea to stop hemorrhages. **RELATED SPECIES:** The Seminoles used root tea of *H. pectinata* (L.) Poit., Comb Bushmint, as a wash for foot and leg sores. The leaves and fruit were thought to benefit insane people. In India, a tea of *H. brevipes* Poit. given to mothers after birth to help the uterus; also used to reduce phlegm and remove skin parasites. Leaf tea considered a refreshing beverage in Java. Leaf juice is given to babies to cure colic. Leaves poulticed for wounds and to heal navel of a newborn. In China, *H. suaveolens* (L.) Poit. is widely used as a folk medicine; stem and leaves poulticed for headaches and skin problems. Leaf tea is used to stimulate mother's milk, relieve intestinal spasms, and for rheumatism.

Desert Lavender (Hyptis emoryi) *has a pouched central flower lobe.*

Pitcher Sage (Lepechinia calycina) *has a distinctive bulblike calyx.*

PITCHER SAGE

Lepechinia calycosa (Benth.) Epling ex Munz   Mint Family

Aromatic evergreen, to 5 ft. Stems with long, silky hairs, sometimes with short-stalked glands. Leaves ovate to oblong, gland-dotted; tips bluntly pointed; bases tapered; margins scalloped to coarsely toothed. Showy, white flowers *purple-veined*, solitary in axils of reduced upper leaves; tubular petals 2-lipped; upper lip 4-lobed; lower lip 1-lobed, longer than upper; Apr.–June. **WHERE FOUND:** Rocky slopes, chaparral, woodland. Cen. and n. Calif. coast ranges. **USES:** Miwok Indians used a plant tea for headaches, fevers, malaria, and colds. **RELATED SPECIES:** *L. caulescens* (Ort.) Epl., used in Mexico to treat diabetes, has been shown to be hypo-glycemic in studies on rabbits. *L. hastata* (Gray) Epling, used to treat uterine infections in Baja California, contains the antimicrobial carnosol.

WHITE SAGE

Salvia apiana Jepson   Mint Family

Strongly aromatic, white-velvety; to 5 ft. Leaves opposite, oblong, mostly basal, crowded at base of current year's growth; margins finely scalloped. *Showy*, white to lavender flowers in loose whorls, arranged in tall racemes; *lower lip expanded, margin wavy, abruptly bent upward; stamens 2, well exserted*; Apr.–July. **WHERE FOUND:** Dry, sandy or rocky areas, chaparral, desert washes or coastal slopes. S. Calif. to n. Baja Calif. **USES:** Leaves eaten, smoked, and used in sweat baths by Cahuilla Indians to treat upper respiratory infections. Considered an expectorant; used for colds, coughs, sore throats, and systemic poison oak rashes. Crushed leaves used in a wash as shampoo, dye, or hair straightener; placed in armpits before bedtime as a deodorant. An important ceremonial plant among southwestern Indian groups. The herb was burned as a fumigant after an illness in the dwelling. **RELATED SPECIES:** Garden Sage, *S. officinalis* L., was an official drug in European herbal tradition and was used for many of the same afflictions for which American Indians used North American sages. Salvias are commonly used in both European and American Indian traditions for stomachaches, indigestion, colds, sore throats, as a gargle to relieve pharyngitis, tonsillitis, sore gums, and mouth ulcers. Sage oil has strong antimicrobial properties, and its rosmarinic acid is anti-inflammatory. Garden Sage used in deodorant products in Europe and North America. The tendency of certain *Salvia* species to dry secretions, including milk, contraindicate its use during nursing; it is useful for decreasing milk production at weaning.

(Left) *White Sage* (Salvia apiana) *has strongly aromatic, white-woolly leaves.* (Above) *Purple Sage* (Salvia dorrii) *has a purplish bract beneath each flower.*

PURPLE SAGE
Leaves, seeds

Salvia dorrii (Kellogg) Abrams
Mint Family

Aromatic, mat-forming or upright, to 30 in. Stems covered in dense, whitish gray *scales*; glandular. Leaves silvery, obovate to *spoon-shaped*; tips rounded, bases tapered; margins without teeth. Flowers blue, 2-lipped, in dense whorls at branch tips; *purplish bract below each flower* hairy on back and margin. Upper lip of flower 2-lobed, upright; lower lip 3-lobed, middle lobe margin wavy; 2 stamens and style extended beyond petals; May–July. **WHERE FOUND:** Dry, rocky sites, ridges, plains, deserts, sagebrush scrub. East of Sierra-Cascade crest from s. Calif. to Wash., Idaho, Nev., Utah, n. Ariz. **USES:** American Indian groups used tea as a wash or inhaled the fumes to treat headaches. The Kawaiisu drank leaf tea for stomachaches and threw the plant on fires to chase away ghosts. Hopi used tea to treat epilepsy and faintness. Sage smoke was used to clear nasal passages. Leaves poulticed for varicose veins, chest colds, and earaches. Other tribes used the tea for colds, flu, coughs, stomachaches, fevers, gonorrhea, syphilis, and as a general tonic for any illness.

BLACK SAGE
Seeds, leaves

Salvia mellifera Greene
Mint Family

Aromatic evergreen, to 7 ft. Stems with dense, soft, light gray hairs, some glandular. Leaves lance-shaped to oblong; margin finely scalloped. Upper leaf surface smooth, green; lower surface with short, woolly gray hairs. Bluish lavender flowers (sometimes white or pale blue) *clustered in whorls* at branch tips; flowers 2-lipped; upper lip 2-lobed, bottom lip deeply indented; sepals with sharp pointed tips. Stamens 2, not appearing beyond upper lip; style forked at tip; Mar.–Aug. **WHERE FOUND:** Coastal sage scrub, chaparral, dry slopes, and hillsides. Cen. Calif. to n. Baja Calif., mostly in coast ranges. **USES:** American Indian groups chewed leaves to relieve gas pains. A hot poultice was used for earache and sore throat. Leaf tea used for coughs, colds, heart ailments, and in a bath to treat paralysis. Poulticed for rheumatism and arthritis. Research confirms antiseptic, sedative, and pain-relieving activity. **RELATED SPECIES:** A tea of Hummingbird Sage, *S. spathacea* Greene, used to reduce fevers and relieve headaches. A hot tea of *S. reflexa* Hornem. (as *S. lanceolata* Wild.) was historically recommended by physicians as a diaphoretic to lower rheumatic fevers, and a cold infusion as a digestive aid and astringent.

WOOLLY BLUECURLS, AMERICAN WILD ROSEMARY
Trichostema lanatum Benth.

Leaves, flowers
Mint Family

Resinous, pleasant-scented shrub to 5 ft. Stems densely woolly when young. Leaves widely linear, nearly stalkless; margins

Black Sage (Salvia mellifera) *flowers are small in tight whorls.*

Black Sage has deeply veined leaves.

Woolly Bluecurls (Trichostema lanatum) *has floral parts with purplish hairs.*

smooth, rolled under. Upper leaf without hairs; lower surface with gray-woolly hairs. Floral parts covered in dense, *purplish woolly* hairs. Flowers blue to lavender, 2-lipped, with 5 spreading petal lobes and 2 pairs of long, slender, arched stamens, much longer than petals; style forked at tip; Apr.–Aug. **WHERE FOUND:** Coastal scrub, chaparral, dry rocky ridges. Outer coast ranges, cen. Calif. to Baja Calif. **USES:** Leaf and flower tea highly regarded for easing stomach problems. The Mahuna used plant as a panacea. American Indian groups washed hair with a strong plant tea to restore black color and promote growth. A tea of flowers and young leaves was used for colds and flu by early Spanish settlers in California, who called the plant Romero because it reminded them of Rosemary (*Rosmarinus officinalis* L.).

OPPOSITE, DECIDUOUS, COMPOUND LEAVES: ELDERBERRIES

COMMON ELDERBERRY

Flowers, berries, inner bark, leaves

Sambucus nigra ssp. *canadensis* (L.) R. Bolli   Honeysuckle Family
[*S. canadensis* L., *S.mexicana* K. Presl ex DC., *S. cerula* var. *mexicana* (K. Presl ex DC.) L. Benson]

Deciduous shrub, to 25 ft., often lacking a main trunk. Leaves pinnately compound; 3–9 leaflets elliptic to ovate, the central midvein often curved, tips abruptly pointed; margins toothed. Numerous creamy yellow flowers in flat-topped clusters; Apr.–Aug. Berrylike fruit appearing blue, but actually nearly black with a dense *white, waxy film.* **WHERE FOUND:** Streambanks, open flats, valleys. Calif. to B.C., Utah, Ariz., N.M., w. Tex.; Mexico. **USES:** The flowers, fruit, bark, and roots of elderberry species have been used extensively throughout the world. Preparations used

Common Elderberry (Sambucus nigra *ssp.* canadensis) *has many flat-topped flower clusters.*

Common Elderberry with its typical loose flower heads.

for skin conditions, to lower fevers, and treat colds and flu. Recent laboratory and clinical studies show that elderberry fruit extracts are protective against different strains of the flu virus, thus supporting traditional use. A poultice of the leaves or bark was used on boils, swelling, bruises, and eczema. Juice of flowers and fresh berries used in salves for wounds, burns, and other skin conditions. Tea of leaves, bark, or flowers used as an antiseptic wash for skin inflammation and wounds. A warm tea of the flowers used for colds, fevers, and headaches. Dried berries once used to treat diarrhea. Inner bark and root are strongly emetic and cathartic, formerly used in minute doses as a cleansing purgative. Tea of the bark and root was used for headache, mucous congestion, and to promote labor. Work on the chemistry and pharmacology of elderberry is still preliminary. The plant is complex, containing bioactive proteins such as lectins, flavonoids, alkaloids, sterols, fatty acids, tannins, and cyanogenic glycosides in varying degrees, depending on the species, variety, and plant part. Proven biological effects include antifungal, antibacterial, antiviral, diuretic, hypotensive, anti-inflammatory, and liver-protective properties. **RELATED SPECIES:** Common Elderberry, *S. canadensis* L., is recognized as a separate species or is lumped with *S. mexicana* L. as

S. nigra L. ssp. *canadensis*. Scientists are still discussing and studying the taxonomy of this complex group. Whatever the taxonomic designation of blue-fruited species or varieties, their uses, chemistry, and pharmacology are similar. European Elderberry, *S. nigra* L., has been used extensively for medicine and food since before the time of Christ. Asian species such as *S. latipinna* Nak. are used to heal bone fractures, and in kidney ailments, dropsy, high blood pressure, and lower back pain. **WARNING:** Most parts of the plant are mildly to moderately toxic, especially the inner bark and root. Only cooked fruits and heated flowers are considered safe for moderate use. Bark, root, leaves, and unripe berries **toxic**; said to cause cyanide poisoning, severe diarrhea and vomiting. Children are especially sensitive, even to slightly unripe berries.

RED ELDERBERRY
Sambucus racemosa L.

Flowers, berries, leaves, inner bark
Honeysuckle Family

Rank-smelling shrub, to 18 ft. Leaves with 5–7 elliptical leaflets; *base generally not symmetrical*, and tip gradually tapering to a sharp point. Flowers small, colored cream to white, pleasantly fragrant, in dense *dome-shaped clusters;* Mar.–Aug. Berries bright *red*. **WHERE FOUND:** Widespread. Moist places below 10,000 ft. Every western state except Tex. **USES:** Many Native American groups used red elderberry for cleansing and purging. The plant contains emetic and laxative compounds. Red berries are considered more toxic than the blue ones of other elderberry species, especially fresh. Other plant parts may be more toxic as well. American Indian groups chewed the roots or drank a tea as a purgative and laxative for ritual cleansing, to cure poisoning, or to purify the body to increase the endurance of hunters. Sometimes a second, weaker brewing of the tea was used for this purpose. The Hesquiat rubbed the crushed roots

Red Elderberry (Sambucus racemosa) *has flowers in dense dome-shaped cluster.*

on aching muscles for rheumatism, and other tribes used tea as a soak for tired, sore legs and feet. **RELATED SPECIES:** S. *melanocarpa* Gray is accepted either as a separate species or as a variety of S. *racemosa* [S. *racemosa* var. *melanocarpa* (Gray) McMinn]. The two species are considered interchangeable here. **WARNING:** All parts, including the berries, are considered potentially toxic.

LOW-GROWING OR MAT-FORMING SHRUBS; LEAVES ALTERNATE, FRUITS FLESHY

BEARBERRY, UVA-URSI
Arctostaphylos uva-ursi (L.) Spreng.

Whole plant
Heath Family

Evergreen, *mat-forming*, branch tips upright to 20 in. Leaves *shiny-leathery*, *spatula-shaped*. Flowers white to pinkish, urn-shaped, in short, dense racemes; Mar.–June. Fruit a dry red berry. **WHERE FOUND:** Rocky outcrops, sandy soils. Calif. to Alaska; every western state in northern U.S.; Eurasia. **USES:** Widely used in American Indian medicine. Leaves were chewed to suppress thirst and dried and mixed with tobacco for smoking. Leaf tea used as a mouthwash for canker sores and weak gums. Leaf tea widely used as a diuretic tonic, antiseptic, and astringent for kidney, urinary tract, and bladder ailments. The entire plant was made into a tea and used as a hair wash for dandruff and scalp disorders; also applied to skin sores. Leaves and stems were ground up and applied to sores and cuts to accelerate healing.

(Above) *Bearberry* (Arctostaphylos uva-ursi) *has urn-shaped, white to pink flowers.* (Right) *Bearberry with evergreen leaves and red fruits.*

Leaf paste poulticed to burns, boils, and pimples. A stem, leaf, and berry tea was taken for chronic back pain and back sprains. Moistened leaves were rubbed on the back for pain. Smoke from the leaves was used for earaches. The fruits were mixed with grease and given to children for diarrhea, and the raw berries were eaten as a laxative. Berries were eaten raw or cooked and considered quite nutritious. Leaves traditionally used by physicians as an astringent and urinary antiseptic for dysentery, diabetes, enuresis, and chronic kidney and urinary disorders. Research confirms strong antimicrobial, diuretic, and anti-inflammatory activity from hydroquinones such as arbutin. In Germany bearberry is approved as a urinary antiseptic. **RELATED SPECIES:** Leaves of *Arctostaphylos manzanita* Parry, White-leaf Manzanita, and probably other species, were used by American Indian groups as a tea for severe colds but are generally considered too strong for internal use. Used externally as a cleansing wash. Leaves formerly chewed for stomachaches and cramps and placed on sores. **WARNING:** Bearberry leaves contain arbutin, which hydrolyzes to the **toxic** urinary antiseptic hydroquinone; use is limited to less than one week in German herbal practice. Leaves are also high in tannins (up to 8 percent).

BLACK CROWBERRY
Empetrum nigrum L.

Leaves, stems, berries
Waterwort Family

Evergreen, with numerous low-creeping, matted branches with upturned tips, to 8 in. Stems with long, woolly hairs. Leaves dark green, linear, crowded, *grooved beneath; margins rolled under.* Flowers small, purplish, 3-parted, in leaf axils; June–July. Fruit a black berry with 2–9 large, white seeds. **WHERE FOUND:** Dry or wet rocky sites, coastal headlands, bogs, alpine tundra. Nw. Calif. to Alaska; Great Lakes; Europe, Asia, Chile. **USES:** The Haida people of British Columbia used a tea of the branches to treat tuberculosis. Leaf tea, with or without berries, was taken as a strong laxative. Tea of leafy branches used as a diuretic for children with fever and for kidney prob-

Black Crowberry (Empetrum nigrum). *Note leaves grooved beneath, with margins rolled under.*

lems. Stem tea or cooked berries taken for diarrhea. The leaves are a European folk medicine for water retention. Research confirms antifungal and antibacterial activity for extract.

LEAVES ALTERNATE, AROMATIC-RESINOUS, EVERGREEN

YERBA SANTA
Leaves, branches
Eriodictyon californicum (Hook. & Arn.) Torr.   Waterleaf Family
Aromatic, resinous evergreen, sometimes forming thickets; to 10 ft. Stems hairless, sticky. Leaves leathery, *sticky,* lance-shaped; lower leaf with woolly hairs; margins coarsely toothed. Flowers purple to white, tubular, in clusters; petals 5-lobed; May–Aug. **WHERE FOUND:** Dry, rocky slopes and ridges, chaparral, roadsides. S. Calif. to s. Ore. **USES:** Yerba Santa, the "saintly herb," has sweet, spicy leaves. Leaf tea used for colds, stomach problems, coughs, gonorrhea, asthma, rheumatism, pneumonia, and as a blood purifier. Leaves were smoked for colds and asthma, poulticed for sores, poison oak, sprains, wounds, insect bites, and broken bones. They were also used in steam baths for hemorrhoids and rheumatism. Some tribes boiled and strained the leaves, then added sugar to make a syrup for colds, pleurisy, and tuberculosis.

Yerba Santa (Eriodictyon californica) *flowers.*

Yerba Santa has sticky, resinous leaves.

Hot rocks were placed in a basket containing the herb and the vapors inhaled for dizziness. Leaves were once listed in the *U.S. Pharmacopoeia* and widely prescribed by physicians in the early 20th century for asthma, hay fever, bronchitis, pneumonia, and coughs with abundant expectoration. Herbalists recommend it for the same conditions today. **RELATED SPECIES:** Leaf and shoot tea of *E. angustifolium* Nutt., Narrow-Leaf Yerba Santa, drunk for indigestion, stomachaches, nausea, and constipation. The tea was used as a wash for tired feet and cuts. This and other western species of *Eriodictyon* often used interchangeably with *E. californicum*.

CALIFORNIA BAYBERRY, PACIFIC WAX MYRTLE
Root bark

Myrica californica Cham. & Schlect.   Wax Myrtle Family
[*Morella californica* (Cham. & Schlect.) Wilbur]

Aromatic evergreen shrub or small tree, to 30 ft. Stems and leaves *densely dotted with black glands.* Leaves shiny, leathery, dark green, narrowly oblong to lance-shaped; margins coarsely toothed. Flowers tiny, densely clustered in leaf axils; Mar.–Apr. Brownish purple fruit hard, rough, *covered in whitish wax.* **WHERE FOUND:** Coastal dunes, canyons, chaparral, moist slopes, along coast ranges. S. Calif. to Wash. **USES:** American Indian groups once used it as a mucous membrane tonic to relieve inflammation and increase the flow of blood and lymph to mucous membrane tissues. **RELATED SPECIES:** Pacific Wax Myrtle is considered to have similar properties to Wax-Myrtle, *M. cerifera* L., which was used as an astringent and stimulant for treating debilitated conditions of the mucous membranes, aphthous stomatitis, gum disease, sore throat, poor digestion, diarrhea, and dysentery. The powdered bark is mixed with water and applied externally for skin ulcers, sores, and fungal infections. Bark tea was especially favored for treat-

California Bayberry (Myrica californica) *has sweet-scented leaves.*

ing coughs and colds. A U.S. patent was registered for a tea of the twigs to relieve the symptoms of arthritis. Laboratory tests show that a terpenoid compound from *M. cerifera*, myriceric acid A, can inhibit endothelin binding, helping to prevent blood vessel constriction and increase blood flow to the body's organs. **WARNING:** May cause nausea in large doses. Wax is irritating. Constituents of the wax are reportedly carcinogenic.

LEAVES ALTERNATE, EVERGREEN;
FLOWERS SMALL IN SHOWY CLUSTERS

CHAMISE
Leaves, twigs

Adenostoma fasciculatum Hook. & Arn.   Rose Family

Evergreen, to 13 ft. Leaves thick, *linear, clustered*, somewhat resinous. Flowers small, white, 5-petaled, arranged in dense panicles at branch tips; Apr.–June. **WHERE FOUND:** Chaparral, dry slopes, and ridges. N. Calif. to n. Baja Calif.; Nev. **USES:** American Indians used a leaf and stem tea to soak or wash infected, sore, or swollen parts of the body. Tea was drunk for stomach or intestinal pain. **RELATED SPECIES:** American Indian groups drank a tea of the twigs of Red Shank, *A. sparsifolium* Torr., to relieve stomach or intestinal pain, apparently as a mild laxative.

CEANOTHUS, CALIFORNIA LILAC,
BLUE-BLOSSOM
Plant, leaves

Ceanothus thyrsiflorus Eschsch.   Buckthorn Family

Evergreen shrub or small tree, to 20 ft. Greenish *stems angled with lengthwise ribs*; hairless. Leaves ovate to oblong, prominently 3-veined from base; raised veins beneath are sparsely hairy; margins gland-toothed. Flowers numerous, small, light to deep blue, with 5 *spoon-shaped petals*; in long, dense clusters at branch tips; Mar.–June. **WHERE FOUND:** Wooded slopes, canyons. S. Calif. coast ranges to sw. Ore. **USES:** American Indian groups used plant tea as a wash for facial blemishes and as a hair rinse. Leaf

Chamise (Adenostoma fasciculatum) has linear, clustered leaves and showy white flowers.

California Lilac (Ceanothus thyrsiflorus) *is one of the showiest California natives.*

California Lilac with lilaclike flowers.

and twig tea used as a wash for newborn babies. **RELATED SPECIES:** American Indians boiled the roots of Deerbrush, *C. integerrimus* Hook. & Arn., to make a diuretic for the kidneys. Tea from this plant was given to women who suffered injury during childbirth. Red Root or New Jersey tea, *C. americanus* L., traditionally used as an important remedy for ailments of the stomach, liver, and spleen. Herbalists consider it a specific remedy for any ailment or symptoms related to congestion of the spleen or lymph, including enlarged spleen or swollen lymph nodes.

SNOWBUSH CEANOTHUS, TOBACCO BRUSH

Twigs, leaves

Ceanothus velutinus Dougl. ex Hook.

Buckthorn Family

Aromatic evergreen, upright to 10 ft. Forming thickets or sprawling, becoming matlike. Bark green. Leaves broadly ovate, *sticky, shiny*, dark green above, paler and gray-hairy beneath; prominently *3-veined from base*; margins finely gland-toothed; often curling under in hot weather.

Snowbush Ceanothus (Ceanothus velutinus) *has sticky, shiny leaves and showy white flowers.*

Flowers small, white, with 5 spoon-shaped petals, in dense clusters; Apr.–July. **WHERE FOUND:** Dry to moist sites; open woods and slopes. Calif. to B.C., eastward to Mont., Colo., Utah. **USES:** American Indian groups used twig and/or leaf tea for general illness, weight loss, arthritis, diarrhea, rheumatism, and gonorrhea. Leaf tea used as a cough remedy and for broken bones. Externally as a wash for pains, sores, eczema, broken limbs, rheumatism, and arthritis. A tea from plant tops and leaves was used for dandruff and to help prevent diaper rash. A whole plant tea was a folk cancer remedy. The dried, powdered leaves were used as a baby powder and mixed with pitch and applied to sores.

WILD BUCKWHEAT
Eriogonum fasciculatum Benth.

Whole plant
Buckwheat Family

Evergreen; branches low, spreading. Leaves narrow, *leathery, clustered*; covered in dense white hairs below, hairless above; margins strongly rolled under. Flowers small, dry, *brownish rust, generally persist after flowering* in dense, round clusters, arranged in umbels at branch tips; flower stalks gray hairy, leafless; May–Nov. **WHERE FOUND:** Dry slopes, washes, canyons, coastal bluffs. Coast ranges of Calif. to w. Ariz., Nev., sw. Utah; Baja Calif., nw. Mex-

Wild Buckwheat (Eriogonum fasciculatum) *flowers turn brownish rust and persist after flowering.*

Winter Sage (Krascheninnikovia lanata). *Note the densely hairy flower spikes.*

ico. **USES:** The Cahuilla drank leaf tea for headache and stomach pain. Hot root tea drunk for colds and laryngitis. Whole plant tea taken internally and applied externally for urinary problems. Flower tea used as a cleansing purgative and given to babies for diarrhea. Root poultice was applied to wounds. A tea of dried flowers or dried roots was taken to prevent heart problems. Studies have identified leucoanthocyanidins beneficial to the heart in other *Eriogonum* species.

WINTER SAGE, WHITE SAGE Whole plant

Krascheninnikovia lanata (Pursh) A. D. J. Meeuse & Smit
[*Eurotia lanata* (Pursh) Moq.] Goosefoot Family

Evergreen, to 3 ft. Stems and leaves densely covered in white, star-shaped hairs; *becoming rust-colored*. Leaves linear, clustered; margins entire, rolled under. Small male and female flowers in densely hairy spikes at branch tips, Mar.–June. **WHERE FOUND:** Rocky, clay, or alkaline soils, flats, gentle slopes. East of Sierra-Cascade crest from s. Calif. to every western state; north to Sask., n. cen. U.S.; n. Mexico. **USES:** Southwestern Indian groups applied the chewed leaves as a poultice to sores, boils, smallpox sores, poison ivy, and sore muscles. Plant tea was taken to treat fevers and spitting of blood, used as a wash or compress for sore eyes, applied as a hot solution for head lice. Still used as a tonic scalp wash to slow hair loss and prevent graying. Powdered roots were applied to burns.

OREGON GRAPEROOT Root bark

Mahonia aquifolium (Pursh) Nutt. Barberry Family
[*Berberis aquifolium* Pursh]

 Evergreen, upright or spreading, to 2–10 ft. *Inner bark and roots bright yellow.* Pinnately compound leaves with 5–11 shiny, green, hollylike leaflets. Leathery, oblong leaflets flat to strongly wavy with sharp, spine-tipped teeth. Yellow flowers in dense racemes at branch tips; Mar.–June. Sour, dark bluish *berries covered with whitish film.* **WHERE FOUND:** Slopes, canyons, coniferous forests, oak woodland, chaparral, open sites. Calif. to B.C., to Colo., N.M.; n. Mexico; eastern U.S. Widely cultivated as an ornamental shrub. **USES:** American Indian groups used the root as a blood purifier and general tonic and in treating "all kinds of sickness," including stomach problems, sore throat, tuberculosis, kidney problems, syphilis, bleeding, and as a wash for arthritis. The stem tips were used to treat upset stomach. Plant tea used as an eyewash. The berries were considered laxative. Traditionally, root and stem bark preparations used by herbalists and physicians as a blood purifier, to treat liver disorders, gallstones, impaired digestion, constipation, respiratory ailments such as pneumonia and bronchitis, as a

(Left) *Oregon Graperoot* (Mahonia aquifolium) *has hollylike leaflets.* (Above) *Algerita* (Mahonia trifolioata) *has leaflets clustered in threes.*

gargle for sore throats, and for chronic skin problems such as eczema, psoriasis, and acne. Externally used as a wash for skin infections and as an eyewash. Recent studies suggest compounds in root are beneficial in treating psoriasis, helping to stimulate immune function, and reducing proliferation of keratocytes. Antioxidant activity also confirmed. **RELATED SPECIES:** All species of *Mahonia* and the closely related genus *Berberis* are used similarly, including *M. repens* (Lindl.) G. Don, *M. fremontii* (Torr.) Fedde, *M. nervosa* (Pursh) Nutt., and the European Barberry, *Berberis vulgaris* L. All contain the alkaloid berberine, which imparts a bright yellow color to the roots. Based on numerous laboratory tests, berberine has antibacterial and amoebicidal activity, stimulates bile secretion, and is mildly sedative. *B. vulgaris* is used in Europe for liver problems, high blood pressure, constipation, and gum and throat irritation. **WARNING:** Avoid use during pregnancy. Do not use berberine-containing herbs for more than a week or two except on advice of a qualified practitioner.

ALGERITA, DESERT BARBERRY

Berries, root

Mahonia trifolioata (Moric.) Fedde

Barberry Family

[*Berberis trifolioata* Moric.]

 Evergreen shrub; 6–9 ft. Leaves elliptical to lance-shaped, to 3 in., strongly 3–7-lobed, or toothed, with spiny-tipped margins. Flowers small, yellow, *saffron-scented*, in tight drooping racemes; Feb.–Apr. Fruits globose, bright red, about ⅜ in. diameter. **WHERE**

FOUND: Rocky slopes, deserts, open woods. S. Tex., s. Ariz., N.M., n. Mexico. **USES:** Used similarly to Oregon Graperoot (above), primarily as a bitter tonic for gastric and mucous membrane irritations, a stimulant to the liver, and antimicrobial for gastrointestinal tract and skin conditions. *M. fremontii*, also referred to as Algerita, used by the Hualapai Indians of the Southwest. Roots also used to prepare a tonic for liver problems, as a laxative, and to stimulate and improve digestion. The fruits are considered edible. **WARNING:** Avoid use during pregnancy. Do not use berberine-containing herbs for more than a week or two without advice of a qualified practitioner.

EVERGREEN SHRUBS WITH ALTERNATE LEAVES; 5-PARTED FLOWERS; FLESHY FRUITS

SALAL
Gaultheria shallon Pursh

Leaves
Heath Family

Evergreen, hairy-stemmed, upright or creeping shrub, to 6 ft. Leaves shiny, *stiff, leathery,* ovate to oval, hairless; margins minutely toothed. Flowers white to pinkish, *urn-shaped,* hanging from horizontal to upright racemes; dense, glandular hairs on branchlets; Apr.–July. Dark, purplish black berry with many seeds; edible. **WHERE FOUND:** Understory in wet to dry coniferous forests, west of Sierra-Cascade crest; generally on acidic soils. Cen. Calif.

(Above) *Salal* (Gaultheria shallon) *has urn-shaped flowers hanging on reddish stalks.* (Right) *Salal has dark purple, edible fruits.*

coast ranges north to Alaska. **USES:** American Indian groups used poultice of chewed leaves on sores, cuts, and burns. Leaves chewed to treat heartburn and colic and to dry the mouth. Leaf tea used to treat coughs, tuberculosis, diarrhea, or as a stomach or convalescent tonic. Newlywed Nitinaht couples ate the leaves to ensure that the firstborn baby would be a boy. **RELATED SPECIES:** Though a close relative of the familiar scented Wintergreen, *G. procumbens* L., Salal lacks aromatic volatile oils.

TOYON
Heteromeles arbutifolia (Lindl.) M. Roemer

Leaves, bark
Rose Family

Evergreen shrub, to 15 ft. Bark gray; young branches with soft, short, dense hairs. Leaves stiff, *leathery*, narrowly oblong to lance-shaped; shiny, dark green above, often with red patches, pale green below; margins sharply toothed. Flowers numerous, white, arranged in flat-topped branched clusters, with 5 separate spreading petals and 5 pairs of stamens; Apr.–July. Clusters of bright red, berrylike fruits with mealy pulp and few seeds. **WHERE FOUND:** Chaparral, oak woodland, mixed evergreen forest. Calif.; n. Baja Calif. A form with yellow berries is found in s. Calif. coast ranges. **USES:** Native American groups used leaf and bark tea for stomachaches and other aches and pains, and as a wash for infected wounds. Costanoan Indians used the leaf tea to treat irregular or suppressed menses.

PALE WOLFBERRY,
PALE MATRIMONY VINE
Lycium pallidum Miers

Root, plant, berries
Nightshade Family

Evergreen, multibranched, to 6 ft. Thorny, spine-tipped stems without hairs. Leaves narrowly obovate, succulent, clustered, covered in *whitish film*; margins entire. Flowers tubular, 5-parted, greenish to white with dark purple veins; petal lobes spreading; Mar.–May. Red to reddish blue berry hard, somewhat fleshy. **WHERE FOUND:** Desert flats, washes, slopes, mesas throughout the southwestern states. S. Calif. to s. Nev., s. Utah, Colo., sw. Tex.;

Toyon (Heteromeles arbutifolia), with leathery leaves and red fruits.

Mexico. **USES:** Navajo used root as a poultice for toothache and also to treat chickenpox; the bark and dried berries were a life medicine and ceremonial remedy. The berries were used as food. **RELATED SPECIES:** The berries of *L. andersonii* Gray., *L. exsertum* Gray, and *L. fremontii* Gray were also used as food. Chinese herbalists add the berries of *L. barbarum* L. or *L. chinense* P. Mill. to prescriptions for treating toothache, night sweats, wheezing, coughing, nosebleed, vomiting of blood, and bloody urine. **WARNING:** Leaves and shoots of *L. barbarum* L. [*L. halimifolium* P. Mill.] contain the toxic alkaloid hyoscyamine. Avoid use during pregnancy.

EVERGREEN HUCKLEBERRY
Leaves, berries, root

Vaccinium ovatum Pursh
Heath Family

Evergreen, to 6 ft. Stems grayish, hairy, not angled. Leaves thick, *leathery*, ovate; margins finely toothed, sometimes rolled under. Flowers *urn-shaped*, white to pink, in clusters from leaf axils; 5-parted with 10 stamens; Mar.–June. Shiny, black berries, many-seeded, with *remnants of petals at tip*, sometimes with whitish film. **WHERE FOUND:** Acidic soils in coniferous forests; dry slopes and canyons. Calif. to B.C. **USES:** Historically, physicians used berries and roots in alcoholic tinctures as a diuretic. Leaf or root tea for diarrhea, ulcerations, leukorrhea, and sore throat. Modern research on *Vaccinium* extracts show antioxidant, blood-vessel-protective, and triglyceride-lowering effects. Both modern herbalists and American Indian groups, who used *V. ovatum* to treat diabetes, claim it is useful in treating hyperglycemia. It contains antiseptic glycosides, which can relieve urinary tract infections. Various *Vaccinium* species have similar properties.

Lycium brevipes, *pictured here, like other* Lycium *species, are important traditional medicines.*

Evergreen Huckleberry (Vaccinium ovatum). *The berries and roots were historically used as a diuretic.*

EVERGREEN SHRUBS WITH ALTERNATE LEAVES; 5-PARTED FLOWERS; DRY FRUITS

ADERLEAF MOUNTAIN MAHOGANY
Cercocarpus montanus Raf.

Whole plant

Rose Family

Evergreen shrub, to 9 feet. Leaves dark green, obovate, sharply toothed above, *lower half wedge-shaped*. Flowers small, cup-shaped, without petals, stamens numerous; Mar.–May. Fruits with *long feathery tail*. **WHERE FOUND:** Dry brushy slopes, sagebrush, aspen and mixed conifer forests, from 4200 to 8000 feet. Common in Rockies. Ne. Calif., e. Ore., to all other western states except Wash., Idaho. **USES:** The Navajo and other tribes considered the plant a general strengthening tonic. Leaf tea used to ease stomach troubles from overeating. Leaves chewed by hunters to bring good hunting. Root was known as a life medicine, or panacea. The Tewa used a cold tea of the leaves as a laxative. **RELATED SPECIES:** Curl-leaf Mountain Mahogany, *C. ledifolius* Nutt., widely used by western tribes. The Gosiute used powdered green wood as a poultice for healing burns. The Kawaiisu powdered the small amber, transparent tears of dried exudate from the plant and applied it to the ears for earaches. For "women's disease" and for gonorrhea, they drank a tea of the bark and leaves. Other tribes used bark tea for stomachaches, diarrhea, and as a blood tonic. Bark tea used for mild to serious respiratory ailments, such as coughs, colds, pneumonia, tuberculosis, and for spitting up blood. A paste made from the bark or wood was spread on sores, cuts, wounds, swellings, and burns. Hardtack, *C. betuloides* Torr. & Gray [*C. montanus* var. *glaber* (S. Wats.) F. L. Martin], from sw. Ore., Calif., Ariz., and n. Baja Calif., was used in similar ways by the Apache and other western tribes. The young plants or leaves of older plants were powdered, salt added, stirred into cold water, then brewed as a laxative. Root tea used for coughs. Tea of leaves and bark used for venereal disease. Charcoal from the burned wood was applied to burns.

Alderleaf Mountain Mahogany (Cercocarpus montanus) *has fruits with a feathery tail.*

Labrador-Tea (Ledum groenlandicum) *is, like its relatives,
potentially toxic.*

LABRADOR-TEA
Ledum groenlandicum Oeder

Leaves, root

Heath Family

⚠ Evergreen, to 2–5 ft. Branches with dense, rusty hairs. Leaves *spicy fragrant*, leathery, narrowly oblong, often drooping; margins entire, *white to rusty-woolly* beneath; *edges turned under.* Flowers white, in terminal cluster, with 5 round spreading petals; May–July. **WHERE FOUND:** Bogs, peat, marshes; generally on acidic or nutrient-poor soils. Alaska to Ore.; Idaho, N.D., S.D.; east to New England, Lab., Greenland. **USES:** One of the most widely used Indian remedies, often used during healing ceremonies. American Indian groups used leaf wash for rashes, chapping, chafing, cracked nipples, itching, poison ivy, stings, sores and burns. Chewed leaves were poulticed on wounds. Dried powdered leaves dusted on a baby's skin for rashes. Internally, tea taken to treat colds, sore throat, pneumonia, tuberculosis, whooping cough, asthma, fever, headaches, nasal inflammation, jaundice, stomach pain, loss of appetite, edema, kidney problems, rheumatism, and as a blood purifier. Many tribes used it as a strengthening tonic and appetite stimulant. Historically, physicians used it for respiratory disease, skin disorders, itching, lice, dyspepsia, rheumatism, gout, and other types of arthritis. Early European settlers used the herb as a substitute for tea. **RELATED SPECIES:** *L. palustre* L. has been used in Europe since the 12th century for arthritic pains, coughs, colds, water retention, and externally for healing wounds.

WARNING: May contain the nerve toxin grayanotoxin (andromedo-toxin). Weak teas apparently contain little of the toxin, with no known reports of human toxicity.

EVERGREEN SHRUBS WITH ALTERNATE FERNLIKE LEAVES; 5-PARTED FLOWERS: ROSE FAMILY

MOUNTAIN MISERY
Chamaebatia foliolosa Benth.

Leaves
Rose Family

Evergreen shrub with *sticky stems*, to 3 ft. Leaves *fernlike*, strongly pungent, obovate, with tiny, oval leaflets. White flowers in loose terminal panicles; May–July. **WHERE FOUND:** Open, coniferous forests; often abundant. S. cen. mountains and nw. Sierra of Calif. **USES:** The Miwok used leaf tea for rheumatism, colds, coughs, chickenpox, measles, and smallpox.

FERNBUSH
Chamaebatiaria millefolium (Torr.) Maxim.

Whole plant
Rose Family

Strong-smelling, glandular-hairy, evergreen, to 6 ft. *Fernlike leaves* oblong in outline; leaflets tiny. Flowers white, in dense terminal panicles; June–Aug. **WHERE FOUND:** Dry, rocky slopes, ridges, sagebrush scrub, pinyon-juniper woodland, pine forests. East slope of s. Sierra Nevada, Calif., to Ariz., Ore., Idaho, Wyo. **USES:** American Indian groups used leaf tea for stomachaches or cramps.

(Above) *Mountain Misery* (Chamaebatia foliolosa) *has sticky, fernlike leaves.* (Right) *Fernbush* (Chamaebatiaria millefolium) *is a strong-smelling, glandular-hairy evergreen with attractive flowers.*

Externally, used for venereal sores. The Ramah Navajo rolled the leaves into a corn husk and smoked it to bring good hunting.

DECIDUOUS SHRUBS WITH ALTERNATE LEAVES; 5-PARTED SHOWY FLOWERS

DESERT PEACH, NEVADA WILD ALMOND
Bark, stems, leaves, roots

Prunus andersonii Gray — Rose Family

Deciduous shrub with spine-tipped stems, to 6 ft. Leaves narrowly oval to obovate, nearly stalkless; hairless; margins finely toothed. Flowers rose-colored, solitary; Mar.–Apr. Fleshy fruit covered in dense, brownish hairs. **WHERE FOUND:** Desert slopes and mesas, scrubland, coniferous forest; 2600 to 8000 ft. E. slope of Sierra Nevada, Calif. to w. Nev. **USES:** Paiute Indians used tea of branches, leaves, or roots for diarrhea. Bark tea for rheumatism, tuberculosis, colds, and preventative for flu. **WARNING:** All parts of *Prunus* species contain varying amounts of highly toxic hydrocyanic acid (producing an almondlike smell).

WESTERN AZALEA
Whole plant

Rhododendron occidentale (Torr. & Gray ex Torr.) Gray — Heath Family

Deciduous shrub, to 13 ft. Leaves thin, oblong to lance-shaped, margins entire, hairy. Flowers showy; color varies from white or cream to pinkish; *upper petal with yellow blotch at base, sweetly fragrant* in umbellike terminal clusters; Apr.–Aug. **WHERE FOUND:** Moist places, seeps, coniferous forests. Coastal Calif., Sierra foothills; Ore. **USES:** Leaves used as a diuretic, narcotic, and poison

Desert Peach (Prunus andersonii) *has solitary rose-colored flowers.*

Western Azalea (Rhododendron occidentale) *is a showy native of coastal coniferous forests.*

antidote. **RELATED SPECIES:** The Okanagan and Thompson Indians used ointment of charred and powdered wood of *R. albiflorum* Hook., Cascade Azalea, to treat swellings. Chinese herbalists prescribe *R. molle* (Bl.) G. Don for rheumatism, headaches, and intractable ringing in the ears, and to ease the pain of fractures. **WARNING:** This and other *Rhododendron* species contain andromedotoxin, which can cause excessive secretions, nausea, vomiting, convulsions, and even death.

LEAVES ALTERNATE, DECIDUOUS; FLOWERS SMALL, 5-PARTED, IN SHOWY CLUSTERS: ROSE FAMILY

OCEAN SPRAY **Leaves, bark, root**
Holodiscus discolor (Pursh) Maxim. Rose Family
Deciduous shrub with *arching stems,* to 20 ft. Leaves oval to triangular; margins shallowly lobed and coarsely toothed. Flowers small, white, arranged in *dense terminal sprays;* turning brown, persistent through winter; June–Aug. **WHERE FOUND:** Dry to moist woodlands, rocky slopes, coastal bluffs. Calif. to B.C., n. Idaho, w. Mont., Wyo., Colo., Utah, Nev., Ariz.; Mexico. **USES:** American Indian groups poulticed powdered leaves to sores, sore lips, and sore feet; bark poultice used for burns. Leaf tea used to treat venereal disease and influenza. Bark tea used as a tonic for convalescents and athletes. Root tea used to ease stomach disorders and diarrhea. **RELATED SPECIES:** Root tea of *H. dumosus* (Nutt. ex Hook.) Heller, Rock Spirea, used for gut disorders, stomachache, and diarrhea.

Ocean Spray (Holodiscus discolor) *has tiny white flowers in showy sprays.*

(Above) *Pacific Ninebark* (Physo-carpus capitatus). *The bark peels off in strips.* (Right) *White Mead-owsweet* (Spiraea betulifolia) *has birchlike leaves.*

PACIFIC NINEBARK
Bark, root
Physocarpus capitatus (Pursh) Kuntze — Rose Family

Deciduous shrub to 15 ft. , with *bark peeling into thin strips.* Leaves round to ovate, 3–5-lobed. Flowers small, white, densely clustered in terminal *umbel cluster*; May–Sept. **WHERE FOUND:** Moist areas, meadows, coniferous forest, coastal marshes, north-facing slopes. Calif. to Alaska, east to Idaho, Mont., Utah. **USES:** Emetic bark tea used as an antidote to poisons and in small doses as a laxative. Externally, used as a wash or bath for rheumatism and rheumatic fever. The root is purgative and laxative. **WARNING:** Large doses of *P. opulifolius* (L.) Maxim are said to be fatal. The bark and leaves of many rose family members contain cyanide compounds in varying amounts.

WHITE MEADOWSWEET
Leaves, stems, flowers, root
Spiraea betulifolia Pallas — Rose Family

Deciduous shrub; slender, upright stems, to 3 ft. Leaves ovate, shiny above, hairless; margins coarsely toothed along *upper half.* Flowers small, white or pink, in dense, *flat-topped* branched clusters; June–Aug. **WHERE FOUND:** Dry, open montane forests, along streams, mostly east of Cascades. Ore. to B.C., to Mont. and Wyo., eastward. **USES:** Flower buds of the European species, *Filipendula ulmaria* (L.) Maxim. [*S. ulmaria* L.] were the original source of the aspirin precursor salicin. The name aspirin comes from a- (for the acetyl group added to salicylic acid to make it more

Douglas's Spirea (Spiraea douglasii) with its showy spire of red flowers.

available to the body) and spiraeic acid (from the genus name *Spiraea*). Salicylic acid formed from salicin in the body has anti-inflammatory properties and is less toxic than acetylsalicylic acid (aspirin). Nineteenth-century pharmacopoeias describe *Spiraea* species as a treatment for diarrhea and as a tonic for treating debility and improving digestion. American Indian groups used tea of leafy stems to relieve menstrual pain and heavy bleeding, colds, abdominal pain, and kidney weakness. Leaf and root tea used for diarrhea and to ease stomach problems; tea of the whole plant for colds.

DOUGLAS'S SPIREA
Spiraea douglasii Hook.
Leaves, seeds
Rose Family
Erect shrub, 3–6 ft. Leaves alternate, oval to elliptical, 1–3 in. long, margins serrated above middle, green above, white-hairy beneath. Flowers rose-pink, in showy pyramidal spikes; June-Sept. **WHERE FOUND:** Moist ground, often along streams. B.C. to n. Calif. **USES:** As in other *Spiraea* spp., leaves probably contain salicin and tannins. Lummi used a tea of seed heads to treat diarrhea. Leaf tea used as a general tonic.

LEAVES ALTERNATE, DECIDUOUS; FLOWERS SMALL, 5-PARTED; FRUITS RED: ROSE FAMILY

UTAH JUNEBERRY, UTAH SERVICEBERRY
Amelanchier utahensis Koehne
Bark, fruit, roots
Rose Family
Deciduous shrub or small tree, to 20 ft.; often forming thickets. Bark gray, smooth; younger stems red. Thin leaves round to oval, ½ to 1½ in. long; margins toothed. Flowers showy, white, fragrant, with 5 upright, oblong petals. Round, tasty, berrylike fruit

initially red, becoming dark purple to black. **WHERE FOUND:** Dry to moist coniferous forest, streamsides, open scrubland, Rocky Mts. Colo., Utah, w. Tex., N.M., e. Calif. to Ore., Idaho, Mont. **USES:** Navajo women drank bark tea during labor and delivery. For snow blindness the green inner bark was boiled with sugar, cooled, then used as eyedrops. **RELATED SPECIES:** *A. alnifolia* (Nutt.) Nutt., Western Juneberry, has a more northerly distribution and is larger in all respects. Widely used by Western American Indian groups. Women used bark tea as a contraceptive, for sitz baths, as a wash following childbirth, and for too frequent menstruation. Root or stem tea used for coughs, chest pains, lung infections, too frequent menstruation, and teething. Berry tea was used as a tonic and for stomach disorders. Fruit a widely used food. In a recent study, a plant extract demonstrated activity against an intestinal corona virus.

HAWTHORN
Flowers, leaves, fruit
Crataegus spp.
Rose Family

Spiny shrub. Leaves simple, toothed; cut or lobed. Flowers mostly white, usually with 5 petals; calyx tube bell-shaped, 5-parted; spring–early summer. Fruit a dry red berry; 1–5 hard seeds. The 100–1000 species of native and cultivated hawthorns in N. America are a very complex, highly variable group. They hybridize readily, and species identification is difficult even for the specialist. The most common western species is *C. douglasii* Lindl., Black Hawthorn or River Hawthorn. **WHERE FOUND:** Streamsides, moist

(Above) *Utah Serviceberry (Amelanchier utahensis) is an early-flowering small tree.* (Right) *Hawthorns are used the world over as heart tonics.* Crataegus douglasii *is pictured here.*

open places, forests, meadows. Calif. to Alaska, west from Wash., Ore. to Great Lakes; Utah. **USES:** American Indian groups ate fruit of River Hawthorn as food and to treat general illness and diarrhea. Thorns were inserted like acupuncture needles into joints with arthritic pain and were allowed to burn down onto arthritic areas as a form of moxibustion. The thorns were also used to pierce and drain boils and to probe ulcers and wounds. **RELATED SPECIES:** The use of fruit for diarrhea echoes the use in Chinese medicine prescriptions of *C. pinnatifida* Bge. or *C. cuneata* Sieb. et Zucc., shan zha, an important remedy to relieve food stagnation accompanied by constipation, diarrhea, and abdominal pain with distension. Hawthorn fruits and flowers are well known in herbal medicine (American Indian, Chinese, European) as a heart tonic. Studies confirm effectiveness in hypertension with weak heart, angina pectoris, arteriosclerosis. Preparations dilate coronary vessels, reducing blood pressure, and act as direct and mild heart tonic. Leaf and flower (though not fruit) of *C. laevigata* (Poir.) DC. and *C. monogyna* Jacq. are approved in Germany for treating early stages of congestive heart failure characterized by diminished cardiac function, sensations of pressure or anxiety in the heart area, age-related heart disorders that do not require digitalis, and mild arrhythmias. Both of these European species have been cultivated and occasionally naturalized in N. America. Effects confirmed by at least 14 controlled clinical studies. The fruits, flowers, and leaves of hawthorn contain active compounds such as flavonoids, proanthocyanidins, phenolic acids, tannins, and amines, all of which contribute to the cardioactive effects. Preparations should be taken for several months, and preferably for a number of years, to derive the most benefit. **WARNING:** Eye scratches from thorns can cause blindness. Heart disease, the number-one killer in America, requires professional medical attention.

ANTELOPE BRUSH, BITTERBRUSH   **Leaves, bark, roots**
Purshia tridentata (Pursh) DC.   Rose Family

Mostly deciduous, to 15 ft. Leaves grayish, *3-lobed at tip*; margins strongly rolled under. Small, yellow to cream flowers solitary at branch tips; May–July. Fruit teardrop-shaped with gray hairs; *blood red when crushed.* **WHERE FOUND:** Dry slopes, chaparral, sagebrush scrub, piñon-juniper woodland, coniferous forest. Calif. to B.C., east to Mont., N.M., Nev. **USES:** Western Indian groups used leaf poultice or wash for itching, rashes, insect bites, chickenpox, and measles. Leaf tea used as a general tonic and for colds, pneumonia, liver disease, to expel worms, and as an emetic and laxative for stomachache and constipation. Twigs, leaves, and berries

(Above) *Antelope Brush, Bitter-brush* (Purshia tridentata) *has small, cream-yellow flowers.*
(Right) *Mountain Ash* (Sorbus spp.) *with showy fruit clusters.*

used as a laxative. Root tea for coughs, lung and bronchial infections, fever, and to facilitate delivery of the placenta. **RELATED SPECIES:** *P. glandulosa* Curran [*P. tridentata* var. *glandulosa* (Curran) M. E. Jones], *P. mexicana* (D. Don) Henrickson, and *P. stansburiana* (Torr.) Henrickson were used similarly.

SITKA MOUNTAIN ASH

Fruits, bark

Sorbus sitchensis M. Roemer   Rose Family

Deciduous shrub, to 10 ft. Leaves p*innately compound* with *7–11 bluish green,* oval to oblong *leaflets,* coarsely toothed, mostly above the middle. Flowers small, white, in dense terminal clusters; May–Aug. *Fruit is bright red berry.* **WHERE FOUND:** Open montane areas; coniferous forest, streambanks, meadow edges. Calif. to B.C.; east to Idaho, w. Mont., w. Nev. **USES:** Tea of root and inner bark of branches used for rheumatism, arthritis, backache, stomach problems, bed-wetting, and weak kidneys with frequent urination. The bark was chewed to relieve cold symptoms. Juice of fruit used in water as a gargle for sore throat and hoarseness. Berries rubbed on head to kill lice and treat dandruff. Fruits eaten as a purgative. **RELATED SPECIES:** Fruits of the European Mountain Ash, *S. aucuparia* L., have been used for piles, urinary difficulty, indigestion, gall bladder ailments, angina, and other coronary problems.

ALTERNATE, DECIDUOUS COMPOUND LEAVES; 5–7 LEAFLETS; ROSES

CALIFORNIA WILD ROSE

Flowers, fruit, leaves

Rosa californica Cham. & Schlecht.

Rose Family

Deciduous shrub, to 8 ft. Often forming thickets. Branches with *stout, flattened, strongly curved prickles*. Leaves pinnately compound, with 5–7 oval to ovate leaflets; margins toothed. Flowers pink; sepals with long, slender tips, hairy on back; May–Sept. Fruit a red rose hip, *with* sepals attached on top. **WHERE FOUND:** Moist areas, streambanks, canyons. Calif., s. Ore.; n. Baja Calif. **USES:** Costanoan Indians used fruit to treat colds, sore throat, fever, indigestion, kidney problems, muscle and joint aches and pains, and as a wash on scabs and sores. Other tribes used flowers for pain and fever in infants and for "clogged stomach." **RELATED SPECIES:** Probably all of the more than 100 species of roses worldwide have been used medicinally. Fruits and flowers of a European red garden rose, *R. gallica* L., used as a heart and nerve tonic, blood purifier, to relieve mouth sores, sore throat, earache, headache, uterine cramps, and as a wash or poultice for sore eyes.

WOOD ROSE, DWARF ROSE

Whole plant

Rosa gymnocarpa Nutt.

Rose Family

Deciduous, mostly *to 4 ft*. Stems with *slender, straight prickles*. Leaves pinnately compound with 5–7 widely oval, hairless

(Left) *California Wild Rose* (Rosa californica) *branches have flattened, strongly curved prickles.* (Above) *Wood Rose* (Rosa gymnocarpa). *The hips do not have persistent sepals at the top.*

leaflets; margins with gland-tipped teeth. Stems and stalks glandular-hairy. Flowers small, pink to rose; May–July. Orange to red hip round, *without* sepals attached at top. **WHERE FOUND:** Dry to moist, open or shaded forest; scrublands. Calif. to B.C.; Idaho, Mont. **Uses:** Okanagan-Colville Indians drank plant tea when taking sweat baths, also as a body and hair wash. Leaves poulticed for bee stings and added to smoking mixtures. Thompson Indians made a tonic for general illness from the stems. They considered the hips of this species unpalatable and somewhat toxic.

ALTERNATE, DECIDUOUS COMPOUND OR PALMATELY LOBED LEAVES: BLACKBERRIES, RASPBERRIES, AND RELATIVES

WHITEBARK RASPBERRY
Leaves, roots, stems
Rubus leucodermis Dougl. ex Torr. & Gray
Rose Family

Deciduous, upright to 6 ft., or arched, rooting at tips. Stems covered in *thick whitish film* and many *curved, flat prickles.* Leaves 3–5-divided, leaflets ovate; margins sharply toothed; lower surface white, prickled on midvein. Flowers small, white; sepals bent backward; Apr.–July. Edible berry initially red, *becoming dark purple;* shallowly rounded, with soft hairs. **WHERE FOUND:** Moist, rocky or open sites, canyons; montane coniferous forest. Calif. to B.C.; east to Mont., Nev., Utah, N.M. **USES:** Pomo and Kashaya Indians treated diarrhea, weak bowels, or upset stomach with tea of leaves

(Above) *Whitebarked Raspberry* (Rubus leucodermis) *berries are red at first, then turn purplish.* (Right) *Black Raspberry* (Rubus occidentalis) *is the familiar blackberry of commerce.*

and roots. Thompson Indians used root tea for influenza. The Shoshone poulticed powdered stems on cuts and wounds. **RELATED SPECIES:** The astringent leaves and roots of many *Rubus* species have been used to treat diarrhea, dysentery, hemorrhage, leukorrhea, and sore gums. Leaves of Red Raspberry, *R. idaeus* L., are still widely used today as a toning tea drunk throughout pregnancy to facilitate childbirth. Therapeutic use has not been approved in Germany because studies have not supported claims of efficacy as a uterine tonic. Extracts of the leaves have demonstrated uterus-relaxing effects in laboratory tests.

BLACK RASPBERRY
Rubus occidentalis L.

Leaves, roots
Rose Family

Deciduous, upright to 8 ft., or arching, rooting at tips. *Stem glaucous, with curved prickles.* Leaves 3–5-divided, leaflets ovate; margins toothed; lower surface white, densely hairy. Flowers white; sepals densely hairy; Apr.–June. *Black berry covered in a whitish, waxy film;* edible. **WHERE FOUND:** Edges of woods and fields; dry, rocky sites. Colo., N.M.; eastern N. America. Cultivated throughout. Alien (Europe). **USES:** Astringent root tea traditionally used for diarrhea, dysentery, stomach pain, gonorrhea, back pain, as a "female tonic," blood tonic, and for boils. Leaf tea used similarly, also as a wash for sores and ulcers. Leaf tea approved in Germany for treatment of diarrhea and mild inflammation of the mouth and throat. Its astringency is due to tannins in both leaf and root. A decoction of the roots, stalks, and leaves was used for whooping cough in children. A concentrated infusion was drunk to ease childbirth pain.

Thimbleberry (Rubus parviflorus) *has maplelike, soft-hairy leaves and white, showy flowers.*

Salmonberry (Rubus spectabilis) *has salmon-colored fruits.*

THIMBLEBERRY
Leaves, roots, berries, galls

Rubus parviflorus Nutt.
Rose Family

Deciduous, to 6 ft. Often forming thickets. *Bark flaky or peeling, without prickles.* Large leaves 5-lobed; *both* surfaces soft hairy; margins finely toothed. Branchlets with dense glandular hairs. Flowers large, white, petals crinkled; May–Aug. Red fruit shallowly rounded with fine hairs; edible. **WHERE FOUND:** Moist, shady sites. Calif. to Alaska; east to w. Mont., south to N.M. **USES:** American Indian groups used tea of various plant parts for its astringent and tonic properties in treating diarrhea, stomachache, vomiting, spitting blood, acne, as a tonic and appetite stimulant for thin people, for prolonged menstruation, anemia, and to strengthen the blood. Leaves poulticed on wounds and burns and to lessen scar formation. Young sprouts eaten as an antiscorbutic and blood purifier. In China, root tea a folk remedy for treating fevers due to colds and flu, tonsillitis, rheumatoid arthritis, hepatitis, diarrhea, water retention associated with kidney infections, urinary stones, blood in stools or sputum, and externally for boils and toxic swellings. Research confirms that extracts shorten bleeding and coagulation time.

SALMONBERRY
Leaves, roots, bark

Rubus spectabilis Pursh
Rose Family

Deciduous, to 13 ft. Often forming thickets. *Bark yellowish to gold brown, shredding.* Stems initially with slender, straight prickles, usually at base; *older stems without prickles.* Leaves with 3 ovate leaflets, without prickles. Flowers showy, reddish to magenta; Mar.–June. *Berry yellow, salmon,* or red; edible. **WHERE FOUND:** Moist sites, streambanks. Calif. to Alaska; Idaho. **USES:** Northwest Indian groups used bark tea for skin, digestive tract, and gynecological complaints. Bella Coola used root bark for stomach problems, specifically those not involving diarrhea or vomiting. Makah Indians poulticed bark on wounds and toothache; leaves poulticed on burns to relieve pain. Bark tea used to decrease labor pain and clean infected wounds. Kwakiutl Indians encouraged the growth of children by putting chewed sprouts on their heads. The bark was considered a remedy for the effects of overeating salmon.

LEAVES ALTERNATE, DECIDUOUS, PALMATELY 3–7-LOBED; FRUIT FLESHY; GINSENG AND GOOSEBERRY FAMILIES

DEVIL'S CLUB
Bark, stem, roots
Oplopanax horridus Miq. — Ginseng Family
[*Echinopanax horridus* (Sm.) Dcne. & Planch. ex Harms]

Upright or sprawling, prickly, ill-scented, to 9 ft.; forming thickets. Stems thick, *covered in large, yellowish spines*. Leaves alternate, large, *palmately lobed*, maplelike, with *spines on veins and petioles*. Tiny, greenish white flowers in *small heads*, in racemes; May–July. *Bright red berries* in dense, oblong clusters. **WHERE FOUND:** Moist woods, old-growth forests, along streams, seeps. S. Ore. to Alaska, Idaho, Mont.; disjunct eastward to Mich. **USES:** American Indian groups used root bark, stems with outer bark and spines removed, or inner bark as a tonic and blood purifier, and to treat virtually any disease. Specifically indicated for body aches and pains, arthritis, rheumatism (used internally or externally in a steam bath or poultice), colds, flu, coughs, bronchitis, tuberculosis, lack of appetite, weight loss, stomach cramps, indigestion, gastric ulcers, constipation, diabetes, broken bones, and in a compound for cancer. Also used to reestablish menstrual flow after childbirth; poulticed on the breasts to reduce milk flow and on the chest for lung hemorrhage. Externally, tea used as a wash for boils, skin ulcers, and wounds. Laboratory and human studies demonstrate a blood sugar–lowering effect. Studies confirm antibacterial, antifungal, antiviral, and antituberculosis activity of extracted components. Herbalists still recommend the root and root bark in tincture form to treat and prevent diabetes.

Devil's Club (Oplopanax horridus). *Note the spiny hairs beneath palmate leaf veins and the heavily armed stems.*

(Above) *Golden Currant* (Ribes aureum) *has delicate yellow flowers.* (Right) *Bristly Black Currant* (Ribes lacustre). *Some tribes considered the plant and thorns toxic.*

RELATED SPECIES: In China, Japan, and Korea, twig tea of *O. elatus* (Nak.) Nak. used as a tonic for progressive emaciation. Also drunk as a digestive tonic. Stem and leaves of *O. japonicus* (Nak.) Nak. are used to lower fevers and treat pneumonia.

GOLDEN CURRANT
Ribes aureum Pursh

Bark, root, flowers
Gooseberry Family

Deciduous; upright to 9 ft. Stems smooth, without hairs or spines. Light green leaves shallowly 3-lobed, bases rounded to tapered; lobes rounded, margins without teeth. Younger leaves with glandular hairs. Yellow, tubular flowers 5-parted with *spicy fragrance*; Apr.–May. Berry yellow, red, or black; hairless. **WHERE FOUND:** Moist places, along streams, lowland thickets; piñon-juniper, Douglas-fir woodlands. All western states; e. Sierra of Calif. to B.C., east to S.D., N.M. **USES:** Paiute and Shoshone Indians used preparation of inner bark for leg swellings. Paiute used the powdered bark on sores. Crushed roots, boiled and gargled, or a piece of the root chewed to ease sore throat. Flower tea consumed to relieve gall bladder problems.

BRISTLY BLACK CURRANT
Ribes lacustre (Pers.) Poir.

Berries, leaves, bark, roots
Gooseberry Family

Deciduous; branches low, spreading or upright, to 3 ft. Stems covered in *straight* spines; *larger spines 3 or more at leaf nodes*. Leaves deeply palmately 3–7-lobed, mostly hairless; bases heart-shaped; lobes coarsely toothed. Flowers small, flat, purple or greenish, in loose racemes from leaf axils; June–July. Black berry covered in gland-tipped hairs. **WHERE FOUND:** Moist, shady sites, along streams, meadow edges. nw. Calif. to Alaska, east to Newfoundland, south to Utah, Colo., Nev. **USES:** Skagit Indians used bark preparation during labor. Bella Coola poulticed leaves or bark for sores caused by thorns. Root tea for constipation. Several tribes used a root and stem tea when not feeling well. Twigs were used for body aches; the berries for strength and health, and a general women's tonic. The thorns were used to lance boils and remove splinters. Saanich made a ritual wash with cherry roots for bathing newborns to insure they become intelligent and obedient. **WARNING:** Some tribes considered the plant and thorns toxic.

LEAVES ALTERNATE, DIVIDED INTO 3 LEAFLETS: MARGINS WITHOUT TEETH; FLOWERS PEALIKE; FRUIT A DRY POD; PEA FAMILY

SCOTCH BROOM
Cytisus scoparius (L.) Link
[*Sarothamnus scoparius* (L.) Koch]

Leaves, flowers
Pea Family

⚠ Evergreen, to 8 ft. *Stems green, 5-angled.* Leaves 3-divided, leaflets oblong ; margins without teeth. Younger branches generally with 1 leaflet, older branches with 3. Flowers yellow, showy, pealike, in open clusters; petals sometimes with maroon or dark

(Above) *Scotch Broom* (Cytisus scoparius), *a serious weed shrub has green stems.* (Right) *California Broom* (Lotus scoparius) *has yellow flowers, turning reddish with age.*

purple veins or blotches; Apr.–June. **WHERE FOUND:** Disturbed sites. Calif. to w. Wash., Idaho, Mont., Utah. Noxious weed native to Europe and North Africa. **USES:** American Indians used tea of dried plant tops as a cardiac depressant and a diuretic in edema, no doubt learning of this use from Europeans. Historically, physicians prescribed extracts and teas of broom tops to slow and strengthen the heartbeat for tachycardia and arrhythmias and as a potent diuretic for edema associated with congestive heart failure. Broom tops contain the alkaloids sparteine and oxytyramine, which affect the conductivity of heart nerves. Sparteine also stimulates uterine contractions and was formerly used as an abortifacient. **WARNING:** Avoid use during pregnancy. Broom should be used only under the direction of a qualified health care provider.

CALIFORNIA BROOM — **Leaves**
Lotus scoparius (Nutt.) Ottley — Pea Family

Upright, sometimes trailing or mat-forming; to 6 ft. Leaves alternate, 3-divided, leaflets *oblong*; margins entire. Flowers yellow, in whorls along upper stems from leaf axils, *maturing to reddish*; *sepals hairless*; Mar.–Aug. Slender pods drooping, not opening; beak curved at tip; seeds 2. **WHERE FOUND:** Dry slopes, deserts, coastal dunes, roadsides. N. to s. Calif. coast ranges; Baja Calif. **USES:** Costanoan Indians used the leaves to treat coughs. Mahuna Indians used leaves and also a plant infusion to build the blood. **RELATED SPECIES:** *L. humistratus* Greene was used as a wash during labor by Karok women. Navajo used *L. wrightii* (Gray) Greene leaves as a cathartic and treatment for stomachache; leaf poultice used for swellings caused by being bewitched by a bull snake. **WARNING:** Avoid taking large amounts internally; not for long-term use.

LEAVES ALTERNATE, COMPOUND, DIVIDED INTO 5 OR MORE LEAFLETS: MARGINS WITHOUT TEETH; FLOWERS PEALIKE; FRUIT A DRY POD; PEA FAMILY

FEATHERPLUME, YERBA DE ALONSO, FEATHER DALEA — **Leaves**
Dalea formosa Torr. — Pea Family

Aromatic, multibranched, to 24 in. *Stems sometimes zigzag.* Leaves odd-pinnate, with 7–11 tiny, oblong leaflets. Leaflets hairless, *gland-dotted beneath*, generally folded lengthwise along midvein. Flowers rose or yellowish, pealike, in dense terminal clusters; with silky hairy sepals; Apr.–July. *Hairy pod gland-dotted*, single-seeded; remaining closed with seeds inside. **WHERE FOUND:**

(Above) *Featherplume* (Dalea formosa) *has multicolored flowers.*
(Right) *Silver Lupine* (Lupinus albifrons), *with silvery-hairy leaflets and bluish flowers.*

Dry, rocky plains and low hills. S. Colo. to Ariz., N.M., Tex.; Mexico. **USES:** Keres Indians used leaf tea as an emetic before breakfast. Tea taken by runners to increase endurance and lung capacity. Leaf tea also considered strongly laxative.

SILVER LUPINE
Plant
Lupinus albifrons Benth. ex Lindl.
Pea Family

⚠ *Silver-haired* shrub or subshrub; to 6 ft. Basal or alternate stem leaves *palmately divided* into 6–10 oblanceolate leaflets, *hairy on both sides*; margins entire. Blue to purple flowers in whorls on racemes; top petal *hairy on back near tip*, with yellow to white patch below; bottom middle petal (keel); Mar.–June. Pods dull yellow, hairy. **WHERE FOUND:** Open, sandy or rocky areas, coastal scrub or inland. S. cen. and N. coast ranges to Sierra foothills. Calif. to s. Ore.; Baja Calif. **USES:** Karok Indians boiled the stems and leaves in a basket with hot stones and drank the tea for stomach problems. To increase effectiveness, a charm was recited or chanted. Plant used as a steam in the sweat lodge for stomach problems. **WARNING:** A number of western tribes used *Lupinus* species for food but not extensively for medicine. Some species were known to be toxic and primarily used externally. Many lupine species contain toxic alkaloids; many are teratogenic. Some have lower amounts of the toxic principles and are consumed as food plants. Experimentation is not advised.

ALTERNATE, DECIDUOUS LEAVES; MARGINS WITHOUT TEETH; FLOWERS INCONSPICUOUS; SEEDS WITH COTTONY DOWN; WILLOWS

NARROWLEAF WILLOW, SANDBAR WILLOW
Salix exigua Nutt.

Bark, leaves
Willow Family

Deciduous, to 20 ft; often forming thickets. Younger stems brown, covered in long, soft hairs. *Linear leaves* with very short petioles; tips pointed, *bases tapered*; margins mostly without teeth. Younger leaves silky-hairy; older leaves *silvery green with grayish hairs*. Tiny male and female flowers in dense, hairy, upright catkins on separate plants; appearing with or after leaves emerge; Mar.–May. *Small bract below each flower yellowish brown*, hairy. **WHERE FOUND:** Wet sites, streamsides, marshes, ditches. Calif. to Alaska, generally east of the Sierra-Cascade crest; Idaho, Utah, Ariz., N.M., Tex.; eastern N. America; Mexico. **USES:** Bark tea used to lower fevers, an action commonly associated with willows because of their aspirinlike salicylate content. Ramah Navajo used leaf and bark tea as a cleansing emetic. Northern Paiute used tea for syphilis and gonorrhea. Zuni used tea to relieve coughs and sore throat.

(Left) *Narrowleaf Willow* (Salix exigua) *has linear leaves with upright catkins.* (Above) *Arroyo Willow* (Salix lasiolepis). *Note the dense, upright catkins.*

ARROYO WILLOW
Bark, leaves

Salix lasiolepis Benth.
Willow Family

Deciduous shrub or small tree, to 40 ft. Bark smooth. Young branches yellowish to dark brown, covered in velvety hairs; generally brittle at base. *Leaf surfaces are of different colors; wider at middle or above.* Obovate to oblanceolate leaves dark, shiny green, and mostly hairless above, with whitish film below; margins without teeth, somewhat rolled under. Younger leaves with long white or sometimes rust-colored hairs. Tiny male and female flowers in dense, hairy, upright catkins on separate plants; appearing before leaves; Feb.–Apr. **WHERE FOUND:** Streambanks, marshes, meadows, springs, bluffs. Throughout Calif. to e. Wash. and Idaho, w. Nev., Ariz., N.M., Tex.; Mexico. Highly variable. **USES:** Costanoans drank tea of immature leaves or flowers to relieve cold symptoms. The Mendocino used leaf tea to relieve diarrhea and a bark tea as a wash for scabies sores, for measles, or to induce sweating to help cure any disease. Many species of willow were used interchangeably.

SCOULER'S WILLOW
Bark, leaves

Salix scouleriana Barrett ex Hook.
Willow Family

Deciduous shrub or small, multistemmed tree, to 40 ft. Branches dark brown, hairless. Younger stems yellowish, densely velvety. Bark and young, densely hairy leaves have a peculiar fetid odor. *Leaf surfaces are different in color; wider above.* Leaves obovate to oblanceolate; upper leaf shiny, dull green, hairless; lower leaf with whitish film and silver or rust-colored, woolly hairs. Tiny male and female flowers in hairy, dense, upright catkins on separate plants; appearing well before leaves emerge; Mar.–June. **WHERE FOUND:** Dry to moist forests, meadows, springs, streamsides, upland thickets. Most of Calif. to s. Alaska, east to cen. Canada; throughout west to N.M.; Mexico. **USES:** The Bella Coola drank bark tea to aid in recovery after childbirth and to facilitate nursing. Crushed bark and sap poulticed on bleeding wounds and over broken bones. A root tea taken to prevent diarrhea.

Scouler's Willow (Salix scouleriana) *has broadly ovate leaves.*

SMOOTH SUMAC
Rhus glabra L.

Berries, leaves, bark, roots
Cashew Family

Deciduous, 3–20 ft. Twigs and leaf stalks *smooth, without hairs.* Leaves with 11–31 *toothed,* lance-shaped leaflets. Small, greenish flowers in very dense panicles at branch tips, May–July. *Red, intensely sour,* berrylike fruits *covered in short, reddish, appressed hairs;* June–Oct. **WHERE FOUND:** Generally dry sites; fields, desert scrubland, riverbanks. Ore. to B.C., Utah; eastward to every state. **USES:** Berry tea a traditional European folk medicine to treat postpartum bleeding, bloody discharges, urinary tract problems, diabetes, fever, vomiting, and bed-wetting. Berry tea gargled for ulcerations of the mouth and throat; used externally to wash ringworm lesions and slow-healing ulcers. Root tea used as a postpartum wash for bleeding and taken internally to relieve painful urination, urinary retention, colds, dysentery, and suppressed appetite and as an emetic. Bark tea used in syrups to stimulate lactation, stop bleeding, for gonorrhea, vaginal yeast infections, dysentery, swollen lymph nodes. Root bark poulticed on old ulcers as a potent antiseptic. Leaves used externally to treat

Smooth Sumac (Rhus glabra) has smooth leaves and stems.

Sugar Sumac (Rhus ovata) has evergreen leaves, folded upward.

sunburn, sore lips, skin sores, rashes, poison ivy, to aid in healing of surgical wounds. Internally, leaf tea used for diarrhea, urinary tract disorders, cystitis, tuberculosis, asthma, and syphilis, and smoked with tobacco for head or lung problems. Fruit preparations used for itchy scalp, frostbite, gonorrhea, and to facilitate labor. The mucilaginous exudate from the cut bark used to soothe urinary inflammation. **WARNING:** Potentially toxic in concentrated or large doses. May cause diarrhea.

SUGAR SUMAC, SUGARBUSH
Rhus ovata S. Wats.

Leaves
Cashew Family

Aromatic evergreen shrub or small tree, to 30 ft. Leaves widely ovate, leathery, generally *folded* upward along midrib; margins without teeth. Flowers small, white to pink, in densely branched terminal clusters; Mar.–May. Reddish green, flattened berrylike fruit, single-seeded with sticky hairs; *sour outside,* pulp sweet. **WHERE FOUND:** Chaparral, canyons, south facing slopes. sw Calif., Ariz., Baja Calif. **USES:** Cahuilla Indians used the leaves to treat colds, coughs, and chest pains. Just before giving birth, Diegueño Indian women took a tea to assure an easy delivery.

SKUNKBRUSH
Rhus trilobata Nutt.

Leaves, berries, bark, roots
Cashew Family

Deciduous, to 8 ft. Young branches with soft hairs. Thin leaves deeply 3-lobed or compound, hairy above and below; margins scalloped to slightly lobed. Flowers small, yellowish, in terminal panicles; appearing before leaves; Feb.–Apr. Red-orange, berrylike fruit *intensely sour,* single-seeded, with sparse, sticky hairs.

Skunkbrush (Rhus trilobata) *has 3 round-toothed leaflets.*

Pacific Poison Oak (Toxicodendron diversilobum) *has oaklike, shiny leaves.*

WHERE FOUND: Dry sites: hillsides, slopes, plains, chaparral. S. Calif. to s. Canada; east to Great Plains; n. Mexico. **USES:** Whole plant tea used for easing bowel troubles; stem tea for relieving coughs and lung ailments. Leaves were used as a tea or chewed to treat bowel and urinary tract problems, stomachache, itching, poison ivy, hair loss, to repel snakes and insects, as an emetic, diuretic, to restore appetite, as a contraceptive, and for head colds. The berries chewed or tea used as a mouthwash, for toothache, stomach problems, and flu. Root-bark tea used to promote expulsion of the placenta after childbirth. **WARNING:** May cause dermatitis.

PACIFIC POISON OAK Leaves, root

Toxicodendron diversilobum (Torr. & Gray) Greene   Cashew Family
Deciduous shrub, to 13 ft., or vine climbing to 80 ft. Stems gray to red-brown, oily. *Leaves compound in 3 leaflets* (sometimes 5), the lateral ones without stalks. Leaflets oval with rounded tips; *upper surface glossy, oily;* margins lobed, scalloped, or toothed. Leaves bright red in fall. Small, yellowish flowers in loose inflorescences from leaf axils; Apr.–May. *White, berrylike fruit* single-seeded, smooth, hairless. **WHERE FOUND:** Shaded, moist to dry sites; streambanks, chaparral, oak woodland, thickets, wooded slopes. Calif. to B.C., Nev.; n. Baja Calif., Mexico. **USES:** American Indian groups reportedly swallowed leaves, buds, or an infusion of the root as protection from rashes brought on by skin contact with the plant. The Karok swallowed a leaf in the spring as a contraceptive aid. A moxa of the leaves or plant juice was used directly on warts, and the juice on ringworm. A tincture of the fresh leaves has been used on eczema, ringworm, and other skin diseases. **WARNING:** Can cause severe, even life-threatening, intensely irritating and pruritic skin and internal mucous membrane eruptions. Poisonings have occurred from ingesting the berries and root.

MISCELLANEOUS SHRUBS: LEAVES ALTERNATE; MARGINS ENTIRE TO 3-LOBED; FLOWERS SHOWY; FRUIT DRY

FLANNELBUSH, CALIFORNIA FREMONTIA Bark

Fremontodendron californicum (Torr.) Coville   Chocolate Family
Deciduous; upright to 20 ft. or with low, spreading branches. Stems and undersides of leaves covered in *dense, brownish felt of star-shaped* hairs. Leaves leathery, 3-lobed; upper leaf dark green with few hairs; margins scalloped, without teeth. Showy yellow flowers with 5 petals and 5 stamens fused together at base; May–June. Petals with silky hairs at base, sometimes with reddish margins. **WHERE FOUND:** Chaparral, rocky ridges, dry slopes, oak or

Flannelbush (Fremontodendron *spp.*). *Mexican Flannelbush* (Fremontodendron mexicanum), *pictured here, differs from other species only in that the sepal pits are without hairs.*

pine woodland. Calif., Ariz.; Baja Calif. **USES:** Kawaiisu Indians used an infusion of the inner bark as a laxative. The inner bark has abundant mucilage and was used as a demulcent externally in poultices for inflammation and internally for soothing throat irritation. **RELATED SPECIES:** *F. mexicanum* Davidson, Mexican Flannelbush (pictured here), differs only in that the sepal pits are without hairs.

WHITE RHATANY, RHATANY
Krameria grayi Rose & Painter

Roots, leaves
Rhatany Family

Densely branched, *spine-tipped*; horizontal or upright to 24 in. Stems, leaves, and fruits grayish, covered in dense, woolly hairs. Leaves linear; tips pointed; margins entire. Flowers large, purplish, 5-parted with 4 stamens, *solitary in leaf axils*; Apr.–May. **WHERE FOUND:** Dry, rocky, or sandy ridges and flats, especially on lime soils; deserts. S. Calif. to s. Nev., Ariz., w. Tex.; Baja Calif., n. Mexico. **USES:** Pima Indians used root tea to treat coughs, pain, and fevers and as a wash for swellings. Powdered root poulticed on a newborn's umbilical stump to prevent infection. Root chewed to relieve sore throats. Paiute Indians put the root powder on sores and used a cold-water root infusion as a wash for swellings and gonorrhea sores and for gonorrheal infections in the eyes. **RELATED SPECIES:** *K. triandra* Ruiz et Pavon, native to Peru, was formerly an official drug in the U.S. and Europe as a gentle tonic and powerful astringent, used for treating bowel complaints, diarrhea, hemorrhoids, hemorrhaging, wounds, menorrhagia, leukorrhea, gum disease, as a gargle for throat infections, and for other conditions in which an astringent would prove beneficial. Antimicrobial procyanidins and benzofurans have been isolated from the root. In Europe rhatany is still a widely used ingredients (for red coloring and for its astringent and antimicrobial activity) in dentifrices such as mouthwash and toothpaste. Other South American species were used interchangeably, as well as Texas Rhatany, *K. lanceolata* Torr. [*K. secundiflora* auct. non DC.].

(Above) *White Rhatany* (Krameria grayi) *has purplish flowers.* (Right) *Texas Rhatany* (K. lanceolata) *is found in the eastern part of our range.*

HORNED MILKWORT, SIERRA MILKWORT — Root
Polygala cornuta Kellogg — Milkwort Family

Generally low-growing to 30 in. or upright to 8 ft.; often forming thickets. Stems slender; *roots with wintergreen fragrance.* Leaves narrowly lance-shaped to linear. Flowers pealike, yellowish to greenish white, *turning dull rose after pollen shed*; petals hairy; stamens 8, with short beak; in dense terminal clusters; June–Sept. Fruit a broad, yellowish brown pod releasing hairy, black seeds with prominent white tissue at tip. **WHERE FOUND:** Open coniferous forest, chaparral, rocky or gravelly slopes, shaded canyons, oak woodland. Klamath Range in nw. Calif., n. Sierra, s. Calif. mountains to n. Baja Calif. **USES:** Root tea used for pains, colds, coughs, and as an emetic. Flowers poulticed on swellings. **RELATED SPECIES:** North American Seneca Snakeroot, *P. senega* L., used as an expectorant for respiratory problems, rheumatism, and to promote menstruation. Extracts show hypoglycemic effects. *Polygala* spp. are high in saponin glycosides that have mucous membrane–stimulating and mucus-thinning properties. **WARNING:** Extracts of *Polygala* spp. stimulate the uterus; avoid during pregnancy.

DESERT RUE, TURPENTINE BROOM — Stems, leaves
Thamnosma montana Torr. & Frem. — Rue Family

Deciduous, *strong-scented*, upright, to 24 in. Yellowish green stems widely branching, covered with glands. Leaves small or narrow, or absent. Dark purple flowers with 4 leathery upright petals;

Horned Milkwort (Polygala cornuta) *forms thickets. The roots have a wintergreen fragrance.*

Turpentine Broom (Thamnosma montana) *has yellowish green, gland-covered stems.*

Mar.–May. **WHERE FOUND:** Dry sandy or rocky ridges. Deserts from s. Calif. to s. Utah, Ariz., N.M.; Baja Calif., n. Mexico. **USES:** Stem tea used as a tonic, to treat colds, smallpox, gonorrhea, chest pains, and as a wash or douche for gynecological problems. Leaf tea considered emetic and laxative. Crushed stems used on open wounds. Dried stems mixed with tobacco were smoked for colds. Tea of whole plant used by medicine men for ritual ceremonies and to aid in hunting.

ALTERNATE LEAVES; MARGINS ENTIRE; FLOWERS INCONSPICUOUS; FRUIT DRY WITH THIN WINGS; GOOSEFOOT FAMILY

SALTBUSH, FOUR-WING SALTBUSH
Atriplex canescens (Pursh) Nutt.

Whole plant
Goosefoot Family

Multibranched evergreen, to 6 ft. Stems and leaves covered in *dense gray to white scales*. Thick leaves linear to oblanceolate; tips rounded, bases tapered; margins without teeth. Tiny male and female flowers on *different plants* in dense spikes; May–Aug. Oblong, single-seeded fruit surrounded by 4 broad, hardened, winglike bracts. **WHERE FOUND:** Sandy, clay, or gravelly soils, desert flats, slopes, washes, scrubland. Generally in alkaline or saline soils. S. Calif. to Wash., east of Sierra-Cascade crest, to e. Colo., Tex.; Baja Calif., n. Mexico, w. Canada. **USES:** American Indian groups boiled fresh roots with a little salt and drank half-cupful doses for stomach pain and as a laxative. Roots ground and applied as a toothache remedy. Leaf or root tea taken as an emetic for stomach pain and bad coughs. Soapy lather from leaves used for itch-

Saltbush (Atriplex spp.) is commonly found in alkaline soils.

ing and rashes from chickenpox or measles. Fresh leaf or a poultice of fresh or dried flowers was applied to ant bites. Leaves were used as a snuff for nasal problems. Smoke from burning leaves used to revive someone who was injured, weak, or feeling faint. Hispanics use the plant for colds and flu.

LEAVES ALTERNATE, FINELY TOOTHED OR ENTIRE, FRUIT BLACK AT MATURITY; BUCKTHORN FAMILY

COFFEEBERRY
Frangula californica (Eschsch.) Gray
[*Rhamnus californica* Eschsch.]

Bark, berries, leaves
Buckthorn Family

Evergreen; upright to 13 ft. or low and spreading. Young stems red. Leaves thick, leathery, oval to oblong; margins finely toothed, sometimes rolled under; shiny beneath with *bright greenish yellow raised veins.* Flowers small, clustered in leaf axils; May–July. Fruit initially red, becoming black at maturity, 2-lobed with 2 seeds. **WHERE FOUND:** Hillsides, ravines, chaparral, woodlands, forests, coastal sage scrub; nonserpentine soils. Calif., Ore., Nev., Ariz., N.M. **USES:** Inner bark is strongly laxative. The Kawaiisu Indians used the mashed berries on burns, infected sores, wounds, and to stop bleeding. Ripe berries used as a laxative or digestive tonic. Bark and leaf tea used as a wash to treat poison oak and ivy and sciatica. Bark of root or stems was used as a panacea for nearly any disease, but especially for flu, kidney problems, rheumatism, gonorrhea, and mania. Neeshenam Indians held a hot piece of root against an aching tooth. Historically, physicians accepted this species as a substitute for cascara sagrada. They prescribed the bark tincture, 15–20 drops every three or four hours, or less, which is below the threshold of laxative action, on a continuous basis to relieve acute rheumatism pain. For chronic cases, as

Coffeeberry (Frangula
californica). *The leaves have
bright greenish yellow raised veins
beneath.*

well as to relieve long-standing
cases of painful menstruation,
the same dose was adminis-
tered for up to four months. They also prescribed the bark of this
species to clear diarrhea with mucus due to sluggish liver conditions. **WARNING:** Some Indian tribes considered the berry poisonous,
others reportedly ate them. The ripe berries are both very sweet and
bitter. Preparations from all species of *Frangula* are contraindicated for people with intestinal obstruction, abdominal pain of unknown origin, or inflammatory intestinal conditions such as appendicitis, colitis, Crohn's disease, and irritable bowel syndrome. Avoid
use during pregnancy or lactation. Avoid using the fresh bark; it
should age for one to two years to moderate its action.

ALDERLEAF BUCKTHORN
Rhamnus alnifolia L'Hér
Bark, berries
Buckthorn Family

Deciduous; loosely branched to 6 ft. Bark gray; stems gray or reddish brown. Leaves very thin, dark green, elliptical to oval; margins finely toothed; with prominent raised *yellowish veins* beneath. Flowers small, greenish, in clusters of 1–3, in leaf axils as
leaves emerge; May–June. Shiny, black fruit 3-lobed, juicy, *bitter-
sweet*, 3-seeded. **WHERE FOUND:** Wet sites; meadows, bogs, marsh and
swamp edges. High mountains
of Calif. to Canada; n. Rocky
Mountains; northern U.S. to
Atlantic Coast. **USES:** Bark tea
used to treat constipation and

Alderleaf Buckthorn (Rhamnus
alnifolia) *has very thick leaves
with yellow veins beneath.*

Graythorn (Ziziphus obtusifolia
var. obtusifolia). *Note the rigid
thorns.*

associated liver and gallbladder
problems. Also used to treat
colic from lead ingestion, obesity, congestive heart failure,
and hemorrhoids. Iroquois gave
Buckthorn to children as a laxative, a tonic and blood purifier, and
to calm them when fussy. Plant tea drunk and applied as a wash
to poisonous swellings. Roots used to treat gonorrhea. Berries
and their juice are strongly laxative.

GRAYTHORN, GRAY LOTEBUSH   Root, thorns
Ziziphus obtusifolia (Hook. ex Torr. & Gray) Gray   Buckthorn Family
[*Condalia lycioides* (Gray) Weberb.]

Deciduous, multibranched, to 10 ft. *Thorn-tipped stems rigid with
short, dense, white hairs.* Bark pale gray-green. Leaves thin, gray,
oval to oblong, clustered on short shoots; margins entire. Flowers
tiny, with 5 yellowish petals clustered in leaf axils; Apr.–July. Dark
blue to black fruits with whitish film; juicy; single-seeded. **WHERE
FOUND:** Sandy desert, creosote bush scrub. S. Calif. to w. Ariz., s.
Nev.; Baja Calif., Mexico. **USES:** American Indian groups treated
rheumatic pains by pricking the skin over sore areas with the
thorns. Many species of *Ziziphus* are used for numerous conditions in other parts of the world, especially Africa, the Middle
East, and China.

LEAVES ALTERNATE, MOSTLY EVERGREEN, AROMATIC, SILVER OR GRAY-HAIRY, WITH YELLOWISH DISK FLOWERS; ARTEMISIAS

COAST SAGE   Whole plant
Artemisia californica Less.   Composite Family

Aromatic evergreen, to 8 ft. Stems and leaves covered in dense,
grayish white hairs. Leaves pinnately divided into long, threadlike
lobes; margins curled under. Flowers small, pale yellow, in *nodding* heads; Aug.–Dec. **WHERE FOUND:** Chaparral, dry slopes,
foothills, coastal scrub. Cen. and lower coast ranges, s. Calif.; n.
Baja Calif. **USES:** An important medicinal plant of the coastal Cali-

Coast Sage (Artemisia californica) *has small, yellowish flowers in nodding heads.*

Silver Sage (Artemisia frigida) *is silver-green and mat-forming.*

fornia Indians, especially for ritual and cleansing during the sexual maturation of women. Plant tea used by Cahuilla Indian for suppressed menstruation, to facilitate childbirth and hasten postnatal recovery, to prevent painful periods and lessen menopausal symptoms. Tea given to one-day-old babies to cleanse their system. Externally tea used as a bath for rheumatism, coughs, and colds; poulticed to aching teeth and wounds. For asthma a poultice of the plant was applied to the back or a tea taken internally. **WARNING:** Of unknown safety. May cause dermatitis.

SILVER SAGE, FRINGED SAGEBRUSH　　　**Whole plant**
Artemisia frigida Willd.　　　Composite Family

Aromatic; mat-forming or upright, to 20 in. Stems soft with woolly hairs. Leaves silvery, finely divided into *linear segments, covered in long, silky, white hairs.* Small, nodding heads of yellowish disk flowers sitting on densely hairy receptacle; July–Sept. **WHERE FOUND:** Dry, open plains and foothills; high elevations. E. Wash., Idaho, Nev., to all other western and central states; Rockies, central plains; New England; Siberia. **USES:** American Indian groups used hot leaf tea for colds, coughs, and venereal disease and for stomach ailments such as indigestion, biliousness, or flatulence. Women took tea internally and as a wash for irregular menstruation. The whole leaf was applied to stop bleeding and for headaches associated with fever. A hot leaf poultice used for toothache. Chewed leaves were placed on wounds to reduce swelling. Leaves were used as a snuff for nosebleeds, and dried leaves burned to disinfect a sickroom or as an inhalant for biliousness. Plant tops chewed and the liquid swallowed as a heartburn remedy. Root tea was taken for convulsions, as a tonic, and applied to bleeding wounds. Plant tea was used for lung problems, cancer, diabetes, menstrual irregularity, and consumption. Smoke from leaves and flowers was used to revive comatose patients. **WARNING**: Of unknown safety. May cause dermatitis.

BIG SAGEBRUSH, CHAMISO

Leaves, stems, seeds

Artemisia tridentata Nutt.   Composite Family

Aromatic evergreen, to 8 ft. Gray-green branches generally twisted, covered in short, whitish gray hairs; bark shredding. Leaves soft, silvery, *3-lobed* at tip; densely hairy. Flowers in small heads, pale yellow, in dense, narrow racemes; July–Oct. **WHERE FOUND**: Dry, sandy to coarse gravelly soils, high valleys, slopes. S. Calif. to B.C., generally east of Sierra-Cascade crest; to Idaho, Wyo., Colo., N.M.; Baja Calif. **USES**: Widely used among American Indians, especially for colds and fever. Green leaf tea used for stomach complaints; in larger doses to induce vomiting. For head colds, branches were burned and fumes inhaled. Green leaves poulticed for chest colds or placed on gums for toothache. For pneumonia, leaves were boiled in water with a pinch of salt and

(Above) *Big Sagebrush* (Artemisia tridentata) *is 3-lobed at leaf tip.*
(Right) *Big Sagebrush occurs over large areas of the West.*

given in tablespoon doses each time the patient coughed. Branches were burned on top of stove as a fumigant for rooms after an illness. Stems and leaves burned to purify the air in both homes and sweat houses. For headache, tea from branches was taken internally and also used to bathe the head, fumes from burning plants were inhaled, and crushed green leaves applied as poultice to the forehead. Tea of branches was taken to relieve diarrhea, stomachaches and stomach cramps, laryngitis, and tuberculosis. Leaf tea used as antiseptic gargle for sore throats and as a wash or poultice for cuts, wounds, sores, or pimples. Leaf tea drunk for gum and mouth diseases, pneumonia, fever, and colds with coughing or bronchitis. Dried leaves were finely pulverized and used as talcum powder for babies. The plant was used both internally and externally for rheumatism. Some tribes chewed and swallowed the leaves for coughs, indigestion, and gas. **WARNING:** Of unknown safety. May cause dermatitis.

LEAVES ALTERNATE, AROMATIC OR RESINOUS EVERGREENS WITH TUBULAR FLOWERS; COMPOSITE FAMILY

RABBITBRUSH, RUBBER RABBITBRUSH   **Whole plant**

Chrysothamnus nauseosus (Pallus ex Pursh) Britt.   Composite Family
Deciduous; resinous, upright, to 9 ft. *Stems covered in whitish gray to greenish felt.* Leaves gray-green, threadlike to narrowly lance-shaped; covered in dense woolly hairs; margins entire. Flower heads with 5 yellow, tubular flowers in dense, flat-topped panicles; Aug.–Oct. **WHERE FOUND:** Open, dry sites, plains, foothills, often in alkaline soils. Calif. to B.C., to Mont., Colo., Tex.; Rocky Mts.; Great Plains; Baja Calif., n. Mexico. Highly variable, with

Rabbitbrush, Rubber Rabbitbrush (Chrysothamnus nauseosus) *produces a profusion of yellow flower heads.*

22 subspecies. **USES:** Leaf or flower tea used by American Indian groups for stomach disorders, colds, coughs, and as a general tonic. Root tea taken for coughs, fever, colds, and menstrual pain. Root and plant top tea taken for bloody diarrhea. Leaf and stem tea used as a cough medicine and applied as a wash to sores and skin eruptions. A twig tea was used to ease toothaches. Smoke from the burning plant was thought to keep away spirits that caused nightmares.

ALTERNATE LEAVES: YELLOW RAY AND DISK FLOWERS; COMPOSITE FAMILY

BRITTLEBUSH, INCIENSO
Leaves, stems, flowers, resin
Encelia farinosa Gray *ex* Torr.
Composite Family
Drought-deciduous shrub with *yellowish, aromatic sap, which dries hard;* 5 ft. Stems brittle, covered in woolly hairs. Leaves silvery gray, narrowly to broadly ovate, densely hairy; margins mostly without teeth. Flowers in numerous heads on long, hairless stalks in panicles; ray flowers yellow, broad, *3-notched at tip;* disk flowers yellow or brownish purple; Mar.–July. **WHERE FOUND:** Open desert, stony hillsides. S. Calif. to Ariz., Nev., sw. Utah; Baja Calif., n. Mexico. **USES:** American Indian groups used plant poultice to relieve pain. A strong tea of blossoms, leaves, and stems was held in the mouth to ease toothaches. The gum resin was used to increase the flow of saliva. **RELATED SPECIES:** A tea of the leaves and flowers of *E. virginensis* var. *actonii* (Elmer) B. L. Turner of the western U.S. was made into a wash to ease rheumatic pains.

Brittlebush (Encelia farinosa) has an aromatic sap that dries yellow.

Brittlebush is common in open deserts of the West.

BROOM SNAKEWEED

Plant, leaves, root

Gutierrezia sarothrae (Pursh) Britt. & Rusby — Composite Family

Slender, grooved stems, sprawling or upright to 2 ft. Gummy, linear leaves dark gray-green, *gland-dotted*; margins entire. Very small heads of few yellow ray and disk flowers in crowded, flat-topped clusters of 2–5; May–Oct. **WHERE FOUND:** Dry, open places, grasslands, deserts, montane areas; often with sagebrush. East of Sierra-Cascade crest from s. Calif. to ne. Wash., to all western states; Great Plains, s. cen. Canada, n. Mexico, Baja Calif. **USES:** An important and widespread remedy for American Indians. Many tribes used plant preparations to treat colds and coughs, muscle aches, headache, dizziness, anxiety, stomach flu, bloody diarrhea, gastrointestinal tract disease in general and as an emetic and cathartic. Used externally as a wash for eye problems, rashes, measles, and sores, or on the forehead for headaches. Flower tea considered good medicine for strengthening the limbs and muscles. Ceremonially, the plant was used to treat snakebites. Leaves poulticed for rheumatism, bruises, sprains, swellings, ant bites, bee and wasp stings, on the top of the head for headache, and around the ear for earache. Juice from chewing the plant was used internally and externally for snakebites. Root tea used for stomachache, diarrhea, and painful urination. Mouth sores and sore throat were treated by sucking on a root. Steam from boiled roots was inhaled for respiratory conditions. Smoke from the burning plant used to fumigate a newborn and mother or women with painful menstruation. An antitumor glycoprotein has been identified from the plant. **RELATED SPECIES:** *G. californica* (DC.) Torr. & Gray, San Joaquin Snake-weed, and *G. microcephala* (DC.) Gray, Threadleaf Snakeweed, were used similarly.

Broom Snakeweed (Gutierrezia sarothrae) has linear leaves and sparse flower heads.

TREELIKE CACTUS

SAGUARO CACTUS, GIANT CACTUS
Whole plant

Carnegia gigantea (Engelm.) Brit. & Rose
Cactus Family

[*Cereus gigantea* Engelm.]

⚠ Large cactus familiar to all who have seen Western movies. Tree-like, up to 40 ft. high, with a simple upright stem or up to 8–12 branches, held upright by 12–24 woody ribs. With a water content of up to 95 percent, the plant may weigh up to 10 tons. Waxy white flowers bloom on specimens from 50–75 years old; May. Egg-shaped fruits, purplish. **WHERE FOUND:** Sonoran Desert. Extreme se. Calif., s. Ariz., n. Mexico. **USES:** Native groups of the northern Sonoran used Saguaro as food and medicine. The fruits were fermented to make an intoxicating beverage, made into preserves, and eaten raw. Seeds also used as food. Thorns were used for tattooing. Pima used plant to stimulate milk flow. Woody ribs from dead cactus were used as splints for broken bones. Saguaro contains alkaloids similar to those found in peyote, including carnegine, gigantine and salsolidine. However, the plant was never used to induce psychoactive experiences. **NOTE:** This vegetative symbol of the American Southwest, though a federally protected endangered species, is still threatened by vandalism and "cactus rustling," mostly for illicit nursery trade in the Southwest.

Saguaro Cactus (Carnegia gigantea) is a familiar symbol of western deserts.

CONIFERS; LEAVES NEEDLELIKE, IN CLUSTERS; PINES AND LARCHES

WESTERN LARCH, TAMARACK
Bark, pitch, leaves, branches

Larix occidentalis Nutt.
Pine Family

Deciduous tree, to 160 ft. Bark of young trees smooth, silver-gray to brownish gray. Bark of mature trees red-brown, is deeply furrowed between scaly plates. *Leaves clustered,* radiating from tips of short branches. Leaf apex pointed to rounded. Oval seed cones *sit upright on short stalks.* Bract below each cone scale has a slender tip that is exserted beyond the cone scale; margins entire. **WHERE FOUND:** Mountain valleys and lower slopes, 1600–5300 ft.; Wash., Ore., Idaho, Mont.; B.C. Mountain Larch resembles Subalpine Larch (*L. lyallii* Parl.), which occurs at higher elevations: 5900–7900 ft. **USES:** Northwest Indians considered the tree a panacea. Bark and pitch used externally for cuts, wounds, and bruises. Bark tea used to treat colds, coughs, sore throats, and tuberculosis. Externally as a soak for arthritic limbs. Pitch and branches used to help set broken bones. Branches and leaf tips used to treat skin sores, cuts, burns, ulcers, severe arthritis, can-

Western Larch (Larix occiden-talis) *is one of our few deciduous conifers. Note leaves turning yellow in autumn.*

Lodgepole Pine (Pinus contorta) *has 2 leaves per bundle and pendent cones (male flowers shown).*

cer. Leaf tea taken for suppressed appetite, as a contraceptive after giving birth, and as a wash for making babies strong, healthy, and good-natured. Arabinogalactan extracted from Western Larch is of scientific interest for delivering diagnostic or therapeutic agents to liver hepatocytes via a unique receptor mechanism. Immunostimulant and potential antitumor activity confirmed in this and other *Larix* species. **RELATED SPECIES:** The eastern *L. laricina* (Du roi) K. Koch and European *L. europea* L. were used similarly. **WARNING:** Sawdust can cause dermatitis.

LODGEPOLE PINE
Bark, pitch, needles

Pinus contorta Dougl. ex Loud.
Pine Family

Shrublike or tree, to 165 ft. Bark brown to gray or red, scaly and shallowly furrowed. Leaves yellow-green, 2 *per bundle*, 2–3 inches long. Small, round seed cones (1–3 in.) *are pendent.* Scale tip knob with sharp prickle. Seed cones mostly require fire for opening. **WHERE FOUND:** Mixed conifer forest; sea level to 11,500 ft. Sierra Nevada, Cascade ranges, coast ranges from s. Calif. north to Alaska. Rocky Mts. from cen. Colo. north to Yukon, including Utah, Wyo., Idaho, Mont.; n. Baja Calif. **USES:** Gum or sap applied externally, alone or mixed with fat or other herbs, for aching muscles, arthritis, psoriasis, sores, cuts, burns, lung congestion, heart problems, coughs, colds and sore throats. Gum preparations used for coughs, colds, sore throat, tuberculosis, stomachache, and ulcers. Needle and bud preparations, such as teas and expressed juice,

used for stomach pain, paralysis, general debility, coughs, colds, and flu. Inner bark was eaten or taken as tea as a cleansing laxative, diuretic, blood purifier; also for coughs, tuberculosis, gonorrhea, and stomachache. Proanthocyanidin polymers from pine pitch demonstrate potent antifungal effects in laboratory experiments.

Two-Needle Pinyon Pine (Pinus edulis) *is a source of pine nuts.*

TWO-NEEDLE PINYON PINE
Bark, pitch, needles

Pinus edulis Engelm.
Pine Family

Small tree, to 70 ft. Bark red-brown, shallowly furrowed. Leaves blue-green, in *bundles of 2*, 1–2½ in. long, and *upcurved*. Upright seed cones are oval to round, 1–3 in. long. Cone scales are few in number *without a prickle at tip*. **WHERE FOUND:** Dry mountain slopes, mesas, plateaus; pinyon-juniper woodland. 4200–8800 ft. Ariz., N.M., Utah, Colo. Rare in Calif., Wyo., Tex.; Mexico. **USES:** Teas of plant parts, especially young leaves and inner bark, which were also chewed and swallowed, eased symptoms of fever, flu, colds, coughs, tuberculosis, headache, and syphilis. Smoke from burning needles or pitch was used to purify the air or inhaled to treat colds. Pitch was used fresh or dried and powdered on sores, cuts, syphilis lesions, infections, and applied to the forehead to protect from sorcery. Seeds a source of pine nuts.

ONE-LEAVED PINYON, SINGLELEAF PINYON
Pitch, bark, needles

Pinus monophylla Torr. & Frem.
Pine Family

⚠ Tree, to 50 ft. Bark red-brown, scaly, furrowed. Leaves blue- or gray-green, in "bundles" of a *single leaf*. Needles often curved, 1–2½ in. long. *Upright* seed cones round with *few cone scales*, 1–4½ in. long. Cone scale tips *without prickle*. Hybridizes with *P. edulis*. **WHERE FOUND:** Dry, montane forest; pinyon-juniper woodland; 3300 to 9200 ft. S. Calif., southeast to Ariz., Nev., Utah, Idaho; Baja Calif. **USES:** Pitch once used as an antiseptic base for external herbal preparations. Internally the boiled pitch used for coughs, colds, congestion, fevers, tuberculosis, flu, nausea, diarrhea, indigestion, worms, and other gastrointestinal tract disorders, to stop menstruation and make one infertile. American Indian groups used tea to keep adolescent girls youthful and long-lived, and as a tonic after childbirth, for general debility, and for venereal disease. Externally, pitch used for sunburn protection, on cuts, sores, boils, swellings, to draw splinters, and to relieve muscle

One-leaved Pinyon (Pinus monophylla) has a single needle per bundle.

Ponderosa Pine (Pinus ponderosa) *is one of the most common pines of the West.*

soreness or sciatica. Needle tea used as a wash on measles and other rashes. **WARNING:** In controlled experiments, cows that ate pine needles often aborted. Avoid use during pregnancy.

PONDEROSA PINE, WESTERN YELLOW PINE
Pitch, needles
Pinus ponderosa P. & C. Lawson
Pine Family

Large evergreen tree, to 240 ft. Bark yellow to red-brown, forming plates between deep furrows. *Bark smells of turpentine.* Yellow Pine is most often confused with Jeffrey Pine (*P. jeffreyi* Grev. & Balf.), which has a butterscotch or vanillalike fragrance. Leaves yellow-green, *long (4½ to 10 in.), generally 3 per bundle but* varying, 2–5. Seed cones *broadly oval,* 3½–7 in., falling at maturity. Cone scales *prickled at tip and generally darker on lower surface.* When cones open, the prickles will poke palms of the hands (hence the nicknames Prickly Ponderosa vs. Gentle Jeffrey, whose spines point inward). **WHERE FOUND:** Dry, open, montane mixed conifer and mixed evergreen forests. Generally absent from serpentine soils. Sea level to 9800 ft. Occurring in all western states; B.C.; Baja Calif. **USES:** The pitch, inner bark, and needles were used in many of the same ways as pines listed above. The pitch or pounded inner bark was mixed with animal fat and applied to sores, boils, cuts, chapped skin, used for earache, backache, muscle and joint pain, and boiled to make an eyewash. Needle tea used for colds, coughs, and fever. American Indian groups used a tea of leaf tips or buds for fevers, headaches, internal bleeding, as an eyewash, and by young women as a beauty wash. One needle was sometimes eaten for heartburn. Nuts were charred, powdered, moistened, and poulticed on burns and scalds. The boughs were used for painful self-flagellation in the sweat lodge. **WARNING:** *P. ponderosa* and other pine species are known to contain "pine needle abortive factor," causing decreased uterine blood flow, abortion, and retained placenta in late pregnancy in cows.

CONIFERS WITH SINGLE, FLAT (OR 4-SIDED) NEEDLES

WHITE FIR

Resin, bark, leaves

Abies concolor (Gord. & Glend.) Lindley ex Hildebr.   Pine Family
Large evergreen tree, to 200 ft. Young bark smooth, white-gray, becoming gray-brown and *deeply furrowed* as tree matures. Leaves generally *all the same length* (to about 1 in.) with rounded tips. *Base of leaf is twisted.* Upper leaf surface light grayish green, lower surface with 2 white longitudinal lines. Branches have smooth, round scars where leaves have fallen off. Olive-green, cylindrical *seed cones sit upright on branches,* but *fall apart at maturity.* **WHERE FOUND:** Mixed conifer and red fir forests; 2900–11,000 ft. N. Baja Calif. to cen. Ore., east to Ariz., N.M., Nev., Utah, Colo., s. Idaho. **USES:** American Indian groups applied fresh pitch to cuts, sores, and boils. Both needles and the bark resin tea used as an expectorant for pulmonary complaints, including tuberculosis. Resin boiled in water was taken for venereal disease. Leaf tea was drunk and used as a wash for rheumatism. Fresh pitch poultice

(Left) *The needles of White Fir* (Abies concolor) *are all the same length.* (Above) *Grand Fir* (Abies grandis) *has alternately short and long needles.*

was applied to cuts. Poultice of warm pitch applied to sores or boils. All parts of the tree contain antimicrobial terpenes and phenolic compounds.

GRAND FIR
Resin, bark, leaves

Abies grandis (Dougl. ex D. Don) Lindl.   Pine Family

Large evergreen tree, to 260 ft. Young bark white-gray, maturing to red-brown. Leaf length noticeably *alternating between short and long on each side of branch*. Tip of leaf *notched and base twisted*. Upper leaf surface dark green, lower surface with 2 longitudinal white lines. Seed cones of various colors *sit upright* and *fall apart at maturity.* **WHERE FOUND:** Redwood, Douglas-fir, and mixed evergreen forests; up to 4900 ft. N. Calif. to B.C., Idaho, Mont. Grand Fir hybridizes with White Fir in s. Ore. **USES:** Elders of the Saanich and Cowichan Coast Salish people of s. Vancouver Island treat, or have treated, respiratory ailments, digestive tract ailments, and gynecological problems with bark. American Indians used root bark or stem tea for tuberculosis. Leaf tea commonly used for colds and to treat cuts. Externally, a bark or pitch poultice applied to treat rheumatism, boils, and ulcers. A piece of the root was held in the mouth for gum boils and canker sores, while the hard pitch was used to clean the teeth. Bark tea used for sore eyes, hair loss, dandruff, and stomach ailments

PACIFIC YEW, WESTERN YEW
Bark, needles

Taxus brevifolia Nutt.   Yew Family

Small tree with *drooping branches*, generally less than 60 ft. Bark red-brown, shredding. *Leaf tip with small bristle;* leaf base flattened and appressed to branch; leaf underside has whitish bands. The female "cone" is a single seed nearly surrounded by a *red, fleshy aril, open at top, resembling a pimento olive.* **WHERE FOUND:** Dense, mixed evergreen forests; streamsides and moist areas of lower slopes, canyon bottoms, and ravines. Coastal to 7000 ft. Calif. to se. Alaska; Idaho, w. Mont.; B.C. **USES:** American Indian groups used twig or bark tea to treat colds, coughs, early stages of tuberculosis, cancer, arthritis, stomachache, bowel problems, blood in urine, internal injuries, finger or leg numbness, and for general health. A leave poultice was applied to wounds. The bark and leaves contain paclitaxel (once called "taxol," but that name is now a registered trademark of Bristol-Myers Squibb). Paclitaxel was first isolated in 1969, and its structure determined by 1971, by Monroe Wall, its discoverer. At first commercially derived from the bark of the Pacific Yew, most paclitaxel now comes from *T. baccata* and its relatives in Europe and India. It is used as an antitumor agent in chemotherapy against several forms of ovarian

(Above) *Pacific Yew* (Taxus brevi-folia). *A red aril surrounds the seeds.* (Right) *Pacific Yew is a scattered understory tree in forests of the Northwest.*

and breast cancer. Sales of the drug exceed $1 billion per year, making it one of the most valuable natural products. **OTHER SPECIES:** *T. canadensis* Marsh., American Yew, has similar uses, but the needles and branches were especially favored in steam baths and as a tea, sometimes with other conifers, to ease rheumatism and paralysis. **WARNING:** Yews are considered toxic, and deaths have been reported from ingestion of the seeds. A review of poison control centers over 10 years shows, however, that yew poisoning rarely results in significant morbidity.

WESTERN HEMLOCK
Bark, needles, branches

Tsuga heterophylla (Raf.) Sarg.   Pine Family

Large evergreen tree, to 200 ft. Top of crown and branches generally *drooping*. Bark reddish to gray-brown, inner bark dark purple. *Leaves unequal in length* with rounded tips and a *small petiole at base*; upper surface grooved; lower surface with 2 whitish bands. *Small* oval seed cones (about 1 in.) *pendent* from branch tips. Cone scales *soft and papery*. **WHERE FOUND:** Coastal to mid-montane conifer and mixed evergreen forests; sea level–2300 ft. N. Calif. to Alaska, n. Mont., Idaho; B.C. The most common forest tree in Alaska and the north coast of B.C. **USES:** American Indian groups widely used a tea of bark or inner bark for colds, sore throat, coughs, flu; as an emetic and laxative; sometimes mixed with other herbs, for internal injuries, bleeding, tuberculosis, syphilis, rheumatic fever, arthritis, phlebitis, gallbladder problems, and di-

Western Hemlock (Tsuga hetero-phylla). *Note the white markings on the undersides of needles.*

Mountain Hemlock (Tsuga mertensiana) *generally has drooping branches.*

arrhea. The powdered bark, fresh crushed bark, or tea preparations used externally for sore eyes, burns, boils, rheumatic joints, burns, bruises, and broken bones. The pitch or gum, often mixed with oil or fat, was used to prevent chapping and sunburn, lice, cuts, and facial sores. Dried, shredded bark was burned directly on the skin as a moxa for warts and moles. Bark and pitch poultice applied to child's chest for colds, as a styptic on wounds and on stubborn sores. Chewed needle poultice was put on burns and swellings. An antichafing powder was made from bark. Bark and boughs used as a disinfectant. Tea of leaf tips used for tuberculosis and to stimulate the appetite.

MOUNTAIN HEMLOCK
Bark, needles, branches

Tsuga mertensiana (Bong.) Carr.
Pine Family

Evergreen tree, to 130 ft., sometimes prostrate at timberline. Bark red- or purple-brown with *deep furrows*. Leaves more crowded on *upper surface of the branch*, spreading in many directions; in dense forests, leaves may be flattened into one plane. Leaves equal in length, with rounded tips and whitish bands on both *upper and lower surfaces*. Oblong, pendent seed cones are *soft and papery* (1–3 in.). **WHERE FOUND:** Coastal, montane, and subalpine mixed conifer and red fir forests; sea level–11,500 ft. Calif. to Alaska, Mont., Idaho, Nev.; B.C. **USES:** American Indian groups used bark tea to treat colds and flu, as an emetic, and as a disinfectant. Chewed leaves poulticed to burns; the warm gum to cuts, and the sap mixed with other herbs to treat syphilis sores. A bark moxa was used for "internal ailments." The warmed seeds were used in a toothache mixture.

CONIFERS WITH SINGLE FLAT NEEDLES ARRANGED SPIRALLY

SITKA SPRUCE
Picea sitchensis (Bong.) Carr.

Bark, pitch, needles, cones

Pine Family

Large evergreen tree, to 260 ft. Bark gray to brown, scaly, with *thin plates*. Leaves rigid, with sharp tips; *painful if grabbed*. Upper leaf surface flattened. Leaves sit atop a *small peg on the branch*, so branches are prickly after leaves fall. Oblong seed cones are *pendent. Soft, papery cone scales* have jagged margins. **WHERE FOUND:** Pacific coastal forests in moist, well-drained sites and mouths of coastal rivers; sea level–3000 ft. N. Calif. to Alaska. **USES:** Northwest Indian groups used boughs and young shoots as important talismans during hunting and cleansing rituals and as a virtual panacea. Pitch or gum used externally on boils, sores, cuts, wounds, infections, rashes, dermatitis, syphilis lesions, arthritis, as a breath freshener; mixed with oil for sunburn and placed on chest for heart problems. Tea of inner bark, buds, new shoots, needles, and gum used to treat coughs, colds, throat problems, tuberculosis, as a diuretic for gonorrhea, for stomach pain, rheumatic pains, as a blood purifier, and laxative. Cones, bark, and needles were put on hot rocks for steam treatment of rheumatic aches and pains and to relieve stomach problems. Cone ash was used to treat dysentery. Boughs rubbed vigorously on the skin to treat aches and pains, burns, headaches. Ritually, the boughs were believed to protect one from death and illness. **RELATED SPECIES:** Like many members of the pine family, the bark, pitch, and needles of Engelmann spruce, *P. engelmannii* Parry ex Engelm. was used to treat coughs,

Sitka Spruce (Picea sitchensis) *has ridge-tipped leaves.*

Douglas-fir (Pseudotsuga menziesii) *is an important timber tree of the Northwest.*

colds, tuberculosis, other respiratory ailments, and cancer. The pitch or twig ash was used on skin afflictions.

DOUGLAS-FIR
Pitch, leaves, bark

Pseudotsuga menziesii (Mirbel) Franco
Pine Family

Large tree, 80–100 ft. (sometimes to 300 ft.). Bark dark brown to red-brown, deeply furrowed. Leaf tip pointed; ¾–1 ½ in. long, base with small petiole, leaf underside with 2 whitish bands. Round leaf scars are *slightly raised,* making *branches feel bumpy.* Pendent, oval cones are green when immature. Bract below each cone scale is *deeply 3-toothed and extends beyond the cone scale.* Bracts resemble a mouse's hind legs and tail or a cobra's tongue. **WHERE FOUND:** Widespread in mixed evergreen and mixed conifer forests. Throughout western U.S., Canada, and n. Mexico. **USES:** American Indian groups extensively used all parts of the tree. Bark still used by the Coast Salish people of British Columbia for respiratory, gynecological, and digestive problems. Formerly, the pitch was poulticed on cuts, boils, sores, and injured or dislocated bones. Internally, bark tea used to treat colds, coughs, sore throats, gonorrhea, excessive menstrual bleeding, and as an emetic and purgative for diarrhea, intestinal pains, and constipation. Needle tea used as a general tonic, for colds, urinary tract ailments, venereal disease, rheumatism, paralysis and as an antiseptic wash. Shoots were placed in the tips of moccasins to prevent athlete's foot. Twigs and shoots used as a purifying wash in sweat lodges. Bark used to make a moxa for rheumatism. Boughs were used ritually in sweat lodges, bereavement ceremonies, and for bringing good luck and good health.

California Nutmeg (Torreya californica) leaves have a distinctly unpleasant smell.

CALIFORNIA NUTMEG, CALIFORNIA TORREYA   **Nuts**
Torreya californica Torr.   Yew Family

Evergreen tree, to 140 ft. *Dioecious.* Bark smooth, dark brown; wood aromatic. Leaves linear (1–3 in.), *rigid, with spine tip;* base is flattened and appressed to branch; upper surface dark green, lower surface with 2 longitudinal yellowish grooves. *Leaves unpleasant-smelling when crushed.* A single oblong seed (less than 2 in.) is surrounded by a *fleshy green or purplish exterior.* **WHERE FOUND:** Mountain streams, creek bottoms, and moist, shady forests in the coast ranges and Sierra Nevada, Calif. Sometimes present in chaparral. 100–6800 ft. **USES:** Nuts chewed by American Indian groups for indigestion. The Pomo soaked the nuts overnight in cold water, then made tea to treat tuberculosis. Nut poultice, mixed with fat, was applied to the temples for headache, to the body for chills, and to increase perspiration. **RELATED SPECIES:** The nuts of *T. grandis* Fort. are an important drug in traditional Chinese medicine to kill tapeworms, pinworms, hookworms, and roundworms and to help ease a dry cough. **WARNING:** Large doses can be toxic. Consult a licensed practitioner of Chinese medicine before use.

CONIFERS WITH SCALELIKE LEAVES

INCENSE CEDAR, POST CEDAR,
WHITE CEDAR   **Seeds, twigs, leaves**
Calocedrus decurrens (Torr.) Florin   Cypress Family

Evergreen tree, to 170 ft. Widely conical in outline with *cinnamon-colored, fibrous shredding bark.* Leaves opposite, *much longer than wide,* with pointed tips; rotated 90 degrees at each node. Oval seed cones are *pendent* at maturity; *3-parted with reflexed outer scales.* **WHERE FOUND:** Montane mixed evergreen and yellow pine forests; 1000–8000 ft. Calif., Ore., Utah, Nev., Baja Calif. **USES:** American Indian groups used seed tea for asthma. Twigs were burned in sweat baths for the ill. Leaf tea inhaled for colds and drunk for stomach disorders.

CALIFORNIA JUNIPER   **Berries, leaves, bark**
Juniperus californica Carr.   Cypress Family

Shrub or tree to 25 ft., male and female cones on separate trees. Typically, older trees have many trunks. Older leaves *very small, scalelike,* with a pointed tip and *noticeable gland at base.* Newer leaves awl-like. *Berrylike seed cones are bluish with a glaucous film;* resinous when bruised and very aromatic. Cones at *branch tips,* maturing red-brown. **WHERE FOUND:** Dry rocky slopes, open woodlands, 150–4500 ft. Calif., Nev., nw. Ariz.; Baja Calif. **USES:**

Incense Cedar (Calocedrus decurrens). *Note the green, fan-shaped stems.*

American Indian groups used leaf tea to treat colds, coughs, high blood pressure, hangovers, pain, and to promote perspiration. Leaf tea taken before labor to relax muscles and facilitate delivery. Convulsions were treated by rubbing scorched twigs on the body. Chewed berries or berry tea used to treat fevers from flu and as a laxative, diuretic, or douche. **WARNING:** Long-term use of the berry tea said to cause permanent sterility.

(Above) *California Juniper* (Juniperus californica) *in fruit.* (Right) *California Juniper has an upright habit.*

Oneseed Juniper (Juniperus monosperma) *is common in the Southwest.*

ONESEED JUNIPER
Fruits, leaves, twigs

Juniperus monosperma (Engelm.) Sarg.   Cypress Family

Small, branching tree, to about 18 ft. Usually branching from base into several small trunks, creating a bushlike crown. Leaves small, in pairs or threes, closely appressed, sometimes spreading, ovate, only 2–3 mm. long, minutely serrated, rough to touch. Male and female flowers inconspicuous. Fruit pale or dark purplish blue, globose-oval with sweetish, resinous pulp, usually one-seeded. **WHERE FOUND:** Steep slopes, canyons, brushlands, plains. Nw. Okla., w. Tex. to Utah, Nev., se. Ariz., N. M. **USES:** Various native groups of the West, including the Apache, Hopi, Paiute, and Shoshone, used leaf tea to treat fevers, colds, and coughs. Also used for gastrointestinal disorders, stomachache, and indigestion. Externally used as a wash, steam bath, or poultice to treat rheumatism, muscle aches, bruises, sprains, and swelling. Berries used in tea as diuretic. **WARNING:** Of unknown safety. However, as in other juniper species, oil of berries is probably irritating to urinary tract if taken in sufficient quantity.

RED CEDAR, WESTERN RED CEDAR
All parts

Thuja plicata Donn ex D. Don   Cypress Family

Evergreen tree to 225 ft. Trunk flared at base with reddish brown, fibrous bark. Branchlets 4-sided. Leaves opposite, *small, about as long as wide*, yellowish green, rotated 90 degrees at each node; *white stripes beneath*. Oval seed cones resemble *tiny, woody rose buds* sitting upright on top of sprays. **WHERE FOUND:** Moist sites, mixed coniferous forest. Sea level to 5400 ft. Nw. Calif. to se. Alaska; Rocky Mts.: B.C. to Idaho and Mont. **USES:** One of the most important trees in the material culture of Northwest Indians. Bough or bark tea was used internally to promote menstruation, for diarrhea, painful joints, coughs, colds, and tuberculosis. Bough tea popular for purification during a sweating ceremony. Tea of seeds or small branches used for fevers. Bark and twig tea

(Left) *Western Red Cedar* (Thuja plicata) *has delicate leaves.*
(Above) *Fruiting cones of the Western Red Cedar.*

for kidney problems. Tea of cones used for leprosy or stomach pain. Bud tea as a gargle or buds chewed for toothache and sore lungs. Leaf tea used for stomach pain. Externally, washes, poultices, and baths made from strong leaf tea were used for sore backs, arthritis, rheumatism, internal pains, stomach pain, skin sores and infections, to reduce swellings, and as an antiseptic and antidandruff hair rinse. Leaf tea used internally for heart problems, upper respiratory infections, coughs, swollen neck, and sore lungs. Small pieces of the dried inner bark were burned on the skin as moxibustion over arthritic or painful areas of the body to promote healing and reduce pain. Some tribes believed that sleeping under a red cedar would bring vivid dreams. **RELATED SPECIES:** Northern White Cedar, *T. occidentalis* L., of the eastern U.S. was used for many of the same purposes. Historically, physicians used preparations for treating enlarged prostate and incontinence in the aged, as well as syphilitic sores. In modern European phytotherapy, preparations are used for upper respiratory and urinary tract infections as an expectorant and immune stimulant, often combined with Echinacea. Research confirms antifungal, antiviral, and immune-activating properties. **WARNING:** Internally, large doses are toxic. Alcoholic extracts should be used only in very small doses for short periods of time for treating infections. The hepatotoxic and mutagenic compound thujone, from the essential oil of *Thuja* spp., is not very water soluble, but abundant in alcoholic extracts. Avoid use during pregnancy or lactation. Plicatic acid in wood dust causes asthma.

MISCELLANEOUS TREES WITH ALTERNATE, SIMPLE, EVERGREEN LEAVES

PACIFIC MADRONE, MADRONO, MADRONA   Leaves, bark
Arbutus menziesii Pursh   Heath Family

Evergreen with broad, spreading crown, to 130 ft. Bark reddish brown to orange-brown, *peeling in strips* during summer to expose a smooth, greenish trunk. Leathery, oblong leaves (3–6 in.) shiny, dark green above, white to pale green below. Panicles of many white, urn-shaped flowers pendent at branch tips. **WHERE FOUND:** Generally dry, sunny, rocky sites in coniferous and oak forests; often on acidic soils. Baja Calif. to w. B.C., west of Sierra-Cascade crest. **USES:** American Indian groups chewed leaves for strength, sore throats, and colds and to relieve stomachache and cramps. The plant was eaten to induce vomiting. Juice of fresh chewed leaves swallowed to ease a bad cold. Leaves were rubbed on skin to treat rheumatism and burns. Bark tea was used for diabetes, stomachaches. Externally as a wash for cuts, wounds, sores, impetigo; gargled for sore or strep throat. Leaf tea drunk for colds, sore throats, and ulcerated stomach.

EUCALYPTUS, BLUE GUM TREE`   Leaves
Eucalyptus globulus Labill.   Myrtle Family

⚠ Evergreen, to 150 ft. Bark smooth, bluish gray, peeling into numerous shaggy strips. Newer leaves *blue-green with a waxy film,*

(Above) *Pacific Madrone* (Arbutus menziesii) *has a distinctive red trunk and urn-shaped flowers.*
(Right) *Eucalyptus* (Eucalyptus globulus) *is an Australian native.*

highly aromatic, opposite, round to oval. Older leaves green, alternate, lance-shaped curving to *sickle-shaped*, tapering to a point. Large, showy flowers with many white stamens, solitary in leaf axils. Fruit a woody capsule with cross-shaped opening at top. **WHERE FOUND:** Widely planted and naturalized. Weedy in Calif. Perhaps the most widely cultivated species of *Eucalyptus*. Native to se. Australia. **USES:** After the tree was introduced to the western U.S. in the early 1800s, Native Americans used the leaves in steam treatments to cure colds and relieve sinus congestion. Modern herbalists use leaves or essential oil similarly. Eucalyptus oil is an approved nonprescription drug ingredient in lozenges and syrups to treat symptoms of colds. Considered strongly antibacterial, expectorant, mildly antispasmotic, diuretic, and anti-inflammatory. Scientists propose that the decongestant and mucus-freeing properties of eucalyptus result from stimulation of mucus-producing cells in the respiratory tract. **WARNING:** Oil may cause burning or irritation.

TREE TOBACCO
Leaves

Nicotiana glauca Graham   Nightshade Family

Evergreen shrub or small tree, to 26 ft. Stems and leaves generally *covered with a whitish film*, without hairs. Leaves gray-green, ovate, with long petioles; margins entire. Flowers slender, yellow, tubular, with 5 stamens. **WHERE FOUND:** Naturalized in open, disturbed flats or slopes. Calif. to s. U.S.; Mexico. Native to S. America. **USES:** Cahuilla Indians used leaves interchangeably with other tobacco species in hunting rituals and as a poultice to treat swellings, bruises, cuts, wounds, boils, sores, inflamed throat, and swollen glands. Steam from heated leaves was used to alleviate rheumatism and nasal congestion. Smoke was blown into the ear for earache. **WARNING:** Contains the toxic and addictive alkaloid nicotine. Ingestion of the leaves can be fatal. Toxins can be absorbed through the skin.

Tree Tobacco (Nicotiana glauca) *is considered poisonous.*

California Bay (Umbellularia californica) *has pungently fragrant leaves.*

CALIFORNIA BAY   **Leaves, nuts**
Umbellularia californica (Hook & Arn.) Nutt.   Laurel Family

 Evergreen tree, to 150 ft. Bark dark reddish brown. Leaves leathery, *pungently aromatic*, narrowly lance-shaped to elliptical, shiny above and below. Flowers yellow-green, with 6 sepals and 9 stamens, are arranged in umbels; Nov.–Apr. Yellowish green fruit, small, 1-seeded. **WHERE FOUND:** Canyons, valleys, chaparral, open slopes. Baja Calif., Calif. to sw. Ore. **USES:** American Indians treated headaches by inhaling the scent of crushed leaves, by applying a leaf poultice to the head, or by drinking leaf tea. Crushed leaves also inhaled to clear the nasal passages. Leaf tea used to treat colds, sore throats, lung congestion, stomachache, colic, menstrual cramps, clotting. Externally as a wash for sores, poison oak, lice, fleas, rheumatism, and neuralgia. Leaves and leaf smoke used as a flea repellent. Boughs burned to fumigate sick houses. A counterirritant leaf poultice used for rheumatic, neuralgic, and chronic abdominal pain. Shamans would repeatedly hit a patient with the boughs while chanting to help heal colds and other ailments. Nuts, used for food, were said to be stimulant; externally poulticed on sores. Historically, physicians recommended a few drops of the leaf tincture to treat nervous headaches, meningitis, colic, and chronic diarrhea. **Warning:** Contains safrole, a potential liver carcinogen. Avoid internal use of alcoholic extracts. Tea contains lower concentrations, but caution should be exercised.

WESTERN REDBUD
Bark, roots

Cercis canadensis var. *texensis* (S. Wats.) M. Hopkins   Pea Family

Small tree or shrub, to 20 ft. Deciduous. Bark smooth, dark brown. Round leaves with *heart-shaped bases*, margins entire. Flowers pealike, showy, pink to magenta, appearing before leaves emerge; Mar.–May. **WHERE FOUND:** Dry shrubby slopes, canyons, ravines, chaparral, riverbanks. Calif., Ariz., s. Nev., Utah, w. Tex. **USES:** Mendocino Indians used bark tea for chills and fever. **RELATED SPECIES:** Historically, Eclectic physicians used the extremely astringent root bark of *C. canadensis* L., Eastern Redbud, to treat diarrhea and dysentery. As a wash or douche, the tea was used for healing chronic gonorrhea and yeast infections. American Indian groups used tea of the roots and inner bark for fevers and respiratory congestion. In China the bark and wood of the related Chinese Redbud, *C. chinensis* Bge., is considered antiseptic and prescribed for treating abscesses and bladder disease.

DESERT WILLOW, MIMBRE
Leaves, bark, flowers, fruit

Chilopsis linearis (Cav.) Sweet   Bignonia Family

Deciduous small tree or shrub, to 30 ft. Long, narrow leaves curved, appearing sickle-shaped, margins entire; sometimes opposite or whorled. Flowers large, tubular, light pink to light purple, sweet-smelling; petals *with 2 yellow ridges and many purple lines*; margins wavy; May–July. **WHERE FOUND:** Sandy washes and streams, creosote bush desert, Joshua tree woodland. Se. Calif.

Western Redbud (Cercis canadensis *var.* texensis). *Note the pealike flowers and heart-shaped leaves.*

Desert Willow (Chilopsis linearis) *has showy flowers.*

Osage-orange (Maclura pomifera) *has softball-sized inedible fruits.*

east to s. Nev., Ariz., N.M., sw. Utah, w. Tex.; n. Mexico. **USES:** Reputed to have antifungal and antibacterial properties. Flowers were used as a tea or poultice to treat coughs. Powdered plant parts used on fungal or bacterial skin inflammation. Teas of plant parts used as anticandidal vaginal douche.

OSAGE-ORANGE
Root, fruit
Maclura pomifera (Raf.) Schneid.
Mulberry Family

Small tree, 30–60 ft. Branches armed with short spines. Leaves lustrous, oval or oblong to lance-shaped. Fruit large (to 6 in.), round, fleshy; surface *brainlike*; Oct.–Nov. **WHERE FOUND:** Roadsides, clearings. Widely cultivated and escaped. Originally from Ark. and Tex. **USES:** American Indians used root tea as a wash for sore eyes. Fruit sections used as a cockroach repellent. Inedible fruits contain antioxidant and fungicidal compounds. **WARNING:** Milk (latex or sap) may cause dermatitis. Lectins in fruits may be carcinogenic.

WHITE WILLOW
Bark, leaves
Salix alba L.
Willow Family

Deciduous tree, to 75 ft. Leaves narrowly lance-shaped, waxy on bottom, and silvery-silky on both sides, especially on back, and with *small glands along edge*. Male and female catkins, spreading or upright, on different trees; Apr.–May. **WHERE FOUND:** Along streams, in yards and fields. Alien (Europe). Escaped from cultivation. Ariz., Mont., Wyo., Colo.; eastward. **USES:** The most widely used willow for medicinal purposes in Europe and North America. With confirmed anti-inflammatory, pain-reducing, fever-lowering, and antiseptic properties, willow bark has an important place in the herbal repertoire of many cultures. The bark and leaves contain salicin, a naturally occurring salicylate, which is

White Willow (Salix alba) *shown on a frosty morning.*

modified into salicylic acid in the body. Chemically related to aspirin, with similar properties. Salicylate content of willow bark varies widely, depending on the species and time of year. Tannins contribute to astringency. Teas and extracts of the bark were prescribed and used as folk remedies for alleviating all types of pain, especially headache and arthritis, and for reducing fevers of colds and flu. American Indian tribes chewed or brewed the bark or leaves for sore mouth and toothache and to treat respiratory illness, to lower fevers, as a gargle for gum and tonsil inflammation, sore throats, laryngitis. Externally as a poultice or skin wash for rashes, itching, cuts, and sores, for treating diarrhea, and to soothe urinary tract irritation. **RELATED SPECIES:** The most widely used *Salix* species among Indian tribes of the western U.S. include S. *bonplandiana* Kunth, Red Willow; S. *discolor* Muhl., Pussywillow; S. *melanopsis* Nutt., Dusky Willow; S. *planifolia* ssp. *pulchra* (Cham.) Argus, Tealeaf Willow; and S. *Sitchensis* Sanson ex Bong., Sitka Willow.

SIMPLE, ALTERNATE LEAVES; LEAVES LOBED; OAKS & SWEET GUM

SWEET GUM   Bark, sap
Liquidambar styraciflua L.   Witch Hazel Family
Deciduous tree, to 130 ft. Leaves large, palmately 5–7-lobed (to 7½ in. long, 6 in. wide), aromatic, margins finely toothed. Flowers inconspicuous. Fruits *spiny balls*. **WHERE FOUND:** Riverbanks, bottomland woods. Tex. and throughout e. U.S. Widely planted as a shade tree throughout the West. **USES:** Sap traditionally used to make a softening and antiseptic ointment for itching, ringworm, scabies, bruises, ulcers, sores, cuts, wounds, and hemorrhoids or

(Left, above) *Sweet Gum* (Liquidambar styraciflua) *has distinctive 5–7 parted, maplelike, fragrant leaves and globe-shaped fruits with beaklike projections.*

fistulas. Gum or balsam (resin) from bark stimulates mucous membranes; used for treating cough, chronic congestion, asthma, bronchitis, leukorrhea, diarrhea, dysentery, and skin conditions. Cherokee used the bark to treat nervous patients and to stop uterine hemorrhage. Considered expectorant, antiseptic, antimicrobial, anti-inflammatory. **RELATED SPECIES:** Various species are used in other parts of the world for similar purposes, including *L. orientalis* Miller and *L. formosa* Hance, used in Chinese medicine to promote circulation, as an astringent to treat skin diseases and wounds, and for low back pain. Essential oil of leaf contains similar components to Australian Tee Tree (*Melaleuca alternifolia* [Maiden & Betche] Cheel), well known for its antimicrobial activity.

VALLEY OAK   **Bark, galls**
Quercus lobata Nèe   Oak Family

Deciduous tree, 80–100 ft. Gray bark becoming deeply checkered with age. Leaves deeply round-lobed, dark green above, pale below, margins entire. Loose yellow catkins of male flowers appear as leaves emerge in early spring. Fruit an oblong acorn, about 2 in. long, gradually tapering to a point. *Acorn cap bumpy and quite deep*, covering up to ⅓ of the nut. **WHERE FOUND:** Valley floors, open grasslands, slopes; generally in rich soils. Calif.: from w. slopes of Sierra Nevada to Pacific Coast, from Trinity R. to Tehachapi Mts. Valley Oak may be confused with Oregon White Oak, *Q. garryana*, which also has deeply lobed leaves but has acorns round

Valley Oak (Quercus lobata). *Note the lobed leaves.*

to oval with *smooth caps of flattened scales*. Blue Oak, *Q. douglasii*, has shallowly lobed, blue-green leaves. The genus *Quercus* is well known for extensive hybridization. Hybrids typically show characteristics intermediate between its parent species. Hybrids may also backcross with either parent species or another hybrid. This web of crossing can lead to populations with considerable individual variation, posing difficulties in identification. **USES:** American Indian groups used diluted juice or solutions of powdered or fresh stem as an eyewash. Ground galls were also used as a poultice on sores, cuts, and burns. Powdered bark was applied to weeping sores and poorly healing umbilical stumps of newborns. Bark was used for treating diarrhea. **RELATED SPECIES:** Juice from crushed bark of *Q. rubra* L., red oak, was applied to the gums to tighten loose teeth. Bark and galls from all species of oak are considered astringent and used to treat mucous membrane and skin inflammation, diarrhea, sore throat, ulcers, hemorrhoids, vaginal leukorrhea, wounds, and sores. Oak galls were formerly official drugs. Galls contain up to 70 percent polyphenolic acids (tannins), some of which show antiviral, antibacterial, and antiparasitic activity, along with a powerful astringent and drying action on local tissue. The green stems of the fresh growth of any *Quercus* species can be chewed ragged to make a chewing stick for massaging the gums and cleaning the teeth. The juice contains potent antibacterial and astringent activity, which may help fight gum disease and tighten gum tissue.

VALLEY WHITE OAK, BLUE OAK

Galls, bark, acorns

Quercus douglasii Hook. & Arn.   Oak Family

Deciduous tree, to 60 feet. Leaves oblong; margins entire or *shallowly lobed*; blue-green above and paler and short-hairy below. Flowers Apr.–May. Acorns with shallow cups; *scales have small warts*. **WHERE FOUND:** Rocky, dry slopes below 3500 feet around interior valleys of Calif. from n. Los Angeles Co. to s. Cascades. **USES:** Native Americans used diluted juice or solutions of powdered or

Valley White Oak (Quercus douglasii). *The acorn scales have small warts.*

fresh stem and leaf galls as an eyewash. Ground galls were also used as a poultice on sores, cuts, and burns. Powdered bark was applied to weeping sores and as a burn dressing. A leaf tea was gargled to ease a sore throat.

SIMPLE, ALTERNATE, TOOTHED LEAVES WITH DRY, CONELIKE FRUITS; BIRCH FAMILY

RED ALDER
Alnus rubra Bong.
[*Alnus oregona* Nutt.]

Bark, stems, sap, buds
Birch Family

Deciduous tree, to 130 ft. Bark white to gray, mostly smooth, but with short horizontal ridges (lenticels), breaking into thin plates as tree matures. *Roots red-orange*, often exposed along creeks, with nodules containing a nitrogen-fixing fungus. Leaves broadly ovate, leathery, coarsely toothed, margins tightly rolled under (3–6 in. long). *Lower surface with rust-colored hairs.* **WHERE FOUND:** Generally forms thick stands in wet areas: streambanks, rich bottomlands. Cen. Calif. north to s. Alaska, n. Idaho **USES:** American Indian groups considered the sap a tonic and blood purifier; externally applied to cuts. The bark was both chewed and made into a tea for tuberculosis and asthma. Bark tea used for tuberculosis, asthma, as a

Red Alder (Alnus rubra) *is common in the Pacific Northwest.*

laxative; externally as a wash for rashes. Bark poulticed to sores, eczema, and aches. Buds chewed and rubbed into sores and wounds. Powder from charred fruit applied to burns. Stem-bark tea used as an emetic and to relieve headaches. Extracts from the catkins have demonstrated antifungal activity. Bark extracts have antibacterial activity. **RELATED SPECIES:** The bark of a European species, *A. glutinosa* (L.) Gaertn., is high in lignins, tannins, and phenolic glycosides. A decoction is gargled to relieve sore throats.

PAPER BIRCH
Betula papyrifera Marsh.

Whole plant

Birch Family

Deciduous tree, 50–70 ft. White bark with prominent horizontal ridges, *peeling into thin strips*. Leaves are oval with acute tips, 2–3 in. long, ½–2 in. wide; base wedge- or heart-shaped; margins doubly serrated; prominent raised midrib is yellow; marked by black glandular dots. Male flowers appear before leaves in early spring in long clusters or pairs; 3–4 in. long. Female catkins are 1–1½ in. long, with pale green lance-shaped scales. **WHERE FOUND:** Moist, rich soils; forests, stream and lake edges, mountain slopes. Ore. to Alaska; Idaho, Mont., Wyo., Colo.; east to New England. Widely planted ornamental. **USES:** American Indians drank the sap as a spring tonic and laxative and to treat colds and coughs. Tea of wood taken for back pain, to induce sweating, and to increase mother's milk. Inner bark tea used as an enema for dysentery; externally as a wash for skin rashes and sores. The dried inner bark was ground, mixed with pitch and grease, and applied to persistent scabs and rashes. Bark or rotten wood was powdered and used for diaper rash and other skin rashes. Bark used as a cast for broken bones as well as for birch bark canoes. Betulinic acid from many species, including birches, is a promising anticancer compound (against melanomas); also anti-inflamma-

Paper Birch (Betula papyrifera) *is easily recognized by its bark.*

tory and antiviral. **RELATED SPECIES:** The leaves and flowers of *B. occidentalis* Hook. were used as an abortifacient. Bark and leaves of a European species, *B. alnus* var. *glutinosa* L., are reported to contain tannins and phenolic glycosides, commonly used in the form of a gargle as a folk remedy for sore throats.

TREES WITH ALTERNATE, TOOTHED LEAVES; STALKS MOSTLY FLATTENED; POPLARS

BLACK COTTONWOOD   Buds, bark, leaves
Populus balsamifera ssp. *trichocarpa* (Torr. & Gray ex Hook.) Brayshaw
[*P. trichocarpa* Torr. & Gray ex Hook.]   Willow Family
Deciduous, to 150 ft. Bark dark gray, deeply furrowed. Winter buds resinous: *very sticky and strongly fragrant*. Leathery leaves narrowly to widely ovate, with slightly scalloped or toothed margins; whitish beneath, often with *brown to rust-colored resin stains*. Petiole round in cross section, making it easy to roll between finger tips. Round, green, 3-parted fruits release numerous hairy, "cottony" seeds. **WHERE FOUND:** Wet sites, streamsides, valleys, floodplains. N. Baja Calif. to Alaska.; Nev., Utah, Ore., Idaho, Wash., Mont.; n. Rocky Mts. **USES:** Resinous buds, and sometimes bark or leaves, used to make salves or poultices for wounds, cuts, sores, infections, chancres, eczema, fungal infections, sunburn, baldness, and dandruff, as a mosquito and fly repellent. American Indian groups used buds, bark, and leaves in baths or poulticed for aches, pains,

(Above) *Black Cottonwood* (Populus balsamifera ssp. trichocarpa). *The sticky buds are used as herbal medicine in many cultures.*
(Right) *Black Cottonwood has leathery leaves.*

Frémont Cottonwood (Populus fremontii) *has leaves that are bright green on both sides.*

sprains, and strains. Tea of buds or inner bark taken for colds, coughs, colic and bowel disorders, worms, rheumatism, headache, venereal disease, and as a blood tonic. Cottonwood's anodyne properties come from its salicin content. **RELATED SPECIES:** Many *Populus* species are used for medicine worldwide. Other western species used include *P. alba* L., White Poplar; *P. balsamifera* L.; and *P. nigra* L., Lombardy Poplar. Extracts of *P. nigra* have antibacterial, antiviral, antifungal, anti-inflammatory, analgesic, fever-lowering, capillary-dilating, and expectorant activity in laboratory tests. Though there is some variation among species in chemical constituents, all *Populus* species have the same active compounds, including flavonoids, phenolic resinoids, natural salicylates, and prostaglandins.

FRÉMONT COTTONWOOD   BARK, LEAVES
Populus fremontii S. Wats.   Willow Family
Deciduous tree, to 100 ft. Bark light gray. Leaves triangular, with coarsely scalloped margins, tips abruptly pointed. *Leaves bright green on both sides.* Petiole flattened, not easily rolled between finger tips. Fruits oval, 3-parted, releasing many *cottony* seeds. Susceptible to mistletoe. **WHERE FOUND:** Wet sites, streambanks, floodplains. N. Calif. south and east to Nev., Utah, Ariz., Colo., N.M., Tex.; n. Baja Calif. **USES:** Cahuilla Indians used the boiled leaves and bark as a poultice or bath, for muscle strains, injuries, cuts, sore throats, saddle sores, and swollen limbs. Kawaiisu Indians and other tribes used an inner bark tea to wash broken limbs or as a poultice for injuries. Diegueños and other tribes infused the leaves to wash bruises, wounds, or insect stings.

QUAKING ASPEN   **Buds, bark, leaves**
Populus tremuloides Michx.   Willow Family
Deciduous, to 100 ft. Bark smooth, greenish white to light gray. Leaves widely ovate to nearly round, with abruptly pointed tips; margins finely scalloped. *Flattened petiole causes the distinctive*

Quaking Aspen (Populus tremu-loides) *is common in western mountains.*

Quaking Aspen is easily recognized by its smooth, light gray bark.

fluttering of leaves. Fruits oblong to conical, 2-parted, releasing many hairy seeds. **WHERE FOUND:** Streambanks, meadows, slopes; montane and subalpine forests, woodlands, sagebrush steppe; sea level to 10,000 ft. All western states; northeastern N. America, across Canada to Alaska. **USES:** Western herbalists use this tree for many of the same purposes that American Indian groups used cottonwood, and for treating fevers and indigestion. American Indian groups made poultices of bark for cuts, wounds, and rheumatism. Bark tea used to treat worms, venereal disease, colds, hernias, stomach pain, indigestion, and heart trouble. The white powder on the bark surface was scraped and used as a styptic. Crushed leaves poulticed on bee stings. Historically, physicians prescribed bark preparations for weak digestion with weight loss, general weakness, chronic diarrhea, and fevers. They thought it especially effective for urinary tract problems such as painful, scanty urination (tenesmus), as a diuretic and antiseptic, for gonorrhea, and for prostate enlargement.

TREES WITH SIMPLE, ALTERNATE LEAVES; JUICY FRUITS

CASCARA SAGRADA, CHITUM
Frangula purshiana (DC.) Cooper
[*Rhamnus purshiana* DC.]

Bark, berries, leaves
Buckthorn Family

Deciduous tree or shrub, to 40 ft. Bark smooth, gray to silver. During winter, buds not covered in protective scales. Leaves broadly elliptic to oblong (3–7 in. long, 2 in. wide), midrib and veins prominent, margins finely toothed, tips and bases rounded.

Umbels of small, greenish yellow flowers *in leaf axils*; May–July. Fruit fleshy, shiny black, 3-lobed with 3 stones. **WHERE FOUND:** Moist woods in lowlands and canyons, coniferous forests, chaparral. Cen. Calif. north to s. B.C., mostly west of Sierra-Cascade crest; n. Idaho, w. Mont. Bark harvested commercially from wild trees in Ore., Wash., and s. B.C. **USES:** Cascara Sagrada is Spanish for "sacred bark." Long used as a laxative by native groups of the Pacific Northwest. Introduced into western medicine in 1877. By 1890 the bark replaced the berries of the European buckthorn (*R. catharticus* L.) as an official laxative. An ingredient in many nonprescription laxatives. Bark contains anthraquinones (cascarosides A and B), which are transformed by intestinal bacteria into substances that increase peristalsis in the large intestine while restoring tone of the bowels. Only bark aged at least one year or heated above 212 degrees F. (100 degrees C.) is used. Fresh or untreated bark is strongly cathartic. American Indian groups also used the bark for chronic indigestion, upset stomach, dysentery, worms, liver, and gallstone problems, rheumatic aches and pains, and gonorrhea. Bark poulticed on wounds and sores. **RELATED SPECIES:** *Rhamnus catharticus* L. in Europe and other *Rhamnus* or *Frangula* species worldwide have similar uses. **WARNING:** Preparations from all species of *Frangula* are contraindicated in case of intestinal obstruction, abdominal pain of unknown origin, or with inflammatory conditions of the intestines such as appendicitis, colitis, Crohn's disease, or irritable bowel syndrome. Avoid use during pregnancy or lactation. Avoid using the fresh bark; it should be aged for one to two years to moderate its action. Use can lead to laxative dependency. Frequent use leads to discoloration of the bowels, a condition often seen by proctologists.

The bark of Cascara Sagrada (Frangula purshiana) *is one of the few tree barks of the West used in commerce.*

WHITE MULBERRY
Morus alba L.

Leaves, inner bark
Mulberry Family

Small tree, 20–60 ft. Leaves heart-shaped or irregular, 3–5-lobed, coarsely toothed, often lobed. Flowers in tight, drooping clusters. Fruit resembles a thin blackberry, whitish to purple; June–July. **WHERE FOUND:** Planted and naturalized in much of our range. Alien (Asia), introduced for silkworm production. **USES:** In China, leaf tea used for headaches, hyperemia (engorgement), thirst, coughs, and as a liver cleanser. Experimentally, leaf extracts are antibacterial. Young twig tea used for arthralgia, edema. Fruits eaten for blood deficiency, to improve vision and circulation, and for diabetes. Inner-bark tea used for lung ailments, asthma, coughs, and edema.

BITTER CHERRY
Prunus emarginata (Dougl. ex Hook.) D. Dietr.

Bark, roots
Rose Family

⚠️ Deciduous tree or shrub, to 30 ft.; forming thickets. *Small branches mostly red*; older bark gray or reddish-brown with horizontal ridges. Leaves oval, wider than tapered bases, margins toothed. Flowers white, arranged in *flat-topped* racemes of fewer than 12, from leaf axils. Fruit fleshy, red to purple, containing a single seed surrounded by a stony outer shell. **WHERE FOUND:** Mixed evergreen or coniferous forests; streambanks, rocky slopes, canyons, chaparral. S. Calif. to all other western states except Colo. and Tex. **USES:** American Indian groups used bark tea to treat colds, tuberculosis, mouth sores, heart problems, respiratory conditions, gynecological problems, constipation, and eczema. Saanich grandparents were said to wash infants with an infusion of cherry and gooseberry roots to make them intelligent and obedient. Children

White Mulberry (Morus alba) *has small, blackberrylike fruits that are relished by birds.*

Bitter Cherry (Prunus emarginata) *branches are reddish.*

wore amulets of the bark for disease protection. **WARNING:** All parts of cherry species contain varying amounts of highly toxic hydrocyanic acid, which has an almondlike smell.

CHOKECHERRY, WILD CHERRY
Bark, roots, leaves, berries
Prunus virginiana L.
Rose Family

⚠ Deciduous small tree or shrub, to 20 ft. Bark gray-brown. Leaves ovate to oval with pointed tips, rounded bases, and finely toothed margins. Flowers white in a thick, many-flowered *elongated raceme*. Fruit dark red to purple to black, *acrid-tasting*. **WHERE FOUND:** Coniferous forests, oak/pine woodland, rocky slopes, canyons. Most of Calif. except along coast, to B.C., Idaho, Tex.; cen. U.S.; n. Mexico. **USES:** Historically, physicians considered chokecherry bark a useful recuperating herb because of its tonic properties and its ability to relieve mucous membrane irritation in the gastrointestinal, respiratory, and urinary tracts. Unripe berries were used for diarrhea, ripe berries for constipation, berry juice for diarrhea, and dried berries to stimulate appetite. *P. virginiana* var. *demissa* (Nutt.) Torr., Western Chokecherry, was widely used by Indian tribes of the western U.S. for similar ailments, and *P. virginiana* var. *melanocarpa* (A. Nels.) Sarg. was used to a lesser extent. **RELATED SPECIES:** *P. ilicifolia* (Nutt. ex Hook. & Arn.) D. Dietr., Hollyleaf Cherry, was used as a cough medicine in California, while the *aromatic* inner bark of *P. serotina* Ehrh., Black or Wild Cherry, native to Ariz., N.M., and eastward, was extensively used in tea or syrup for coughs, as a blood tonic, for fevers, colds, sore throats, diarrhea, lung ailments, bronchitis, pneumonia, inflammatory fever diseases, and dyspepsia. Chinese herbalists use vari-

Chokecherry (Prunus virginiana) has delicate racemes of white flowers.

Chokecherry fruits range from red to black.

ous species of cherry bark for coughs, hemorrhage, constipation, diarrhea, worms, menstrual irregularities, and other disorders. **WARNING:** All parts of cherry species contain varying amounts of highly toxic hydrocyanic acid, which has an almondlike smell.

TREES WITH ALTERNATE COMPOUND LEAVES; WALNUTS

CALIFORNIA BLACK WALNUT
Juglans californica S. Wats.

Leaves
Walnut Family

Deciduous tree, to 80 ft. Bark gray to dark brown. Leaves odd-pinnate, to 9 in.; 11–19 leaflets, narrowly lance-shaped to ovate, with an *obvious terminal leaflet*, Small male flowers hang in catkins; solitary female flowers sit in leaf axils; Mar.–May. Large, green fruits (1 ½ in. diam.) have a smooth, fleshy husk surrounding a smooth to shallowly grooved nut; *flesh quickly bruises dark.* **WHERE FOUND:** Canyons, valleys, streamsides, slopes. S. to n. Calif., west of Sierra-Cascade crest. **USES:** Costanoan Indians took an infusion of the leaves for "thin blood." **RELATED SPECIES:** The inner root bark of Butternut, *J. cinerea* L., was an official drug in the U.S. to treat dysentery and diarrhea. Since ancient times the leaves of the Eurasian English walnut, *J. regia* L., have been used as a laxative, as an astringent for treating skin problems, and to kill worms. The Chinese used nuts of *J. regia* to treat constipation, kidney problems, and chronic coughs and wheezing. **WARNING:** Fruit husks and leaves can cause severe contact dermatitis.

BLACK WALNUT
Juglans nigra L.

Bark, leaves, fruit
Walnut Family

Deciduous, to 150 ft. Bark black to dark gray, deeply furrowed. Long, pinnately compound leaves (to 2 ft.) have lance-shaped to sickle-shaped leaflets with toothed margins. Most of the 9–11 paired leaflets are nearly opposite; *terminal one absent or reduced.*

Flowering Apr.–May. Smooth, green fruit (to 3 in. diam.) encloses nut with a deeply longitudinally grooved shell. **WHERE FOUND:** Native to eastern N.

California Black Walnut (Juglans californica) *has 11–19 leaflets.*

Black Walnut (Juglans nigra). *The terminal leaflet is often absent or much reduced.*

America. Common ornamental throughout western U.S., often persisting around old home sites. **USES:** American Indian groups rubbed leaves or juice from hulls on fungal infections, skin inflammations. Nut meats mixed with bear grease as a mosquito repellent and to treat scabies. Root-bark tea used to expel worms and prevent dysentery; a strong laxative and emetic. Poulticed to treat headaches and mental instability. Leaves scattered to repel flies. Historically, physicians used the juice and a tincture of the nut rind to treat eczema, herpes, and other skin conditions; tea for intestinal worms. The hulls contain a strong antifungal agent, juglone, and black walnut preparations are used in herbal practice for candida yeast infections, diarrhea, and intestinal parasites. Scientific studies have found that the leaf extracts have strong antiviral activity against cold sores; have a protective effect on the vascular system; and inhibit certain forms of tumors. **WARNING:** Fruit husks and leaves can cause severe contact dermatitis.

MISCELLANEOUS TREES WITH COMPOUND, ALTERNATE LEAVES

TREE-OF-HEAVEN, STINKTREE   **Bark, root bark**
Ailanthus altissima (P. Mill.) Swingle   Quassia Family

⚠ Smooth-barked tree, 20–100 ft. Leaves compound, similar to those of sumacs; crushed leaves *smell like peanuts*. Each leaflet with 2 *glandular-tipped teeth at base* (on underside). Flowers small, yellow; June–July. Male flowers *foul-smelling*. Fruits are winged "keys," persisting through winter. **WHERE FOUND:** Waste places. Throughout. This Chinese native introduced in the late 19th century is a persistent weed tree in many American cities. **USES:** Bark tea used in traditional Chinese medicine for diarrhea, dysentery, leukorrhea, tapeworm. Contains several antimalarial compounds, five of which are more potent than the standard antimalarial drug chloroquine. **WARNING:** Large doses potentially **poisonous.** Cutting trees or handling leaves may cause dermatitis.

Tree-of-Heaven (Ailanthus altissima). *Note the gland on the underside of the prominent tooth at base of leaflet.*

Tree-of-Heaven fruits are winged samaras like maples, but the seed is in the center of the wings.

ELEPHANT TREE, TOROTE

Bursera microphylla Gray

Sap

Torchwood Family

Small, deciduous, *resinous, aromatic* tree or shrub, to 13 ft. Mature bark white, younger branches reddish, spreading. Leaves odd-pinnately compound, with 7–33 small, oval to oblong leaflets. White to cream-colored flowers, singly or in clusters of 2–3 in leaf axils. Flowering before leaves emerge; June–July. Fruit

(Left) *The trunk of Elephant Tree (Bursera microphylla) looks like elephant skin.* (Above) *Elephant Tree has tiny leaves and reddish brown fruit.*

with *aromatic, resinous pulp* surrounds a yellow, single-seeded pit. **WHERE FOUND:** Desert regions, rocky slopes. s. Calif. east to s. Ariz., n. Baja Calif., and n. Mexico. **USES:** Found only in rare, isolated spots in s. California, this plant was considered a powerful panacea by American Indian groups. Sap, leaves, and twigs were kept hidden and administered only by shamans. The light red, resinous sap was rubbed on the body to cure skin diseases but was believed useful against many conditions. **RELATED SPECIES:** The dried sap, bark, and leaves of a number of Indian species such as the Turpentine Tree, *B. gummifera* L., are used for incense and perfume and medicinally for protecting against worms, lowering fevers, for dysentery, gonorrhea, and as a diuretic. *B. tomentosa* Trian. et Planch. and other Mexican and South American species are used for their tonic, astringent, and antispasmodic properties against rheumatism and colds. Frankincense, *Boswellia serrata* Roxb.; Myrrh, *Commiphora myrrha* Engl., and Guggul, *C. mukul* (Hook. ex Stocks) Engl., are related members of the Torchwood Family.

HOPTREE, WAFERASH
Ptelea trifoliata L.

Root, leaves
Rue Family

Aromatic large shrub or small tree, 10 to 20 ft. Leaves 3-divided into ovate to slender, lance-shaped leaflets, finely wavy-margined. Flowers small, greenish white, in clusters; Apr.–June. Fruit oblong to round, *hoplike*, surrounded by a thin, broad-veined wing. **WHERE FOUND:** Dry arroyos and canyons. Ariz., Utah, N.M., Tex., east to Fla, N.Y. **USES:** Traditionally herbalists and physicians used hop tree preparations to improve health and vitality lowered by febrile diseases, for it soothes stomach and gastrointestinal tract irritation and helps to invigorate appetite and digestion. Historically, root used to expel worms, lower fevers, relieve rheumatic pain and asthma. Externally poulticed to wounds. Late 19th- and early

Hoptree (Ptelea trifoliata) *has three leaflets and waferlike fruits.*

Black Locust (Robinia pseudoacacia) *in flower.*

20th-century physicians prescribed an extract for asthma and digestive weakness. Menominee and Meskwaki Indians considered it an especially valuable medicine and used it to strengthen effects of other herbs. Root tea used for lung ailments, and a leaf tea rubbed on abdomen of a child with stomachache. *Ptelea* extracts show antibacterial, antifungal, and anticandida activity in laboratory experiments. **WARNING:** Do not confuse leaves of this small tree with Poison Ivy leaves. Coumarins in the leaves can induce photodermatitis.

BLACK LOCUST **Root bark, flowers**
Robinia pseudoacacia L. Pea Family
To 70–90 ft.; armed with stout, *paired thorns*, ½–1 in. long. Leaves *pinnately compound*; 7–21 elliptic to oval leaflets. Fragrant white flowers in racemes; May–June. Pods *smooth*, flat. 2–6 in. **WHERE FOUND:** Dry woods of eastern N. America. Planted and escaped elsewhere. **USES:** American Indians chewed root bark to induce vomiting, held bark in mouth to allay toothache. A folk tonic, purgative, and emetic. Flower tea used for rheumatism. In China the root bark is also considered purgative and emetic and the flowers are considered diuretic. Experimentally, shows diuretic activity. **WARNING:** All parts are potentially toxic. The strong odor of the flowers has been reported to cause nausea and headaches in some persons.

PERUVIAN PEPPERTREE **Leaves, bark, fruit, seeds, sap**
Schinus molle L. Cashew Family

Evergreen tree with drooping upper branches. Wood and *leaves resinous, aromatic.* Leaves pinnately compound with up to 15 sessile, lance-shaped to linear leaflets. Female plants with *small, red, berrylike, single-seeded fruits.* **WHERE FOUND:** Washes, slopes, abandoned fields. Sierra Nevada foothills; cen. and s. Calif. to Tex.;

Peruvian Peppertree (Schinus molle) has linear leaflets and red fruits.

Mexico. Alien (South America). **USES:** In Peru, other South American countries, and Mexico, the leaves, fruits, and white, acrid pitch are used to treat upper respiratory infections, urinary tract infections, gastrointestinal problems, cholera, rheumatism, tuberculosis, bronchitis, menstrual problems, premenstrual syndrome (PMS), arthritis, high blood pressure, hemorrhages, and depression. The shell of the red fruit tastes sweet at first, then acrid and peppery. In Chilean folk medicine, the whole fruits are fermented or soaked in hot water to make a drink that is taken as a diuretic, to ease gas pains, as a digestive tonic, for cleansing the system, for hemorrhoids, and externally for wounds. The kernels are used to adulterate black pepper, for which they make a good substitute. Extracts have been shown to have potent broad-spectrum antibacterial, antifungal, and diuretic properties. **RELATED SPECIES:** The Brazilian peppertree, *S. terebinthifolius* Raddi, a serious invasive weed in Florida, is used similarly. **WARNING:** May cause contact dermatitis.

TREES WITH ALTERNATE, DECIDUOUS, PINNATELY COMPOUND LEAVES; SHOWY FLOWERS WITH PROMINENT STAMENS; PEA FAMILY

CATCLAW ACACIA, GREGG CATCLAW **Pods**
Acacia greggii A. Gray Pea Family

Deciduous shrub or small tree, to 16 ft.; often forming thickets. Branches grayish brown, rigid, with scattered, *small, stout, downward-curved prickles*. Gray-green leaves, pinnately 2-compound, hairy; margins entire. Leaflets oblong, usually 4–6 pairs. Pale yellow, fragrant flowers arranged in dense, cylindrical spikes from leaf axils, typically extending beyond leaves; stamens showy; Apr.–June. Grayish pod flat, twisted, contracted between seeds.

(Above) *Catclaw Acacia* (Acacia greggii). *Note the cat-clawlike thorns.* (Right) *Mesquite* (Prosopis glandulosa) *is a dominant tree in Texas.*

WHERE FOUND: Desert flats, washes, canyons, dry streambeds. S. Calif. to Utah, Colo., w. Tex.; Baja Calif., n. Mexico. **USES:** Sap from stems and branches infused in warm water and used as a demulcent to soothe coughs and throat irritation or externally for burns or rashes. The ripe fruit is still an important food. **WARNING:** The leaves and twigs contain cyanogenic glycosides, which have been responsible for cattle poisoning in some parts of its range.

MESQUITE, HONEY MESQUITE
Prosopis glandulosa Torr.

Leaves, fruit
Pea Family

Deciduous shrub or small tree, to 20 ft. Trunks crooked; branches arched. *A single pair of pinnately compound leaves and 1–2 spines occur at each branch node.* Many bright green, oblong leaflets, hairless or nearly so; margins entire. Yellow flowers, each with 10 showy stamens, densely clustered in long, cylindrical racemes; Apr.–Sept. Straw-colored pods long, straight or somewhat curved, *slightly narrowed between seeds.* Pods remaining unopened; seeds separated by spongy partitions. **WHERE FOUND:** Desert washes, grasslands, mesas, alkali flats, bottomlands, creosote bush scrub. S. cen. coast ranges to Sierra foothills of Calif. to s. Calif., north to Nev., Ariz., Utah, Colo., N.M., Tex.; nw. Mexico. **USES:** Several Native American groups made an eyewash from the leaf juice or a decoction of the leaves and pods after the beans had been removed. The leaves are chewed and the juice swallowed for indigestion; an infusion of bark given to children to stop bed-wetting.

Screwbean Mesquite (Prosopis pubescens) has an unusual twisted fruit.

SCREWBEAN MESQUITE, TORNILLO
Leaves, fruit
Prosopis pubescens Benth.
Pea Family

Deciduous shrub or small tree, to 30 ft. Stems slender, softly hairy, with stout spines at leaf nodes. Leaves pinnately compound in pairs; leaflets oblong, with soft gray hairs; margins entire. Flowers yellow, with 10 showy stamens, arranged in dense spikelike racemes; May–Aug. *Pods tightly coiled with dense, fine hairs.* **WHERE FOUND:** Sandy or gravelly washes, ravines, or canyons, along creeks, creosote bush scrub. S. Calif., Nev., Utah to w. Tex.; Baja Calif., n. Mexico. **USES:** Pima Indians used powdered bark on wounds and sores, root tea for menstrual irregularities. Wash from powdered gum used for sores and eye ailments. Apache and Tewa used a cold pod tea for earache. Papago used a tea of inner bark for chronic indigestion.

SIMPLE, OPPOSITE LEAVES

BIGLEAF MAPLE
Bark, gum
Acer macrophyllum Pursh.
Maple Family

Deciduous tree, to 115 ft. Bark gray-brown, furrowed, often covered in mosses, ferns, and lichens. Leaves large, palmately lobed (4–12 in. wide), with 5 toothed, pointed segments. Yellowish green flowers in pendent clusters as new leaves emerge. The light brown fruit breaks into 2 single-seeded units, *each with a large wing attached.* **WHERE FOUND:** Moist soils, streambanks, canyons; S. Calif. to Alaska., mostly west of the Cascades Sierra Nevada. **USES:** American Indians used bark tea for tuberculosis. Gum from buds was used as a hair tonic; raw sap as a tonic.

Bigleaf Maple (Acer macrophyllum) *has large palmately lobed leaves.*

TREES WITH COMPOUND, OPPOSITE LEAVES

CALIFORNIA BUCKEYE, CALIFORNIA HORSECHESTNUT

Fruit, bark

Aesculus californica (Spach) Nutt.

Horsechestnut Family

Deciduous tree, to 40 ft. Leaves palmately compound with 5–7 *oblong to lance-shaped leaflets*; margins finely toothed. Showy sprays of white to pale rose flowers sit on erect, upturned stalks, *musty-sweet-smelling*. Pear-shaped fruits generally hang solitary at tip of inflorescence. **WHERE FOUND:** Dry slopes and hillsides, canyons, stream borders; Calif., generally west of Sierra-Cascade crest. **USES:** American Indians leached the bark, then boiled it to treat toothaches and loose teeth. The bark also placed in cavity for toothache. Pulverized fruits applied to hemorrhoids. Seeds and fresh fruit are considered poisonous. Crushed seeds, high in saponin, were thrown into streams to stun fish. After being ground and repeatedly water-leached, seeds were an important food source. **WARNING:** See warning under Horsechestnut, below.

HORSECHESTNUT

Nuts, leaves, flowers, bark

Aesculus hippocastanum L.

Horsechestnut Family

Large deciduous tree, to 100 ft. Leaflets 5–7; to 12 in. long; *without stalks*, toothed. Buds large, *very sticky* Flowers white (mottled red and yellow); May–June. Fruits *spiny or warty*; Sept.–Oct. **WHERE FOUND:** Widely planted as an ornamental. Occasionally naturalized

California Buckeye (Aesculus californica). *Note the sprout from the large nut.*

The showy flowers of California Buckeye.

in West. **USES:** Horsechestnut seed extracts widely prescribed in European phytomedicine for edema with venous insufficiency to treat varicose veins and improve vascular tone, strengthen weak veins and arteries to reduce leg edema, nighttime calf muscle spasms, thrombosis, and hemorrhoids. Effectiveness confirmed by several clinical studies. Contains aescin, which reduces capillary-wall permeability, lessens diameter and number of capillary wall openings, regulates the flow of fluids to surrounding tissue, and increases blood circulation. Topically, aescin-containing gels or creams are widely used to allay swelling and pain in bruising, sprains, and contusions. Injectable forms of aescin used in European trauma centers to help stabilize brain trauma patients. Only chemically well-defined products are used, not the crude drug. **RELATED SPECIES:** Red Buckeye, *A. pavia* L., occurs as far west as cen. Tex. The ground nuts were applied externally for tumors and infections, and a cold infusion of the bark was used to stop bleeding after delivery. **WARNING:** Outer husks poisonous; all parts can be toxic, and fatalities have been reported. Seeds (nuts) are used as a foodstuff only after toxins have been removed.

Horsechestnut (Aesculus hippocastanum) *is often grown as a shade tree.*

Oregon Ash (Fraxinus latifolia) *has single-seeded fruits with a wing attached.*

OREGON ASH

Bark, roots, twigs

Fraxinus latifolia Benth.

Olive Family

Deciduous, to 80 ft. Bark gray to grayish brown, shallowly furrowed. Leaves pinnately compound with 3–9 leaflets, narrow to broadly oval, sessile. Yellow to greenish flowers are borne in tight clusters on stems before leaves emerge; Apr.–May. Fruit pendulous from long, slender stalks, single-seeded *with an attached wing*, up to 2 in long. **WHERE FOUND:** Moist to wet soils at lower elevations; valleys, streambanks, floodplains, woodland. S. Calif. to B.C., west of Sierra-Cascade crest. **USES:** American Indian groups soaked twigs in cold water for fevers and as a diuretic. Bark tea used for worms. Roots poulticed to wounds. Leaves were placed in sandals as a snake repellent. Leaf tea used for arthritis and as a laxative. **RELATED SPECIES:** The bark of *F. americana* L., White Ash, and other species used as a folk medicine tonic and mild astringent for diarrhea and edema. The bark was soaked in wine and used to treat an enlarged spleen. The seeds were taken to prevent obesity. *F. rhynchophylla* Hance used in Chinese medicine for dysentery, to relieve redness, swelling, and pain in the eyes, and for rheumatism.

VINES WITH OPPOSITE LEAVES

WESTERN WHITE CLEMATIS, WHITE VIRGIN'S BOWER

Whole plant

Clematis ligusticifolia Nutt

Buttercup Family

Deciduous vine climbing by twining petioles, up to 50 ft. Leaves on slender petioles divided into 5–7 ovate to lance-shaped leaflets. Leaflets lobed or coarsely toothed. White to cream flowers in crowded, showy panicles from leaf axils; June–Sept. Single-seeded fruits with dense, stiff hairs and long, *feathery tails*. **WHERE FOUND:** Moist places, along streams, riparian woodland, forest edges. Every western state; B.C., Midwest, Southeast. **USES:** American Indian groups used leaf tea as a wash for skin eruptions, sores, boils; a sitz bath or wash for edema and foot bath for tired feet. Cold plant tea applied for aching backs and swelling of limbs. Leaves poulticed for rheumatic pain, swellings, bruises, wounds, boils, and spider and sand cricket bites. Powdered dried leaves were used as a snuff or fresh leaves inhaled for headaches. Root tea drunk to treat headaches, stomachaches, or cramps. Leaves and stems chewed for sore throat and colds. Navajo used the plant to treat pain and as a postpartum tonic. Stalk and roots used as a female contraceptive. Shoshone whipped sore, painful areas with the branches as a counterirritant. Seeds poulticed for burns. Dried stem pieces applied to aching tooth. Plant tea given to children to cure bed-wetting. **RELATED SPECIES:** American Indian groups also used tea of whole plant of *C. occidentalis* (Hornem.) DC. as a wash for scabs and eczema. Eclectic physicians used the dried leaves or highly diluted fresh leaf preparations of *C. virginiana* L., *C. recta* L., and other species as a diuretic, for rheumatic pain, pain and spasms of the uterus, cystitis, urethritis, gonorrhea; externally for eczema, herpes, and other

Western White Clematis (Clematis ligusticifolia) *has numerous stamens.*

Hops (Humulus lupulus). *Note the papery fruit.*

skin eruptions. In Chinese medicine the roots of *C. chinensis* Osbeck and other species are known as the drug wei ling xian; used in prescriptions for arthritic pain and to soften fish bones stuck in the throat. A folk remedy for malaria, rheumatism, menstrual irregularities, and colds, among other uses. **WARNING:** Avoid use of the fresh plant, which contains the toxic antibacterial compound protoanemonin. This unstable compound breaks down to yield anemonin, which is less toxic. The plant loses its acrid, irritating qualities when dried or prepared as a hot tea. May cause contact dermatitis or blistering when fresh.

HOPS
Humulus lupulus L.

Plant, roots, fruit
Hemp Family

Rough-haired, twining perennial. Leaves opposite, *palmately 3–5-lobed; base of lobes rounded*; margins coarsely toothed. Male and female flowers on separate plants. Female flowers densely clustered with *greenish, papery* bracts below; forming soft, hanging, inflated fruits (strobiles) with yellow resinous granules; July–Aug. **WHERE FOUND:** Disturbed sites; escaped garden ornamental. Throughout most of N. America. Alien (Eurasia). Commercially cultivated in the Pacific Northwest. **USES:** Hops has long been used in the treatment of anxiety, restlessness, insomnia, pain, fever, dyspepsia, gas, intestinal cramping, and diarrhea. Historically, physicians also used it as a diuretic for urinary stones, and externally to treat pneumonia, pleurisy, painful swellings and tumors, eczema, and skin ulcers. American Indian groups adopted it for similar uses and for breast and uterine problems, earaches, toothaches, and protection against witches. Laboratory studies demonstrate muscle-relaxing, digestive-stimulating properties. Approved in Germany to treat restlessness or anxiety and sleep disturbances. Considered calming and sleep-promoting. Widely used to relieve mood disturbances, nervous tension, anxiety, and unrest. Also used to flavor beer. **WARNING:** Handling plant often causes dermatitis and can cause fatigue. Hop-picker fatigue is believed to result from release of the essential oil during harvest. Dislodged hairs may irritate eyes. Crystalline resin in fruits causes rare allergic reactions.

ORANGE HONEYSUCKLE
Lonicera ciliosa (Pursh) Poir. ex DC.

Leaves, bark, flowers

Honeysuckle Family

Twining or trailing, deciduous vine, to 20 ft. Stems hollow, mostly without hairs. Leaves ovate, tips pointed to rounded; whitish beneath; margins entire, hairy. First pair of leaves beneath flowers (and often second pair) are *fused around stem* at leaf base, with flower stalk arising from center. Flowers orange, long–tubular, petal tips spreading; May–June. Pollinated by hummingbirds. Red to orange-red berry with several seeds. **WHERE FOUND:** Forests, thickets. N. Calif. to s. B.C., Idaho, Mont., Utah, Ariz. **USES:** American Indian groups used leaf or bark tea to treat colds, sore throats, and tuberculosis. Externally, leaves poulticed on bruises, used in steam bath and as a tea to stimulate milk flow, for uterine problems, and as a wash to strengthen the body and make hair grow. Vine used in bath or flowers sucked to treat epilepsy. Dried vines placed under pillow to assure sound sleep. The Chehalis used leaf tea as a contraceptive. Conversely, Thompson Indian women used the vines to help conceive.

(Above) *Orange Honeysuckle* (Lonicera ciliosa) *with orange tubular flowers.* (Right) *Japanese Honeysuckle* (Lonicera japonica) *with "gold and silver" flowers.*

JAPANESE HONEYSUCKLE

Flowers

Lonicera japonica Thunb.

Honeysuckle Family

Evergreen, climbing or trailing vine. Leaves oval, entire. Flowers white or buff, lobes strongly spreading from throat, sweetly fragrant. White blossoms fade to yellow on second day, earning it the Chinese name "Gold and Silver Flower"; Apr.–Sept. **WHERE FOUND:** Widely cultivated ornamental. Occasionally escapes from cultivation into disturbed sites. Abundant in Se. U.S. Alien (Asia). **USES:** Chinese herbal practitioners categorize the flower as an herb that removes heat which contributes to disease. Widely used in prescriptions and patent medicines in traditional Chinese medicine to treat colds and flu. Flower tea prescribed to treat fever, sore throat, mouth sores, headache, conjunctivitis, keratitis, corneal ulcers, breast infections, muscle and joint pain, stomach problems, diarrhea, and painful urination. Stem tea used for abscesses, sores, and to reduce joint pain and heat of arthritis. Leaves and flowers a beverage tea in Japan. Research confirms that leaf and flower extracts have antiviral, antibacterial, and cholesterol-lowering effects. Flower extracts inhibit an enzyme associated with Crohn's disease and other inflammatory conditions.

VINES WITH ALTERNATE LEAVES

CALIFORNIA DUTCHMAN'S PIPE

Whole plant

Aristolochia californica Torr.

Birthwort Family

Sprawling or climbing, soft-haired, deciduous vine; woody stems to 15 ft. Leaves alternate, *heart-shaped*; margins entire. Tubular, *pipe-shaped, green to brownish flowers with dark veins*, pendent from leaf axils; unpleasant-smelling; Jan.–Apr. **WHERE FOUND:** Streambanks, forest thickets, chaparral. Coast ranges and nw. Sierra of Calif. **USES:** Miwok used tea of this extremely bitter plant to cure colds. **RELATED SPECIES:** *A. serpentaria* L., Virginia Snake Root, is an important Native American remedy used by early physicians for treating loss of appetite, the common cold, fever, suppressed menses, and indigestion. The Chinese drug guang fang ji, *A. fangchi* Wu, is used in prescriptions to relieve pain of arthritis and other conditions. Other species of *Aristolochia* are used medicinally in Europe, India, and many other parts of the world. Use now banned in several countries because of toxicity. **WARNING:** May cause nausea, intestinal pain, and vomiting. Recent studies show that *Aristolochia* spp. contain aristolochic acid, a compound toxic to the kidneys as well as carcinogenic and mutagenic. According to systems of medicine that use members of this genus in a traditional healing system, very small amounts are used for only a few days to a week to relieve acute symptoms of the common cold and arthritis.

The distinctive flowers of California Dutchman's Pipe (Aristolochia californica).

Wild Cucumber (Marah macrocarpus). *Note the small white flowers and spiny fruit.*

Woody Nightshade (Solanum dulcamara). *Flowers are back-curved.*

Woody Nightshade fruit is glossy red.

WILD CUCUMBER

Marah macrocarpus (E. Greene) E. Greene   Gourd Family

Perennial vine, to 20 ft. Leaves alternate, *deeply palmately 5—7-lobed, bristle-tipped; tendrils branched.* Flowers *star-shaped*; sepals none; Jan.–Apr. Fruit an *oval* gourd covered in *stout, flattened spines.* **WHERE FOUND:** Open areas, hillsides, canyons, washes. S. Calif. to Baja Calif. **USES:** Luiseño Indians used roots as a purgative. Mahuna Indians rubbed plant juice on skin for ringworm and seed oil on the head for diseases of the scalp and hair roots. Costanoans made a paste from the seeds for treating acne and skin sores.

WOODY NIGHTSHADE, BITTERSWEET
Root, leaves, berries

Solanum dulcamara L.   Nightshade Family

☠ Woody, climbing vine, to 10 ft. Leaves ovate, *generally with 2 basal lobes*; margins entire. Flowers violet (or white) stars, petals reflexed backward, each with *2 yellowish green spots at base*; May–Sept. Berries bright red or orange-yellow, oval, many-seeded. **WHERE FOUND:** Widespread weed throughout U.S.; disturbed, moist sites, roadsides, clearings, thickets. Alien (Europe). **USES:** Used for several millennia in Europe as a folk remedy, mostly externally as a poultice, but also internally, for arthritic pain, coughs, stuffy nose, sinus headaches, bruises, sprains, eczema, herpes sores, vaginal yeast infections, jaundice, and stopped menses, especially due to exposure to cold. The controversial 17th-century English herbalist Nicholas Culpeper wrote that the juice was useful to help dissolve stagnant blood caused by "falls from high places and from being beaten." The plant was said to be a favorite of shepherds, who hung it around the necks of their animals to protect them from the "evil eye" of witches. Historically regarded as having narcoticlike effects, used as an anaphrodisiac to ease sexual mania. In Germany the relatively nonpoisonous stems have been approved for use in supportive treatment of acne, eczema, boils, and warts. Stems contain much lower amounts of toxic alkaloids than other parts of the plant. Steroidal saponins in the leaves have shown antifungal activity in laboratory tests. **WARNING: Toxic.** *Solanum* species contain the toxic alkaloid solanine in varying amounts, especially the leaves and unripe berries. It has anticholinergic effects and disrupts the gastrointestinal tract and nervous system, and can lead to symptoms such as a feeling of dryness and heat in the throat, nausea, and diarrhea. Deaths have been reported. Solanum alkaloids have potential teratogenic effects.

FIELD HORSETAIL

Stems, roots

Equisetum arvense L.   Horsetail Family

Perennial from creeping rhizome, often *forming large colonies*; to 2 ½ ft. Stems hollow, *ridged, jointed*. Sterile stems green, with *whorled branches at nodes*; leaves reduced to *brownish, papery, toothed sheath* around node; sheath with fewer than *14 teeth*. Fertile stems brownish to whitish, with large "cone" at tip, formed by spore-producing scales; cone produced in early spring. *Bottom sheath shorter than lowest internode.* **WHERE FOUND:** Moist places, meadows, streambanks, disturbed areas, roadside ditches. Widespread throughout N. America, except Fla. **USES:** American Indian groups used a stem tea as a diuretic, kidney tonic, and laxative. Poulticed for underarm and groin rashes. Powdered stems were put in moccasins to prevent foot cramps when traveling long distances. Burned stem ash used on sore mouths or as a wash for itching or open sores. Commonly used in European herbal medicine to prevent and treat urinary stones, to increase urine flow, and to stop bleeding. Studies confirm hemostatic and mild diuretic properties. Because of high silica content (up to 80 percent water-soluble silicic acid), horsetail extracts used in products for strengthening hair, nails, and bones. Approved in Germany for treatment of post-traumatic edema and in irrigation therapy for bacterial and inflammatory diseases of the lower urinary tract

(Above) *Field Horsetail* (Equisetum arvense) *is about 1 ft. tall.* (Right) *Scouring Rush* (Equisetum hyemale) *stems do not branch.*

Giant Pacific Horsetail (Equisetum telmateia) *grows up to 6 ft. tall.*

and kidney and bladder stones; externally for wounds, burns. **WARNING:** Correct identification may be essential for safe use of *Equisetum* spp. *E. palustre* L. is known to contain alkaloids that interfere with thiamine synthesis and may break it down. Data on human toxicity is incomplete, and human poisonings have not been reported. Teas or powdered extracts made from dried horsetail are not likely to be toxic.

SCOURING RUSH, GREATER HORSETAIL   Whole plant
Equisetum hyemale L.   Horsetail Family

⚠ Evergreen, hollow-stemmed, rough-surfaced, jointed primitive perennial; to 5 ft. Variable. The jointed, apparently leafless, rough, finely ribbed, nonbranching stems make it easy to distinguish from other species of horsetail in our range. **WHERE FOUND:** Moist, sandy soils, along streambanks, moist depressions, and pond edges throughout our range and beyond. **USES:** Essentially the same as for *E. arvense* (above), though this species is considered stronger by some authors. Rough stems are used like sandpaper to give a very fine, satiny finish to wood. Early settlers used the stems to scour pots and pans. A number of flavonoids in the plant may contribute to diuretic activity. In Chinese medicine, prescribed for swelling, redness of the eyes, and bleeding. **WARNING:** See *E. arvense,* above.

GIANT PACIFIC HORSETAIL   Stems, leaves
Equisetum telmateia Ehrh.   Horsetail Family

⚠ Very similar to *E. arvense,* but much larger; resembling *giant green horse's tail.* Stout stems to 6 ft., up to ¾ in. in diam.; forming dense stands. Leaf sheaths with more than *14 teeth; bottom sheath longer than lowest internode.* **WHERE FOUND:** Wet areas, streambanks, marshes, roadside ditches. Cen. coast ranges and se. Calif. to sw. B.C., Idaho. **USES:** American Indians applied a poultice of rough stems to cuts and sores. Tea of fresh plant tops was used as a diuretic. Tender young shoots were eaten raw or boiled to build up the blood. **WARNING:** See *E. arvense*, p. 371.

RUNNING CLUBMOSS, RUNNING PINE

Spores, plant

Lycopodium clavatum L. Clubmoss Family

Mosslike evergreen with long, creeping runners; 3–15 in. Upright stems branched with *small, clublike cones at tip.* Leaves tiny, linear to narrowly lance-shaped, *tightly spiraled along stem, finely bristle-tipped.* **WHERE FOUND:** Moist or dry, open areas; forests, rocky sites. N. coast ranges of Calif. to Alaska; Idaho, Mont., N.M.; eastern N. America. **USES:** Historically used by physicians as an antispasmodic, diuretic, and fever reducer. Specific indications included fevers, intestinal and urinary tract disorders such as cystitis, water retention, indigestion, and gastritis. Seldom used today. American Indian groups used plant for postpartum pain, weakness, fever. Spore powder used as a styptic and absorbent powder, especially for babies. Spores, called "vegetable sulfur," formerly used as lubricant to coat pills and suppositories; still used as a coating for condoms. Spores are explosive and were used historically as a photographic flash powder. **RELATED SPECIES:** *Huperzia serrata* (Thunb. ex Murr.) Trevisan [*L. serratum* Thunb. ex Murr.] is used in Chinese herbal medicine as an anodyne, to stop bleeding, and for hemorrhoids. Recently the plant has been receiving international attention because its alkaloids, the huperzines, show promise for treating dementia and Alzheimer's disease. Human and laboratory studies support this use. **WARNING:** Related species contain toxic compounds. Identification is difficult, even for trained bot-anists. Poisonings have been reported from individuals mistaking a toxic species for an

Running Clubmoss (Lycopodium clavatum). *Note the linear leaves tipped with soft, hairlike bristles.*

apparently safe one. Spores may cause asthma (an occupational hazard reported from condom factories). Widely used as a hospital dusting powder in the 1920s and '30s; if spores enter surgical wounds, they may cause *Lycopodium* granulation, lesions that resemble tuberculosis sores or cancers. The condition may occur many decades after surgery.

FERNS: FRONDS ONCE-CUT

CALIFORNIA POLYPODY **Root**
Polypodium californicum Kaulfuss Polypody Family

Very similar to *P. glycyrrhiza* (below). Summer-deciduous. *Rhizome not tasting sweet or of licorice*, but rather acrid or bland. Leaflet tips *rounded* to acute; wider than *P. glycyrrhiza*. **WHERE FOUND:** Shaded forests, streambanks, coastal bluffs; *generally not growing on trees under moss*. Southern mountains, cen. and s. coast ranges and n. Sierra of Calif.; Baja Calif. **USES:** Wailaki Indians rubbed the root juice on areas affected by rheumatism, applied it to skin sores and as an eyewash. Root considered expectorant, used for sore throats, colds, and stomach problems. Used over a long period, it was once thought to be beneficial in the treatment of venereal disease. **RELATED SPECIES:** An extract from *P. leucotomos*, called Anapsos, from Central America has potent immunomodulating and protective effects against ultraviolet solar radiation. Anapsos products have been approved in Spain to treat psoriasis, and several positive controlled clinical trials indicate that the extract might be useful as an oral sunscreen and preventative for skin cancer; it may also be of potential use in treating multiple sclerosis as an immune suppressant.

California Polypody (Polypodium californicum) is found from California south to Baja California.

Licorice Fern (Polypodium glycyrrhiza) has a licorice-scented root.

Giant Chain Fern (Woodwardia fimbriata) *is a large evergreen fern up to 10 ft. tall.*

LICORICE FERN
Root, leaves
Polypodium glycyrrhiza Eaton — Polypody Family

Creeping rhizome *tasting of licorice*. Fronds arising singly, to 2 ½ ft. Stipe glabrous. Leaves nearly 1-pinnately compound. *Leaflets narrowly lance-shaped*, tapering to acute tip, margins finely serrate. Sori round, *rather large*. **WHERE FOUND:** Generally coastal; moist forests, mossy rocks and slopes; *often growing on deciduous trees under moss*. Cen. and n. coast ranges of Calif. to Alaska; Idaho. **USES:** Northwestern Indians chewed rhizomes and swallowed the juice or drank tea of rhizome to treat colds, coughs, chest pains, shortness of breath, vomiting of blood, gas, sore gums, as a uterine tonic, and to sweeten the breath and mouth. **RELATED SPECIES:** Historically, physicians and eastern tribes used the closely related *P. virginianum* L. (*P. vulgare* L.) for similar conditions, especially for dry coughs, loss of voice, as a laxative, for poor appetite, and skin and liver ailments. Tea with added sugar used as a European folk remedy for whooping cough, also for rheumatism.

GIANT CHAIN FERN
Root
Woodwardia fimbriata Sm. — Chain Fern Family

Evergreen, 3–10 ft. tall, up to 1 ½ ft. across. Fronds from *basal rosette*. Large scales on stipe are yellow to orange to brown. Leaflets 6–12 in. long, *deeply lobed. Sori end to end (chainlike) and covered by oblong flaps*. **WHERE FOUND:** Shady, wet areas and streamsides in coniferous or mixed evergreen forests. Most of w. Calif., transverse ranges of s. Calif. to Ore., Wash., Ariz., Nev. **USES:** Native Americans used a root decoction to treat wounds, sores, and ulcers. Luiseño Indians used a root infusion to relieve pain. **RELATED SPECIES:** A rhizome decoction of *W. radicans* (L.) J. Sm., Rooting Chain Fern, was used internally and externally to relieve the pain of injuries.

VENUS MAIDENHAIR FERN

Whole plant

Adiantum capillus-veneris L.   Maidenhair Fern Family

Short, creeping rhizome. Fronds *drooping*, 6–30 in. tall. Stipe thin, *black, shiny*, glabrous. *Leaflets fan-shaped and lobed*, with terminal margin rolled under. **WHERE FOUND:** Shaded, rocky or moist banks along streams and rivers. Along s. coast ranges, s. Calif. deserts, Klamath range of n. Calif., east to Va., Fla. This species grows throughout the world in temperate climates. Some botanists say it is an alien in the western U.S. **USES:** Maidenhair fern has long been used in Europe, China, India, and the Philippines as an expectorant and demulcent for coughs, colds, flu, hoarseness, mucous congestion, asthma; also for easing fevers, removing worms, kidney problems, and jaundice. Externally, Asians poultice leaves for snakebites and impetigo. American Indians used plant tea for rheumatism and insanity. Externally, as a wash for bumblebee or centipede stings. Insane persons were encouraged to smoke dried leaves of maidenhair to drive out bad spirits. Some tribes used it to treat colic, menstrual irregularities, hemorrhages, and liver disorders. The leaves were chewed for internal bleeding from wounds and stomach troubles. Maidenhair extracts contain flavonoids and cinnamic esters and demonstrate hypoglycemic and diuretic properties experimentally.

(Left) *Venus Maidenhair Fern* (Adiantum capillus-veneris). *Note the black stems and triangular leaf shape.* (Above) *California Maidenhair Fern* (Adiantum jordani) *occurs mostly in California.*

CALIFORNIA MAIDENHAIR FERN

Whole plant

Adiantum jordani C. Müll.   Maidenhair Fern Family

Slender, creeping rhizome. Fronds *upright*, 8–20 in. tall. Stipe thin, *dark brown, shiny*, nearly as long as blades. *Pinnules roundish or semicircular, slightly lobed.* Sori linear or straight. **WHERE FOUND:** Rocky canyons, moist soils at low elevations. S. Calif to sw. Ore. Rare in Sierra Nevada. **USES:** Used similarly to Venus Maidenhair. Costanoans also used plant tea for pain, as a blood purifier, for stomach ailments, and to expel afterbirth. Stems also used in basketry.

RATTLESNAKE FERN

Root

Botrychium virginianum (L.) Swartz   Adder's-tongue Family

Delicate, lacy, nonleathery, broadly triangular leaf (sterile frond); to 10 in. long, 12 in. wide. Fertile frond on a much longer stalk, bearing bright yellow spores. **WHERE FOUND:** Rich moist or dry woods. Lab. to B.C., south to Ore., n. Calif. **USES:** American Indian groups used root poultice or lotion for snakebite, bruises, cuts, sores. Root tea used to induce sweating and as an expectorant and emetic. Early settlers adopted root tea as an emetic, to induce sweating; also as an expectorant and used for lung ailments.

MALE FERN

Rhizomes, roots

Dryopteris filix-mas (L.) Schott   Wood Fern Family

Deciduous, 1–3 (4) ft. Fronds arise from *basal rosette* and are *narrowly elliptical in outline*. Stipes with dense brown to red scales. *Kidney-shaped flaps cover round sori.* **WHERE FOUND:** Moist, rocky woodlands, granitic cliffs, shaded talus slopes. Every western state; rare in Calif.; northeastern N. America. **USES:** American Indians ate the raw rhizomes to lose weight and to neutralize plant and shellfish

Rattlesnake Fern (Botrychium virginianum) *is called "seng pointer" because its habitat is similar to that of ginseng* (Panax *spp.*).

poisoning. An oleoresin extracted from the roots was once used as a worm expellent. Though toxic to tapeworms, it is considered too toxic for use. **RELATED SPECIES:** A decoction of the roots of *D. arguta* (Kaulfuss) Watt, Coastal Woodfern, was used by California Indians for cleansing ceremonies and to stop internal bleeding and spitting of blood. A hair wash was made by infusing the fronds. The rhizomes of the Chinese species *D. crassirhizoma* Nakai. are prescribed for killing intestinal worms, resolving carbuncles and mumps, and stopping internal bleeding. Scientific studies show the root to have antibacterial, antiviral, and antiparasitic effects. **WARNING:** All species of *Dryopteris* should be considered toxic. Do not use internally.

BIRDFOOT CLIFFBRAKE, BIRD'S FOOT FERN

Leaves, rhizomes

Pellaea mucronata (D. C. Eat.) D. C. Eat   Maidenhair Fern Family
Evergreen, 3–18 in. Fronds clustered, *scales brown with black center.* Stipe dark brown to black, *shiny, glabrous.* Leaflets *narrowly oblong with small point at tip,* margins rolled under. Undersides of leaflets with *yellowish to white powdery exudate.* **WHERE FOUND:** Dry cliffs and rocky slopes. S. mountains, along cen. coast ranges, and n. Sierra of Calif., Nev., Ore.; Baja Calif. **USES:** Western American Indian groups used this fern to make a beverage tea used medicinally as a spring tonic and blood purifier and to treat fevers, colds, internal injuries, bleeding, and facial sores. Dried,

(Left) *Male Fern* (Dryopteris filix-mas) *root was formerly used to expel worms.* (Above) *Bird's Foot Fern* (Pellaea mucronata) *leaflet margins are rolled underneath.*

powdered leaves were applied to sores. Pieces of the rhizomes were "scattered about the house to keep animals and enemies away, and encourage friends to visit." A tea made from small sprouts used to lower fevers. **RELATED SPECIES:** The fronds of *P. mucronata* ssp. *mucronata* (D. C. Eat.) D. C. Eat. [*P. ornithopus* Hook.], Tea Fern, were used medicinally and as a pleasant beverage by the Luiseño.

BRACKEN FERN
Pteridium aquilinum (L.) Kuhn

Root, leaves
Bracken Fern Family

Deciduous, 3–6 ft. *Fronds arise singly from long creeping rhizome;* stem glabrous, grooved on underside. Leaf large, *broadly triangular in outline.* Leaflets cut into narrow segments that have margins rolled under. **WHERE FOUND:** Open forests, meadows; partial to full sun. Extremely common; found in every state except Neb.; throughout temperate and tropic zones; cosmopolitan. **USES:** American Indian groups used the rhizomes and roots to treat uterine problems, including prolapsed uterus, to stimulate milk production, for caked breasts, chest pains, to relieve nausea and stomach cramps, anemia, vomiting of blood from internal injury, and to stimulate appetite. Externally, as a poultice on burns. The whole plant was used to treat diarrhea, dysentery, worms, colds, tuberculosis, night sweats, in a steam bath for arthritis, and as a poultice or bath for broken bones. Shoots were used to treat uterine cancer. Fronds were used to make an antiseptic wash for sores, and to make beds to strengthen weak babies and old people. Herbalists historically used it for treating diarrhea, dysentery, worms, night sweats, hemorrhage, ulcers, mouth ulcers, and as a vaginal douche for leukorrhea. **WARNING:** Contains thiaminase (which destroys vitamin B_1) and carcinogens. Populations that use bracken as food have high rates of stomach and esophageal cancer.

Bracken Fern (Pteridium aquilinum) is common in much of North America.

CALAMUS, SWEET FLAG
Rhizomes, roots

Acorus americanus (Raf.) Raf.
Arum Family

[*A. calamus* L., *A. calamus* var. *americanus* (Raf.) H. D. Wulff.]

⚠ Perennial from stout, creeping, fleshy rhizome, whitish pink; sweet, spicy fragrance; forming large clumps. Sword-shaped leaves *folded along off-center midrib*, up to 5 ft.; margins undulating. Tiny, greenish yellow *flowers in dense, elongated spikes* emerging laterally from 3-angled stem. *A. americanus* differs from *A. calamus* in having a central midvein, plus 1–5 additional veins raised above leaf surface. *A. calamus* has only one prominently raised midvein and does not produce fertile fruits. **WHERE FOUND:** Fresh, shallow water, swamps, marshes, moist ground at water's edge. Native to eastern U.S. Introduced from e. Wash. to n. Calif., Nev., Tex., Colo. Sometimes cultivated. The fingerlike flower heads, jutting at an angle about one-third up the stem, are found only on a low percentage of plants in a given population. **USES:** The aromatic rhizomes are used in traditional medicine. Calamus was an important Native American trade item and the plant's wide distribution in N. America is probably a result of that trade. The root chewed as a stimulant and to assuage thirst on long journeys. Tea of the pleasantly spicy and fragrant roots widely used as a carminative. Tea drunk for fever and colds. Regarded as a panacea, the rhizomes were chewed for colds, coughs, and toothache and rubbed on the skin for any malady. Poultice of roots used for cramps and sore chest. Still used in modern herbal practice as a warming medicine for colds, headache, toothache, sore muscles, skin disorders and as a bitter aromatic for stomach complaints and flatulence. Calamus contains a complex volatile oil with antiarrhythmic, hypotensive, vasodilatory, antitussive, antibacterial, and expectorant activity. **WARNING:** Some chemical types of the plant contain the potentially hepatotoxic and mutagenic terpene beta-asarone.

Calamus, Sweet Flag (Acorus americanus) *has sweet-scented leaves.*

CATTAIL

Typha latifolia L.   Cattail Family

Perennial from creeping, tuberous rhizomes. Pithy stems unbranched to 10 ft., forming dense stands. Swordlike leaves light green, about 1 in. wide; bases sheathing. *Tiny flowers in long, dense, cylindrical spikes at stem tips*; May–Aug. Lower spike dark brown, spongy, wider; upper spike tan to yellow, narrow, falling away early; no break between sections. **WHERE FOUND:** Shallow, still or slow-moving fresh water; marshes, pond and lake edges, wet ditches. Widespread in northern N. America; Europe. **USES:** Traditionally a root poultice was made by pounding the root until a gel was released. This was applied to burns, scalds, infections, tumors, ulcers, inflammations, and eye problems. Native Americans used it for sores, inflammation, wounds (to stop bleeding), infections, and strains. Root simmered in milk and drunk for dysentery and diarrhea. Root tea drunk for abdominal cramps, as a cleansing emetic, for kidney stones and gonorrhea. Flower heads ingested to treat diarrhea. The down from the flowers was used as a dressing for burns, scalds, sores, and wounds, and to prevent chafing on infants. Lying on a mat made of cattail was thought to be beneficial to yellow fever patients. Chinese herbalists prescribe rhizome and dried pollen to promote pus drainage, and treat bloody stools, hemorrhoids, cystitis, urethritis, and irregular menses. The abundant bright yellow flower pollen is gathered, toasted, and taken in a tea to stop excessive menstrual bleeding, vomiting blood, nosebleeds, coughing of blood, and blood in the urine or stool. **WARNING:** The fresh root, if dug during or after flowering, is acrid and burning; drying and cooking renders it edible.

Cattail (Typha latifolia) *is easily recognized by its cigar-shaped seed heads.*

GRASSES AND GRASSLIKE PLANTS;
SPIKELETS IN DENSE SPIKES

CHUFA
Root, tuber

Cyperus esculentus L.
Sedge Family

⚠️ Perennial, *triangular stems solid*, unbranched, to 2 ½ ft. *Scaly rhizomes ending in small, round tubers.* Basal leaves flat, linear. Tiny florets, each with a single bract below, in dense, flat, *yellowish brown spikes*; June–Oct. Spikes in clusters, on stalks radiating umbellike from stem tip. **WHERE FOUND:** Moist, low ground or drier sites, ditches, croplands, disturbed sites. Widespread weed across North America; every state except Mont., Wyo. Alien (Eurasia). **USES:** Pima Indians chewed the roots for colds and coughs. Chewed roots were polticed to snakebites. In Southeast Asia, Cyperus is used as a folk remedy to encourage good digestion. In India, root used in food as a stimulant and aphrodisiac. **RELATED SPECIES:** Nut grass, *C. rotundus* L., is used in India, China, and other countries as a spice and important medicine. The plant grows throughout the U.S., especially in sandy river bottoms. In Chinese medicine the dried rhizome is the drug xiang fu, which is added to prescriptions to relieve pain under the ribcage and poor digestion associated with liver ailments. The herb is widely prescribed in formulas to ease menstrual symptoms such as pain and cramps and irregular flow associated with a liver imbalance. The rhizome contains a complex aromatic essential oil that shows an estrogenlike activity in animals. **WARNING:** Avoid use during pregnancy.

(Above) *Chufa* (Cyperus esculentus) *has a nutty edible root.* (Right) *Couch Grass* (Elytrigia repens) *is a troublesome weed throughout the United States.*

COUCH GRASS, QUACK GRASS

Elytrigia repens var. *repens* (L.) Desv. Ex B. D. Jackson
[*Agropyron repens* (L.) Beauvois, *Elymus repens* (L.) Gould]

Roots

Grass Family

Aggressively spreading perennial; yellow rhizomes scaly. Stems green or with whitish hue, often hairy, to 3 ft. Flat leaves thin, bright green, hairy; base clasping stem with earlike flaps. Several florets clustered, flat to stem, *alternating on each side of round spike, closely overlapping*; June–Aug. Floret bracts often bristle-tipped. **WHERE FOUND:** Disturbed places, fields, lawns, roadsides, cultivated areas. Widespread weed across the U.S.; every western state except Tex. Alien (Europe). **USES:** This Eurasian native traditionally used as a demulcent and diuretic in the treatment of kidney and bladder inflammation, intestinal problems, gout, high cholesterol, and liver and gallbladder disorders. Cherokee Indians used it to treat incontinence, bed-wetting, and urinary tract calculi; a decoction used as a wash for swollen legs. The Iroquois used it as a worm treatment and to improve urine flow. Approved in Germany in irrigation therapy for inflammatory conditions of the urinary tract and prevention (not treatment) of kidney stones.

FOXTAIL BARLEY, SQUIRREL TAIL BARLEY

Hordeum jubatum L.

Roots

Grass Family

Clumped annual or perennial. Stems upright or bent at base, to 2 ft. Leaves rough-hairy, *without earlike flaps at base*. Dense, bristly spikes nodding, long and thick, easily falling apart at maturity; May–July. Bristles purplish red, to 3 in. long. **WHERE FOUND:** Open, moist, or disturbed sites, roadsides. Widespread across U.S. **USES:** Chippewa Indians used a root poultice on sties and other eyelid inflammations. **RELATED SPECIES:** Costanoan Indians used a tea of *H. murinum* L. to treat bladder problems. Chinese herbalists use *H. vulgare* L. seeds as a digestive aid and to inhibit lactation. In European tradition, Barley seeds were used to treat fever and inflammatory conditions and, mixed with hops, used as a tonic and to make beer or ale. Historically, physicians prescribed Barley for its nutritive and demulcent properties in convalescence; to

Foxtail Barley (Hordeum jubatum) *seed heads resemble a fox's tail.*

treat mucous congestion, dysentery, gonorrhea, and bladder inflammation; and as beer or ale to treat chronic diseases with exhaustion.

GRASSES WITH SPIKELETS ARRANGED IN OPEN INFLORESCENCES

GIANT REED
Arundo donax L.

Stems
Grass Family

Tall, robust, bamboolike perennial, to 20 ft; often forming large stands. Large leaves, to 3 ft. long and 2½ in. wide, distributed along stems with long, sheathing bases. Plumelike panicles white to purplish, compact; Mar.–Sept. *Bracts below each floret covered in dense, silky hairs.* **WHERE FOUND:** Moist places, ditches, streams, seeps; Calif., Nev., Utah, Ariz., N.M., Tex. Alien (Europe). **USES:** Cahuilla Indians used the plant as a splint for broken limbs. Giant reed was known to the Egyptians and Greeks, who used it for spitting of blood and as a diuretic to relieve water retention. In Chinese medicine, the roots and rhizomes are used for stomachaches. The root is used in Burma as a diuretic and in Southeast Asia to stop the flow of mother's milk.

WILD OATS
Avena fatua L.

Seeds
Grass Family

Annual; stems hollow, to 4 ft. Leaves with rough hairs. Florets 2–3, surrounded by 2 large, papery bracts with several veins,

forming small, elliptical *spikelets*; drooping; arranged in loose, open panicles with horizontal branches; Apr.–June. Lower bract of each floret with stiff, brownish hairs below and a *bent, twisted bristle from middle. Immature grain milky inside when crushed.* **WHERE FOUND:** Disturbed sites, roadsides, fields. Widespread across U.S.; every western state. Alien (Europe). **USES:** The fruits (seeds)

Giant Reed (Arundo donax) *is a robust, bamboolike grass.*

(Left) *The immature fruits of Wild Oats* (Avena fatua) *are milky within.* (Above) *Mature fruits of Wild Oats.*

of Wild Oats were eaten as an energy source for breakfast by some American Indians. The unripe fruits or *spikelets* are commonly used in herbal formulas for smoking cessation. Herbalists consider the spikelets useful as a long-term tonic for treating drug addictions and any nerve weakness. The whole plant used in formulas, most commonly in teas or tinctures, to support the nervous system during times of stress. The dried stalks are used to make a mineral tea. **RELATED SPECIES:** Slender Wild Oats, *A. barbata* Pott. ex Link, and Cultivated Oats, *A. sativa* L., are often used interchangeably.

SWEET GRASS
Plant, leaves

Hierochloe odorata (L.) Beauv.
Grass Family

Perennial from slender, creeping rhizomes; *vanilla-scented when crushed*. Stems solitary, base purplish, to 24 in. Leaves basal, less than 2 in. long and ½ in. wide. Single floret hard, shiny, surrounded by 2 broad, boat-shaped, straw-colored bracts; drooping; without bristles; arranged in open panicles. **WHERE FOUND:** Moist meadows, lake edges, streambanks, forest openings. N. Calif. to Alaska, Canada, eastern U.S.; Eurasia. **USES:** Native Americans used an infusion as a wash to deodorize body and hair. Also to treat coughs, sore throats, fevers, sharp internal pains, as a wash for chapping and windburn, as a wash for venereal infections in men, and as an eyewash. The plant was chewed to enhance endurance. The smoke from the burning leaves was used to bring guardian spirits, to protect one from thunder and lightning, as an insect repellent, and inhaled to treat colds.

COMMON REED
Phragmites australis (Cav.) Trin. ex Steud.
[*P. communis* Trin.]

Plant, root
Grass Family

Tall, robust perennial, to 11 ft., forming dense stands. Leaves to 1½ ft. long and 2 in. wide, mostly one-sided on stem. Plumelike panicles initially purple-brown, becoming straw-colored; densely hairy from *base* of bracts below florets; July–Nov. **WHERE FOUND:** Pond and lake edges, marshes, sloughs; every state except Ark. Widespread worldwide. **USES:** Cheyenne used root and plant for diarrhea and stomach problems, as an emetic, and as a poultice for boils. The dried sugary sap was used as an expectorant in pneumonia, to loosen phlegm and ease pain. The bundled plants have been used as splints for fractures. The Western Keres crushed the young shoots and gave the juice to children with diarrhea. Preparations from the rhizomes are prescribed in Chinese medicine to treat nausea and fever, especially during lung infections with thick yellow or green mucus, as a diuretic for urinary tract infections, and for food poisoning. The rhizomes are used in India for diabetes and to allay nausea.

Sweet Grass (Hierochloe odorata) *has been overharvested and is declining.*

Common Reed (Phragmites australis) *has plumelike flower heads.*

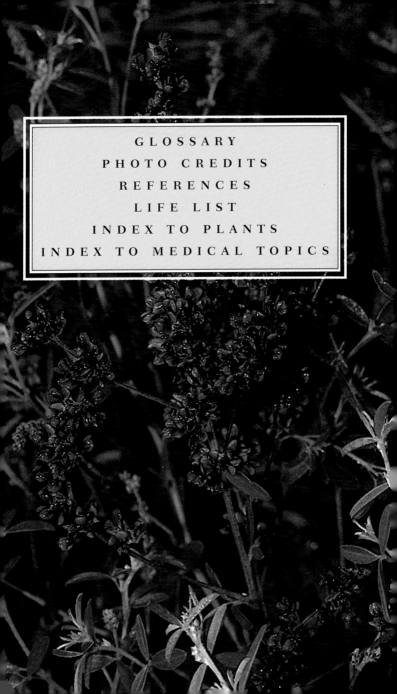

GLOSSARY

MEDICAL TERMS

ALKALOID: Any of a large, varied group of complex, usually alkaline, nitrogen-containing compounds, including nicotine, cocaine, and caffeine, that react with acids to form soluble salts, many of which have physiological effects on humans.

ALTERATIVE: A medicinal substance that gradually restores health.

AMENORRHEA: Abnormal cessation or absence of the menses.

AMOEBICIDAL: An agent that kills amoebas.

ANALGESIC: A pain-relieving medicine.

ANAPHRODISIAC: An agent that quells sexual desire.

ANODYNE: A pain-relieving medicine, milder than an analgesic.

ANTIAMOEBIC: An agent that kills or inhibits growth or multiplication of amoebas.

ANTIANGINAL: A medicine used to lessen or treat angina.

ANTIARRHYTHMIC: A medicine used to lessen or treat arrhythmia (irregular heartbeat).

ANTIBIOTIC: An agent that kills or inhibits growth or multiplication of a living organism, especially bacteria or other microorganisms.

ANTICANDIDAL: An agent that inhibits or kills candida fungi, most often *Candida albicans.*

ANTICHOLINERGIC: An agent that antagonizes the action of parasympathetic or related nerve fibers.

ANTICONVULSANT: An agent that reduces or relieves convulsions or cramps.

ANTIFUNGAL: An agent that kills or inhibits growth or multiplication of fungi.

ANTIHISTAMINE: An agent that neutralizes the effect or inhibits production of histamine, an immune-system substance that promotes inflammation.

ANTI-INFLAMMATORY: An agent that reduces or neutralizes inflammation.

ANTIMICROBIAL: An agent that kills or inhibits growth or multiplication of microorganisms.

ANTIMUTAGENIC: An agent that inhibits mutations at the cellular level.

ANTIOXIDANT: Preventing oxidation; a preservative or agent that scavenges singlet oxygen radicals known as free radicals.

ANTISCORBUTIC: An agent effective against scurvy.

ANTISEPTIC: Preventing sepsis, decay, putrefaction; an agent that kills microbes.

ANTISPASMODIC: Preventing or relieving spasms or cramps, mostly in smooth muscles such as the bronchial airway, uterus, intestines, or urinary bladder.

ANTITUMOR: Preventing or effective against tumors (cancers).

ANTITUSSIVE: Preventing or relieving cough.

ANTIVIRAL: An agent that kills or inhibits growth or multiplication of viruses.

APHRODISIAC: Increasing or exciting sexual desire.

ARTERIOSCLEROTIC: A medicine that helps to prevent or reduce arteriosclerosis.

ASTRINGENT: An agent that causes tissue to contract, often associated with chemical compounds called tannins.

BACTERICIDAL: An agent that kills bacteria.

BRONCHODILATING: An agent that dilates bronchial tubes.

CALMATIVE: An agent with mild sedative or calming effects.

CARDIOACTIVE: Affecting the heart.

CARMINATIVE: An agent that relieves and removes gas from the digestive system.

CATHARTIC: A powerful purgative or laxative, causing severe evacuation, with or without pain.

CNS: The central nervous system.

COUNTERIRRITANT: An agent, such as a mustard plaster or liniment, that produces inflammation or irritation when applied locally to stimulate circulation in another, usually irritated, surface.

CYTOTOXIC: An agent that is toxic to certain cells and thus toxic to organs, tissues, or other cells.

DECOCTION: A preparation made by boiling or simmering a plant part in water. Compare infusion.

DEMULCENT: An agent that is locally soothing and softening.

DIAPHORETIC: An agent that induces sweating.

DIGESTIVE: An agent that promotes digestion.

DITERPENES: A chemical subdivision of terpenes, with a specific number of hydrogen atoms and 20 carbon atoms; found in aromatic components of plants.

DIURETIC: An agent that induces urination.

DYSMENORRHEA: Difficult or painful menses.

ECLECTIC: A medical movement that thrived from 1850 to 1940 in the United States. The doctors who trained at Eclectic medical schools relied heavily on American medicinal plants in their practice. They were responsible for introducing popular herbs used today such as Echinacea and Black Cohosh.

EMETIC: An agent that induces vomiting.

EMMENAGOGUE: An agent that induces or increases menstruation or menstrual flow.

EMOLLIENT: An agent that softens and soothes the skin when applied locally

ESTROGENIC: A substance that induces female hormonal activity and that binds to and activates cells sensitive to the human hormone estrogen, which is found in the breasts and uterus.

EXPECTORANT: An agent that induces the removal (coughing up) of mucous secretions from the lungs.

FUNGICIDAL: An agent that kills fungi.

HEMATURIA: A medical condition involving red blood cells in the urine.

HEMOPTYSIS: Spitting of blood from the lungs.

HEMOSTATIC: An agent that checks bleeding.

HEPATOTOXIC: An agent that causes liver toxicity.

HOMEOPATHIC: Relating to homeopathy, a system of medicine founded in the late 1700s by Samuel Hahnemann. The system is based on the principle that "like cures like." Practitioners believe that a substance that produces a set of symptoms in a well person will, in minute, "potentized" doses, cure those same symptoms in a diseased individual.

HYPERTENSIVE: Causing or marking a rise in blood pressure. An individual with hypertension.

HYPOCHONDRIASIS: Unfounded concern about disease or mental health.

HYPOGLYCEMIC: Causing a lowering of blood sugar.

HYPOTENSIVE: Causing or marking a lowering of blood pressure, as in hypotension.

IMMUNOMODULATING: An agent activating the immune system, usually in a positive direction.

IMMUNOSTIMULANT: Stimulating various functions or activities of the immune system.

INFUSION: A preparation made by soaking a plant part in hot water (or cold water, for a cold infusion); in essence, a "tea." Compare decoction.

LAXATIVE: A mild purgative.

LEUKORRHEA (OR LEUCORRHEA): Discharge of white or yellow fluid from the vagina, often caused by an overgrowth of *Candida albicans.*

MENORRHAGIA: Excessive loss of blood during menstruation.

MONOTERPENES: A chemical subdivision of terpenes, with a specific number of hydrogen atoms and 10 carbon atoms. They are an important part of the aromatic essences of plants. Menthol is an example.

MOXA: A dried herb substance burned on or above the skin to stimulate an acupuncture, energy, or immune trigger point or to serve as a counterirritant. Thought to stimulate healing and reduce pain and inflammation of arthritis and other painful conditions. A famous technique of traditional Chinese medicine, using dried pressed leaves of certain *Artemisia* species.

MOXABUSTION: The practice of using moxa.

MUCILAGINOUS: Pertaining to or resembling or containing mucilage; slimy.

NEPHROTOXIC: An agent that is toxic to the kidneys.

NERVINE: An agent that affects, strengthens, or calms the nerves.

PANACEA: An agent good for what ails you, or what doesn't ail you. In American Indian traditions a "life" medicine. Ginseng is the most famous example. Panax, the genus name for ginsengs, derives from the word panacea.

POULTICE: A moist, usually warm or hot mass of plant material applied to the skin, or to a cloth next to the skin, to effect a medicinal action.

PHYTOESTROGENS: Plant compounds (often isoflavonoids) that have estrogenlike activity or that compete with other estrogens at cellular estrogen receptor sites, often found in members of the pea family, such as soy and red clover.

PURGATIVE: An agent that causes cleansing or watery evacuation of the bowels, usually with griping (painful cramps).

RUBEFACIENT: An agent that causes reddening or irritation when applied to the skin.

SAPONIN: A steroid glycoside compound common in plants, which, when shaken with water, has a foaming or "soapy" action.

SPASMOLYTIC: Checking spasms or cramps.

SPERMATORRHEA: Involuntary discharge of semen.

STIMULANT: An agent that causes increased activity of another agent, cell, tissue, organ, or organism.

STOMACHIC: A medicine that improves appetite and digestion.

STYPTIC: Checking bleeding by contracting blood vessels.

TINCTURE: A diluted alcohol solution of plant parts (see p. 9).

TERATOGEN: A substance that can cause deformity of a fetus.

TERPENES: A class of chemical compounds containing a certain structure of carbon and hydrogen atoms often found in aromatic components of plants. It is the largest group of secondary plant compounds. All terpenes are made up of the same basic building block of a 5-carbon, 23-hydrogen "isoprene" unit. A very diverse and widespread chemical class in plants.

TONIC: In the West, an ambiguous term referring to a substance thought to have an overall positive medicinal effect of an unspecified nature. In Asian cultures, an herb having a sweet flavor and fortifying effect on various organs and functions of the body.

TRITERPENES: A chemical subdivision of terpenes with a specific number of hydrogen atoms and 30 carbon atoms; found in aromatic components of plants. Steroids are triterpenes.

TRYPANOCIDAL: An agent that kills protozoa (trypanosomes) responsible for certain mostly tropical diseases, such as sleeping sickness.

VASODILATOR: An agent that causes blood vessels to dilate.

VERMIFUGE: Having worm-killing properties; an agent that kills worms.

VULNERARY: An agent used for healing wounds.

BOTANICAL TERMS

ACHENE: A small dry fruit that does not split at maturity, containing a single seed that is attached to the ovary wall.

APPRESSED: Pressed flat (or nearly so) against another surface.

AWN: A narrow, elongated appendage, usually at the tip of an achene.

AXIL: The point at which a leaf (or other plant part) forms an upper angle to a stem.

BASAL ROSETTE: Leaves radiating directly from the crown of the root.

BRACT: One of the leaflike structures of a grouping or arrangement of flowers (inflorescence).

CALYX: The sepals collectively; the external floral envelope.

CILIATE: Having a fringe of hairs along a margin.

COROLLA: The petals collectively.

DIOECIOUS: Having male and female flowers borne on separate plants.

EXSERTED: Protruding beyond a particular point, such as a stamen that is longer than a petal.

FLORET: A very small flower, especially one of the disk flowers of plants in the Composite family.

GALL: An abnormal, usually inflated growth on a plant caused by an insect.

GLABROUS: Smooth and shiny; without hairs.

GLAND: A structure that exudes an oily, resinous, or sticky substance.

GLANDULAR: Pertaining to a gland.

GLAUCOUS: Covered with a fine, white, often waxy film, which rubs off.

GLOBOSE: Globe-shaped.

HERBACEOUS: Nonwoody.

LANCEOLATE: Lance-shaped.

LIGULE: A strap-shaped structure, such as a single petal of a ray flower of a sunflower (see also rays).

MONOECIOUS: Bearing male and female flowers on the same plant.

MYCORRHIZA: A symbiotic relationship between a plant root and soil fungus.

OBLANCEOLATE: Of leaves, lance-shaped but broader toward the apex.

OBOVATE: Of leaves, oval but broader toward the apex.

OVATE: Oval but broader toward the base; egg-shaped.

PALMATE: With 3 or more leaflets, nerves, or lobes radiating from a central point.

PANICLE: A flower group, with branches that are usually in racemes.

PAPPUS: An appendage (a modified calyx) at the apex of a seed in the aster family, consisting of awns, bristles, or scales.

PERFECT: Of a flower, one that has a full complement of male and female parts as well as a floral envelope (petals *and* sepals).

PERFOLIATE: Of a leaf, perforated by the stem.

PINNATE: In a featherlike arrangement, usually referring to a compound leaf with leaflets arranged on each side of a central axis.

PINNULE: The ultimate division of a twice-pinnate leaf.

RACEME: An unbranched, elongated flower grouping, with individual flowers on distinct stalks, with most mature flowers at bottom of stalk.

RAYS (RAY FLOWERS): The straplike, often sterile flowers (commonly called petals) surrounding the flower head (disk) of a plant in the Composite family, such as the yellow rays of Sunflowers or the purple rays surrounding the cone of Purple Coneflower.

RECURVED: Curved backward.

REFLEXED: Bent downward or backward.

RHIZOME: A creeping underground stem.

ROSETTE (BASAL): Leaves radiating directly from the crown of the root.

SAPROPHYTIC: Of a plant, usually lacking chlorophyll, that lives on dead organic matter.

SCAPE: A flower-bearing leafless stalk arising from the root.

SEPALS: The individual divisions of the calyx (outer floral envelope).

SESSILE: Of a leaf or flower, lacking a stalk.

SILIQUE: A dry, long, narrow seedpod separating into two halves that fall away, leaving an erect central membrane to which the seeds are attached, as in the mustard family.

SORUS (PLURAL, SORI): A cluster of spore-bearing sacs (sporangia) on the underside of a fern leaf.

SPADIX: A thick, fleshy flower spike (usually enveloped by a spathe), as in members of the arum family.

SPATHE: A modified leaflike structure surrounding a spadix, as in members of the arum family (Skunk Cabbage, Jack-in-the-Pulpit, Dragon Arum).

SPIKE (FLOWER): An unbranched, elongated flower grouping in which the individual flowers are sessile (attached without stalks).

STAMENS: The pollen-bearing anthers with attached filaments (sometimes without filaments).

STIPE: A stalk that supports a plant structure, such as the petiole of a fern or the stalk of a mushroom.

STIPULES: Appendages resembling small or minute leaves at the base of leaves of certain plants.

STOLON: A horizontal stem that travels along the ground, rooting at nodes or tips to produce new plants.

SUBSHRUB: Usually a plant with stems that are woody at the base but mostly herbaceous.

TENDRIL: A modified leaf or branch structure, often coiled like a spring, used for clinging by plants that climb.

UMBEL: A flower grouping with individual flower stalks or groups radiating from a central axis, often flat-topped and umbrella-like.

PHOTO CREDITS

left, right; 289; 294; 297 right; 299 right; 300; 302; 304 left, right; 306 left; 307 right; 309 left, right; 310 left, right; 312; 313 right; 315; 319 left, right; 323; 325; 328 left; 330 left, right; 333; 335 top, bottom left, right; 336; 337 left; 340; 342; 343; 344 left, right; 347; 348 left, right; 350 left, right; 351; 352 left; 355; 356 top left, right, bottom left, right; 357; 358; 359; 362; 364 left; 365; 366; 367 left, right; 369 top left, right, bottom left, right; 371 left, right; 372; 373; 374 left; 376 left; 377; 378 left; 379; 380; 381; 383; 385 left, right; 386 top left, right, bottom left; 389; 396; 398; 415; 433

CRAIG C. FREEMAN: 25 right; 382 right

PAMELA HARPER, HARPER HORTICULTURAL LIBRARY: 147

WILLIAM R. HEWLETT/CALIFORNIA ACADEMY OF SCIENCES: 171 top;

CHRISTOPHER HOBBS: v; 20; 26; 28 right; 30; 31 right; 32 left, right; 36; 45; 46 right; 47 right; 50; 51; 55; 57 bottom left, right; 59; 63; 64 left, right; 65; 66; 67 left, right; 69; 70 left, right; 72 top left, right; 81; 82 top, bottom left; 85 left; 86 right; 88 bottom; 90; 96 right; 104 right; 106; 110; 111 left; 112 right; 113 right; 115; 118 right; 120; 122 top, bottom; 123; 125; 126 left, right; 127; 132 left; 143 left; 148 left; 149 left, right; 150 left, right; 151; 153 right; 154; 155 left, right; 157 right; 160; 161 left; 162; 163 left, right; 164 left; 173 left, right; 176; 177 right; 178 left, right; 180; 181 right; 187 right; 188; 190; 191; 193 left; 197 right; 198 left, right; 206 right; 210 left; 213; 214 left; 215 right; 223 left; 225 left, right; 228; 231 left, right; 232 left, right; 233 right; 235 left; 239; 241 left; 247 left; 248; 251; 254 bottom; 258 top, bottom right; 260; 263; 265; 266 right; 267; 268 left, right; 269 right; 271 left, right; 274 left; 275; 277; 278 left; 279; 280; 281 bottom; 282 right; 286; 287 left, right; 288; 290 left, right; 291 left, right; 292; 293 left, right; 295 left, right; 297 right; 298 left, right; 299 left; 301; 303 left; 306 right; 307 left; 308; 313 left; 314 left; 316 top, bottom; 317; 318 left; 320; 321 left, right; 322; 324 right; 326; 327; 328 right; 331 left, right; 332 left, right; 337 right; 338 left, right; 339; 341 left, right; 345; 346 bottom; 349; 352 right; 353 left, right; 354; 360 left; 361; 363 left, right; 364 right; 374 right; 375; 376 right; 378 right; 384

J. E. & BONNIE MCCLELLAN/CALIFORNIA ACADEMY OF SCIENCES: 314 right

H. WAYNE PHILLIPS: 42 right; 83; 121; 168; 175 right; 211 left; 219 left; 264; 303 right; 318 left; 324 left;

ROBERT SKOWRON: 94 bottom

STEPHEN L. TIMME, SPERRY HERBARIUM: 75 right; 100; 184 right; 185; 192 right; 234;

CHARLES WEBBER/CALIFORNIA ACADEMY OF SCIENCES: 382 left

BURR WILLIAMS: 128 left; 386 right

FRANCES WILLIAMS: 35; 49 right; 102 right; 136; 184 left

REFERENCES

POPULAR GUIDES

Craighead, John J., Frank C. Craighead, Jr., and Ray J. Davies. 1963. *A Field Guide to Rocky Mountain Wildflowers*. Boston: Houghton Mifflin.

Foster, Steven. 1993. *Herbal Renaissance: Understanding, Using and Growing Herbs in the Modern World*. Layton, Utah: Gibbs Smith.

————.1998. *101 Medicinal Herbs*. Loveland, Colo.: Interweave Press.

Foster, Steven, and Roger Caras. 1994. *A Field Guide to Venomous Animals and Poisonous Plants of North America Exclusive of Mexico*. Boston: Houghton Mifflin.

Foster, Steven, and James A. Duke. 2000. *A Field Guide to Medicinal Plants and Herbs: Eastern and Central North America*. 2nd ed. Boston: Houghton Mifflin.

Foster, Steven, and Varro E. Tyler. 1999. *Tyler's Honest Herbal*. 4th ed. Binghamton, N.Y.: Haworth Press.

Foster, Steven, and Yue Chongxi. 1992. *Herbal Emissaries: Bringing Chinese Herbs to the West*. Rochester, Vt.: Healing Arts Press.

Hobbs, Christopher. 1995. *Medicinal Mushrooms*. Williams, Ore.: Botanica Press.

————. 1998. *Herbal Remedies for Dummies*. Chicago: Hungry Mind Press.

Kraft, Karin, and Christopher Hobbs. 2001. *Herbal Medicine: A Pocket Guide*. New York: Thieme Medical Publishers.

Moore, Michael. 1977. *Los Remedios*. Santa Fe, N.M.: Red Crane Books.

————. 1979. *Medicinal Plants of the Mountain West*. Santa Fe: Museum of New Mexico Press.

————. 1989. *Medicinal Plants of the Desert and Canyon West*. Santa Fe: Museum of New Mexico Press.

———. 1993. *Medicinal Plants of the Pacific West*. Santa Fe: Red Crane Books.

Niehaus, Theodore F., and Charles L. Ripper. 1976. *A Field Guide to Pacific State Wildflowers*. Boston: Houghton Mifflin.

Niehaus, Theodore F., Charles L. Ripper, and Virginia Savage. 1984. *A Field Guide to Southwestern and Texas Wildflowers*. Boston: Houghton Mifflin.

Petrides, George A., and Olivia Petrides. 1998. *A Field Guide to Western Trees*. Boston: Houghton Mifflin.

SCHOLARLY WORKS

Abrams, Leroy, and R. S. Ferris. 1923–1960. *Illustrated Flora of the Pacific States*. 4 vols. Stanford, Calif.: Stanford University Press.

Barbour, M. G., and N. L. Christensen, 1993. "Vegetation," in *Flora of North America, North of Mexico*. Vol. 1. New York: Oxford University Press.

Barkley, T. M., ed. 1986. *Flora of the Great Plains*. Lawrence: University Press of Kansas.

Bean, Lowell John, and Katherine Siva Saubel. 1972. *Temalpakh: Cahuilla Indian Knowledge and Usage of Plants*. Banning, Calif.: Malki Museum Press.

Bensky, Daniel, and Andrew Gamble. 1986. *Chinese Herbal Medicine*. Seattle: Eastland Press.

Blumenthal, Mark, Alicia Goldberg, and Josef Brinckmann. 2000. *Herbal Medicine: Expanded Commission E Monographs*. Newton, Mass.: Integrative Medicine Communications.

Bocek, Barbara R. 1984. "Ethnobotany of Costanoan Indians, California, Based on Collections by John P. Harrington." *Economic Botany*. 38(2):240–55.

Chadha, Shri Y. R., ed. 1952–1988. *The Wealth of India (Raw Materials)*. 11 vols. New Delhi: Publications and Information Directorate, Center for Scientific and Industrial Research.

Chang, Hson-Mou, and Paul Pui-Hay But. 1986–1987. *Pharmacology and Applications of Chinese Materia Medica*. 2 vols. Philadelphia: World Scientific.

Cheatum, Scooter, Marshall C. Johnston, and Lynn Marshall. 1996. *Useful Wild Plants of Texas*. Vol. 1. Austin: Useful Wild Plants of Texas.

Chestnut, V. K. 1902. *Plants Used by the Indians of Mendocino County, California*. Washington, D.C.: Government Printing Office.

Correll, David S., and Marshall C. Johnston. 1970. *Manual of the Vascular Plants of Texas*. Renner, Tex.: Texas Research Foundation.

Coville, Frederick V. 1897. "Notes on the Plants Used by the Klamath Indians of Oregon." U.S. Department of Agriculture, Division of Botany. *Contributions from the U.S. National Herbarium* 5(2).

Cronquist, Arthur, et al. 1972–1977. *Intermountain Flora*. 6 vols. New York: Hafner.

Curtin, L. S. M. 1947. *Healing Herbs of the Upper Rio Grande*. Los Angeles: Southwest Museum.

Elmore, Francis H. 1943. *Ethnobotany of the Navajo*. Albuquerque: University of New Mexico Press.

Felter, Harvey W., and John Uri Lloyd. 1898. *King's American Dispensatory*. Cincinnati: Ohio Valley Co.

Ford, Richard I. 1985. "Anthropological Perspective of Ethnobotany in the Greater Southwest." *Economic Botany* 39(4):400–415.

Foster, Steven. 1995. *Forest Pharmacy: Medicinal Plants in American Forests*. Issues series no. 2. Durham, N.C.: Forest History Society.

French, David H. 1965. "Ethnobotany of the Pacific Northwest Indians." *Economic Botany* 19(4): 378–82.

Fuller, Thomas C., and Elizabeth McClintock. 1986. *Poisonous Plants of California*. Berkeley: University of California Press.

Gunther, Erna. 1945. *Ethnobotany of Western Washington*. Seattle: University of Washington Press.

Hänsel, R., K. Keller, H. Rimpler, and G. Schneider, eds. 1992–1994. *Hagers Handbuch der Pharmazeutischen Praxis*. 3 vols. In German. Berlin: Springer-Verlag.

Hardin, James W., and Jay M. Arena. 1974. *Human Poisoning from Native and Cultivated Plants*, 2nd ed. Durham, N.C: Duke University Press.

Hickman, James C., ed. 1993. *The Jepson Manual*. Berkeley: University of California Press.

Hitchcock, C. Leo, and Arthur Cronquist. 1973. *Flora of the Pacific Northwest*. Seattle: University of Washington Press.

Hitchcock, C. Leo, Arthur Cronquist, Marion Ownbey, and J. W. Thompson. 1955–1969. *Vascular Plants of the Pacific Northwest*. 5 vols. Seattle: University of Washington Press.

Hultén, Eric. 1968. *Flora of Alaska and Neighboring Territories*. Stanford, Calif.: Stanford University Press.

Kartesz, John. 1994. *A Synonymized Checklist of the Vascular Flora of the United States, Canada, and Greenland* 2nd ed. Portland, Ore.: Timber Press.

Kearney, Thomas H., and Robert H. Peebles. 1942. *Flowering Plants and Ferns of Arizona*. U.S. Department of Agriculture, Miscellaneous Publications no. 423. Washington, D.C.: Government Printing Office.

Kingsbury, John M. 1964. *Poisonous Plants of the United States and Canada*. Englewood Cliffs, N.J.: Prentice-Hall.

Krochmal, Arnold, S. Paur., and P. Duisberg. 1954. "Useful Native Plants in the American Southwestern Deserts." *Economic Botany* 8(1):3–20.

McGuffin, Michael, Christopher Hobbs, Roy Upton. and Alicia Gold-berg. 1997. *Botanical Safety Handbook*. Boca Raton, Fla.: CRC Press.

McKelvey, Susan Delano. 1956. *Botanical Exploration of the Trans-Mississippi West 1790–1850*. Jamaica Plain, Mass.: Arnold Arboretum of Harvard University.

Moerman, Daniel E. 1998. *Native American Ethnobotany*. Portland, Ore.: Timber Press.

Munz, Philip A. 1974. *A Flora of Southern California*. Berkeley: University of California Press.

Munz, Philip A., and David D. Keck. 1968. *A California Flora*. Berkeley: University of California Press.

Rafinesque, Constantine Samuel. 1828, 1830. *Medical Flora or Manual of the Medical Botany of the United States of North America*. 2 vols. Philadelphia: Samuel C. Atkinson.

Robbins, Wilfred William, John Peabody Harrington, and Barbara Freire-Marreco. 1916. *Ethnobotany of the Tewa Indians*. Washington, D.C.: Government Printing Office.

Smith, Harlan I. 1928. "Materia Medica of the Bella Coola and Neighbouring Tribes of British Columbia." *National Museum of Canada Bulletin* 56: 47–68.

Stevenson, Matilida C. 1915. "Ethnobotany of the Zuni Indians." *Annual Report of the Bureau of American Ethnology* 30: 31–102.

Stuckey, Ronald L., and William R. Burk. 2000. "Emmanuel D. Rudolph's Studies in the History of North American Botany." *Sida Botanical Miscellany* no. 19.

Stuhr, Ernest T. 1933. *Manual of Pacific Coast Drug Plants*. Lancaster, Pa.: Science Press.

Taylor, Mary Susan. 1976. "Some Native Medicinal and Edible Plants of Butte County, California." Master's thesis, Chico State University.

Thomas, John H. 1961. *Flora of the Santa Cruz Mountains of California*. Stanford, Calif.: Stanford University Press.

Train, Percy, James R. Henrichs, and W. Andrew Archer. 1957. *Medicinal Uses of Plants by Indian Tribes of Nevada*. Reprint. Lincoln, Mass.: Quarterman Publications.

Turner, Nancy Chapman, and Marcus A. M. Bell. 1971. "The Ethnobotany of the Coast Salish Indians." *Economic Botany* 25(1): 63–99.

———. 1973. "The Ethnobotany of the Southern Kwakiutl Indians of British Columbia." *Economic Botany* 27(1): 257–310.

Turner, Nancy J., R. Bouchard, and Dorothy I. D. Kennedy. 1981. *Ethnobotany of the Okanagan-Colville Indians of British Columbia and Washington*. British Columbia Provincial Museum Occasional Paper no. 21.

Turner, Nancy J., and Barbara S. Efrat. 1982. *Ethnobotany of the Hesauiat Indians of Vancouver Island.* Victoria, B.C.: British Columbia Provincial Museum Cultural Recovery Paper no. 2.

Turner, Nancy J., John Thomas, Barry F. Carlson, and Roger T. Ogilvie. 1983. *Ethnobotany of the Nitinaht Indians of Vancouver Island.* Victoria, B.C.: British Columbia Provincial Museum Occasional Paper no. 24.

Turner, Nancy J., Laurence C. Thompson, M. Terry Thompson, and Annie Z. York. 1990. *Thompson Ethnobotany: Knowledge and Usage of Plants by the Thompson Indians of British Columbia.* Victoria, B.C.: Royal British Columbia Museum Memoir no. 3.

Vogel, Virgil. 1970. *American Indian Medicine.* Norman: University of Oklahoma Press.

Weber, William A., and Ronald C. Wittman. 1996. *Colorado Flora: Western Slope.* 2nd ed. Niwot, Colo.: University of Colorado Press.

———. 1996. *Colorado Flora: Eastern Slope.* 2nd ed. Niwot, Colo.: University of Colorado Press.

Welsh, Stanley L., N. Duane Atwood, Sherel Goodrich, and Larry C. Higgins, eds. 1987. *A Utah Flora.* Great Basin Naturalist Memoirs no. 9. Provo, Utah: Brigham Young University.

Whiting, Alfred F. 1939. *Ethnobotany of the Hopi.* Flagstaff: Museum of Northern Arizona.

WEB SITES FOR PLANT RANGES, TAXONOMY, AND ETHNOBOTANY

James A. Duke's Phytochemical and Ethnobotanical Database: http://www.ars-grin.gov/duke/

Flora of California database: http://www.calflora.org

Integrated Taxonomic Information Service (current scientific names of all plants and animals in the United States): http://www.itis.usda.gov/plantproj/itis/access.html

Daniel Moerman's Native American Ethnobotany database: http://www.umd.umich.edu/cgi-bin/herb/

"A Synonymized Checklist of the Vascular Flora of the United States, Canada, and Greenland": http://www.mip.berkeley.edu/bonap/ checklist_intro.html

Steven Foster's Herb Information Site: http://www.stevenfoster.com

Christopher Hobbs's Herb Information Site: http://www.christopher-hobbs.com

LIFE LIST

ORANGE

PINK/RED

____PEYOTE, 153 _____to_____

____BEAVERTAIL PRICKLYPEAR CACTUS, 153 _____to_____

____SPOTTED CORALROOT, 154 _____to_____

____SNOWPLANT, 155 _____to_____

____CRIMSON COLUMBINE, 155 _____to_____

____PACIFIC BLEEDING HEART, 156 _____to_____

____LONG-TAILED WILD GINGER, 157 _____to_____

____GIANT TRILLIUM, 158 _____to_____

____FIREWEED, 158 _____to_____

____RED CLOVER, 159 _____to_____

____SHOWY MILKWEED, 160 _____to_____

____GREAT BASIN CENTAURY, 161 _____to_____

____REDSTEM STORKSBILL, 161 _____to_____

____CAROLINA GERANIUM, 162 _____to_____

____RICHARDSON'S GERANIUM, 163 _____to_____

____CHEESEWEED, 163 _____to_____

____REDWOOD SORREL, 164 _____to_____

____COPPER GLOBEMALLOW, 165 _____to_____

____SPREADING DOGBANE, 165 _____to_____

____MADAGASCAR PERIWINKLE, 166 _____to_____

____DESERT FOUR O'CLOCK, 167 _____to_____

____LONGLEAF PHLOX, 167 _____to_____

____DESERT TRUMPET, 168 _____to_____

____PIPSISSEWA, 169 _____to_____

____LIVERLEAF WINTERGREEN, 170 _____to_____

____NETTLELEAF HORSEMINT, 171 _____to_____

____MOTHERWORT, 172 _____to_____

____MOUNTAIN MONARDELLA, 173 _____to_____

____CALIFORNIA HEDGENETTLE, 173 _____to_____

____CARDINAL FLOWER, 174 _____to_____

____ELEPHANT'S-HEAD LOUSEWORT, 175 _____to_____

____CALIFORNIA FIGWORT, 176 _____to_____

____HYSSOP LOOSESTRIFE, 177 _____to_____

____LADY'S THUMB, 178 _____to_____

____BITTERROOT, 178 _____to_____

____WESTERN PEONY, 179 _____to_____

____PEREZIA, 179 _____to_____

____SPREADING FLEABANE, 180 _____to_____

____DAISY FLEABANE, 180 _____to_____

____GREATER BURDOCK, 181 _____to_____

____COMMON BURDOCK, 182 _____to_____

____COBWEB THISTLE, 183 _____to_____

____YELLOWSPINE THISTLE, 183 _____to_____

____DOTTED BLAZING-STAR, 184 _____to_____

____RUSH SKELETON WEED, 185 _____to_____

VIOLET/BLUE

____COMMON CAMAS, 186 _____to_____

____ROCKY MOUNTAIN IRIS, 186 _____to_____

GREEN/BROWN

GRASSES OR GRASSLIKE

INDEX TO PLANTS

Numbers in **bold** refer to the page numbers of photographs.

INDEX TO MEDICAL TOPICS

330, 331, 333, 347, 355, 358, 377, 385. *See also* Vomiting

Emphysema, 164

Enema, 347

Enteritis, 164, 226

Enuresis, 277

Epilepsy, 25, 67, 73, 92, 119, 138, 150, 169, 181, 228, 247, 252, 271, 367

Erysipelas, 68, 85

Expectorant, 33, 43, 54, 108, 151, 175, 191, 267, 270, 328, 344, 374, 376, 377, 380, 385. *See also* Antitussive

Eyes. *See* Ophthalmia

Eyewash, 22, 32, 45, 78, 79, 81, 89, 93, 120, 134, 139, 147, 161, 165, 169, 180, 185, 219, 260, 283, 284, 374, 385

Fainting, 68, 193, 271, 315

Fatigue, 258

Feet, 20, 41, 60, 120, 134, 190, 258, 264, 269, 276, 279, 292, 365, 371

Female ailments, 22, 300. *See also* Childbirth; Gynecological problems; Menstruation

Fertility, 109

Fever, throughout

Fibroid, 22

Fistula, 215, 344

Fits, 17. *See also* Epilepsy

Flatulence, 56, 125, 142, 203, 318, 380. *See also* Carminative; Gas

Fleas, 79, 340

Flu, 22, 41, 56, 64, 65, 75, 86, 87, 119, 126, 131, 135, 217, 244, 245, 246, 271, 273, 274, 291, 301, 302, 311, 315, 322, 325, 326, 330, 331, 335, 343, 368, 376. *See also* Influenza

Fracture, compound, 123, 228. *See also* Bones

Frostbite, 310

Fullness, 232

Fumigant, 196, 250, 270, 340

Fungal infection, 37, 97, 176, 279, 348, 355

Gallbladder, 37, 119, 159, 190, 192, 204, 218, 237, 245, 267, 297, 303, 317, 330, 383

Gallstones, 37, 102, 216, 232, 264, 283, 351

Gas, 21, 58, 67, 125, 126, 140, 173, 190, 192, 195, 203, 233, 240, 254, 272, 320, 359, 366, 375. *See also* Carminative; Flatulence

Gastrointestinal disorders, 29, 93, 103, 124, 134, 141, 153, 162, 164, 165, 187, 235, 246, 250, 285, 302, 326, 353, 357, 359, 373, 3365

Genitourinary tract ailments, 110, 132, 133

Glands, 32, 100, 106, 108, 140, 264, 339

Glaucoma, 222. *See also* Ophthalmia

Goiter, 192

Gonorrhea, 19, 21, 26, 33, 39, 42–43, 96, 98, 110, 114, 133, 146, 168, 169, 170, 184, 187, 198, 229, 233, 243, 256, 264, 266, 268, 271, 278, 282, 288, 300, 307, 309, 310, 312, 314, 315, 317, 325, 332, 333, 350, 351. *See also* Venereal disease

Gout, 21, 37, 44, 50, 78, 93, 106, 111, 115, 129, 182, 219, 228, 242, 250, 289, 383

Gums, 81, 106, 208, 238, 268, 270, 276, 279, 284, 300, 312, 320, 329, 375

Gynecological problems, 30, 32, 35, 39, 56, 67, 249, 258, 259, 301, 314, 329, 333, 352

Hair, 45, 68, 80, 82, 94, 97, 130, 153, 156, 192, 228, 230, 242, 261, 263, 270, 273, 276, 280, 283, 299, 311, 329, 367, 370, 371. *See also* Baldness

Hands, chapped, 89

Hangovers, 335

Hay fever, 123, 243, 257, 279. *See also* Allergies

Head, effects on, 206, 310, 311

Headache, throughout

Hearing, 195, 233. *See also* Ears, effects on

Heart, effects on, 22, 29, 32, 46, 54, 89, 98, 119, 140, 146, 165, 169, 176, 178, 179, 192, 196, 208, 211, 226, 228, 237, 252, 267, 272, 283, 296, 297, 298, 305, 317, 325, 328, 332, 337, 350, 352

Heartburn, 22, 125, 139, 185, 187, 192, 255, 286, 319, 327

Heat prostration, 43

Hematuria, 174

THE PETERSON SERIES ®

PETERSON FIELD GUIDES ®

BIRDS

ADVANCED BIRDING North America 97500-x
BIRDS OF BRITAIN AND EUROPE 0-618-16675-0
BIRDS OF TEXAS Texas and adjacent states 92138-4
BIRDS OF THE WEST INDIES 0-618-00210-3
EASTERN BIRDS Eastern and central North America
74046-0
EASTERN BIRDS' NESTS U.S. east of Mississippi River 93609-8
HAWKS North America 67067-5
HUMMINGBIRDS North America 0-618-02496-4
WESTERN BIRDS North America west of 100th
meridian and north of Mexico 91173-7
WESTERN BIRDS' NESTS U.S. west of Mississippi
River 0-618-16437-5
MEXICAN BIRDS Mexico, Guatemala, Belize,
El Salvador 97514-x
WARBLERS North America 78321-6

FISH

PACIFIC COAST FISHES Gulf of Alaska to Baja California 0-618-00212-x
ATLANTIC COAST FISHES North American Atlantic coast 97515-8
FRESHWATER FISHES North America north of Mexico 91091-9

INSECTS

INSECTS North America north of Mexico 91170-2
BEETLES North America 91089-7
EASTERN BUTTERFLIES Eastern and central North America 90453-6
WESTERN BUTTERFLIES U.S. and Canada west of 100th
meridian, part of northern Mexico 79151-0

MAMMALS

MAMMALS North America north of Mexico 91098-6
ANIMAL TRACKS North America 91094-3

ECOLOGY

EASTERN FORESTS Eastern North America 92895-8
CALIFORNIA AND PACIFIC NORTHWEST FORESTS 92896-6
ROCKY MOUNTAIN AND SOUTHWEST FORESTS 92897-4
VENOMOUS ANIMALS AND POISONOUS PLANTS) North America north of
Mexico 93608-x

PLANTS

EARTH AND SKY

REPTILES AND AMPHIBIANS

SEASHORE

AUDIO AND VIDEO

EASTERN BIRDING BY EAR
cassettes 97523-9
CD 97524-7

WESTERN BIRDING BY EAR
cassettes 97526-3
CD 97525-5

EASTERN BIRD SONGS, Revised
cassettes 53150-0
CD 97522-0

WESTERN BIRD SONGS, Revised
cassettes 51746-X
CD 97519-0

BACKYARD BIRDSONG
cassettes 97527-1
CD 97528-X

EASTERN MORE BIRDING BY EAR
cassettes 97529-8
CD 97530-1

WATCHING BIRDS
Beta 34418-2
VHS 34417-4

PETERSON'S MULTIMEDIA GUIDES: NORTH AMERICAN BIRDS
(CD-ROM for Windows) 73056-2

PETERSON FLASHGUIDES™

ATLANTIC COASTAL BIRDS 79286-X
PACIFIC COASTAL BIRDS 79287-8
EASTERN TRAILSIDE BIRDS 79288-6
WESTERN TRAILSIDE BIRDS 79289-4
HAWKS 79291-6
BACKYARD BIRDS 79290-8
TREES 82998-4
MUSHROOMS 82999-2
ANIMAL TRACKS 82997-6
BUTTERFLIES 82996-8
ROADSIDE WILDFLOWERS 82995-X
BIRDS OF THE MIDWEST 86733-9
WATERFOWL 86734-7
FRESHWATER FISHES 86713-4

PETERSON FIELD GUIDES can be purchased at your local
bookstore or by calling our toll-free number, (800) 225-3362.

When referring to title by corresponding ISBN number,
preface with 0-395, unless title is listed with 0-618.

PETERSON FIRST GUIDES®

PETERSON FIELD GUIDE COLORING BOOKS